*The Unruly Facts of Race*

# The Unruly Facts of Race

## THE POLITICS OF KNOWLEDGE PRODUCTION IN THE EARLY TWENTIETH-CENTURY IMMIGRATION DEBATE

Sunmin Kim

THE UNIVERSITY OF CHICAGO PRESS
CHICAGO AND LONDON

The University of Chicago Press, Chicago 60637
The University of Chicago Press, Ltd., London

Published 2026
Printed in the United States of America

35 34 33 32 31 30 29 28 27 26    1 2 3 4 5

ISBN-13: 978-0-226-84590-6 (cloth)
ISBN-13: 978-0-226-84592-0 (paper)
ISBN-13: 978-0-226-84591-3 (ebook)
DOI: https://doi.org/10.7208/chicago/9780226845913.001.0001

Library of Congress Cataloging-in-Publication Data

Names: Kim, Sunmin (Sociologist) author
Title: The unruly facts of race : the politics of knowledge production in the early twentieth-century immigration debate / Sunmin Kim.
Description: Chicago ; London : The University of Chicago Press, 2026. | Includes bibliographical references and index.
Identifiers: LCCN 2025021893 | ISBN 9780226845906 cloth | ISBN 9780226845920 paperback | ISBN 9780226845913 ebook
Subjects: LCSH: United States. Immigration Commission (1907–1910) | Emigration and immigration—Research—United States—History—20th century | Racism—United States—History—20th century | Race discrimination—United States | United States—Emigration and immigration—History—20th century | United States—Emigration and immigration—Government policy | United States—Race relations—History—20th century
Classification: LCC JV6483 .K53 2026 | DDC 305.800973/0904—dc23/eng/20250708
LC record available at https://lccn.loc.gov/2025021893

♾ This paper meets the requirements of ANSI/NISO Z39.48-1992 (Permanence of Paper).

Authorized Representative for EU General Product Safety Regulation (GPSR) queries: **Easy Access System Europe**—Mustamäe tee 50, 10621 Tallinn, Estonia, gpsr.requests@easproject.com
Any other queries: https://press.uchicago.edu/press/contact.html

*For Sujin Eom*

# Contents

[ INTRODUCTION ]

# Race, Legitimacy, and Facts

On June 16, 2015, Donald Trump launched his first presidential campaign with a speech vilifying Mexican immigrants: "When Mexico sends its people, they're not sending their best. They're not sending you. . . . They're sending people that have lots of problems, and they're bringing those problems to us. They're bringing drugs. They're bringing crime. They're rapists." With these lines, the future forty-fifth and forty-seventh president of the United States effectively shattered the decades-long political and social consensus on immigration. Ever since John F. Kennedy's "a nation of immigrants" proclamation in 1964, both elites and the public in the United States have been paying due respect to the nation's immigrant origins, even if it was only a symbolic gesture. In direct contrast, Trump drew a clear, insurmountable divide between "immigrants" and "Americans," blaming the former for the latter's supposed suffering.[1]

With this rhetoric, we see once again immigrants serving as a blank screen onto which the nation's worst fears and fantasies are projected. Trump essentialized, and thereby effectively racialized, immigrants: Rather than arguing that immigrants do not contribute to the economy or that they take advantage of welfare, he defined all immigrants as categorically different from "Americans" and perceived them as inherently threatening to the nation.[2] Supporters of immigrants argued back by debunking his statements with facts, demonstrating through empirical data that immigrants had lower crime rates and that most of them were good, hardworking people who simply wanted to feed their families. As Trump's eventual victory would tell us a year later, this rebuttal strategy had limited success, if any. In the following decade, through his time in office and in his next two presidential campaigns, Trump made the attack against immigrants the centerpiece of his platform, in the process expanding his list of targets beyond Mexicans to include Muslims, Chinese, El Salvadorans, and Haitians. In 2024, during his third presidential campaign, Trump dialed up his rhetoric and called immigrants "not human"—"animals" that are "destroying the blood of our country." His second victory, according to his supporters, gave him a mandate to act on this hateful rhetoric, starting with mass deportation operations throughout the country. In 2025, as fear and fantasy triumph over facts, we find ourselves once again in the middle of another "unsettled time" in terms of race, immigration, and national belonging.[3]

This book has been inspired by this course of events, but it is a study of a different time, one when, despite the familiar denigration of immigrants, facts were able to partially dispel the myth of race and lead to a new system of racial governance. As the twentieth century began, immigration restrictionists[4]—a loose coalition of powerful politicians and influential intellectuals who dubbed immigrants unredeemable members of an "undesirable race"—engaged in a similar political project. Immigrants, according to their thinking, were the source of every possible social problem, ranging from crime and poverty to prostitution and the decline of democracy. Restrictionists saw them as fundamentally at odds with the American ideal and sought to exclude them from the country by enacting federal-level immigration restrictions. Motivated by and responding to the agitations of immigration restrictionists, American politicians, bureaucrats, and social scientists sought knowledge about, and a solution to, the "immigration problem," to borrow the phrase of historian Katherine Benton-Cohen.[5] In 1907, a group of powerful politicians launched a congressional inquiry on immigration, a fact-finding project of unprecedented scale. After four years of work, the United States Immigration Commission, also known as the Dillingham Commission, published the result of its inquiry in forty-one volumes of reports.[6] Restrictionists saw the work as an opportunity to use the facts to categorize certain immigrants, particularly those from southern and eastern Europe, as members of an "undesirable race" unfit for inclusion in the nation. The facts, however, did not support this conclusion and, instead, became the touchstone for a prolonged, decades-long debate on race, immigration, and national belonging. In the process, advocacy for immigrant assimilation was ironically grafted onto premises upholding immigrant exclusion, a merger that led to distinguishing immigrants into assimilable and nonassimilable groups.[7] What's more, the clash between racial ideology and the unruly facts would influence how Americans conceived of and dealt with the immigration problem throughout the twentieth century and beyond. The social scientific infrastructure for answering questions about race, immigration, and national belonging that still undergirds our thinking about these matters emerged in these tumultuous but vibrant decades.

I am not telling this story to highlight the contrast with our times or to reminiscence about the good-old days when social science persuaded the public and policymakers through the primacy of facts. I am telling this story so we can understand the origin and limitations of our tool kit for addressing racial demagoguery. Recently, many scholars have debated why some people refuse to accept facts and cling to their false beliefs.[8] While this is certainly an important line of inquiry, I am asking a somewhat different question: Why do we assume that facts would and should dispel a myth, in our case that of the racialized immigrant? What are we *not* seeing when we see ourselves as rational and righteous actors and label others as irrational, misguided, and prejudiced? Throughout this book, I show that the idea of looking to the facts—and, in turn, social sciences—to dispel the myth of race stems from a particular sequence of events in the early twentieth century and, as a product of those events, retains a particular set of limitations when it comes to the debate about race and national belonging. By understanding those limitations, I argue, we can move beyond the naive worship of facts and start imagining different ways of pursuing freedom from race.

Scholars agree that race has been an important—if not the most important—force in the founding and development of the American nation and that, although definitions, norms, and expectations surrounding race have changed, its political centrality has not diminished in the twenty-first century.[9] Two intersecting strains of racial ideas, which I dub racial essentialism and racial liberalism, would come to inform the political meaning of race over the course of the twentieth century.[10] Racial essentialism posits race as an unchanging, all-encompassing marker that represents *categorical* difference and regards racial others as forever determined by their race. Because the difference is categorical, there is no middle ground or room for change; therefore, the only solutions the so-called race question allows for are exclusion, segregation, and even, in horrific scenarios, genocide. In contrast, racial liberalism presents race as a less deterministic, *gradual* difference that can be overcome through time and effort. Because the difference is gradual, with many intermediary layers between extremes, racial others are imagined to be capable of taking steps to change their ways to better fit into the existing social order. With racial liberalism, individuals are encouraged to break free from their racial destiny. When it comes to immigration policy, whereas racial essentialism offers contemptuous exclusion for immigrants, racial liberalism fosters pity for their plight and advocates eventual assimilation.[11] The former is well represented by the nineteenth-century anti-Chinese movement and its slogan—"The Chinese Must Go"—and the latter by the Progressive reform movement, whose ethos is best characterized by Emma Lazarus's "The New Colossus."[12]

Up to the late nineteenth century, race was the governing principle of belonging to the body politic in the United States: Whites were citizens and Blacks were second-class citizens, if by name only. The rapid surge of immigration on both the East and West Coasts disrupted this simple guideline: Whereas southern and eastern Europeans challenged the unity and consistency of the White category, Asians and Mexicans[13] stood outside the binary itself. As people landed on American shores and crossed borders, those who were already in the country were faced with the question of difference: Are newcomers different from us, and, if so, how? And are they all one and the same, or are there different kinds of immigrants? What do differences mean for the nation?

In the early twentieth century, with the rise of social sciences, the answers to these questions began to take new forms. Politicians, bureaucrats, and intellectuals formulated theories, collected facts, and, consequently, produced a body of knowledge that explained who immigrants were and what should be done about them. This body of knowledge became the foundation on which the two competing strains of racial ideas could engage in a debate with each other: Racial essentialism had to contend with facts that did not support its negative caricature of immigrants, and racial liberalism provided a counterargument to address the discrepancy between the hypothesis and data. This debate, I argue, led to the conceptual (i.e., race and ethnicity) and institutional (i.e., the Johnson-Reed Act of 1924) constructs to address the immigration problem that still direct our understanding of race and immigration today.[14] In the end, the immigration debate led to a new system of racial governance that combined a more flexible approach to racial categorization and a more restrictive and compulsory immigration policy. This transformation in racial governance was a key component of the expansion of federal executive power and the American state's evolution toward a global empire.[15] The objective of this book is not to use the story as a model to follow in the future but to assess how we came today to think and talk the way we do about race, immigration, and national belonging. Perhaps by understanding this history we can move beyond the contemporary impasse between race and facts to imagine new ways of talking about difference.

To sketch out this process, I begin with a particular organization and trace the networks of ideas and people stemming from it. My starting point is an agency of the federal government: the United States Immigration Commission (1907–11), also known as the Dillingham Commission. The commission conducted a comprehensive inquiry on immigration to provide a scientific foundation for future immigration policy and, in the process, became a focal point of the immigration debate during the early twentieth century. The Dillingham Commission is important in two respects. First, in terms of its scale, visibility, and legitimacy, the commission had no rival in previous or ensuing decades and thus exercised lasting influence on immigration discourse and policy. Many of the people who worked for the commission became notable participants in the immigration debate, and the commission's data became a common reference point in their discourse. Furthermore, as is discussed more in chapter 7, the idea for national quotas—arguably one of the most consequential policies in US immigration history—emerged directly out of the commission's inquiry. In this sense, the Dillingham Commission is a historically important institution in its own regard. Second, in terms of our study, the commission provides a unique opportunity to observe racial ideas in flux—that is, how race as a concept clashed with empirical data and faced challenges in its legitimacy. These challenges transformed racial ideas, specifically in terms of how racial essentialism related to racial liberalism. In a nutshell, the Dillingham Commission provides a strategic vantage point to observe how American policymakers, bureaucrats, and intellectuals contended with the question of race, immigration, and national belonging.[16]

Many of the existing accounts of the commission highlight political contention and racial essentialism, focusing on how those who supported immigration restriction prevailed over immigrants and their allies to steer the commission's inquiry to their liking.[17] In the process, the commission is typically depicted as a product of collaboration between restrictionist ideology and Progressive Era social sciences, in which the authority of science was invoked to amplify theories about the purported undesirability of immigrants. In other words, the Dillingham Commission was a racist instrument for immigration restrictionists, one among many in the early twentieth century.[18]

This book challenges this one-dimensional portrayal by drawing on underexamined archival sources to articulate a new theoretical model of understanding race.[19] In brief, "racist" is too simple a way to characterize what happened in the commission and as a result of the commission. The racial essentialism of immigration restrictionists was not substantiated by the empirical data collected by the commission, and so the commission members were forced to revise their understanding of race, nation, and belonging. Although restrictionists did win the legislative battle over immigration in the short term, hence ushering in an era of racist immigration policy, their racialized vision of what the American nation should look like underwent a transformation over the course of the fact-finding inquiry, and they could not completely manage the long-term fallout from that upheaval.

The ironic and contradictory coexistence of racial essentialism and racial liberalism—represented in persistent political scapegoating of immigrants and the emphasis on their eventual assimilation—can be accounted for in this light. The unruly facts derived from the commission's process of knowledge production grafted a good amount of racial liberalism into racial essentialism, leading to the emergence of concepts such as ethnicity, culture, and assimilation. These concepts, developed mainly in sociology and anthropology, explained how a particular subset of immigrants could cease to be the racial other and get incorporated into the body politic while implicitly designating another set of immigrants as ineligible for such a transition. The divide between assimilable immigrants and unassimilable racial other, or White immigrants and non-White immigrants, emerged through these developments. By narrating this history, I urge readers to ponder the irony and contingency inherent in American immigration rhetoric and policy—namely, the fact that racial liberalism was grafted onto the exclusive impulse of racial essentialism as a haphazard solution to address the clash between anti-immigrant ideology and unruly facts. Hopefully, this understanding will lead us to imagine an alternative to racial liberalism, which seems to have reached its limit in the early twenty-first century based on the revival of racial essentialism and demagoguery targeting immigrants.

In the following sections, I parse out this argument through a series of steps. First, I elaborate on how the focus on racial knowledge production allows us to comprehend a neglected dynamic in the transformation of racial ideas. Second, I define my use of racial essentialism and racial liberalism within the context of the early twentieth century, followed by a more detailed exposition of my argument around the notion of unruly facts. Third, I explain my sources and methods followed by a summary of chapters.

## Race, Knowledge Production, and Legitimacy

There is a convention in sociology of treating race and immigration as two separate research topics, which has resulted in two separate scholarly traditions and networks. The research on race largely focuses on African Americans and revolves around the themes of inequality, discrimination, and violence; the research on immigration is typically about Europeans of the past or Asians and Latinos of the present and centers on such characteristics as assimilation, mobility, and cultural difference. While many scholars have lamented the lack of dialogue between the two scholarly communities, there has actually been an ample amount of cross-fertilization of ideas between the two fields.[20] For instance, recent works on immigrants from the Caribbean and Latin America have analyzed how they constantly rearticulate and negotiate the established ideas about race in the mainland United States.[21]

When we take a historical perspective, however, we can better grasp the reason why such a divide exists among scholars in the first place. Simply put, the separation of race and immigration as belonging to separate domains of inquiry stems not from analytical necessity but from a sequence of events during a particular historical period, that of the early twentieth century. As I make clear through further discussion of racial essentialism and racial liberalism, the separation opens itself up to one set of governing principles about population difference while suppressing others. Connecting these two domains is, as Mahmood Mamdani has poignantly observed, the American state's attempt to "define and rule" its population: In designating certain populations as domestic racial minorities and others as immigrants, the American state devised two different sets of governing strategies pertaining to the two groups and thereby reified their divide through the exercise of its power over decades. Social scientists have—sometimes willingly and other times unwittingly—cooperated with those strategies while reproducing the epistemological limitation that comes with them.[22] Departing from this tradition, this book reconstructs the early twentieth-century immigration debate through the lens of governing strategies, drawing on the abundant literature about the regulation of population difference in modern societies.[23] When I refer to *race*, I am invoking this analytical stance more than our contemporary usage of the term.[24]

Historians have shown that the meaning of race has varied widely depending on the parameters of discussion, not only centering on biological differences between groups but often encompassing culture and collective history under its umbrella.[25] Ultimately, the definition of race is inseparable from the very social process through which it emerges, and many sociologists of race have built their theories around this insight. For instance, under the rubric of "racial conceptualization," Ann Morning has observed how biological scientists contend with race, and how different social contexts can lead to radically different definitions and applications of the race concept. In their theory of racial formation, Michael Omi and Howard Winant have provided a model in which different social groups engage in political struggles over the definition and use of race. Moon-Kie Jung, in his work focusing on the labor movement in Hawaii, contends that collective struggle and ensuing rearticulation redefines the meaning of race in each historical moment. Sociologists have thus shown that race is something that is socially constructed, as different individuals and groups engage with each other to shape its meaning and application.[26]

Knowledge production is one example of this process, but it occupies a special place because of what I call an inherent contradiction in race as an idea. Contrary to popular understanding, race does not solely derive from a set of prejudices held by individuals. Nor is it a natural, physical fact that exists "out there" to be discovered and measured through scientific means such as DNA testing.[27] However flawed, the idea of race presents itself as an explanation of human population differences, and oftentimes this explanation is a foundation for a social and political vision that prioritizes one racial group over another.[28] Considerable amount of work goes into substantiating this explanation of differences and connecting it to real-life examples, regardless of whether such connection is factually valid. In other words, race does not have to make perfect sense, but it has to make *some sense* to at least *some people*, enough to justify its legitimacy as a vision for the social world. The tension between "anything goes" and "makes perfect sense" exists at the heart of any idea of race, and those who are invested in a racial ideology try their best to neutralize this tension. When I posit race as a product of knowledge production, I am referring to this work of building and manifesting legitimacy.[29]

The focus on knowledge production and legitimacy calls for a new model of thinking about the social construction of race. The existing theories largely rely on the motifs of contest or struggle to describe how race is socially constructed: On the one side are those who attempt to racialize populations and exercise power; on the other side are those who are being racialized, as well as their sympathizers, and are fighting against it. These two sides compete against each other in different spaces—such as electoral politics, social policy, the Census Bureau, and the media—in order to shape the definition and use of race in society.[30] Building on this model of contest, many scholars have documented the power play between different groups over the meaning of race. Rebecca Jean Emigh and her coauthors, in a comprehensive study that spans two thousand years of censuses around the world, have documented how different groups compete to influence censuses and their classification systems.[31] Scholars focusing on more recent cases, including the emergence of the Hispanic category, have highlighted the way activists, bureaucrats, and intellectuals participate in a "field of classification struggle" to produce new ideas about race.[32]

To a certain extent, the motif of contest works well with the social constructionist approach. In this perspective, race is not a given fact in nature but a product of our own making—a fulcrum at the heart of political struggle between groups with conflicting visions of human differences. Contest rhetoric, however, provides a limited scope in accounting for the process of knowledge production. If race is nothing but an irrational bias held by those in power, the winner of a struggle can readily change the meaning of race without any restriction, unilaterally enforcing their vision while squashing the resistance. History teaches us that things are not as straightforward when it comes to race. For instance, when White supremacists attempted to enforce antimiscegenation laws in early twentieth-century Virginia, they wanted to neatly divide the population into either the White or "colored" category and prevent union between the two. But the extensive history of intermarriage in the state between early White settlers and Indigenous people made such a clear-cut divide impossible, and White supremacists had to concede to having exceptions to their definition of being White.[33] In other words, White supremacists who controlled the legislature could not have the "pure" White race they dreamed of not because others directly challenged them but because of the historical reality in which they were operating.[34]

Episodes of "confusion, contradiction, and unintended consequences"[35] like this show that there is a distance between race as an idea and its practical realization. Race indeed is an absurd idea, but its manifestation is a serious business that requires much footwork and compromise. A degree of internal logical coherence and some form of external validity check—evidence, facts, data, anecdote, or whatever one calls it—are necessary to strike a negotiated balance between "anything goes" and "makes perfect sense." For instance, to racialize a group as criminals, one needs to provide statistical data to prove group members' supposed criminality. If no data is available, one has to at least come up with a tale of crime committed by group members, even if one ends up fabricating the specifics.[36] Even antebellum southern slaveholders, not known for their intellectual rigor, provided a justification for slavery by invoking the biblical tale of stewardship: Because God designed and entitled masters to lead and protect slaves, slavery apologists argued, the peculiar southern institution should be protected from impious, capitalistic Northerners. Of course, they had to distort reality and sometimes plainly lie to validate this argument, but they did have to put forward a thesis and back it up with the authority of the Bible to legitimize the highly repressive, unequal system of power ridden with horrific violence.[37] Obviously, this rendered them vulnerable to challenges not only from abolitionists but also from conservative clergy who cared about biblical orthodoxy, creating an unexpected and cumbersome controversy they could not foresee.

Herein lies the ultimate contradiction of racial ideas. The human population is far too diverse to be classed into a few categories.[38] Building a simple, intuitive hierarchy among those categories is not a straightforward task. To use race as a meaningful social force, however, one must overcome these challenges to provide a vision of human differences that magically constructs a coherent structure out of disparate shards. Sociologists have long puzzled students by teaching that race is a social construction, that race is not a real thing but still a powerful maker of reality. This statement is admittedly confusing, but it does contain a kernel of truth: Any racial idea is an exercise of building something out of nothing, and this impossible task usually requires many rounds of discussion and painstaking efforts to discover—or, one may say, construct—evidence when there is none.

Granted, the work of "making sense" of race is situated within the larger confines of political struggles, and the logic of racial knowledge production is conditioned by dynamics of power.[39] Or, more precisely, the two distinctive yet interconnected dynamics of knowledge production and political struggle represent different social forces underpinning the concept of race. In their study of scientific experimentation and modern social order, Simon Schaffer and Steven Shapin famously proclaim that "solutions to the problem of knowledge are solutions to the problem of social order."[40] By the same token, a properly justified concept of race mirrors a secure coalition of political forces behind the concept, which would constitute grounds for successful race making. However, a not-so-properly justified concept of race will create instability in this formula, leading to the transformation of racial ideas and the coalition that undergirds them.

In many cases, this transformation will result in mere window dressing, or justify violence and repression under a slightly different cover. In some cases, however, the transformation will amount to meaningful changes in the modes of racial governance by altering the terrain on which struggle over race occurs. Whereas political struggles revolve around competing intentions—that is, actors fight for what they want—knowledge production follows its own logic built around contingency: The whole point of asking a question is to find an answer that one did not know already. Even if the question is a rhetorical one, the act of asking it opens up the space of indeterminacy and vulnerability; that is, someone may hijack the rhetorical question and supply an answer one does not expect. In other words, knowledge production is premised on the notion of autonomy, however purported; it is neither an unprocessed reflection of "things out there" nor just a function of power. Because of this presumed autonomy, knowledge production can yield unexpected outcomes, ones that were not foreseen or desired by the actors involved.[41]

To be clear, I do not argue that all accounts of racial governance can be explained through this framework. We have gained much insight by focusing on violence and the underlying power dynamics, as the history from the Reconstruction and Jim Crow to the civil rights movement attests. The analysis focusing on legitimacy and justification pales in comparison to the cruelty and ruthlessness of the violence embedded in this historical sequence.

However, the narrative of power struggle cannot tell the entire story, and my focus on knowledge production complements existing accounts from a different angle. For example, Khalil Gibran Muhammad traces how the northward migration of African Americans in the early twentieth century led to a new way of criminalizing the migrants. Of course, we are well aware of how police violence and incarceration substituted lynching in northern cities. At the same time, social scientists began to argue that African Americans were prone to criminal activity not because of their race per se but because of their culture and social circumstances, such as poverty and joblessness. The cultural theory of Black criminality not only justified increased policing but also made possible the coalition of White and African American reformers in northern cities, which effectively disciplined the Black poor through the language of law and safety. In this formulation, the connection between race and crime were ostensibly severed, while the system of racial domination persisted. This move allowed its supporters to claim that the new regime of racial governance had nothing to do with race. Without understanding the previously described transformation in racial ideas and their justification process, we cannot properly comprehend the historical trajectory leading up to the emergence of "colorblind racism."[42]

My goal is to factor contingency from knowledge production into the larger arc of political history around race and the American nation, especially in the context of immigration: Americans fought over the right to define and use race in immigration policy, but neither restrictionists nor their critics could completely control the outcome of the struggle. In the early twentieth century, those who dreamed of a White, Anglo-Saxon, and Protestant (WASP) nation and campaigned for immigration restriction won the struggle, closing the gates for decades. Yet instead of the WASP nation that they dreamed of, they arrived at a White nation that partially embraced the contributions of some immigrants while categorically excluding others. Thus, New England WASP supremacists' racial essentialism came to incorporate, at least partially, pro-immigrant reformers' racial liberalism emphasizing assimilation. How did this come about? I turn to a congressional investigative commission during the era for an answer.

## The State and Investigative Commissions

The Dillingham Commission and Progressive Era expert commissions in general represent a unique institutional sphere in which dynamics of power and the logic of knowledge production intertwine to produce a particular form of governance, one that is undergirded by the notion of facts.[43] The uniqueness stems from these commissions' relationship with the larger bureaucratic structure of the American state. Investigative commissions were not a part of the regular organizational structure of the federal government; they were established as a response to urgent and contentious issues to first determine facts around the particular problem before the government could properly devise policy solutions. Politicians, typically ranking members of the Senate and House, occupied executive positions, and civilian experts, including professors from major universities, worked as advisors, while federal employees and other street-level bureaucrats collected data in the field.[44] Because their subject matter was facts, impartiality and empiricism were assumed to be the core values of these commissions, and conspicuous pursuits of partisan interests were discouraged. To guarantee such impartiality, political factions with different views on the subject were usually invited to participate. In many cases, ensuing policy discussions occurred based on what commissions had determined as facts.[45]

When Timothy Mitchell characterized the boundary between the state and society as "a line drawn internally within the network of institutional mechanisms through which social and political order is maintained," he could just as well have been articulating the location and nature of investigative commissions during the Progressive Era.[46] Although expert commissions were propelled by the power and administrative capacity of the government—usually Congress, but sometimes the executive branch—each commission's operational logic was independent of its origin. And such independence granted some level of autonomy both in terms of its activity and overall findings. As Oz Frankel demonstrates with his study of investigative commissions in the nineteenth century, the state engaged in fact-finding activities through these commissions when it recognized the limits of its own power. When facing a particularly thorny issue such as policies concerning emancipated slaves after the Civil War, for example, the state established organizations such as the American Freedmen's Inquiry Commission (1863) to gather information and determine the relevant facts before implementing a policy solution.[47]

By doing so, the state officially recognized that certain things were not under its full jurisdiction. These investigative commissions, Frankel writes, "facilitated unforeseen encounters and dealings between governments and legislatures and their local interlocutors."[48] Oftentimes, "facts and knowledge proved elusive and occasionally ungovernable." Their objects of inquiry—in the case of the Dillingham Commission, immigrants—chose to "talk back," to borrow the phrase from historian of science Ian Hacking:

Sometimes subjects mobilized against the attempts to study them; other times, they just said too much, providing answers that investigators did not anticipate or appreciate.[49] In fact-finding activities, the power of the state provisionally ceded itself to other factors and, in so doing, faced its limitations while aiming to develop a better means of dealing with the problem at hand. In short, investigative commissions were "space[s] for the modern state's self-invention and self-reflection" through engagement with the limit of its power.[50]

In *The Racial State*, David Theo Goldberg puts race at the heart of the modern state, noting that the regulation of inclusion and exclusion by race is one of the founding functions of the institution. Rogers Smith and Desmond King concur based on the history of American political development.[51] Investigative commissions bring an interesting twist to this formulation by introducing an empirical challenge to the state—that is, the state initiates fact-finding activities to substantiate and legitimize racial governance, yet the process ironically reveals that the Leviathan is not omnipotent, exposing vulnerabilities to the forthright execution of its aims. In this light, the Dillingham Commission became a site in which the American state faced its limits in terms of its ability to base race on facts. There were competing forces pressuring the commission, including anti-immigrant and pro-immigrant ones, and they wanted the commission to scientifically support their respective positions. Yet as nineteenth-century positivists would often proclaim, "facts are facts": Once the inquiry began, the commission ventured into an unknown territory, and competing forces could not completely control what would transpire from the data collection effort or, ultimately, how the uncovered facts would configure race and nation. In short, in investigative commissions, the quest for legitimacy forced the state to inadvertently become something that it did not foresee.

In narrating the genealogy of "the modern fact," Mary Poovey presents the political function of facts in modern times as providing the basis for, as well as demarcating the boundary of, ensuing political discourse.[52] The Dillingham Commission's inquiry carried out a similar function: There could be debates as to how to interpret the facts, but no actor in the commission could completely control what kind of facts would be found, and the terms of the ensuing immigration debate in and outside of the commission would be structured by those facts. The "tension between government's desire to master social knowledge and knowledge's endemic ungovernmentality" opened up a possibility of the idea of race being transformed through knowledge production.[53] The grafting of racial liberalism onto the strain of racial essentialism occurred on this basis.

## Race at the Turn of the Twentieth Century

According to historian Robert Wiebe, the first two decades of the twentieth century were a period in which the United States engaged in a "search for order."[54] A rural, agricultural society was evolving into an industrial empire at the center of global commerce and relation. The minimal system of governance, or what scholars called "the government of parties and courts," was being increasingly eclipsed by the centralized power of federal agencies. Federal bureaucrats were beginning to establish networks with experts to produce knowledge about social problems of various kinds.[55] In the process, the nascent disciplines of social sciences—economics, political science, sociology, and anthropology—formed a symbiotic relationship with the government to obtain funding and legitimacy.[56]

Social as well as physical mobility abounded in all regions of the country during this period. The dynamic nature of westward expansion was coming to a halt, leading historian Frederic Jackson Turner to proclaim the end of the so-called frontier expansion.[57] The failure of Reconstruction and subsequent return of the violent Jim Crow regime in the South propelled many African Americans to move to northern industrial cities. Territories outside of the North American continent, including Hawaii, Guam, and Puerto Rico, were incorporated into the federation, sparking the debate about whether the United States was willing to embrace its role as a de facto empire.[58] The Chinese Exclusion Act (1882) barred Chinese laborers from entry, but people from other regions of Asia, including Japan, Korea, and the Indian subcontinent, arrived to take their place. But the most prominent source of mobility was European immigration. Although European immigrants continued to arrive on eastern shores throughout the country's history, the late nineteenth century saw a notable transformation in both the configuration and size of immigration from Europe.

Figure 1 summarizes this transformation, as understood by the Dillingham Commission. Late nineteenth-century and early twentieth-century immigrants, according to those who campaigned for their restriction, were very different from the early settlers of the nation or even the "old immigrants" who had arrived earlier in the nineteenth century. The old immigrants were typically Protestants from northern and western Europe. The "new immigrants" were Catholics and Jews from southern and eastern Europe. According to restrictionists, the former typically settled on the frontier and became settler-farmers, helping expand the nation. The latter, however, gravitated toward the industrial cities of the East Coast, looking to make quick money in factories rather than settling in the country for good through farming. In other words, in the imagination of restrictionists, the figure of the new immigrant was squarely antithetical to the nineteenth-century Jeffersonian ideal of citizen-farmer. According to this ideal, land-owning farmers were the backbone of a democratic nation because they did not rely on government or anyone else to make a living and thus were free of outside influences.[59] Catholic factory workers from the poor nations of Europe, on the contrary, lacked autonomy, relying instead on employers, religious leaders, and corrupt politicians to survive in the United States. Hence, they were categorically unfit for a democratic polity like the United States. According to restrictionists, these immigrants were at the root of many social problems in cities, including poverty, crime, and prostitution.[60]

Responding to this purported social divide, many early American social scientists invoked race to explain the difference embodied by these new immigrants. They relied mostly on a strain of racial essentialism: The new immigrants were a fundamentally different kind of people from the previous ones, and this difference manifested in their problematic behaviors, precluding any hope for their inclusion in the nation. The notion of "race suicide," coined by sociologist Edward Ross, is a good example of this line of thinking.[61] Ross raised an alarm about the difference in fertility rates of women from different backgrounds. While native-born Protestant women were giving birth to fewer children than in previous generations, immigrant Catholic women were birthing many more, resulting in a rapid demographic transition. Compounding this trend, "Asiatic" immigrant workers were pouring in from the West Coast, threatening "the American standard of

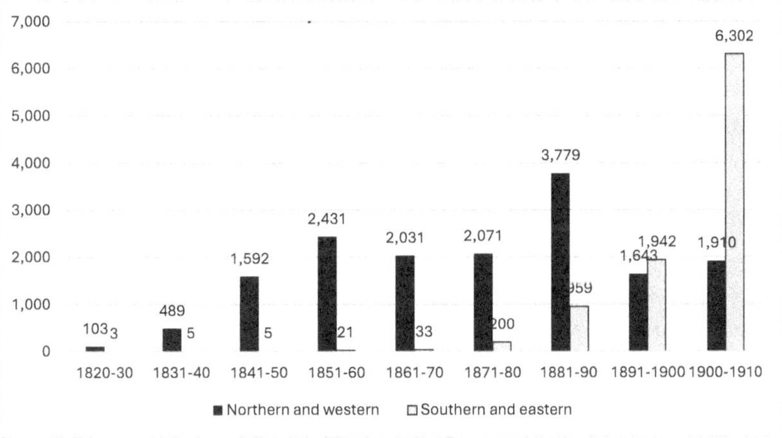


FIGURE 1. The number of European immigrants admitted (in thousands). The *Dillingham Commission Reports*, 1:64.

living" by putting downward pressure on wages of American workers, further contributing to the decline in fertility.[62] Whereas WASP families were disillusioned by the increasingly harsh living conditions, riddled with crime and immorality, brought forth by industrialization, the new immigrants and "Asiatics" thrived in this environment, driving away the more "desirable" population by outnumbering them.[63] Here, the two groups, immigrants and "Americans," were fundamentally at odds with each other, with no hope of peaceful coexistence. Progressive reformers, intellectuals, and government officials, including President Theodore Roosevelt, embraced the pseudo-Darwinian narrative and called for a comprehensive immigration restriction that would curtail the influx of immigrants, supposedly to protect the WASP "essence" of the nation.[64] The Chinese Exclusion Act of 1882 had already set a precedent for federally mandated race-based exclusion, and in the last decades of the nineteenth century restrictionists were beginning to imagine a similar measure for new immigrants on the East Coast.[65]

However, the meaning of the term *race* at the time was markedly different from how we perceive the concept today. Up to the late nineteenth century, the concept of race in the United States had two distinctive axes of racial others—African Americans, or emancipated slaves and their descendants, and "Indians," as members of the Indigenous populations of North America were then called. In the former case, racial essentialism loomed large because the whole economic system of slavery relied on clearly defining and confining the slave population by ancestry. Hence all Blacks, including free persons, were excluded from virtually all White institutions. In the latter case, the practical necessity of the settler-colonial project controlled the selective application of racial essentialism and allowed the limited possibility of Native Americans living among White settlers. For instance, courts sometimes acknowledged interracial marriages between White men and Native women despite antimiscegenation laws to ensure White ownership of land through inheritance.[66] However, when it came to matters of territory and sovereignty, both the federal government and individual settlers regarded "Indians" as fundamentally unfit to become members of the body politic and attempted to erase their existence all together, both physically and culturally.[67]

In the period following the Civil War, the key question about race focused on the social status of emancipated slaves—whether and how they should be integrated into the institutions designed and controlled by Whites. Yet the immigration debate introduced a new dimension to the question of group difference. The difference embodied by African Americans or Native Americans was one thing, but, as many scholars of Whiteness noted, the difference represented by the new immigrants was considered a distinct kind.[68]

These immigrants were legally White in that they hailed from the European continent and were clearly not descendants of slaves. But they were not exactly the same as the Anglo-Saxon Protestant elites of the country—or, as historian Matthew Frye Jacobson puts it, they possessed "whiteness of a different color."[69] Race was invoked to categorize them as a fundamentally different kind of people, but in the process the coverage of the concept grew exponentially. In addition to skin color, hair texture, and descent, race came to encompass a wide variety of traits, including language, food, habits, religion, place of origin, and any other features that could define a group. While the old strain of racial essentialism was enlarged to address the difference represented by the new immigrants, this expansion undermined its conceptual coherence. Early proponents of racial liberalism, such as W. E. B. Du Bois and Franz Boas, began to challenge these contradictions largely on scientific grounds.[70] These scholars were yet to mount a full-blown rebuttal of racial essentialism, but they were amassing evidence to contradict some of its core claims. Other scholars within the strain of racial essentialism experimented with the concept of "ethnic" regarding the new immigrants, but the public overwhelmingly preferred *race*, even though confusion over the actual meaning of the word abounded. In short, the early twentieth century was an "unsettled time" in terms of the meaning of *race*, with cracks beginning to show in the hegemony of racial essentialism.[71]

## Unruly Facts and Racial Liberalism

The call for an independent scientific inquiry on immigration emerged against this backdrop. The congressional debate on immigration had been at a stalemate, with restrictionists turning up the heat and their opponents slowly losing ground, but not enough to allow a major reform to pass. The restrictionists believed that social science was on their side and that a properly executed scientific inquiry on immigration would provide them with a stronger footing going forward. Indeed, during the time, many social scientists were deeply invested in the idea of race, and many notable scholars, such as Edward Ross, supported restriction. Pro-immigrant politicians in Congress begrudgingly agreed, because they thought such an inquiry would at least buy them some time to thwart the political momentum of the restrictionists. Bridging a deal between the warring factions in Congress, President Theodore Roosevelt initiated a social scientific study of the "immigration problem," appointing Senator William P. Dillingham (R-VT) as the chairman of the United States Immigration Commission.[72]

The existing scholarship referring to the commission mostly characterizes its work as an extension of scholarship on racial essentialism—that is, scholars found that racial ideology prevailed in the commission, and evidence and facts did not exercise much power over predetermined conclusions about the supposed undesirability of new immigrants. Most notably, historian Oscar Handlin writes, after closely analyzing the executive summary, policy recommendations, and main volumes of the *DCR*, that the commission "began with the preconceived ideas as to the difference between the old and new immigration . . . [and] . . . devoted much of its effort to bending what evidence it could find to that end."[73] Daniel Tichenor writes, "Deeply informed by racial theories, [the commission's] expert findings offered a portrait of southern and eastern newcomers that legitimized the xenophobic narrative and policy agenda of Progressive Era restrictionists."[74]

Others have noted the discrepancy between the commission's overall conclusion and the data it collected, although they did not theoretically elaborate on the mismatch. John Higham, in his history of nativism in the United States, argues that the commission reified "an invidious contrast between the northwestern and southeastern Europeans."[75] Reviewing the forty-one volumes of its reports, however, Higham points out that the commission's overall emphasis on the "invidious contrast" did not match its own data. In a similar vein, Desmond King submits a nuanced take on the commission, acknowledging how its conclusion appealed to restrictionists while pointing out the many diverging strands in its reports, such as concerns for immigrant assimilation.[76] Lastly, Aristide Zolberg, in his sweeping history of nation building in the United States, writes that "although the Commission has been deservedly demonized for its egregious stereotypes regarding nationality and race and its firm commitment to Asian exclusion, by early twenty-first-century standards its outlook would be located on the relatively 'liberal' side of the immigration policy spectrum."[77]

More recent works have picked up on the multifaceted character of the commission's inquiry to present a much more complicated picture while unearthing extensive additional archival evidence. Robert Zeidel's pioneering monograph on the commission has established the basic timeline and historical details while generally supporting the conclusion presented in the works previously citied.[78] In his book on the classification of immigrants, Joel Perlman provides a detailed analysis of the commission's scheme, "races or peoples," along with a discussion of the Jewish question in the commission's period.[79] Lastly, Katherine Benton-Cohen has delivered the most comprehensive account of the commission to date, picking up and elaborating on many of the strands discussed in other works. *Inventing the Immigration Problem* (2018) recognizes the importance of going beyond the restrictionist talking points in understanding the diverse backgrounds and motivations of the commission participants, highlights women's previously neglected contributions, sheds a light on the global consideration behind American immigration discourse and policy, and analyzes how the commission defined immigration as a "problem" to which federal power and social science expertise could provide an answer, among other contributions.[80]

While building on these works, I take a step in a different direction by focusing on how the commission articulated its vision of race. Rather than presuming that the meaning of *race* was certain during the period, as some of the aforementioned scholars have done, I posit that the concept itself was subject to reformulation in the Dillingham Commission's inquiry and set out to observe how exactly such reformulation was possible. Earlier scholarship attributed the mismatch between the commission's overall conclusion and the data it procured to the power of executive committee members' restrictionist ideology—that is, the powerful politicians were bad scientists but good partisans, and they effectively lied their way through empirical findings. On the contrary, I exploit the mismatch as an opportunity to analyze how the objects of inquiry in the commission—race and nation—transformed through engagement with facts, propelling ideological transformations that no participants intended or foresaw.

Because the Dillingham Commission was a state-sponsored social science inquiry, neither racial ideology nor political calculations alone could dictate the outcome of its work. Instead, at least on the surface, empirical data and scientific reasoning served as guidelines for its data collection activity. I am not arguing that the commission was free of ideological and political interventions from the outside. On the contrary, there were both external and internal attempts to appropriate the commission's work to serve certain ideological goals throughout its four-year tenure. However, as becomes clearer in the following chapters, these attempts never exerted a unified force, and there were instead multiple ideological and political influences competing for control of the commission.

From this open space emerged facts that did not conform to racial essentialism, and the data led to the "reworking" of certain racial ideas, to borrow the term from Moon-Kie Jung—or, more specifically, to a process I describe as the *grafting* of racial liberalism onto racial essentialism.[81] The commission's internal documents show that challenges to restrictionists' racial essentialism mounted as soon as data collection efforts began. Singling out southern and eastern European immigrants as an undesirable race was, as it turned out, not as straightforward a task as it would seem. First, it was not easy to distinguish southern and eastern Europeans as belonging to a different race from other immigrants, especially those from other

European countries. They were different from WASPs, but their difference was not the same as that of Blacks or Asian immigrants. The commission had to clarify the conceptual ground on which to distinguish southern and eastern European immigrants from other European immigrants, on the one hand, and from non-White immigrants, on the other. As it turned out, racial essentialism was unable to provide such fine-grained distinctions. Second, empirical data suggested that the new immigrants were not always undesirable; instead, they often appeared to be decent, hardworking individuals not much different from their American counterparts. The commission participants who did not necessarily subscribe to racial essentialism—not only pro-immigrant activists but also social scientists and field agents who oversaw data collection—reported these instances faithfully, endangering the ideological motivations of the restrictionists who attempted to control the inquiry through the executive committee. Granted, the research team did not challenge racial essentialism outright, but it brought forth unruly facts that demonstrated the concept's shortcomings. In sum, the restrictionists sought legitimacy of their argument through empirical data, but the unruly facts undermined that legitimacy by showcasing the inconsistencies in their notions about race and immigration.

While most of these unruly facts were either ignored or tucked away in remote corners of the forty-one-volume final report, their existence and persistence made possible the consolidation of racial liberalism. Facts became the central locus around which new ideas and networks concerning national belonging would emerge. Pro-immigrant intellectuals and activists debated restrictionists using the commission's data, and the shared facts enabled dialogue across the boundaries of class, gender, and immigration status. Whereas restrictionists were largely confined to the traditional elites of upper-class WASP men, mostly based in New England, the Dillingham Commission's unruly facts invited immigrant intellectuals, women reformers, and young, low-level bureaucrats to weigh in on the immigration problem, effectively expanding the discursive network through which policy discussion was conducted. In the process, the participants in the immigration debate came to distinguish *categorical* and *gradual* difference between population groups. According to their thinking, non-European immigrants were categorically different and had no chance of assimilating, so they needed to be excluded; European immigrants, on the other hand, were only gradually different and could assimilate given the right opportunity. From the murky terrain of various strains of racial ideas emerged a faint yet firm divide between race and ethnicity, a divide between racial essentialism and racial liberalism. Together the two strains of racial ideas formulated a new way of thinking about the immigration problem, which manifested institutionally through the Johnson-Reed Act of 1924. Most importantly, this transformation was triggered by the unruly facts gathered through the Dillingham Commission's inquiry.

The impact of racial liberalism became even more prominent in the ensuing decades. While the Johnson-Reed Act seemed to signal a victory for restrictionists and their racial essentialism, the 1930s and 1940s would also point to the ascendancy of racial liberalism. As the dust settled on the immigration restriction debate, European immigrants from different nations were encouraged to embrace the American language, customs, and habits of mind to become "indistinguishable" from the WASP "mainstream." Even the most scapegoated European immigrant groups—eastern European Jews and Italians—were given a chance to assimilate, to shed their old ways and celebrate the new. The Americanization movement combined carrots and sticks to accelerate a process that seemed to rest on this premise.[82] Meanwhile, non-White immigrants stayed outside of this dynamic, excluded from the national community and vulnerable to physical and symbolic violence. In short, race ceased to be a destiny for some people, while others were still bound by its grip.

American social sciences provided the intellectual foundation for this transformation by developing a new set of concepts that explained the dynamics of group difference. As noted previously, race had been central to the social scientific understanding of group difference up to the 1920s, although the precise definition of the concept remained elusive. In the 1910s, eugenics rapidly gained popularity among the public and helped restrictionists pass the national origin quotas act by lending the authority of science to the legislation.[83] At the same time, somewhat orthogonal to these political developments, racial liberalism was increasingly overtaking racial essentialism in academia. Moving away from the all-encompassing idea of race, new concepts clearly distinguished the biological from the social and established the latter as an object of inquiry for social sciences. *Ethnicity* represented the kind of difference assigned to and embodied by European immigrants—*cultural* difference that can become obsolete through the process of *assimilation*. Together, these concepts provided a theoretical pathway for European immigrants to become American by freeing them from racial essentialism: By forgoing their culture and assimilating, these *ethnic* groups would be able to achieve national belonging. Of course, racial essentialism did not disappear completely in this line of theorizing. Non-White *races* could not assimilate and therefore remained outside the boundary of national belonging and citizenship.[84]

Previous scholarship has different terms for this process: "the ethnicity paradigm," "the ethnic project," "unfixing race," and "the invention of ethnicity."[85] However, all point to a similar direction in historical development. My point is that this process was first initiated in the Dillingham Commission and its fact-finding operation; the resulting unruly facts were central to grafting racial liberalism onto racial essentialism. As I elaborate more in the conclusion, this contention broadens the timeline of racial liberalism and challenges the ways we think about race, immigration, and national belonging in the twenty-first century.

## Sources, Method, and Disclaimers

My account of the Dillingham Commission and the ensuing immigration debate draws from three different kinds of sources.

First, I refer to the forty-one volumes of the Dillingham Commission's final reports. Much of the prior work in immigration history focuses on the executive summary and policy recommendations, which has led to a relatively simplistic portrayal of the commission. Even the works that discuss the main volumes dwell much on the discrepancies between the commission's data and conclusion, while forgoing the question of why such discrepancies existed and how they transpired. On the contrary, I engage in an in-depth reading of the main volumes, which feature diverse topics and showcase a range of epistemological approaches to immigration. I leverage the discrepancies between the commission's data and analysis to venture into the contradictions brought to light by racial knowledge production, elaborating how they result in unintended consequences in symbolic and institutional manifestations of race.

Second, I also engage with archival materials concerning the commission. The records of the Immigration and Naturalization Services (RG85), housed in the National Archives in Washington, DC, contain only a handful of scattered documents with references to the commission. Instead, I rely more on personal papers of the commission members, including those of executive committee members, experts, and middle-level managers. In addition to containing official documents not preserved in the National Archives, these personal paper collections often include personal correspondence and internal memos concerning the commission's work, and they provide valuable information on the behind-the-scenes operations of the commission. I also refer to the archives of immigration restrictionists, most notable of which are the papers of the Immigration Restriction League (IRL). In addition to referring directly to the commission and its executive committee members, these papers showcase how restrictionists thought about immigrants more generally during the time. Plus, some of the letters they received feature the opinions of those who challenged them. Here I am indebted to the works of other scholars, such as Robert Zeidel, Joel Perlmann, and Katherine Benton-Cohen.[86]

Lastly, I refer to academic works published during and after the commission's time. To properly make sense of the theoretical foundation of the commission's inquiry, I review late nineteenth-century scholarly debates on race, especially those explicitly mentioned in the commission reports. Academic publications and policy reports that used the commission's data provide information on what kind of different analyses could have been possible for the commission.[87] In addition, I draw on a broad range of academic publications in the first half of the twentieth century to trace the impact of the commission's work on the immigration debate.

The primary object of my inquiry is ideas about group difference, which I classify into the two camps of racial essentialism and racial liberalism, as they manifest in the commission's inquiry as well as in the immigration debate in ensuing decades. These beliefs, respectively, undergirded how American politicians, intellectuals, and bureaucrats conceived the relationship between race and nation and thereby had an impact on immigration policy. In parsing out this object and tracing its development through time, I rely on genealogy, as espoused by Michel Foucault and other scholars, as my overarching method. Contrasting his approach to linear, teleological studies of historical origins, Foucault described genealogy as concerned with nonlinear paths toward an outcome, or what he described as a constellation of "accidents, the minute deviations . . . the errors, the false appraisals, and the faulty calculations that gave birth to those things that continue to exist and have value for us."[88] By attending to these seemingly disorganized entities, genealogy attempts to "reconstruct a whole network of alliances, communications, and points of support" that make possible our present.[89] In my case, that present is racial liberalism—or our understanding that we can effectively do away with racial prejudice by sharing facts and open up a pathway for the racialized to become no longer different.[90] Facing the moment of its crisis, I present an account of how it came about so we can imagine otherwise.

Ian Hacking notes in his essay "Making Up People" that ideas about group difference (i.e., race and ethnicity) readily lend themselves to this kind of history because "the category and the people in it emerge hand in hand" through a process of race making that is ripe with "confusion, contradiction, and unintended consequences."[91] That is, a particular process of knowledge production makes it possible for us to put together theory, data, and politics to render a collection of individuals into a legible group, with its own unique tendencies, demarcation points, and name. Because human diversity does not easily lend itself to simple categorization, this process is bound to be messy and confusing. W. E. B. Du Bois understood this and opined that "perhaps it is wrong to speak of [race] at all as 'a concept' rather than as a group of contradictory forces, facts, and tendencies."[92] I argue that genealogy, with its focus on nonlinear sequences, enables us to fully comprehend those "forces, facts, and tendencies."

This methodological choice is inspired by the recent discussion in historical sociology on "emergence," "formation stories," and "constitutive claims."[93] The previous generation of historical sociologists attempted to explain an important outcome (e.g., revolution) through a configuration of variables (e.g., economic conditions, class composition, etc.) by observing variations across cases (e.g., comparing different revolutions across time and space). The studies of "emergence" instead prioritize narrative explanations of how we come to arrive at a certain entity (e.g., the state) that make it possible for us to appreciate a particular outcome of importance (e.g., democracy). My genealogical inquiry of the Dillingham Commission resonates with this framework: By tracing how the commission engaged in the transformation of racial ideas, I narrate how grafting racial liberalism onto racial essentialism happened through gathering unruly facts in the early twentieth century, and how it became possible for us to think through the conceptual framework of race and ethnicity. In the process, unlike many previous renditions of genealogy, I rely much on the repertoire of a sociologist's tool kit—explicit and implicit comparison, negative case method, and even ethnography—to construct my explanation.[94]

The common challenges to genealogical method are well known. Where do we start our investigation, and where do we end? How are we sure that we are not "selecting on the dependent variable" and privileging the evidence that supports our argument, as critics sometimes point out? Many casual readers of Foucault have leveled this line of criticism against his work and other similar endeavors as cherry-picking anecdotes from archives to present a grand theory that is not supported by solid evidence. I find this line of criticism ultimately misleading,[95] but there are valid points to consider. Some of the common data analysis techniques in historical sociology and other subfields of sociology can be useful in scaffolding a broader genealogical argument, provided that their requirements do not overtake the entire direction of the inquiry.

My choice of the Dillingham Commission as a strategic entry point to the immigration debate speaks to these concerns.[96] By grounding my analysis in a specific institutional context, I can temporarily bound my inquiry, at least enough to concretely grasp my analytical object of racial ideas. As becomes clear in the following chapters, my historical explanation does sometimes exceed the immediate scope of the commission, but it is still anchored by the commission and social networks that it spurred through its collection of unruly facts. In other words, the commission as a case study functions as a centripetal force holding together ever-expanding networks of knowledge production. In a sense, this methodological strategy is analogous to ethnography, in terms of grounding general theoretical concerns in a particular place and time. In any case, I attempt to strike a balance between the specificity of a particular historical case and the broader aims of genealogical inquiry by positing the Dillingham Commission as a strategic entry point into more general discussions about race and nation in the early twentieth-century United States.

Lastly, a disclaimer about this study is in order. I try to avoid the presentist bias in understanding racial ideas. It is tempting to understand the concepts of race and ethnicity as defined in contemporary sociological literature, as representing biological and cultural differences, respectively. Seen from this vantage point, the actors in the Dillingham Commission's time appear "misinformed"—namely, they did not understand these concepts properly in not distinguishing the biological from the social, failing to comprehend the socially constructed nature of the categories at their disposal. Worse, some of them appear to have been driven by racial prejudice that we find abhorrent, which, in some popular and scholarly accounts, renders their intellectual work as something not to be taken seriously. This kind of anachronistic imposition is not helpful in understanding the past, especially as it pertains to race. By succumbing to the temptation to make a quick judgment, we are left with an empty charge of "racist" and not much else, and we do not gain insight into how we arrived at our current way of thinking about race. As I show, it is due to these actors' ventures, ignorance, and mishaps that we came to attain the "correct" conception of race and ethnicity. The people of the commission's time, regardless of where they stood politically on matters of race and immigration, took their theoretical work seriously, no less than we do today. Of course, they were not perfect; sometimes, they strictly followed the norms of scientific inquiry as they understood it, but in other instances, they bent those rules and favored explanations that suited them better. And there were various degrees of bending that different actors were willing to allow themselves to engage in. Only by putting ourselves in their shoes—not necessarily sympathizing with their political ideology but grasping the limitations and choices they faced—can we understand how they came to graft, unwittingly, racial liberalism onto racial essentialism. As opposed to brushing them collectively aside as racists as some commentators have done, I take their intellectual endeavors seriously and attend to their internal logics of development. Taking so-called racists seriously is not equivalent to paying them respect. On the contrary, serious engagement leads to a more comprehensive understanding, which allows us to not just criticize them but deconstruct and overcome their harmful legacy.[97]

## Summary of Chapters

This book consists of three parts. The first part presents background information. While chapter 1 showcases the strains of racial ideas available to the commission, chapter 2 describes the immediate political context of its operation. The second part lays out the emergence of racial liberalism, told through the journeys of Daniel Folkmar (chapter 3) and Franz Boas (chapter 4), as they make critical contributions toward the concepts of ethnicity and assimilation, respectively. Chapter 5 broadens the focus and traces how the commission's data enabled the expansion and diversification of the discursive network that facilitated the consolidation of racial liberalism. The third part explain why racial liberalism did not replace racial essentialism altogether, instead opting to become its component. Chapter 6 elaborates how race still mattered, as told through the story of Yamato Ichihashi and his advocacy on behalf of Japanese immigrants. Chapter 7 traces the trajectory of the national quota idea from the commission to the 1920s, analyzing how the Johnson-Reed Act embodied both racial liberalism and racial essentialism. Lastly, the conclusion discusses the limit of racial liberalism as it pertains to the immigration debates of the past and present.

Chapter 1 presents a brief historical overview of the idea of race from the sixteenth century to the late nineteenth century. The modern conception of race first emerged in the context of Europe's violent colonial expansion into Africa, Asia, and the Americas. Early naturalists used color schemes to represent peoples in these continents, associating skin tone with purported aptitude for civilization. After the French Revolution, reactionary intellectuals from fallen noble families started to project their class politics onto this color-coded classification system, advocating for the supremacy of White men over others. In the aftermath of the Civil War, young New England WASP elites, threatened by the rise of industrial capitalism, embraced a similar worldview while targeting European immigrants. By the late nineteenth century, race was a scientifically validated, cutting-edge theory for understanding both the natural and the social worlds, especially for WASP men educated in elite institutions. Consequently, many powerful actors subscribed to racial essentialism and strived to preserve the United

States as a nation of WASPs. However, their concern for European immigration gradually opened up a space for racial liberalism.

Chapter 2 details the political context surrounding the immigration debate in 1907, charting out how various interest groups situated themselves in relation to the so-called immigration problem. Progressive politicians, reformers, and labor leaders called for restriction while old-guard politicians, representing the interests of big capital, opposed the idea. The latter's hold on the House of Representatives led to a stalemate around immigration for two decades at the turn of the century. In addition to this long-standing divide, Theodore Roosevelt also had to pay attention to anti-immigrant mobilization targeting Japanese immigrants in California, not wanting to risk offending Japan given his expansionist agenda in the Pacific. The Immigration Act of 1907, which launched the Dillingham Commission and granted the president the power to enforce the Gentlemen's Agreement with Japan, was a compromise in this complicated context. Somewhat ironically, these multiple layers of influence around the commission gave it some autonomy, making the commission's data collection efforts a no-man's-land in which facts and scientific inquiry prevailed—at least on the surface. As I discuss at the end of the chapter, a diverse set of racial ideas held by the executive committee members also contributed to this autonomy.

Chapter 3 analyzes the racial classification scheme featured in volume 5 of the *DCR*, titled *The Dictionary of Races or Peoples*, to trace the emergence of ethnicity. The story starts with Daniel Folkmar, the anthropologist who authored the report. After having worked as a race scientist for the Philippines' colonial administration and making head casts of different "races" in the archipelago, he was hired by the commission to oversee its theory of racial classification. Folkmar encountered a logical dilemma in singling out southern and eastern Europeans as a different race from the rest of Europeans. Because the existing theories of race did not support this distinction, Folkmar had to resort to language and geography to pinpoint and codify differences within Europe but, in the process, risked de-essentializing the concept of race. Hypothetically, anyone can move to a different place and pick up a new language to become a member of a different race. Facing this logical conundrum, Folkmar had to carefully balance essentialism and liberalism in devising a new scheme to single out southern and eastern European immigrants. This "unfixing" of race would provide an opening for racial liberalism.

Franz Boas was a German-born Jewish anthropologist who became famous for spearheading the discipline's transition from racial science to cultural analysis. Less well-known is his participation in the Dillingham Commission as a principal investigator for the project on immigrant children's head shapes. Chapter 4 focuses on how the commission inadvertently contributed to the demise of racial essentialism in the social sciences by funding his work. Boas proposed a physical anthropology project studying the skull sizes of immigrant children, a proposal that seemed to be squarely within the tradition of racial essentialism. Using time series data collected in New York City, Boas showed that two of the supposedly most stable indicators of race, shapes and sizes of skulls, transformed rapidly under the influence of different environments, undermining racial essentialism. He argued that immigrant children may appear different initially but that they would quickly develop into a new racial type, as indicated by the rapid transformation of their skulls. He called the result of such transformation "the American race," implicitly celebrating hybridity and providing an early iteration of racial liberalism. In the following decades, Boas's students in anthropology would go on to conduct studies with a similar design, further discrediting racial essentialism and instead putting culture at the center of the discourse on group difference. In sociology, W. I. Thomas was inspired by Boas and used his study to formulate the Chicago school's race-relations cycle theory. By the second decade of the twentieth century, cultural relativism and assimilation theory became the dominant paradigms in their respective disciplines of anthropology and sociology, thereby strengthening the hold of racial liberalism in the social sciences.

The theoretical challenges to racial essentialism also entailed the expansion and diversification of discursive networks formerly dominated by upper-class WASP men, and chapter 5 charts this development. Facts collected by the commission proved to be crucial in this process. According to the commission's data, immigrants in many cases appeared to be indistinguishable from—or, in some cases and by some measures, better than—their native-born American counterparts. While the final report of the commission does not highlight these findings, pro-immigrant intellectuals and activists—who were often immigrants or women from modest backgrounds—seized on them to engage in a debate with restrictionists. Although neither side was able to change minds, the debate established discursive networks that crossed boundaries of class, gender, and national origin, leading to conceptual innovations associated with ethnicity, culture, and assimilation. Racial liberalism consolidated around these new ideas and networks.

Shifting the focus to the West Coast and Japanese immigrants, chapter 6 tells the story of a failed challenge to racial essentialism. Yamato Ichihashi migrated from Japan in the 1890s as a teenager and later received a PhD from Harvard and became the first tenured professor of Asian descent at Stanford University. In his twenties, he worked as a field agent for the commission, collecting data on Japanese immigrants living on the West Coast. Ichihashi took great pride in working for the US government and set out to tell the American public the true story of much-maligned Japanese immigrants. He found that Japanese immigrants were much more desirable than any other immigrant groups—they were hardworking farmers and merchants who spoke English at home and were respected members of their communities who sent their kids to American public schools and read English newspapers on Sundays. Yet because of their race, they were categorically barred from naturalization and excluded from the body politic more generally. Based on the supposed desirability of Japanese immigrants, Ichihashi advocated for their naturalization rights, thereby criticizing racial essentialism. Contrary to what we have seen in the previous chapters, Ichihashi's argument did not connect to the larger undercurrent of racial liberalism, and his advocacy for Japanese immigrants did not garner much support. During World War II, he was subjected to incarceration, and he later died stateless. Ichihashi's story tells us that not all unruly facts spurned racial liberalism and that racial essentialism continued to confine the lives of non-White immigrants.

Ideas and networks built around the commission's facts found their institutional manifestation in national quotas, the most important restrictionist policy in US history. Chapter 7 centers on this often-neglected historical development. Archival evidence shows that William Husband, the executive secretary of the commission, was the first person to come up with the idea of quotas. After having encountered unruly facts in the commission's inquiry, he understood that immigration restriction needed a new and effective means of *sorting*—not simply excluding—immigrants. Quotas thereby emerged as an alternative to the then commonly favored literacy test. Quotas embodied both racial liberalism and racial essentialism by applying different means of restriction to European and Asian immigrants. The admission of European immigrants was tied to their likelihood of assimilation, which was deduced from the history and size of settlement by national origin. Immigrants from Asia, on the other hand, were categorically excluded because they were deemed too different to assimilate into the national community. By applying different principles of restriction for "ethnic" versus "racial" immigrants, the quota laws effectively provided a legal and discursive infrastructure by which the contemporary understanding of race and ethnicity became possible. The grafting of racial liberalism onto racial essentialism manifested through this two-tiered sorting system.

Overall, the new ideas, networks, and laws governing race and the American nation emerged in unforeseen ways from the unruly facts gathered by the Dillingham Commission, and restrictionists struggled to reconcile their racial essentialism with empirical evidence from the commission's inquiry. Racial liberalism consolidated around a new set of concepts and networks, thereby challenging racial essentialism. Together, the two strains of racial ideas formulated the foundation for the way we think about immigrants—namely, that there are assimilable White immigrants and nonassimilable non-White immigrants and that the former merit gradual inclusion into the nation, while the latter should be subject to categorical exclusion. This book's key contention, based on archival evidence, is that this transformation was neither engineered by restrictionists nor brokered by pro-immigrant advocates. Instead, it was more powerful and durable because the contingency in knowledge production—which I dub the unruly facts—facilitated it. In the conclusion, I reflect on the limits of this framework in the twenty-first century.

[ CHAPTER ONE ]

# The History of Race-Thinking

## Categories and Hierarchy

The Dillingham Commission had two core working assumptions in designing its inquiry on immigration: First, immigrants could be classified into discrete groups, which the commission called "races or peoples"; second, by collecting statistical and ethnographic data using this classification scheme, it was possible to compare "races or peoples" and discern which groups were "undesirable" and, therefore, should be excluded from the country.

These two assumptions correspond to what Tukufu Zuberi has identified as the two core tenets of a racial stratification system: "racial reification" and "racial ranking."[1] Following these tenets, the idea of race consists of two distinctive epistemological principles—one about what kind of races there are and the other about what relationship exists among those races. I use the terms *categories* and *hierarchy*, respectively, to denote these principles. As with any intellectual inquiry, the Dillingham Commission did not start from scratch: Although the commission did not follow the typical academic protocol of citations, it did mobilize existing theories about race and immigration to build categories and hierarchies. In this chapter, I attempt to elucidate this process of mobilization by reviewing the theoretical strands that preceded the Dillingham Commission's race-thinking.

There is a long history behind the belief that human beings can be classed into mutually exclusive groups and that those groups can be ordered into a hierarchy. I use the term *race-thinking*[2] to reference this tradition and *race-thinkers* to designate the individuals who affirmed this premise through their participation in an influential conversation about race. While the theories and scholarship taking up race do not constitute a coherent intellectual tradition, the two core tenets of categories and hierarchy nevertheless served as the rallying point for the various spectrums of race-thinking.

Up to the time of the Dillingham Commission, there existed three distinctive camps of race-thinking, each with a different purpose in engaging with race. First, naturalists, who initially came up with the idea of biological human differences, were interested in studying differences in humankind and attempted to determine the number of races that existed in nature. The key question for them was how to find the best measure for racial differences, and, as it turned out, for them the answer to this question became collecting and measuring human skulls. Although the emphasis on skulls gradually faded among race-thinkers throughout the nineteenth century, this tradition was revived, albeit for a radically different purpose, in the Dillingham Commission through Franz Boas's work on the head shapes of immigrant children. As discussed in more detail in chapter 4, however, Boas criticized the notion of essential group differences based on biology through his work, effectively dismantling the core tenet of naturalists.

Second, polygenists attempted to develop a metatheory of race in addition to merely documenting and describing biological differences. Their key contention was that different races were different species and not variations of *Homo sapiens*. In their theories, the natural order became a model for a desirable, God-given social order in which Whites governed and other races followed. Invoking both science and religion, polygenists used their theories to justify reactionary political ideologies that defended slavery and colonialism. However, by arguing that different races were different species, polygenists defied the commonly accepted biblical doctrine of monotheism—that is, God created humans as one unified species. As a result, polygenism's popular appeal was limited, and the overly biological theory of human difference lost traction, giving way to theories that emphasized social and historical grounds of group differences.

Lastly, the rise of social sciences in the Progressive Era led to the emergence of a new generation of race-thinking that conceptualized human group differences not as a natural fact or a divine creation but as a statistical construct, obtained through analytical induction from empirical data. Reform-minded social scientists put aside metaphysical questions about race and instead pursued the "practical" use of the concept to provide solutions to key social problems of the time, such as immigration. In the process, race became an all-encompassing entity that addressed both biological and social dimensions of human group differences. The men who were directly linked to the Dillingham Commission—Henry Cabot Lodge, Theodore Roosevelt, and Daniel Folkmar (see chapter 3)—were all heavily influenced by this tradition.

It should be noted that all three traditions lean heavily toward racial essentialism and that racial liberalism was still in its infancy by the late nineteenth century. As Zuberi makes clear with the concept of racial reification, the point of labeling something as race is to signal its immutability, its decisive command over other characteristics. Therefore, it makes sense that the majority of race-thinkers espoused racial essentialism. Between polygenists and the Progressive Era social scientists, however, there were notable Black leaders and intellectuals, such as Booker T. Washington and W. E. B. Du Bois, who debated the possibility of "racial uplift" for newly emancipated enslaved persons and their descendants. These visionaries espoused an antithesis to racial essentialism—namely, that Black people could improve their status by education and collective effort. Race-thinkers, all of them White, virtually ignored this line of thinking in their musings about race and adhered to racial essentialism.

Nevertheless, at the end of the nineteenth century, racial essentialism was witnessing its own limit: The existing repertoire of categories and hierarchy could not effectively single out southern and eastern European immigrants. Race-thinkers faced a catch-22 of sorts: They needed to make a compromise between the political potential and theoretical validity of the race concept, and from this compromise sprang racial liberalism, which highlights a mutable—therefore, not essential—nature of race. As we see throughout this book, with the help of immigrant intellectuals and women reformers, the new iteration of racial liberalism was able to effectively complement racial essentialism as a scientific understanding of human difference—at least within the nascent disciplines of the social sciences.

As I detail in chapters 3, 4, and 5, the Dillingham Commission selectively drew from past repertoires of race-thinking to make sense of the data it was collecting. The commission participants had to work far more on their project than any of the race-thinkers mentioned in this chapter because the amount of their data was unprecedented and the data did not always tell them the story they wanted to hear. Thus, they had to reach deep into the tool kit of race-thinking and summon the ideas of many race-thinkers, from Johann Friedrich Blumenbach to Theodore Roosevelt. In the process, the contradiction within racial knowledge production intensified, giving voice to the unruly facts garnered from the field.

## The Origin Story

It is not easy to determine when and where the idea of race originated. Setting aside the genetic account,[3] most scholars attribute global changes associated with the rise of modernity as key factors in the foundation of race thinking. José Itzigsohn and Karida Brown, following W. E. B. Du Bois, center "racialized modernity" as the key object of inquiry for sociology, situating "colonialism and the creation of race" as well as the ensuing "global denial of humanity and multiple forms of exclusion" at the heart of modern society.[4] According to anthropologist C. Loring Brace, in a simple but provocative account, categorical group differences originated from the development of transportation—that is, long-distance navigation, in the context of colonial ventures.[5] Before the era of European naval expansion, any travel—be it explorations by adventurous individuals or large-scale military campaigns by empires—was characterized by its gradual pace. People moved slowly—no more than one hundred kilometers per day at a maximum on land mass—and, in the process, they might encounter a panorama of human differences in biological characteristics, such as skin color and hair texture, and culture, such as settlement patterns, housing, and customs. For example, in Marco Polo's travelogue, human differences from Italy to China are described as a panorama of different sceneries and customs, not as neatly packaged categories. Even aggressive military campaigns waged by belligerent empires, such as those of Rome or Genghis Khan, were limited by the physical mobility of their troops, and thus the groups they conquered were regarded as reflecting the incremental differences of human societies across different places and climate zones, not categorical differences among humankind.[6]

The great European naval expansion and Christopher Columbus's so-called discovery of the American continent, however, led to a watershed in how human differences were perceived. After years of lonesome voyage on the high seas, European sailors crossed an unprecedented distance and arrived at a different climate zone, encountering those whose looks and habits were far different from their own. To be clear, the difference was striking only because they had been subjected to isolation for months before encountering new people. Had they been moving across the continent, the sailors would have encountered all kinds of peoples between "us" and "them." Yet on the high seas, there was no middle ground, only seabirds and waves. In these extracontinental encounters, human group differences were perceived not as gradational but as categorical—that is, sharply divided and without overlapping characteristics. Ensuing colonial expansion and violent conflict between groups with diametrically opposing interests and destinies (e.g., colonialists and Indigenous groups) also contributed to this way of thinking about human differences, which turned out to be a ground for racial essentialism.

In *Modern Peoplehood*, John Lie argues that the notion of categorical difference alone is not sufficient to warrant the development of race-thinking. Lie rightly points out that categorical difference was widely invoked in any society with a hierarchical caste structure, usually in order to explain the differences between groups with different social statuses, such as peasants and aristocrats. In his account, race emerged as a "fact of nature" only in the nineteenth century, as a collaborative project between the modern state apparatus and the ascending science of biology.[7] Previously, human differences, whether categorical or incremental, were explained through a variety of factors, such as climate, history, religion, and social institution. Yet by separating nature from all other factors and characterizing it as immutable—that is, given at birth, heritable through reproduction, and impervious to environmental influences—the nineteenth-century race-thinkers turned the notion of categorical differences into an *essentialist* theory about human characteristics, firmly siding with racial essentialism. In their thinking, groups were different because they were different *in nature*, and their respective characteristics would never change. These differences could be measured through "the idea of progress," a hierarchy of civilization that placed different races within a ladderlike scale in terms of their supposed level of achievements. European civilization, which was expanding globally through colonial ventures, stood at the top of the hierarchy, while all other races ranked below. In other words, *hierarchy*, as well as *category*, in association with modernity and civilization, enabled the concept of race, and by deeming itself as "natural"—that is, an irresistible fact proven by science—race-thinking obtained authority and power in the broader intellectual discussion about culture and society.

## Race in Nature: Linnaeus, Blumenbach, and the Color Races

Carl Linnaeus (1707–1778), the Swedish botanist known as the father of modern taxonomy, spent his career classifying everything he could think of, from animals and plants to rocks and supernatural beings. Not satisfied with the haphazard classification system of the Middle Ages, he aspired to build a reliable and systematic order of nature distinguishing "species" and "varieties": Species concerned proper distinctions among different organisms as God almighty had intended, while varieties were different expressions of those species that reflected differences not in essence but in their contexts, such as climate or geography.[8] In other words, Linnaeus devised a two-tiered system of classification, one that is not unlike race and ethnicity, of essence and of expression. For instance, dogs come in a variety of breeds, ranging from Siberian husky to shih tzu, but all breeds still belong to a single species.[9] Linnaeus separated *Homo sapiens* into four categories, using color and continent to distinguish these varieties as "white Europeans," "red American," "brown Asian," and "black African." Yet this classification scheme remained a marginal topic in his vast classification system, which included an impressive number of known plants and animals and even "monsters," such as phoenixes, dragons, hydras, and sirens.

Many race-thinkers, including those of the Dillingham Commission, however, credit Johann Friedrich Blumenbach (1752–1840) as the founder of modern race-thinking. Blumenbach's key contribution was conceptualizing race as difference in essence and not in expression (the inverse of Linnaeus's system), thereby cementing the concept of race as an immutable, inherent characteristic of different human groups. In addition to making popular the labels of the "color races"—Caucasian (white), Mongolian (yellow), Malayan (brown), Ethiopian (black), and American (red)—Blumenbach also utilized observational data to substantiate these categories. Regarding the application of this scheme, he argued that visible indicators of race, such as skin color, were unreliable because they could easily be influenced by environment, as evidenced by the cases of European colonialists becoming dark-skinned after spending time in the tropical sun as well as European farmers being darker than their lords and kings. Instead of superficial features such as skin color or hair texture, Blumenbach reasoned that essential features, such as the shapes of skulls, could serve as the core measure of different racial types.

In *On the Natural Variety of Mankind* (1795), Blumenbach documented the process through which his theory of race developed. Central to the book were racial categories based on shapes of skulls, which he substantiated by presenting drawings from his extensive collection of human crania. As historian Nell Irvin Painter recounts, Blumenbach's academic reputation allowed him to mobilize supporters among the wealthy and powerful, and his influential friends assisted the respected professor by sending him human skulls they had obtained from their overseas adventures. With help from his friends, the young, devout naturalist became the "father of craniology"[10] and race-thinking by "placing scores of human skulls from around the world in a line and measuring the height of the foreheads, the size and angle of the jawbone, the angle of the teeth, the eye sockets, the nasal bones."[11]

Like many gentlemen scientists of his time, Blumenbach's observations often combined scientific empiricism with a romantic, aesthetic appreciation for the objects of study—in his case, skulls. It is a well-documented fact that Blumenbach was the first person to use the label "Caucasian," supposedly based on the single skull of a woman from the Eurasian country of Georgia in the southern region of Mount Caucasus. As Painter's fascinating account notes,[12] Blumenbach's thinking was informed by the aesthetics of his prized possession. Selectively drawing on the travel writings of seventeenth-century gentleman explorers, Blumenbach asserted that Central Asia was a region that featured many beautiful individuals, especially

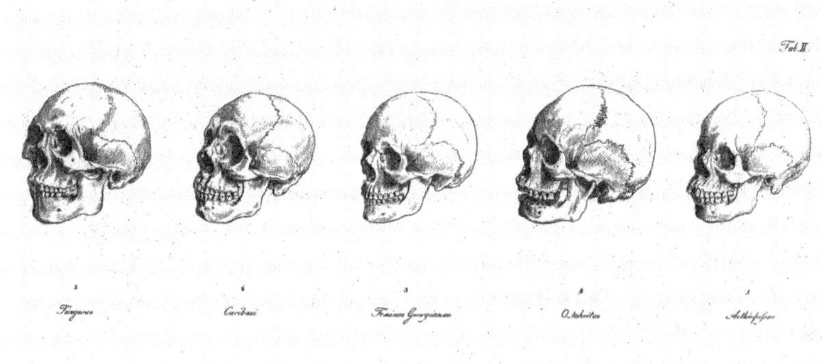

FIGURE 2. Plate IV of Blumenbach, *On the Natural Variety of Mankind*, 3rd ed. Reproduced from Bophal, "The Beautiful Skull."

women. Obsessing over this supposed fact, he declared, "My beautiful typical head of a young Georgian female . . . always attracts every eye, however little observant."[13] Hence, the Georgian skull became an inspirational cornerstone for his racial classification scheme, representing the ideal from which all other races would degenerate. The skull in the middle (3) of figure 2 is "Feminae Georgianae," the famed "Caucasian" skull of a woman from Georgia.[14] Many other skulls in his collection did not receive such appreciation.[15] By combining empiricism and romanticism with the biblical narrative of the fall from grace, Blumenbach presented a basic template for race-thinking: science accompanied by aesthetic obsessions and supported by those in power, although not without contradiction.[16] Many race-thinkers would follow his footsteps and project their desires onto the idea of race.

## The Skull Collector: Samuel Morton and the Limits of Craniology

Building on Blumenbach's foundation, Samuel George Morton (1799–1851) created a stronger and bolder platform for race-thinking through his infamous skull collection. Born in Philadelphia and educated in the Quaker tradition, Morton was trained in the influential medical school of Edinburgh as a physician. His European education introduced him to the emerging tradition of empiricism, and he learned to appreciate nature by observing it with his own eyes as opposed to merely contemplating abstract concepts about it. Like Linnaeus and Blumenbach, Morton felt he was obligated to decipher the logic of God's order of creation, and he pursued his calling throughout his life while practicing medicine in Philadelphia. Morton had a peculiar passion, however: collecting and measuring human skulls. Following the example set by Blumenbach, Morton argued that skulls could provide a reliable and valid indicator of racial essence.

Morton likely became interested in human skulls through his exposure to phrenology while attending the University of Edinburgh's medical school.[17] Although now seen as a pseudoscience, phrenology was once regarded as the finest example of eighteenth-century empiricism: By connecting the physical features of the head with its owner's character, phrenology implied that observation could provide a window into understanding traits that were not directly observable. According to Steven Shapin, this seemingly straightforward, unmediated empiricism challenged a classical intellectual tradition that privileged the musings of distinguished individuals—that is, even aristocrats were no different from peasants and workers in having brains inside their skulls, and anyone with trained eyes and equipment could decipher the genius of the human mind through direct observation. Inspired by the promise of a more democratic and antiestablishment kind of science, Edinburgh factory workers and professionals filled the seats in phrenology lectures with remarkable enthusiasm. By debunking the aura around the notion of genius—the term literally means "noble in birth" in Latin—phrenology provided intellectual catharsis to working- and middle-class residents in the highly polarized, hierarchical society of Edinburgh.[18]

Morton wrote to merchants, travelers, and professional grave robbers asking for skulls and gave almost all of his disposable income to sketchy characters who promised to procure human remains from exotic corners of the world. When he died in 1851 at the age of fifty-two, he left behind 867 skulls from all over the globe. Ann Fabian notes the significance of his collection: "Anatomists had long compared animal skulls, but until Morton came along, no naturalist or anatomist had human skulls in anywhere near a number that approached his."[19] As one might expect, however, the geographical origins of the skulls were confined to certain regions, the list of which closely overlapped with the spatial distribution of colonial violence: "In the category of the English 'race' there were five skulls, in the American seven, and in the German eighteen. On the other hand, there were 338 Indian and 85 Negro skulls."[20] Being a fair-minded scientist, Morton always looked out for opportunities to collect more "White" skulls, yet they were hard to come by, because White lives and skulls were more valued and therefore more closely guarded than those of the colonized. Regardless, the collected skulls were carefully preserved, labeled, measured, and featured in his most influential publication, *Crania Americana; Or, A Comparative View of the Skulls of Various Aboriginal Nations of North and South America* (1839). Adorned with detailed sketches of skulls and their measurements, the 484-page monograph displayed the cutting-edge lithography techniques of antebellum Philadelphia and instantly became a must-have coffee-table book of the time.

With his formidable skills of recordkeeping and meticulous observation, Morton brought about momentous developments in race-thinking, advancing the credibility of a model for racial essence. First, unlike Blumenbach, who had focused on overall shape and a few measurements in comparing skulls of different races, he developed an elaborate set of indexes to note numerous features of skulls, in addition to increasing the sheer number of skulls from which the data was drawn. Along with the sketches of the skulls, he presented tables to display how differences between races could be stated in numerical terms (see fig. 3). These numbers nicely complemented high-quality drawings of skulls and provided an aura of scientific legitimacy as well as visual appeal to the idea of race (see fig. 4). Second, reflecting the influence of phrenology, Morton attempted to measure the "capacity" of his skulls. Size and shape of skulls could vary due to various environmental factors; however, Morton argued, the average volume of skulls for each racial group was constant, therefore representing racial essence. A skull with larger volume indicated a larger brain and, according to Morton, an enhanced faculty of reasoning. Morton filled skulls with grain to accurately measure the average volume of each racial group, and, not surprisingly for Morton, Caucasian male skulls had the highest average volume, or "capacity" for reasoning, followed by various other races. As William Stanton observed, "Morton's quantitative distinctions were also qualitative," and the differences in degree were easily converted into qualitative differences in kind.[21] Whereas Blumenbach moved the focus of race-thinking from the superficial (e.g., skin color and hair texture) to the essential (as thought to be indicated by skull shape), Morton went a step further by locating the essence of race in a differing "capacity" of reason for different races, a conclusion that gained credence because of his in-depth empirical observation of skulls. Hence, race became something more than looks or numbers; it became tied to the ability of each racial group to reason. In other words, Morton made it clear that the question of categories was intrinsically tied to the question of hierarchy, because races differed in their capacity for higher reasoning. However, as we see in the late nineteenth century and in the Dillingham Commission, this emphasis on empirical data would come back to haunt race-thinkers in unexpected ways.

MEAN RESULTS OF THE FOREGOING TABLE.

| | *Toltecan nations*, including skulls from the mounds. | | *Barbarous nations*, with skulls from the Valley of Ohio. | | *American Race*, embracing the Toltecan and barbarous nations. | | Flathead tribes of Columbia river. | | Ancient Peruvians. | |
|---|---|---|---|---|---|---|---|---|---|---|
| | No. of skulls. | MEAN. | No. of skulls. | MEAN. | No. of skulls. | MEAN. | No. of skulls. | MEAN. | No. of skulls. | MEAN. |
| Longitudinal diameter. | 57 | 6.5 | 90 | 7. | 147 | 6.75 | 8 | 6.7 | 3 | 6.8 |
| Parietal diameter. | 57 | 5.6 | 90 | 5.5 | 147 | 5.55 | 8 | 6. | 3 | 5. |
| Frontal diameter. | 57 | 4.4 | 90 | 4.3 | 147 | 4.35 | 8 | 4.9 | 3 | 4.2 |
| Vertical diameter. | 57 | 5.3 | 90 | 5.4 | 147 | 5.35 | 8 | 4.8 | 3 | 4.8 |
| Inter-mastoid arch. | 57 | 14.9 | 90 | 14.6 | 147 | 14.75 | 8 | 14.6 | 3 | 13.3 |
| Inter-mastoid line. | 57 | 4.1 | 90 | 4.2 | 147 | 4.15 | 8 | 4.1 | 3 | 4. |
| Occipito-frontal arch. | 57 | 13.6 | 90 | 14.2 | 147 | 13.9 | 8 | 13.1 | 3 | 14.3 |
| Horizontal periphery. | 57 | 19.4 | 90 | 19.9 | 147 | 19.65 | 8 | 20. | 3 | 18.8 |
| Length of head and face. | 53 | 7.8 | 78 | 8.1 | 131 | 7.45 | 8 | 8.3 | 3 | 8.4 |
| Zygomatic diameter. | 49 | 5.3 | 64 | 5.3 | 113 | 5.3 | 8 | 5.7 | 3 | 5.1 |
| Facial angle. | 55 | 75° 35′ | 83 | 76° 13′ | 138 | 75° 45′ | 8 | 69° 30′ | 3 | 67° 20′ |
| Internal capacity in cubic inches. | 57 | 76.8 | 87 | 82.4 | 144 | 79.6 | 8 | 79.25 | 3 | 73.2 |
| Capacity of the anterior chamber. | 46 | ‡32.5 | 73 | 34.5 | 119 | 33.5 | 8 | 32.25 | 3 | 25.7 |
| Capacity of the posterior chamber. | 46 | ‡43.8 | 73 | 48.6 | 119 | 46.2 | 8 | 47. | 3 | 47.4 |
| Capacity of the coronal region. | 46 | ‡14. | 71 | 16.2 | 117 | 15.1 | 8 | 11.9 | 3 | 14.6 |
| Capacity of the sub-coronal region. | 46 | ‡61.8 | 71 | 66.5 | 117 | 64.5 | 8 | 67.35 | 3 | 58.6 |
| The total capacity being estimated at 100, gives the following proportionate results as parts of 100. Ant. chamb. | | 42.6 | | 41.5 | | 42.1 | | 40.63 | | 35.1 |
| Post. chamb. | | 57.4 | | 58.5 | | 60. | | 59.37 | | 64.9 |
| Coronal reg. | | 18.47 | | 19.6 | | 19. | | 15. | | 20. |
| Sub-cor. reg. | | 81.53 | | 80.4 | | 81. | | 85. | | 80. |

† These three heads are artificially moulded.

‡ The seeming discrepancy in the sums of these two pairs of measurements, arises from the fact that only 46 of the 48 heads measured, enter into each series.

FIGURE 3. A table from Morton's *Crania Americana*, 259.

Lastly, but most important, Morton made a bold argument that each race was an independent species and that God had created each of them in different continents as separate beings. Before Darwin, species were understood as God's creations: They were created perfectly, and thus any change in their design, except for minor modifications in superficial elements, was both unnecessary and impossible. Arguing otherwise would amount to blasphemy or, at least, an open invitation to quarrel with the church. But given the measurements he had taken, and in view of the qualitative conclusions he had drawn about skull volume (which was, he assumed, independent of environmental influence like nutrition), Morton concluded that different races were, in fact, different species. The doctrine of polygenism, or the belief that human beings were created as multiple species, was a dangerous idea: In the nineteenth-century United States, even mentioning such possibility could easily taint one's reputation as a decent Christian.[22] Thus, Morton refrained from openly proclaiming his ideas. Yet there were other gentlemen scientists who were willing to embrace Morton's heresy: As the Civil War approached and the conflict around slavery intensified, at least one slavery apologist rallied behind Morton's polygenism, citing the evidence of Morton's skull collection to make a defense of slavery.

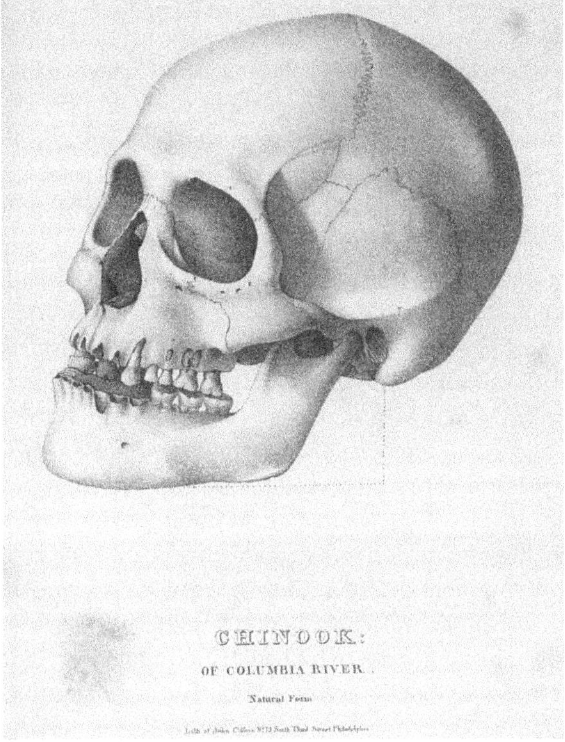


FIGURE 4. Picture of a skull from *Crania Americana*, plate 42.

Polygenist theory would eventually survive the Civil War and find its way into a current of progressive social thought by way of the nation's most prestigious colleges in New England, becoming the intellectual backbone of the anti-immigrant campaign in the early twentieth century.

## Polygenism and the American School of Ethnology

In *Crania Americana*, Morton's polygenism remained less pronounced. After all, the book was designed to showcase his skull collection, and its emphasis was on sketches and numerical data, not the origin theory of race. George Robbins Gliddon (1809–1857), a British-born Egyptologist who grew up in Alexandria, Egypt, served as the key spokesperson promoting the political potential of Morton's theory. In the first half of the nineteenth century, after Napoleon's conquest and forced extraction of the country's vast collection of ancient artifacts, Egypt became the subject of much popular and academic interest in Europe and North America. Gliddon worked as a contractor for Morton, procuring over one hundred skulls and a few mummies from Egypt for the Philadelphia physician. In the process, Gliddon came to appreciate Morton's polygenism and launched his own career as a public intellectual by embarking on a lecture tour of major American cities with his loot from Egypt. Many respected academics, including Louis Agassiz, the Harvard naturalist whom I discuss in detail later, attended Gliddon's talk with the wide-eyed public to listen to his tales of the world's oldest civilization.

Even before the rise of Egypt as an object of intellectual fascination, the ancient empire on the Nile remained a conundrum for European race-thinkers. Before Greece and Rome, in which "White" Europeans founded the "Western" civilization, so to speak, Egypt had built a much more elaborate empire, adorned with such spectacles as pyramids, hieroglyphics, mummies, and grand temples. The case of Egypt presented a puzzle, or more of a dilemma, for race-thinkers: Africans were supposed to lack in their aptitude for building advanced civilization; ancient empires in Asia—regardless of how the region was demarcated—were respectable, but the so-called dark continent should not have had such a commanding display of grandeur and urbane complexity. Gliddon found an answer to this puzzle in Morton's polygenism. In front of his bewildered audience, Gliddon argued that the discrepancy could be accounted for by recognizing that Egypt was a racially segregated society, much like the antebellum United States: "Caucasian" Egyptians, who were actually from the European continent, were rulers who designed all the grand buildings and monuments; dark-skinned Africans from the region today known as Sudan worked as slaves for the rulers, building the monuments as they were instructed. The two groups remained socially and biologically separate without much mixture between them. This arrangement, according to Gliddon, reflected God's intention of creating two different species of humans, one to lead and the other to build. Conveniently for southern slaveholders, this narrative mapped squarely onto the social order of the antebellum South.[23]

After Morton's premature death, Gliddon teamed up with Josiah Nott (1804–1873), a physician in Mobile, Alabama, and together they published *Types of Mankind* (1854), which caused a stir in the contemporary intellectual scene by popularizing the idea of polygenism. Nott encountered Morton's theory while he was attending medical school at the University of Pennsylvania. Combining Morton's empirical style and southern political ideology, Nott became the standard-bearer of the American School of Ethnology, the core doctrine of which was polygenism.[24]

Whereas Morton confined his discussions to skulls and the implication of their measurements, Nott did not hesitate to explicitly address the pressing questions of his time, including slavery. He firmly supported the existing racial hierarchy and believed that slavery was inevitable. Yet unlike other slavery apologists of the South, Nott invoked the authority of science, including that of an internationally acclaimed northern scholar, Morton of Philadelphia, to bolster his case. Different races, according to Nott, were designed differently by God at the Creation, and each race remained the same through millennia without any change because God had intended them to be so. Relying on Morton's work, Nott asserted that Caucasians had the capacity for civilization and "Negroes" did not. In addition, the mixing of different races would result not only in a betrayal of God's intentions but also in the biological degeneration of "hybrid off-springs." Therefore, slavery—in which White men ruled and "Negroes" worked while the two groups remained socially segregated—was the best possible social institution for all those involved, an institution that would simultaneously appease God and prevent biological disasters. Morton's skull collections and Gliddon's Egyptology neatly provided pseudoscientific grounds for this line of reasoning: Cranial measurements supposedly showed that race was immutable; moreover, Egypt proved that a social order based on racial domination could achieve spectacular things like pyramids. In other words, racial essentialism and racial segregation complemented each other.

While preaching this political gospel, Nott came into a collision course with contemporary biblical orthodoxy, because such an account of human origin openly contested the explanation provided in the book of Genesis. By placing the question of race at the intersection of two powerful institutions of the time—slavery and religion—Nott became a sort of self-proclaimed freedom crusader—or, more precisely, "a fervent southern polemicist who defended white supremacy with all the zeal of a South Carolina slave owner while urging the freedom of scientific inquiry from religious orthodoxy."[25] With the controversy, the American School of Ethnology soon gained notice from European naturalists and race-thinkers as well. In the emerging world of nineteenth-century modern science, the United States was usually regarded as a periphery where surprising evidence was brought to view but no creative theorizing was expected. The American School of Ethnology challenged that expectation by providing a provocative hypothesis about the origins of, and differences among, humankind.[26]

However, polygenism remained a contentious idea for the time, and its popular and political appeal was limited at best. Many southern intellectuals found enough reasons to justify slavery without seeming to put biblical doctrine into question. Conservative clergymen from both the North and South attacked Nott as preaching heresy, a charge he was willing to accept as a price to pay for intellectual freedom—the freedom to defend slavery.[27]

Nevertheless, the American School of Ethnology and polygenism left a lasting legacy in an unlikely place: At the nation's most prestigious educational institutions, elite academics held on to polygenism and taught the idea to the next generation, whose members would eventually forge their own race-thinking out of old examples. But before we turn to that story, we should take a brief detour to another strand of race-thinking: reactionary, royalist political ideology from Europe.

## Gobineau: Projecting Race onto Class

As Nott transitioned from his study of varieties of mankind in nature to expressing his opinions about contemporary affairs, he came across an esteemed European author who, just like Nott himself, had attempted to explain world history in terms of race. Joseph Arthur, Comte de Gobineau (1816–1882), had produced a 1,400-page book, *Essay on the Inequality of Human Races* (1853), that was instantly translated into English and published in the United States under Nott's supervision only three years after its original publication in France.

Gobineau was not a famed scholar like Morton. His contemporary influence was minimal, and his work did not circulate outside a small circle of royalists in Paris and slavery apologists in the American South. Yet as Hannah Arendt correctly recognizes in *The Origins of Totalitarianism,* Gobineau gave new life to the old political ideas of European aristocrats by repackaging their reactionary class politics in the language of race.[28] Through the work of Gobineau, the largely provincial quibbles about skull sizes evolved into a full-fledged political ideology that explained the past, present, and future of civilizations across the globe. As many scholars have pointed out, his work was important because it viewed the class conflicts after the French Revolution through the prism of race. Naturalists like Blumenbach and Morton mostly focused on the category question, asking how many varieties of men existed in nature. However, Gobineau was more concerned about the hierarchy question. While incorporating the language of "nature" developed by naturalists and thereby effectively grounding himself in racial essentialism, Gobineau largely ignored biology and instead brought in broad-sweeping generalizations about world history. In doing so, Gobineau's work functioned as a link between skull collecting and political agitation.[29]

According to *Essay,* race was the primary factor driving world history. There were three races: The White race was inclined toward intellect and organization, thus suitable for leading and governing; the Yellow race opted for utility and materialism, making them ideal practitioners of commerce and manufacture; and the Black race displayed sensual and artistic qualities while lacking discipline, hence providing good candidates for artists and manual workers. Contrary to many of his contemporaries, who abhorred the idea of race mixture, Gobineau reasoned that all civilization originated from a mixture of the White race, which was supposed to be the civilizing element, and other races. For instance, the White race on its own would not have produced art; only with the contribution of the sensual Black race did aesthetic creation become possible. Gobineau explained the rise and fall of various nations and empires across history as functions of different forms of race mixture. The rise was generally attributed to the White race, in particular the "Aryan" stock and the contributions of the aristocratic families within that stock; the fall was the inevitable outcome of their mixture with other races, through which the White race lost the vigor in its bloodlines and succumbed to degeneration.[30] In other words, race for Gobineau was a vision for creating a world, a blueprint dictating where different groups belong in the division of labor. Using sensory terms, Gobineau wrote of this vision: "The two most inferior varieties of the human species, the black and yellow races, are the crude foundation, the cotton and wool, which the secondary families of the white race make supple by adding their silk; while the Aryan group, circling its finer threads through the noble generations, designs on its surface a dazzling masterpiece of arabesques in silver and gold."[31]

In short, much of Gobineau's work represented the personal grumblings of a dilettante nobleman who witnessed the downfall of his world in the French Revolution. However, as the dedication of the American translation of *Essay* notes, the work was the first of its kind written "from the point of view of the statesman and historian rather than the naturalist."[32] In other words, those who sought a natural and scientific foundation for social analysis found what they needed in *Essay*. The appeal was especially strong for those who shared Gobineau's social origin and trajectory—the men who found security in their power and privilege, which they felt were gradually sliding away from them through rapid social change. *Essay* provided a metaphysical outlook on their feeling of loss by projecting their particular social circumstances onto world history.

The lineage from Gobineau to the Third Reich is well documented by many scholars, most famously Hannah Arendt, yet its connection to the United States, and more specifically to the immigration restriction movement in the early twentieth century, has often been neglected. Although Gobineau's initial influence was largely confined to Josiah Nott and his friends, the reactionary political ideology he articulated survived through the Civil War and Reconstruction and would eventually reach the Boston Brahmins. The New England aristocrats revived him from obscurity by publishing a new translation of *Essay* in 1915.

## Race-Thinking at Harvard: Louis Agassiz and Nathaniel Shaler

Louis Agassiz (1807–1873) and Nathaniel Shaler (1841–1906), two influential scientists at Harvard, served as unlikely purveyors of polygenism during the period between the Civil War and the end of the nineteenth century. Louis Agassiz made his name in Europe with his studies in geology and was invited to become the head of the Lawrence Scientific School at Harvard in 1847. Agassiz's trajectory represents a story of an immigrant learning the craft of race in America through socialization. His biographers agree that Agassiz, who was born in a Swiss canton and worked mostly in Germany, had no impetus to develop specific opinions on race before his migration to the United States. Upon his arrival, however, Agassiz quickly came into the orbit of the members of the American School of Ethnology, which led him to recognize the importance of the concept in everyday life as well as in the natural sciences.

Agassiz's stance on race was, according to his biographer Christoph Irmscher, an expression of "the desire to align himself, as an immigrant, as firmly as he could with other whites of European descent in America."[33] In addition, there was a clear affinity between Agassiz's conception of natural order and the racial order envisioned by polygenists. Combining his expertise in geology and biology, Agassiz divided the world into a set of climate zones, each corresponding to a different group of plants and animals. God designed the specific configurations of species and environments, and, according to Agassiz, the order of nature should be respected without further human interference. By extension, different races were also created to fit into different climate zones, and they should not intermix with each other, for such interaction would only cause chaos in God's otherwise perfect design.

Historian Toledo Machado, who conducted a detailed study of Agassiz's work on Brazil, summarizes Agassiz's stance on race by highlighting three key viewpoints: creationism, polygenism, and opposition to "hybridism" or any form of interracial marriage.[34] The first two views were largely supported by his studies of the animal kingdom and geology. In his research projects on race, Agassiz focused on the third viewpoint, highlighting the dangers of hybridism. In his expedition to Brazil in 1865, he took pictures of "pure races" and "mixed races," attempting to establish that race mixture was in fact a mixing between different species rather than between variations within a species. He wanted to demonstrate that "mixed races" were less fertile (i.e., have fewer children) than "pure races." In other words, Agassiz sought to reinforce the theme of degeneration, common among many race-thinkers of past and future: When different races interact, the consequences are negative; therefore, races, just like plants and animals, should be confined to their respective habitats and remain separate, without close contact.

Agassiz could hardly be considered an expert on the biology of race, much less its social implications. Nevertheless, he actively engaged with the topic, and as one of the most famous natural scientists of the nation, his voice carried the authority of science. The American Freedmen's Inquiry Commission (1863), which was organized during the Civil War to study possible policies regarding the emancipated slaves, consulted Agassiz about the racial characteristics of the formerly enslaved. The famed Harvard scholar fully supported abolition but at the same time maintained that any extended contact between Blacks and Whites was unnatural and undesired, for it would lead to the degeneration of both races. In other words, he advocated that "freedmen should be assured legal equality, but social and especially political equality [should] be checked."[35]

Nathaniel Shaler (1841–1906) can be considered the direct successor to all that Agassiz represented, even though he altered and updated some of his teacher's core ideas to better incorporate the changing realities of the late nineteenth century. Just like Agassiz, Shaler actively engaged with race, providing his supposedly expert opinions on a scientific basis for the complicated social issue. His position generally mirrored Agassiz's: Different races were created differently by God, and they were to remain separate. Although Shaler firmly denounced slavery, the embattled aftermath of Reconstruction gave him occasion to doubt the capacity of the ex-slaves to govern themselves. While not categorically denying African American potential, Shaler proscribed that only extensive social engineering would ensure a positive, "civilized" future for former slaves and their children. And in the process, echoing Agassiz's revulsion of race mixture, Shaler maintained that Blacks and Whites should remain socially apart: Political equality and social contact were two different things, and nature, according to Shaler, provided a chance for the former but strictly prohibited the latter. In a sense, on the question of Reconstruction, Shaler wavered between racial essentialism and full-fledged racial liberalism, clearly leaning toward the former but showing signs of the latter as well.[36]

In the 1880s and 1890s, as the dust of the Civil War settled and immigration once again increased, Shaler's race-thinking gradually shifted its focus to immigration. Here we see Shaler's unique contribution to Agassiz's polygenism: He distinguished southern and eastern European immigrants from the previous generations of immigrants and characterized them as racially unfit for inclusion in the nation, affirming racial essentialism. In the process, he drew from the Teutonic theory of democracy as well as long-standing beliefs about the Anglo-Saxon cultural identity of New England.

To understand Shaler's perspective on the so-called new immigrants in the 1880s, we need to first understand his primary audience. Essentially, Shaler was engaged in a conversation among men from privileged families in Boston and Cambridge, who worried about the rapid transformation of the country—or, more precisely, about social change taking place in New England.[37] In her seminal work, *Ancestors and Immigrants* (1956), historian Barbara Miller Solomon points out some of the core characteristics of these men, who called themselves "Boston Brahmins": They were heirs of the esteemed families in Boston, some of whom proudly traced their roots to the *Mayflower* and the American Revolution. They saw themselves as equally devoted to the ideals of democracy and God; in their worldview, American history and its democratic ideals were the manifestation of God's vision, and New England, more specifically Boston, was at the center of this vision as the religious, moral, and intellectual capital of the New World.

However, the democratic ideals that lasted till the mid-nineteenth century, according to Solomon, withered over the course of the Civil War and eventually turned into cynicism and despair by the 1880s. To the later generation of Brahmins, all the great things had been achieved in the past by their fathers and grandfathers. Suddenly their cherished homeland, Boston and New England, had turned into a strange place they did not recognize. Rapid industrialization and mass immigration from southern and eastern Europe were transforming the town into a metropolis with slums, just like New York City, and the progress of science was challenging the Christian way of looking at the world along with the cultural and moral authority of men like themselves.[38]

In short, the elite men of Shaler's generation saw themselves as "strangers in their own land," to borrow Arlie Hochschild's phrase, much like Gobineau did in the postrevolution years of France and Europe.[39] This sense of insecurity and isolation drove them to reactionary ideas, some of which were directly borrowed from old-world aristocrats like Gobineau and their American counterparts, such as Josiah Nott. Facing the seeming erosion of their values and ideals, Boston Brahmins searched for the root cause of this decline. They found an easy target in the back alleys of Boston: immigrants. Yet they distinguished themselves from previous waves of anti-immigrant mobilizations, such as that led by the Know-Nothings, by presenting immigration as a social problem to be addressed through appropriate social policy, not through violence and hatred.[40] To this end, they used their knowledge, power, and networks to organize a systemic inquiry of immigrants in order to produce a scientifically grounded solution based on empirical evidence. Eventually, Boston Brahmins' existential concerns about their own decline would initiate the sequence of events that would lead to the Dillingham Commission. Henry Cabot Lodge, as the most esteemed Brahmin of his generation, represented this lineage on the commission.

Shaler was the catalyzing authority figure at the beginning of this sequence. Extending Agassiz's favorite theme, Shaler argued that there was an essential correspondence between different races and different environments—a certain race could prosper in a given environment, while others could not. Obviously to him, the United States represented a particular kind of environment, in which only a few selected races could prosper. Blending what we today perceive as nature and culture, Shaler argued that since the key features of the American environment were freedom and self-government, only those races inherently suited to thrive under these conditions were fit to live in the American environment.

In this argument, Shaler was borrowing from the Teutonic theory of democracy and combining it with his science of environment. Initially the musing of European historians searching for metaphysical forces driving history, the Teutonic theory of democracy proposed that the Germanic tribes of the late Roman Empire were by nature suited for freedom. According to this line of thinking, as the first self-governing peoples who resisted despotic repression, these Germanic tribes supposedly had a deep, inborn craving for freedom and autonomy, best expressed through fraternal bonfire gatherings in the wild forests of Germania, an inherent passion that led them to challenge and dismantle the cosmopolitan, hedonistic Roman Empire. The urge to rebel for freedom ran through the blood lineage of the Teutons, as their descendants were known, and to one of their subgroups in the British Isles, Anglo-Saxons, who conquered the land. The Puritans of the *Mayflower* were, according to this theory, direct descendants of these noble freedom seekers, and the United States was the destination of their journey to self-government: In a land seemingly free of despotism and aristocracy, the descendants of the Teutons established democratic institutions and flourished.

Boston Brahmins loved this theory. It gave them a sense of entitlement, a feeling of self-affirmation that gained luster from the Old World.[41] In the last decade of the nineteenth century, Boston Brahmins saw chaos everywhere. The democratic institutions, it seemed, were not functioning very well. The descendants of the Teutons might have prospered until their fathers' generation, Boston Brahmins thought, but not anymore. Immigrants who were not Teutons—Italians, Jews, Irish, and so forth—did not possess the inherent craving for freedom and self-government and were, thereby, unfit for the American environment, yet they were flocking into the country, further damaging the declining democratic institutions. "Lacking the necessary sociobiological equipment," Shaler asserted, "the eastern European, for example just simply could not respond either to the stimulus of 'American air' or to the equally bracing American way of life." Therefore, "America, in short, was only suitable for the Teutons."[42] To save the nation's democratic institutions, the elite men who understood the danger should do something about the unchecked flow of immigrants, especially those who were unfit for democracy. By combining Teutonic theory and his science of environment, Shaler equated race and nation, and "by conflating biological constitution, social identity, and cultural heritage," his ideas "helped reinforce the confusion between natural history and national history."[43]

## Racial Uplift: Seeds of Racial Liberalism

A very different set of racial ideas were brewing concurrently in this period, albeit not in a prominent place like Harvard. While the high-profile race-thinkers discussed previously reluctantly recognized early incarnations of racial liberalism—they did not altogether shut out the possibility of the racialized achieving civilization, especially in the case of former slaves during Reconstruction—they did not budge on their racial essentialism. Their stance mirrored the broader political circumstance after the demise of Reconstruction: As violence and repression against formerly enslaved people returned in the South, the rest of the nation ignored their plight and decided to look away.[44]

African American leaders and intellectuals, on the other hand, articulated the clearest incarnation of racial liberalism yet as a rebuttal to this development. Virtually all of them were associated with the reform and self-help movement for formerly enslaved people, and their racial ideas took the shape of practical, moral doctrines rather than academic theories about race. That is, they did not muse about how many races there were or how best to measure them; they discussed what was to be done from the perspective of African Americans. Yet those ideas, which Keidrick Roy calls "Black Liberalism," clearly refuted racial essentialism by highlighting formerly enslaved people's potential to better their situation through collective effort.[45]

In *Uplifting the Race*, historian Kevin Gaines provides a comprehensive account of this development while highlighting its class and gender politics.

Black liberalism originated from the folk religious tradition and on-the-ground struggle against slavery in the antebellum South. After the sudden demise of Reconstruction, however, the desire for liberation took a different turn, as newly emerging Black elites emphasized education and enlightenment for the Black masses. In their thinking, African Americans were far behind in every aspect compared to Whites, but that did not mean they were trapped in this position forever. While White race-thinkers emphasized essentialism through the notion of "natural" Black inferiority, Black leaders seized on the Darwinian motive of struggle to counter the assertion, noting that African Americans could indeed struggle against other races for their survival and prosperity in the world. Even if doing so would take time and effort, they could obtain the level of civilization that approximated, if not matched, that of Whites. In the process, Black elites would lead the way through education and community self-help. Until then, political power, as espoused in Reconstruction, could wait while economic and social uplift took primacy. Booker T. Washington's ideas—vocational training, economic self-determination, and acceptance of segregation—were the culmination of this line of thinking.[46]

Admittedly, as Gaines makes clear, the sequence of events leading to this development is quite complex and merits further discussion than is possible here. The important point is that the idea of racial uplift, or progress of the racialized over time through effort, was present in the political thoughts of African American leaders in the late nineteenth century. As Lee Baker discusses, some federal officials and Indigenous leaders applied a similar framework to the situation of "Indians," arguing for the possibility of Indigenous individuals accepting White civilization and living among Whites.[47] These early seeds of racial liberalism, however, remained largely outside the purview of the academic discussion on race, and the hegemony of racial essentialism held steadfast until the early twentieth century.

## The Immigration Restriction League and Henry Cabot Lodge

Oblivious to these developments, some elite students at Harvard took the racial essentialism of men like Shaler to heart. In 1894, soon after graduating from the college, Prescott Hall, Robert DeCourcy Ward, and Charles Warren founded the Immigration Restriction League (IRL), the most influential restrictionist organization during the early twentieth century. They invited Shaler, whom they considered a mentor to their cause, to serve as one of the senior members of the civic organization. The three young professionals represented the new generation of Brahmins who had decided to stop worrying and instead seek a policy solution to the changes they were witnessing. In the process, unlike the previous generation of race-thinkers, they relied on the scientific education they had received from the likes of Shaler and Agassiz: They gathered evidence, devised a solution, and attempted to sway public opinion by reasoning. They prided themselves on "reject[ing] nativist baiting in the 1850s, and in the 1880s"[48] and "not condon[ing] crude group bigotry."[49] While facing strong opposition from the pro-immigrant lobby concerned about its support base and the executive branch mindful of diplomatic relations, the IRL remained committed to this supposed scientific approach to policy. Eventually, by building a wide-ranging coalition—of employers and unions, southern Democrats, and western anti-immigrant activists—the league finally succeeded in passing the Immigration Act of 1917,[50] which would allow entry only to immigrants who could read and write in their own languages. Although the league disbanded in 1921 after Prescott Hall's death, the group was the engine of the restrictionist movement from the early 1890s to the 1920s.[51]

The league's evidence-based policymaking efforts went into motion from the outset. As one of its first activities, Hall, Ward, and Warren obtained statistics from the Massachusetts Bureau of Statistics of Labor and other agencies to carefully study the data on crime, delinquency, pauperism, and illiteracy among the new immigrants. After seizing on literacy rate as the most significant characteristic that separated the new immigrants from the old immigrants and native-born, the three gentlemen invited themselves to Ellis Island in 1895 and administered literacy tests to a sample of incoming immigrants. They found a "close connection between illiteracy and general undesirability" of the new immigrants and thus decided on the test as the most practical and effective means of controlling immigration.[52]

In addition to being a hub of activity for organizing influential citizens concerned about immigration, the league's most distinctive contribution to the restrictionist cause were these kinds of evidence-gathering and brainstorming. In many ways, the organization's activities preceded the Dillingham Commission's inquiry. For instance, in 1904, the IRL conducted a mail survey of its members across the country. The survey asked respondents to check the "classes of persons not desired in your State" and proceeded to give choices such as "1. Foreign Born; 2. Southern and eastern European; 3. Asiatics; 4. Illiterates; 5. Those settling in the cities and averse to country life; 6. Immigrants distributed from eastern cities." Some respondents felt that these categories were not enough and wrote their own answers in the margins of their response letters. The summary of the survey results presented additional categories of immigrants to the given list, including "7. Poles; 8. Persons who can't speak English; 9. Latin race (except French); 11. All but best classes; 12. Any at all." Many included personal letters along with their responses, which offered documentation of the immigration situations in their respective communities.[53] The survey results were summarized and delivered to policymakers through the league's extensive lobbying network, strengthening the appeal of its policy proposals.

Henry Cabot Lodge (1850–1924), a senator from Massachusetts, spearheaded the lobbying efforts of the league. Born into a wealthy merchant family in Boston, Lodge attended Harvard and joined the infamous exclusive final club, the Porcellian.[54] As a powerful politician and close confidant of Theodore Roosevelt, Lodge exercised much power over important issues, including international relations and immigration, through his long tenure in the House (1887–1893) and Senate (1893–1924).[55] Although Lodge is primarily known today as a power broker who orchestrated the emergence of the American empire, he also cared deeply about immigration, from his early days as a junior member of the House all the way to his final days in Congress. In short, if there was a dean of the Boston Brahmins, it would be Lodge.

Lodge grew up in the heart of what is now the Boston downtown area and witnessed firsthand changes to his city's urban landscape. In the mid-nineteenth century, the Irish and Italians flocked to the city, and the demographic transition was evident even to a young boy. His autobiography, published in 1913 when he was sixty-three, carefully treads away from matters of race, presumably out of concern for respectability. However, there is a poignant episode that hints at the origin of his restrictionist position. While writing affectionately of his father and grandfather as "Olympians" who embodied all the glory of the old New England elite, Lodge recalls how his generation lost some of that glory. He describes how he and his friends ceded Boston Common, their favorite playground, to immigrant boys. "On the Common we also waged Homeric combats with snowballs against the boys from the South cove and the North End, in which we made gallant fights," writes Lodge, continuing with the ancient Greek theme. Eventually, according to the Brahmin senator, "the ever increasing number of our opponents gradually by sheer weight pushed us, and still more our successors, from the Common hills and the Frog Pond to seek coasting and skating in the country." Lodge's family had multiple vacation homes in the coastal areas as well as the western part of Massachusetts, and it was not a huge problem that he and his friends were not playing on the Common. They could always play among themselves in the countryside at their family's vacation homes. But the symbolic aspects of the loss stayed with the future executive committee member of the Dillingham Commission. Southern and eastern Europeans, by "the ever increasing numbers," took from him what was rightfully his, and he saw himself as a demigod driven out from Mount Olympus—or the city of Boston—by lowly mortals.[56]

Lodge's Greek-themed fantasy about his family and the city is clearly absurd, just like Blumenbach's obsession over his beautiful Georgian skull. However, it had real consequences, especially as he made his way into politics. He wanted to protect what he inherited from his grandfather and father to the extent that he could by controlling the numbers of immigrants. Lodge first proposed the Literacy Test Bill in 1891 when he was a junior congressman from Massachusetts. The bill was clearly intended to exclude certain new immigrants whom Lodge found unfit for the national character of the United States. He was not necessarily a progressive but still saw himself as a reformer. He championed the American ideal of democracy and American workers' rights, and in his view the new immigrants were ruining both by corrupting democratic institutions through party machines, on one hand, and bringing down the standard of living for working men through wage competition, on the other. Lodge saw both the robber baron capitalists and the new immigrants as representing what was wrong with social change in the late nineteenth century.[57]

Thus, Lodge's race-thinking was somewhat different from that of his predecessors: While carefully balancing biological accounts with cultural and environmental explanations of race, he sided with neither but took a "practical" stance toward the issue. In his 1896 speech in the Senate, Lodge acknowledged that there was "no such thing as a race of original purity according to the divisions of ethnical science," thereby distancing himself from racial essentialism. He could, however, for practical purposes, acknowledge "artificial races," like the English, the Germans, and the Jews. Although these "races" were, Lodge argued, forged by mixing different "elements" over a long period of time, the United States was founded and shaped by the German-English—or more precisely, the Teutonic—tradition. But he was willing to entertain the idea of racial liberalism, if only in very limited fashion. In theory, it may be possible to assimilate other groups under the guidance of the democratic, Teutonic tradition, yet such an endeavor, Lodge envisioned, would take a very long time, not to speak of the enormous effort and cost associated with the process. Therefore, Lodge argued for immigration restriction not based on the essentialist theories about fundamental differences but on practical grounds—to protect American people, institutions, and culture, not to express his personal prejudices toward the unfamiliar.[58] Or at least that was what he himself claimed. Lodge's careful, "practical" balancing of racial essentialism and racial liberalism was transplanted into the Dillingham Commission, which adopted a "races or peoples" classification system based not on theory but on the "practical grounds" of data collection.

To be clear, Lodge did not regard race as unimportant. The practical stance meant that, unlike his predecessors, he did not have to engage in theoretical debates in the science of race. As a politician, not an academic, his primary objective was not to answer questions such as how many races there were or how best to measure differences between races. Yet race was still a concept of utmost importance for him because the concept encompassed all that he deemed consequential about the collective lives of human beings. The practical stance was anchored to the weight of the race concept in his worldview, not from its insignificance: Because the immigration problem was so important, Lodge implied, actions were prioritized over scholarly precision.

In the same speech, Lodge expressed his all-encompassing, almost transcendental perspective on race: Race consisted of "moral and intellectual characters, which in their association make the soul of a race, and which represent the product of all its past, the inheritance of all its ancestors, and the motives of its conduct." These characteristics were in fact, in his thinking, more sociohistorical than biological. Because they were forged over a long period of time through a series of collective experiences, however, they were just as immutable as, if not more so than, biology: "The men of each race possess an indestructible stock of ideas, traditions, sentiments, modes of thoughts, an unconscious inheritance from their ancestors upon which argument has no effect." Lodge used the example of India and the British Empire to further elaborate his point: "You can take a Hindoo and give him the highest education the world can afford. He has a keen intelligence. He will absorb the learning of Oxford, he will acquire the manner and habits of England, he will sit in the British Parliament," Lodge mused, "but you cannot make him an Englishman." It is not that the two groups were irreversibly different, as polygenists had argued a generation ago: "Yet he, like his conqueror, is of the great Indo-European family." The problem was the time horizon: "It has taken six thousand years and more to create the differences which exist between them. You cannot efface those differences thus made, by education in a single life because they do not rest upon intellect."[59] While it was theoretically possible to engage in an "argument" to change the racial characteristics of the new immigrants, for example, Lodge pursued a more practical solution to the problem: control immigration to preserve the American "race" as he saw fit. Those who abided by the Teutonic tradition, including the English, Germans, Scandinavians, and Irish, were included, and all others should be excluded.[60] In other words, Lodge shut down the potential challenges to racial essentialism from racial liberalism on practical grounds. With the advent of empirical data, however, these challenges would come back to haunt him in the Dillingham Commission.

## Progressive Social Science and Eugenics: The Data Turn in Race-Thinking

In the previous sections, we have witnessed how gentlemen scientists' musings about human variety partnered with aristocratic, reactionary political ideology and how the ideas resulting from these partnerships gained prominence at elite educational institutions in the United States. The lineage connecting Gobineau, Nott, Agassiz, and Shaler represents this thread in American race-thinking in which natural scientists took the lead while ideologues and dilettantes followed. There was a contrasting trend of racial liberalism among Black leaders of the late nineteenth century, yet their influence was limited. Social scientists were late to this gathering, but they contributed a critical component to modern race-thinking: numbers or, more precisely, a quantitative way of looking at the world.

In the later decades of the nineteenth century, the emerging discipline of the social sciences started to produce a new group of race-thinkers.[61] Just like Lodge, the newcomers shunned prejudices and emotion, pursuing instead a more pragmatic solution to the problem of race: In their framework, race was neither a feature of God's creation nor an object of revulsion but a matter of practical concern. To be precise, they did not deny the biological foundation of race altogether, nor did they underplay the importance of race in determining individual and group outcomes. However, social scientists tended to bracket off fundamental theoretical questions—for example, how many races there were and how race could be measured accurately—and focused more on documenting how race manifested itself in social settings. The emerging science of statistics provided the necessary tools for such documentation, and race-thinking slowly moved from its roots in the biological domain toward the social domain by way of what Ian Hacking termed the "avalanche of numbers."[62]

Francis Walker's (1840–1897) pointed argument about immigrant and native fertility hit a nerve for intellectuals worried about immigration, such as Lodge. As one of the first economists of the nation, Walker served in prestigious positions such as president of the American Economic Association and Massachusetts Institute of Technology. As an expert on statistics, Walker oversaw the 1880s census and, based on the experience, argued that the inflow of the new immigrants was undermining the fertility of the native-born, thereby diminishing the vitality of the nation as a whole. If the trend continued, Walker warned, the United States would inevitably face decline—meaning that the nation would turn out to reflect not its past or ideal future but the miserable condition of the countries from which immigrants were coming. This line of argument was markedly different from previous agitations, which, according to Walker, worried about "the wards of our almshouses, our insane asylums, and our jails from being stuffed to repletion by new arrivals from Europe." Instead, what was at stake was "the American rate of wages, the American standard of living, and the quality of American citizenship."[63] In other words, it was not a matter of separating the harmful elements—the poor, the insane, and the criminal—from the general inflow of immigrants; the problem was the inflow itself and its impact on the American average of various indicators. If the immigrants as a group were lower in averages—whether it was wages, living standards, or the quality of citizenship—their continued addition to the nation would only lower the "American" average overall and in various dimensions. In other words, Walker's reasoning represented what Katherine Benton-Cohen termed the "from quality to quantity" turn in American immigration discourse and policy: Officials and intellectuals were starting to pay less attention to the individual features of immigrants and focus more on the overall trends and numbers.[64] Although Walker's argument relied more on sentiments than on precise statistical inference, his calling cry against the "beaten men from beaten races" had an enormous popular and intellectual appeal.

Many progressive intellectuals concerned about the problems caused by industrialization took a similar stance against immigration. Edward Ross (1866–1951), one of the most famous early sociologists in the United States, was a champion of labor rights and other progressive causes. He opposed immigration precisely on those grounds: Chinese workers, and later Japanese immigrants, were hampering labor's capacity to unionize and negotiate effectively with employers because of their willingness to accept lower wages and worse working conditions than the standard American worker. Joining forces with popular union leaders, Ross mounted harsh criticisms against "Asiatic," "coolie" laborers during the anti-Asian labor campaigns in the 1880s and 1890s. His employer, Stanford University, was not pleased with his position: As a major railroad tycoon, university founder Leland Stanford had built his fortune on the labor of Chinese workers, and Ross's attack against the Chinese was perceived as an indirect criticism of those who employed the Chinese workers.[65] As Daniel Tichenor has observed regarding immigration policymaking, the strange bedfellows of reform-minded intellectuals, labor leaders, and New England elites engineered the social science turn of race-thinking in the United States.[66]

As the focus of American race-thinking shifted to new immigrants, their supposed difference became the primary concern for the newly emerging race-thinkers. Whereas most of nineteenth-century race-thinking had focused on the difference between Europeans and non-Europeans, such as Africans, Asians, and "Indians," the new generation of race-thinkers delved into the difference among Europeans, most aptly represented by the new immigrants. These scholars would directly provide the Dillingham Commission with a theoretical jumping-off point to classify and categorize southern and eastern European immigrants as a separate, undesirable race distinct from northern and western European immigrants and native-born Americans. In the process, they realized that the overarching category representing Whiteness—for example, "white," "European," or "Caucasian"—was not very useful in capturing the supposed difference of the new immigrants and began to develop new concepts, including "peoples" or "ethnic groups."

Daniel G. Brinton (1837–1899) authored *Races or Peoples: Lectures on the Science of Ethnography* (1890), which provided a comprehensive review of European race-thinking, along with his own contributions on what he called "the American race," or the Indigenous peoples of North America. In the book, Brinton discusses characteristics of various "peoples" within the European continent, showcasing the internal diversity among what was formerly categorized as "whites" without distinction.[67] William Z. Ripley (1867–1941), a well-known Harvard economist who spearheaded the Progressive Era criticisms of big businesses and banks, wrote *The Races of Europe: A Sociological Study* (1899), which argued that there are multiple races within Europe. Amassing a wide range of physiological and geographic data and compiling numerous maps and graphs in six hundred pages, Ripley wrote that Europeans consist of three races—Teutonic, Alpine, and Mediterranean—instead of just one "white" or "Caucasian" race. By doing so, he placed himself in the opposite camp from the previous generation of race-thinkers, such as Blumenbach and Agassiz, who assumed the unity of the "white" race. He engaged in a lively debate with Joseph Deniker (1852–1918), a French anthropologist who took the racial classification among Europeans to a new level: In *The Races of Man* (1900), while criticizing Ripley's undiscriminating use of the term *race*, Deniker posited that *race* should be based on "somatic character"—meaning physiological traits, such as skin color and skull shape—while *peoples* should "take into account *ethnic characters* (linguistic and sociological), and above all *geographical distribution*."[68] He proceeded to suggest *ethnic groups* as a proper term for the groups classified on the basis of their language and geography. In short, facing the practical challenge of classifying the new immigrants, race-thinkers at the turn of the twentieth century were moving away from biology and embracing cultural factors in conceptualizing race. As we see in chapter 3, these developments had a direct bearing on how the Dillingham Commission classified and collected data on immigrants.

In the meantime, eugenics was slowly gaining traction among intellectuals. As historian Daniel Kevles has noted, eugenics covered a wide variety of ideas and practices on both sides of the Atlantic as well as in some colonial and postcolonial settings.[69] Yet the gist of the enterprise came down to the scientific understanding of, as well as interventions in, human heredity. In other words, the urge to understand and control individual- and society-level reproduction informed the core tenets of eugenics.

At its foundation, race was not a primary concern for eugenicists, at least in the ways in which contemporary Americans used that term. The founders of eugenics, Francis Galton (1822–1911) and Karl Pearson (1857–1936), were concerned more about "geniuses" and how they were reproduced through generations.[70] After all, the etymology of eugenics can be traced back to the study of the exceptional individuals who were "good in birth" or "noble in heredity."[71] In tracing those with outstanding ability through family trees, Galton and Pearson developed key concepts and techniques in modern statistics, including normal distribution and linear regression: Whereas the former captured how ability was distributed across populations, the latter explained how the ability of offspring reverted back to the parental mean.[72] By studying ability and its patterns of reproduction, eugenicists attempted to develop a scientific means of improving the "stock" of a society, mainly by intervening in individual decisions about childbearing. Not surprisingly, the proposed interventions were concentrated disproportionately on the socially vulnerable—for example, the poor, women, the incarcerated, and the disabled. Yet many British socialists, feminists, and radicals embraced the idea, thinking that the scientific gospel of eugenics would bring about a utopian society by eliminating the root cause of social problems. Likewise, American progressives were attracted to the doctrine because it represented freedom from the burdens and constraints of biology and reproduction: If society were able to remake itself, a decisive and fundamental reform would become possible.

One may expect eugenics to be another version of "scientific racism," essentially a different variation of skull collecting with more numbers and formulas. Yet there is a subtle but important difference in how eugenics conceptualized race as opposed to how previous waves of race-thinking formulated it: In eugenics, "instead of speculative definitions of alleged archetypes"—for example, Blumenbach's skull-based model or Agassiz's assertion that races were created by God—"species or races might be defined in terms of the quantitatively certain distribution of a given character around a mean and by the statistical correlation of character pairs."[73] In other words, true to the scientific spirit of the late nineteenth century, race was presented not as a Platonic ideal but as a product of analytical induction from statistical data. Therefore, unlike Blumenbach or Agassiz, who sought to approximate the essence of race through observations of nature, race-thinkers informed by eugenics would treat statistical data as an integral part of what race was: Race was a pattern in statistical data, not an archetype existing "out there" in nature.[74]

Along with an emphasis on history and culture, this transition to numbers meant that race-thinkers needed an additional process to substantiate their racial argument. That is, they should collect data first to demonstrate that racial categories and hierarchy exist as opposed to deductively reasoning their existence and engaging in a world-historical narrative about their implication. As we see in the case of the Dillingham Commission, this transition opened up a whole range of new possibilities, as well as problems, for race-thinking. Namely, race-thinkers did not anticipate that the statistical turn would dethrone racial essentialism and instead call for racial liberalism.

British eugenicists were interested in mapping the differences between population groups but, reflecting their own biases, selected these groups in a way that replicated the racial divide in British and colonial societies. However, it was Galton and Pearson's American protégé, Charles Davenport (1866–1944), who maximized the potential of eugenics to produce further innovations in race-thinking. Kevles points out that "eugenics enthusiasts in the United States" were "largely middle to upper class, white, Anglo-Saxon, predominantly Protestant, and educated."[75] Thus, it is not surprising that their anxiety about formerly enslaved people and the new immigrants shaped the application of the newly imported scientific trend. Following the prevalent restrictionist reasoning, Davenport argued that the "new blood," or the southern and eastern European immigrants, would make Americans "darker in pigmentation, smaller in stature, more mercurial . . . more given to crimes of larceny, kidnapping, assault, murder, rape, and sex-immorality."[76]

Unlike the previous generations of race-thinkers, however, Davenport thought of race in less essentialist terms. That is, he understood that there was a normal distribution of ability or "desirability" within a particular race and that not all members of a certain race were "undesirable." Davenport "may have argued against barring the entry of particular national groups, but he believed that the European nations sent over disproportionately large numbers of their worst human stock, that immigrants rapidly outbred the native population, and that they supplied an excess of public charges."[77] In an ideal world, Davenport would have preferred a method of selecting the "best" individuals of any given race, yet such a selection process would be impossible to implement. Instead, Davenport and the eugenicists argued for the next best thing—categorical exclusion of certain races that had higher numbers of undesirables among its members. While the specific list of races to be excluded reflected the popular prejudices of the day, Davenport and eugenicists argued that race was merely a statistical proxy for weeding out the undesirable element within a population group. Just as one would avoid consuming too much of a food that contained harmful elements, Davenport and the eugenicists argued, the nation should also exercise caution in what it ingested, and categorically denying access to some groups was an easy solution to a complicated problem.

Once again, we witness the unholy alliance between a reactionary political ideology and scientific language: "In part, [Davenport's] negative eugenics simply expressed in biological language the native white Protestant's hostility to immigrants and the conservative's bile over taxes and welfare."[78] Established with major support from the Rockefeller Foundation, the Eugenics Records Office in Cold Spring Harbor, New York, became a hub for race-thinking during the first half of the twentieth century. Influential intellectuals such as Prescott Hall, the founding director of the IRL, and Theodore Roosevelt, the former president, would pass through its circuits, strengthening their personal ties as well as adding another layer of sophistication to race-thinking. Eventually eugenics served as the key justification for passing the Johnson-Reed Act of 1924, which allocated different quotas for different European nations while excluding Asian immigrants all together.[79]

## Theodore Roosevelt

A final major race-thinker who paved the way for the Dillingham Commission is Theodore Roosevelt, the president who launched the commission's inquiry by signing off on the Immigration Act of 1907.[80] Like many of his contemporaries, including Lodge, Roosevelt grew up in a prosperous household and developed an infatuation with German mythology at an early age. The young Roosevelt projected the heroic struggle of Siegfried in Richard Wagner's *Der Ring des Nibelungen* onto stories from the American West, fantasizing about a world in which the descendants of the Teutonic Gods were expanding the frontier of civilization by struggling against nature.[81] At Harvard, just like Lodge, who would later become his lifelong best friend, he was deeply influenced by Shaler's ideas, inheriting his theoretical inclinations as well as his obsession over new immigrants.[82] As a race-thinker, Roosevelt's key contribution came from the fact that he revised the

Teutonic doctrine and Anglo-Saxon fetish into a nationalism of a distinctly American variety, producing a more dynamic notion of race and nation that would fully blossom in the Dillingham Commission.

Roosevelt's focus was on equating national identity with race and conceptualizing race as a mixture of various "stocks" that have melted together to produce a political community. Following the Herderian tradition and German romanticism,[83] *race*, defined as political community in Roosevelt's thought, meant more than the shared allegiance of its members to a common flag; it also meant that they shared "the blood," a transcendental identity forged through both actual and metaphorical experiences of fighting collectively against other political communities and natural obstacles. Race—and its equivalent, nation—was a community of those who shared a fate, a sense of one's destination and purpose in the world.[84] Although the American nation, Roosevelt argued, was forged out of diverse European stock, the resulting political community collectively engaged in a set of decisive struggles, such as western frontier expansion and the Spanish-American War, and therefore formed a different race from its European ancestors'. In this sense, Roosevelt stood apart from the essentialist strand in race-thinking, including the Teutonic theory, Anglo-Saxonism, and the Aryan myth: The American race, and by extension the American nation, was not simply another variety of the glorious, best European race; rather, it was an independent branch of the family that was forged through its own adventures in the new world and, through those experiences, became better than its European predecessors. Roosevelt thought that "races that did not move or migrate following their original settlement ran the risk of degenerating into physical and moral weakness."[85] In contrast, the American race, according to Roosevelt, was strong because it kept moving toward the west. Implicitly criticizing previous traditions in race-thinking, Roosevelt saw race as always in the making, thereby formulating an early incarnation of racial liberalism, his favorite terms like *blood* and *destiny* notwithstanding.

Roosevelt thus subscribed to Lamarckianism—the belief that an organism can change to adapt to a new environment—and nominally supported the equipotentiality of all races: Given a proper process and time, any race could bring itself up to the level of the highest civilization. He saw the world as a playing field for different races, all struggling against each other and natural obstacles in their quest for greatness. Contrary to his friend Lodge, Roosevelt had a worldview that was far from aristocratic; it was that of a fighter, who achieved everything through struggle, not privilege—or at least that was how he perceived himself. If the White race, or Americans, were better than others, it was because they won the struggle, not because they were born better. By the same logic, Roosevelt was willing to entertain the possibility—however remote it might be—that any race could be on equal ground with the American race or other European races.[86]

At the same time, however, old influences did not completely vanish. Although he denounced Anglo-Saxon supremacism and the Teutonic doctrine, Roosevelt often referred to "the English-speaking race" to note the special ties among the older generation of Americans, many of whom came from the British Isles and retained an emotional bond with their old country. These original immigrants had struggled the most, according to Roosevelt, and had rightfully obtained their positions as the political leaders of the American nation. Therefore, Roosevelt reasoned, all other races who came later should and would follow their lead and adapt to their ways of life, not attempt to maintain the old-world traits they brought from Europe. In other words, although Roosevelt championed the possibility that races could change, adapt, and melt into a new race, at the same time he was realistic about who would lead the process of Lamarckian evolution: The English-speaking race, or the old-stock Americans, would absorb and digest "foreign" stocks to produce a healthy, vigorous race-nation out of the mixture, and the American nation would maintain its hegemony against both domestic and international threats. His famous wartime cry against "hyphenated Americans" and for "100 percent Americanism" was not just an impulsive jingoism but a theoretical notion that explained how a country born of successive waves of immigration could become a unified race-nation against threats from outside. In other words, the tension between racial essentialism and racial liberalism was managed by power and empire building, spearheaded by "vigorous" Anglo-Saxons like the president himself.

## Conclusion

As discussed throughout this chapter, nineteenth-century race-thinking featured a variety of ideas, as represented by three camps: naturalists, polygenists, and the Progressive Era race-thinkers. Although race-thinking began as largely innocuous quibbles about skull sizes and group differences, political ideologues used it as supposedly scientific grounds to bolster their reactionary theory about world history. Against the backdrop of slavery and colonialism, race-thinking highlighted the distinction between Whites and non-Whites, or Europeans and people outside the continent. However, as American intellectuals at the turn of the century started to focus more on the new immigrants—the most visible racial other in front of them—they realized that the overarching category of "White," supposedly based on biology, could not properly capture the difference represented by southern and eastern European immigrants. This led them to move away from racial essentialism and embrace culture and history as bases for racial classification, thus hinting at the possibility of racial liberalism. In other words, the balance between nature and reactionary political ideology tilted toward the latter in the face of "the immigration problem" in the early twentieth century. The social sciences and its claims on empirical evidence came to fill the void left by nature, further sustaining the scientific authority of race-thinking. Combined with the nationalistic zeal of politicians like Theodore Roosevelt, *race* became a term for an all-encompassing metaphysical dimension of group identity, and intellectuals and bureaucrats embraced the concept in advancing their evidence-based policymaking attempts in the Progressive Era.

However, as we see in the following chapters, the turn toward the social proved to be challenging in its own regard, and race-thinkers had to confront unexpected consequences of their emphasis on empirical data. The Dillingham Commission, central to this transition in race-thinking, was the primary site in which these confrontations occurred. And in these confrontations, we see the clash of, as well as compromises between, racial essentialism and racial liberalism.

[ CHAPTER TWO ]

# The Strange Bedfellows of the Immigration Debate

## Political Calculations and Strange Bedfellows

While the first chapter focuses on the intellectual origins of the Dillingham Commission's work—namely, the genealogy of the racial ideas employed in the commission's project—this chapter highlights the more immediate context of its inquiry. Theodore Roosevelt had multiple layers of political concerns when he signed the Immigration Act of 1907 and launched the commission. The various factions that had engaged for decades in the contest of immigration policy were also highly invested in the inquiry, hoping to use the facts to bolster their cause.[1]

The goal of this chapter is to show that while these complex layers surrounded the commission, competing influences in and around the commission allowed for a space of contingency in which contradictions in racial knowledge production could be amplified. Because so much was at stake and many different actors were trying to control the process, the commission ironically became a no-man's-land governed by, at least ostensibly, the logic of fact-finding and scientific inference. Although backstage political manipulation was a constant threat, the curtain separating center stage from what went on behind the scenes was opaque enough to grant some autonomy to the inquiry. Moreover, even within the commission, there existed divergent views on race, immigration, and national belonging, as evidenced by the range of perspectives held by the executive committee members. And as we see in the following chapters, racial essentialism clashed and reconciled with racial liberalism in this liminal, contingent space between racial ideology and state power, amplifying the voices of the unruly facts to pave a way for a new system of racial governance.

## The Immigration Debate Up to 1907

Daniel Tichenor has characterized US immigration policy up to the 1870s as largely a laissez-faire system: Until the federal judiciary voided the ability of states to implement their own system of screening immigrants, both local and federal government exercised limited control over immigration inflow.[2] Before then, periodic surges of grass-roots mobilization against various immigrant groups—French, Irish, Germans, and French Canadians, to name a few—had a difficult time scoring any legislative victory, mainly because the regulatory structure around immigration was decentralized and activists could not find an effective political target for their grievances. According to Tichenor, "In the early 1870s, official efforts to regulate European immigration remained largely the province of state governments with major ports of entry."[3] A radically different story would play out for Asian immigrants in California: A sustained effort by the coalition of local labor leaders, progressive intellectuals, and restrictionists would eventually triumph over those business and farm owners and political representatives who favored the laissez-faire immigration policy, leading to the Chinese Exclusion Act of 1882. Restrictionists saw the act as a hopeful promise that a federal restriction on immigration based on race was possible.[4]

Yet the European immigrants on the Atlantic coast presented a somewhat different problem. There were two major roadblocks to immigration restriction against European immigrants in the late nineteenth century. First, there were multiple social divisions within the participants of immigration politics, or what Tichenor called "the politics of alien admissions and rights," which made it extremely difficult to build an effective legislative coalition to advance the restrictionist cause. Table 1 presents those divisions, identifying the positions of specific figures and organizations in late nineteenth-century immigration politics.

The strange bedfellows of immigration politics can be classed into four distinctive factions, distinguished by their respective stances toward labor rights and the admission of immigrants. Labor rights were tied to the protection and well-being of both native-born and immigrant workers who were already within the United States; immigrant admissions involved the control of immigration, usually at the federal level. Cosmopolitans were usually left-leaning, radical intellectuals and their organizations and advocated for the common humanity of all workers, regardless of their citizenship status; they believed that a person of any nationality deserved protection and that their right to move freely should not be restricted by the federal government. On the opposite side were the classic exclusionists, consisting of

TABLE 1. Immigration Coalitions of the Progressive Era

| | NO RESTRICTION | RESTRICT ENTRY |
|---|---|---|
| | *Cosmopolitans* | *Nationalist egalitarians* |
| More labor protection | Horace Kallen | Samuel Gompers |
| | Jane Addams | Terence Powderly |
| | Immigrant Protective League | John R. Commons |
| | American Jewish Committee | American Federation of Labor |
| | "Social justice" progressives | Knights of Labor |
| | Franz Boas* | Jeremiah Jenks* |
| | William Bennet* | |
| | *Free-market expansionists* | *Classic exclusionists* |
| Less labor protection | William Howard Taft | Madison Grant |
| | Joseph Cannon | Albert Johnson |
| | National Association of Manufacturers | Immigration Restriction League |
| | Steamship companies | Eugenicists |
| | US Chamber of Commerce | Asian Exclusion Leagues |
| | | Henry Cabot Lodge* |
| | | John Burnett* |

Note: Reproduced with modifications from Tichenor, *Dividing Lines*, 121. Asterisks denote the participants of the Dillingham Commission.

aristocratic social conservatives who strongly believed in the Anglo-Saxon, Protestant identity of the nation. Henry Cabot Lodge, a member of the commission's executive committee, was a prime example of this faction. Classic exclusionists often blamed immigrants for many of the contemporary social problems such as poverty and crime. They were not interested in labor rights—instead, they argued that with proper immigration control, the labor problem would disappear because wages and working conditions would improve without the downward pressure from immigrant workers willing to work for very low wages.

Whereas these two factions roughly map onto the twenty-first-century ideological divide between pro- and anti-immigration constituents, other cells in the table make matters more complicated. Nationalist egalitarians included labor leaders and progressive reformers who championed workers' rights and put faith in the collective regulation of unfettered capitalism. From their perspective, the continuing influx of nonunionized, inexpensive labor from Europe posed a threat against a unified, strong labor movement.

Therefore, just as they demanded state intervention in the market and workplace, they also called for federal regulation of immigration in order to protect "the American standard of living" for American workers.[5] Across the aisle from them were free-market expansionists, composed largely of big business owners and their political spokespersons. Immigrant labor was the most important source of their profit, and this otherwise socially conservative group maintained a liberal attitude regarding alien admissions—that is, they wanted laissez-faire immigration policy so that they could continue to hire nonunionized, inexpensive immigrant labor for their businesses.

Unlike other political issues, immigration politics in the early nineteenth century featured two axes of division: one around labor protection and the other around maintenance of national boundary. This complicated political terrain made it extremely difficult to organize an effective coalition that could overcome pressure from the opposing groups, leading to the stalemate on federal-level immigration policy regarding European immigrants. This stalemate continued well until the 1910s, even as a small group of committed activist groups, led by the IRL, repeatedly attempted to pass restrictionist legislation such as a literacy test.

The second major roadblock to restriction was the legislative process itself, or what Tichenor has identified as the distinctive feature of American political institutions in the prereform era.[6] Due to an emphasis on the checks and balances of power, the American legislative branch contained many veto points at which opposing groups could effectively thwart any legislation with relatively little effort. This included the two-tiered system of the House and Senate; various committees and chairman positions, many of which could sabotage a proposed piece of legislation for months and years, if not sink it all together; hierarchies within the party system that amplified the voices of senior leaders over more numerous junior members; and, lastly, the presidential veto power that stood apart from the direct influences of both Congress and the electorate. All these institutions favored the status quo over change, and immigration was a perfect example of this institutional inertia: Many agreed that something had to be done about immigration, yet no one could amass enough political capital to bulldoze through all the veto points. In this context, relatively small but highly motivated pro-immigrant lobby organizations were able to impede many attempts at immigration control by restrictionists.

The legislative history leading up to the Immigration Act of 1907, which established the Dillingham Commission, is a perfect example of how these two political roadblocks thwarted even highly coordinated legislative efforts to change immigration policy. As previously discussed, the nineteenth-century restrictionist effort had been unable to score any major legislative victory in terms of immigrant restriction, largely due to the veto points previously described and, more importantly, due to immigrant voters who supported the vetoing politicians. In the steps leading up to the formation of the Dillingham Commission, however, Henry Cabot Lodge and the IRL brought new ammunition to use in the old battle: Distancing themselves from the previous waves of anti-immigrant mobilizations, which they characterized as driven mainly by irrational fear and prejudice against the unfamiliar, the new generation of activists saw immigration as a practical social problem, the solution to which should be provided by scientific reasoning. Enlisting the support of natural and social scientists—Nathaniel Shaler, Francis Walker, and Edward Ross, to name a few (see chapter 1)—Lodge and the IRL provided a comprehensive perspective on how immigration was impacting the national identity and how it should be controlled by federal power. Their argument rested on the idea of "fit" between race and nation: According to Shaler and his student Lodge, the United States was founded by the Anglo-Saxons and thus provided a more fitting environment for the descendants of those groups. Southern and eastern Europeans, whose numbers were rapidly increasing in the 1890s and 1900s, would only contribute to the problems of the nation due to lack of fit and therefore should be prevented from entering the country. Starting in 1891, Lodge repeatedly introduced to Congress the literacy test as a means to weed out the undesirables of those races that were a supposed mismatch for the American environment.[7] Of course, his proposal suffered multiple defeats over the course of the decade, stalling out at many of the aforementioned veto points.

The most interesting—and frustrating, from the perspectives of Lodge and his allies—episodes in those defeats come from the early 1900s, from the notorious, ever-powerful Republican House Speaker Joseph Cannon (1836–1926) of Illinois, known as "Uncle Joe." Learning from the repeated failures of the 1890s, the restrictionists amassed a strong coalition of supporters behind their cause, including labor leaders such as Samuel Gompers of the American Federation of Labor and the southern social control conservatives who believed that immigration was as great a race problem as African Americans in the South. With the rise of Theodore Roosevelt, the progressive president, restrictionists had high hopes for enacting federal-level immigration regulation, which was then regarded as a core progressive policy agenda. In 1906, Lodge introduced the literacy test proposal one more time, on this occasion in the form of an amendment to the immigration bill proposed by Senator William P. Dillingham (R-VT), the moderate restrictionist chairman of the Senate Immigration Committee.[8] The bill passed through the Senate with ease, garnering support from the majority of Republicans and even some of the southern Democrats.

In the House, however, Uncle Joe Cannon stood firmly in opposition. According to Tichenor, Cannon was supported by naturalized immigrants: "Lobbied intensely by ethnic associations and the Liberal Immigration League, House party managers worried that the measure would provoke electoral reprisals from foreign-born voters. Cannon's own district contained a large and active constituency of naturalized voters."[9] As the chairman of the Rules Committee, Cannon had unilateral power to decide which legislation would reach the House floor for a debate or whether a specific piece of legislation made it at all. In a show of sheer force against the rank-and-file progressive Republicans, Cannon sat on the Literacy Test Bill for several months in 1906 without allowing debate. When he finally gave in to mounting pressure from the progressive-restrictionist coalition, he countered by removing the literacy test and adding an amendment: establishing a new investigative commission. The proposed commission would conduct impartial fact-finding activities to ensure that future immigration policy debate would be based on the solid foundation of empirical evidence.

This whole episode can be seen as one of the many battles reform-minded politicians engaged in during the Progressive Era, which placed more established, well-connected, and often corrupt party bosses on the one side and the new generation of maverick, activist-minded junior politicians, most aptly represented by Theodore Roosevelt, on the other. In this context, the Dillingham Commission was part of a delay tactic employed by the old guard to fend off challenges to its monopoly on power, if only for the time being. From the perspective of progressive reformers, it was a second-best option that allowed them to keep their agenda alive while garnering more evidence to support it. During the Progressive Era, the authority of science, reason, and facts had, at least on the surface, higher ground over politics and self-interest. Reformers, given their enthusiasm over data and empirical evidence, were happy to engage in an investigation although it meant they would have to wait a few more years to pursue legislation around immigration control.

The enthusiasm for data, however, was not the only reason why reform-minded restrictionists such as Lodge agreed to the compromise. To understand how and why they accepted it requires us to move beyond Washington, DC, politics and pay attention to another arena of conflict, which had repercussions across the Pacific. The diplomatic crisis over Japanese schoolchildren in San Francisco—and the resulting Gentlemen's Agreement of 1907 between Japan and the United States—played a key part in the launch of the Dillingham Commission.

## The Gentlemen's Agreement of 1907, or How Japan Differed from China

The year 1905 was monumental for Japan. The new empire had just emerged victorious from the Russo-Japanese War, much to the surprise of the world, which had expected otherwise. Admiral Tōgō Heihachirō and the Japanese imperial navy destroyed the Baltic Fleet of the Russian Empire, securing Japan's dominant position in the Far East. With firm support from Great Britain and a tacit approval from Theodore Roosevelt, Japan placed Korea under its military protection, just like the European empires had done for their colonies in the first stages of occupation.[10] Finally, it seemed, the time had come for Japan to reap the fruits of its ongoing expansion campaign, in effect since the Meiji Restoration in 1868: The nascent empire finally stood alongside other Western superpowers on equal terms, not as an exotic, barbarian island country on the edge of the map but as a legitimate, sovereign member of the imperialist world order.

Japanese immigrants in the United States, who had been gradually arriving on the West Coast by way of Hawaii since the early 1880s, also took great pride in the rise of their home country.[11] Perhaps they saw their personal trajectories overlapping with that of the empire: They had worked hard and rapidly risen through the ranks of immigrants in the American West; some of them had accumulated enough capital to own farms and small businesses, and they hoped that they would finally be able to get some respect from Americans—White Americans, to be precise—for their hard work and success.

Japan's rise on the global stage coincided with the resurgence of anti-immigrant activism targeting Japanese immigrants in San Francisco. Popular mobilization against Asian immigrants was not a new phenomenon. Since the gold rush, Chinese immigrants had occupied the bottom strata of the working class on the West Coast, doing the hardest work for the lowest pay. Economic competition led to racial resentment and consequently to violence against Chinese workers, until the Chinese Exclusion Act of 1882 practically barred their entry except for trickles of unauthorized migrants.[12] The rise of anti-Japanese agitation was only a matter of time: Japanese immigrants were replacing the aging Chinese workers as a cheap and reliable source of labor, and they soon became the new target of the White working class and its leaders.[13]

In the first decade of the twentieth century, international relations and domestic racial politics were on a collision course in San Francisco. The Roosevelt administration was more than willing to recognize Japan as a partner in keeping order in the Pacific. However, the White working class in California, as well as its representatives in the state and federal government, was not ready to accept Japanese immigrants as permanent members of the local community. As Katherine Benton-Cohen shows in her detailed account of the clash, this collision would trigger the end of the legislative stalemate between Lodge's and Cannon's lieutenants, launching the Dillingham Commission's investigation of immigrants.[14]

The sequence started in San Francisco, with the city's board of education. Responding to anti-Japanese agitations, the board decided to concentrate Japanese students across the city in a school in Chinatown, unofficially designated the "oriental school." Japanese immigrants were furious, and the Japanese government protested through diplomatic channels. The newly emergent empire in the Far East strongly resisted association with China, which was the symbol of corruption and backwardness in the imperial world order. Roosevelt had a dilemma: He could not risk shaking up the friendly relationship with Japan, given American territorial interest in the Pacific, including Guam, the Philippines, and Hawaii; at the same time, his party could not afford to lose the support of restrictionists in California, who had remained loyal to the administration throughout the years. As historian Eric Love has noted, Roosevelt faced a dilemma of "race over empire": American expansionism could not coexist with insistence on a Whites-only nation at home because expansion would naturally bring non-Whites into the fold.[15] In a sense, the global dominance of White supremacy necessarily led to problems for White purity through the conquest and incorporation of non-Whites, just like racial knowledge production for scientific racism led to confusion and contradictions by surfacing unexpected empirical evidence that defied racial ideology. Some measure had to be created to control Japanese immigration without offending the Japanese government.

The Gentlemen's Agreement of 1907 was devised to solve this dilemma. As its title suggests, the agreement relied on the mutual trust of both parties. Japan would stop issuing passports to workers moving to the United States and therefore try its best to curtail further emigration and economic competition in California; the US government, on the other hand, would seek the best measure to deal with anti-Japanese agitation and guarantee equal protection for the Japanese subjects already living within its jurisdiction. The fact that the United States was willing to sign a gentlemen's agreement with Japan was in itself an achievement for the island nation. Japan was no longer among the colonized; it had its place at the table of gentlemen nations of Europe and North America, discussing and deciding the fate of the world.

At the same time, Roosevelt mobilized the Republicans in Congress to add an amendment to the Immigration Act of 1907, the discussion of which was ongoing between the Senate restrictionists and the Cannon surrogates from the House. The amendment would provide the president with the authority to enforce the Gentlemen's Agreement by allowing him to block the entry of Japanese immigrants harming the economic prospects of American workers. Cannon accepted the amendment, and, in return, Lodge and the Senate Republicans conceded to the idea of establishing an investigative commission on immigration while forgoing the literacy test for the time being.

In short, the Dillingham Commission was a product of the legislative struggle between anti-immigrant and pro-immigrant politicians over restriction, yet it was also a product of compromise orchestrated by Roosevelt, who had to appease various constituents and interests. Different groups agreed to the idea of an investigative commission because they all thought that empirical evidence would help their goal: Restrictionists welcomed the opportunity to bring the authority of science and empirical evidence to their side; pro-immigrant politicians were somewhat skeptical yet believed a supposedly objective inquiry was better than a straightforward restriction. In addition, Roosevelt was genuinely curious about the West Coast Japanese immigrant situation, which might continue to cause problems for his expansionist ambition.

## The People of the Dillingham Commission

In a sense, the commission was surrounded by complex political calculations, but none projected decisive power. Hence, the people who participated in the commission were able to exercise a considerable amount of autonomy in their work, and deference to facts and social sciences was one lens through which they made sense of such autonomy. In *Inventing the Immigration Problem*, Katherine Benton-Cohen provides thorough biographical sketches of people who participated in the commission. While I refrain from citing all of the biographical details, in the following I present a few relevant ones, focusing especially on diverging perspectives on race held by different executive committee members.

There were three major groups among the people who participated in the Dillingham Commission (see fig. 5). First, there were politicians—three senators and three congressmen—who were nominated by the Senate Majority Leader and House Speaker. They oversaw the general direction of the fact-finding activity while making decisions on all financial and personnel

FIGURE 5. The executive committee and key staff members of the Dillingham Commission. *From left, front row*: Asbury Latimer, Henry Cabot Lodge, William P. Dillingham, Benjamin F. Howell, and Charles P. Neill; *back row*: William R. Wheeler, Jeremiah Jenks, Morton E. Crane, William S. Bennet, William W. Husband, and John Burnett. George Grantham Bain Collection, Library of Congress (LC-DIG-ggbain-04554).

matters of the commission. Although they did not devote too much time to the Dillingham Commission—they met every month or other week, at best—they were in power, and the decisions that mattered, such as what kind of topics to study and whom to hire as expert investigators, had to go through their vote. They understood that immigration was an important policy subject and invested considerable energy and political capital in the work of the commission, although some members were clearly more interested in its activity than others. But this does not indicate that their perspectives on race and national identity were uniform. As we have seen in chapter 1, Lodge was focused on defending the WASP culture of New England and obsessed over the democratic fitness of new immigrants, and, therefore, he was more closely aligned with the restrictionists led by the IRL. As we see in the next section, however, other members had somewhat different perspectives on race, immigration, and national belonging.

## WILLIAM PAUL DILLINGHAM

Senator William Paul Dillingham (R-VT, 1843–1923) is less well known than Lodge. Dillingham came from an old, established Vermont political family whose heritage could be traced back to the early Puritan colonies of the sixteenth century. According to historian Robert Zeidel, Dillingham was a "regular" Republican "who consistently opposed progressive reforms, such as woman's suffrage and direct election of senators" and was "committed to preserving the remaining vestiges of an older America."[16]

In terms of immigration, he maintained a rather careful stance as a "moderate restrictionist."[17] Although he served as the chair of the Senate Immigration Committee and sponsored numerous bills geared toward immigration restriction, including the 1907 bill that launched the commission, personally and politically he remained aloof from the anti-immigrant activists who openly expressed their hostility toward southern and eastern European immigrants. He was somewhat sympathetic to the new generation of restrictionists, best represented by the IRL and Lodge, but he did not actively advocate for their cause, either. Dillingham approached the issue strictly as a policy question, focusing on the social harms and benefits of immigration, and largely refrained from making any statements that could be construed as based on prejudice. Of course, he did believe and invest in the idea of the United States as a White, Anglo-Saxon, and Protestant nation, in both his public and personal life, but his Vermont nativism had unique characteristics originating from the rural environment of his home state.[18]

Just like any predominantly rural state, Vermont witnessed a surge of Know-Nothings in the 1850s, and antipathy toward Irish and Catholic immigrants was a common theme in both local politics and everyday life of the state. This antipathy mapped squarely onto the rural-urban divide: As opposed to the virtue of quiet rural life that Vermonters appreciated, Irish immigrants were associated with an intensification of urban social problems in the state, such as poverty, disease, prostitution, and anarchism. Born in 1843, Dillingham came of age in the post-Know-Nothing period, presumably under the strong influence of anti-Catholic, anti-urban sentiment. When he was elected the governor of the state in 1888, however, the situation had changed somewhat: With the rise of industrial production in neighboring states such as Massachusetts, the agricultural communities in Vermont suffered a labor shortage. As much as the people of Vermont cherished their heritage and the virtue of quite rural life, the economic realities of rapidly developing capitalism forced them to look for factory jobs in emerging industrial towns near big cities like Boston. As governor, Dillingham established a commission to study the agricultural sector in

Vermont, and he asked the commission to collect data on immigrants living in the state to assess which group would be the best candidate for replacing the Vermont farmers who had left for work in the factories. The commission concluded that "the hard-working, honest Scandinavian" could be the group, given the "geographical similarities between Scandinavia and Vermont." Based on this recommendation, the Vermont commission ended up recruiting twenty-seven families from Sweden to immigrate to farm towns across the state.[19]

In short, while advocating for the literacy test and immigration restriction, Dillingham remained focused on the distribution of immigrants—that is, he believed immigrants only become problems when they concentrated in cities, so the government should devise a proper method of distributing them across rural areas to facilitate their smooth and quick assimilation.[20] In fact, in a speech advocating for his immigration bill in 1906, he specifically explained how his stance differed from other restrictionists:

> There are in this country two classes of persons who differ in judgment as to the policy to be adopted to control immigration. One is made up of pronounced restrictionists who favor drastic measures for the reduction of the numbers admitted. The other class think that the demand for labor should govern the numbers admitted, but we should select from those who offer themselves, and permit only those to enter who are sound in mind, sound in body, sound in morals, and fit to become fathers and mothers of American children. The present law was based on this latter principle—the principle of selection—and the amendments proposed in this bill were framed in accordance with this principle.[21]

One may perceive Dillingham's move to distance himself from the restrictionists as an attempt to disguise his true intentions or personal feelings toward immigrants. In fact, as we have seen in the case of Lodge, some progressive restrictionists did maintain personal prejudices against southern and eastern Europeans and personally desired to see fewer of them occupying their cherished hometowns as opposed to treating the issue of immigration as another policy concern. Among these different spectrums of restrictionists, however, Dillingham appears to be one of the more disinterested figures in his participation in immigration-related matters.

## JOHN LAWSON BURNETT

On the other hand, Congressman John Lawson Burnett (D-AL, 1854–1919) was more firmly in the restrictionist camp but for different reasons from people like Lodge.[22] Like Dillingham, he was familiar with the southern scheme of recruiting immigrants for agriculture—in fact, after the Civil War, the Alabama state legislature had many times attempted to secure "white reinforcements" from Europe through such efforts. Yet by the 1900s, these ventures turned out to be largely futile, mainly because the pull factors in the industrial North were much stronger. Thus, in 1906, speaking in the House, Burnett did not mince words on immigration and the South, characterizing the recent immigrants as a "contamination" to "our white civilization." While Burnett "believe[ed] that we have partially solved one race question" of African Americans through Jim Crow policies, a new race problem was emerging with "this horde of Italians, Austrians, Hungarians, Syrians, Bohemians, and others of that class." He imagined an apocalyptic scene in which the members of the "negro" and "dago" races met up in great numbers in the South, warning that "there will be the devil to pay" in social consequences if such an encounter occurred.[23]

If judged on the basis of these statements, Burnett comes across as a stereotypical southern White politician from the Jim Crow era who did not hesitate to express his contempt for all groups other than his own. However, while speaking in favor of the literacy test, he specifically denied the charge that his position was based on prejudice. After appealing to the notion of southern purity, Burnett quickly added that he had "nothing against foreigners" and that "many of [his] best friends" were "foreigners." In fact, he thought that the literacy test was the best means of selectively excluding problematic classes of foreigners as opposed to a blanket exclusion against a group: "Not all Italians are illiterate or bad, and I would not exclude them merely because of their name." As a rhetorical strategy to represent the literacy test as a rational means of immigration control, he used the example of one of his best friends: "As good a friend as I have in my home city was born beneath Italian skies. So excellent a character does he bear that he is a member of one of the secret orders to which I myself belong. And as a brother, I am glad to meet and greet him; and were all Italians like Mike Costa, I would never raise my voice against their admission. But I have no doubt but that he would join me in my desire to shut out the illiterate hordes from entering our sunny South."[24]

On the contrary, his stated objection to immigration stemmed from his devotion to the people he represented, so-called American workers. A congressman from Alabama described Burnett's constituents as "old-fashioned Americans . . . whose ancestors came to this country so long ago that they have lost track of when they came, whose ancestors were the hardy pioneers who carved this Republic out of its original virgin wilderness." The congressman added that "no finer people live in America than those of the seventh congressional district of Alabama," and "if there are any real Americans, these are they."[25] When others characterized Burnett as "sprung from the ranks of great common people and . . . himself a man of the people," they were using "people" in this socially and historically specific manner, meaning the people of a certain race, class, region, and possibly generation.[26] Of course, it should be added that whether this lineage of "people" had really "carved this Republic out of its original virgin wilderness" was up for debate, especially considering the fact that southern attempts at secession had nearly broken apart the nation.

In short, Burnett may have been the standard-bearer of sorts when it came to racial animosity toward immigrants, but his support of the literacy test and immigration restriction had an idiosyncratic side rooted in the particular social milieu of the South. In fact, along with William Bennet, whom we learn more about in the next section, Burnett formed an unlikely alliance of resistance to the Senate Dillingham bill following the Dillingham Commission's inquiry, holding off the literacy test in conference committee. He was fully supportive of immigration restriction and the literacy test. At the same time, however, he was against a provision added to the bill that granted the president the power to exclude an entire nationality in the event of fraudulent use of passports by some members of the group. At the time, the United States did not require a passport for entry, and the measure was regarded as largely inconsequential. Burnett, however, perceived this authority to be another instance of expanding unchecked federal executive power over the states and Congress.[27]

After the Dillingham Commission finished its work, Burnett took the lead in the legislative effort to implement its primary recommendation, the literacy test. After a drawn-out series of congressional battles in the House and Senate and vetoes from three successive presidents, Burnett finally saw his persistent advocacy for the measure yield fruit when the legislation bearing his name became law in 1917.[28]

## WILLIAM STILES BENNET

Representative William Stiles Bennet (D-NY, 1870–1962) was the lone advocate for immigrants in the commission. Born in New York City, Bennet practiced law before entering politics at thirty-five. Representing the seventeenth congressional district of upper Manhattan and the Bronx, which was home to many of the city's immigrant and Black populations, Bennet championed the rights of those he represented. In the House Immigration Committee, Bennet opposed the literacy test and squared off against the Senate restrictionists led by Lodge; while working in the commission, Bennet once again clashed with Lodge and Dillingham on various issues, cautioning against possible prejudice that the commission may hold against immigrants. In the executive summary of the *DCR*, Bennet refused to sign off on the literacy test recommendation and instead opted to add a single page titled "Views of the Minority." He wrote a paragraph noting the discrepancy between the commission's data and its policy recommendations and championed immigrants as future citizens who would make a distinctive and positive contribution to the nation.[29]

## EXPERTS

In sum, there was a notable diversity in racial ideas among the politicians on the executive committee that could not be reduced to the binary opposition between pro- and anti-immigrant forces. This diversity contributed to the autonomy of the commission's inquiry, in the sense that no coherent, unified racial ideology determined its data collection efforts, although there were certainly restrictionist undertones in some of its framings.

The second of the three groups that made up the commission were experts[30]—namely, social scientists who were either professors at universities or research staff in relevant federal agencies.[31] Three experts were specifically appointed by the president to participate in the executive committee; the others were hired by the executive committee to work on particular subsections of the inquiry, and they often took charge of a certain area of investigation in addition to authoring the final report. In many cases, much like what we see in contemporary government-funded research projects, the commission provided funding, and the professors worked with their students and hired staff to obtain data and write reports. It is fair to say that, as experts, they had a considerable amount of autonomy: Once the outline of investigation was submitted to and approved by the executive committee, the politicians had no direct control over the project. The executive committee received reports and approved (or denied) additional funding and, in the process, provided some feedback, but the inquiry itself was largely in the hands of the experts. Upon receiving the final report, the executive committee technically had to vote on whether to accept or reject it, yet with hectic schedules and given the resources invested, the committee accepted all of the reports it commissioned. As we see in more detail in chapters 5 and 6, the committee may have chosen to put less emphasis on an unexpected outcome by placing it somewhere in the middle of the forty-one volumes, yet once a report was written by experts, it was difficult to bury the results altogether. Daniel Folkmar and Franz Boas—who are discussed in detail in chapters 3 and 4, respectively—fall into this second group.

### STAFF MEMBERS

Lastly, there were staff members, who managed the administrative tasks of the Dillingham Commission and collected data in the field. In some cases, experts managed their own personnel, but most field researchers were hired by the commission and received their salary directly from the executive committee.[32] In both cases, the staff members were provided a badge and employment certification in the name of the United States Immigration Commission (see chapter 6 for further details). Aligning with stereotypical gender roles of the time, many of the staff members hired to conduct statistical analysis and tabulating were women, while the vast majority of field researchers were men.[33] Yamato Ichihashi, who we meet in chapter 6, belonged to this group, although in later life he tried to occupy an expert position by way of the work he conducted for the Dillingham Commission.

## Conclusion

Much of the existing historiography on the commission has depicted it as somewhat static, although recent works have diverged from this perspective. Some scholars have regarded the commission as a delay tactic used by pro-immigrant politicians to hold off the restrictionist lobby and have seen its members as motivated by prejudice and animosity toward southern and eastern European immigrants.[34] Although these assessments convey a grain of truth, the story of the Dillingham Commission is much more complicated. First, domestic and international political calculations undergirded the commission's establishment, and the struggle between the restrictionist lobby and pro-immigrant politicians were only one factor among many in its creation. Second, while some members of the executive committee were clearly restrictionists, diverse perspectives and experiences were represented. Even when we confine our observation to the restrictionist contingent—namely, Lodge, Dillingham, and Burnett—we see that their ideas on race and immigration featured diverse ideological elements, drawn from their different backgrounds and reflecting their idiosyncratic intellectual tastes, as Robert Zeidel and Katherine Benton-Cohen make clear in their respective monographs on the commission.[35]

In short, the Dillingham Commission was a complicated organization, and the complexity entailed the possibility of unexpected outcomes. Because many forces were competing for control of the commission's inquiry—some direct, some more subtle—the voice of the unruly facts was, ironically, amplified. Different sides found themselves appealing to the same data to make their cases. In this way, they could argue that they spoke from the perspective of the empirical data even while drawing markedly different conclusions. In other words, ideological heterogeneity provided a fertile ground for confusion and contradiction in the commission's knowledge production, and on this foundation the competing social forces proceeded to engage in a theoretical and political struggle that would lead to unforeseen outcomes—namely, the grafting of racial liberalism onto racial essentialism.

[ CHAPTER THREE ]

# Ethnicity

## A New Kind of Difference

### Problems with Classification Scheme

The first two chapters focus on the intellectual and political context of the Dillingham Commission. Because divergent forces put the commission into motion, each seeking to wrest a somewhat different outcome from the data, the commission's inquiry acquired some autonomy; the findings, which lay claim to empirical objectivity, provided a contestable landscape amid competing social forces.

This chapter discusses how this dynamic manifested in the commission's racial classification scheme. As discussed in chapter 1, race-thinking operates with two core tenets: what kind of races there are and what kind of relationship exists between those races.[1] Within the scheme of race-thinking, the human population is divided into a few categories, usually in a manageable number (such as fewer than five).[2] Then an intuitive, obvious hierarchy composed of the categories would follow to explain how different races occupied their place within that hierarchy. In the early twentieth-century United States, the ideology of WASP supremacy was articulated following this formula: In terms of category, there were different races, more or less corresponding to different European nations and colonized regions of the world, and these races marked clear-cut, never-changing boundaries between different groups of people. The WASPs stood apart from other groups—most notably, southern and eastern Europeans—in their *essence*. As Henry Cabot Lodge argued (see chapter 1), this essence was grounded not only in their biological origin but also in centuries of historical experiences that rendered them more fit for self-government than other races. Lodge and other powerful leaders of the commission wanted to procure empirical evidence affirming the undesirable nature of southern and eastern European races, thereby proving the supremacy of the WASPs with the authority of science.

In other words, a racial classification scheme was the foundation of the commission's inquiry, especially for restrictionists. In order to warrant WASP supremacy, first the WASPs and others needed to be properly categorized as belonging to distinctive racial categories. Only then could data collection and comparison by those categories become possible. The commission came up with a scheme called "races or peoples" and used it through all forty-one volumes of its report. The commission devoted volume 5, titled *The Dictionary of Races or Peoples* (henceforth *Dictionary*), to the justification of this scheme. In *Dictionary*, the commission sought to legitimize its choice of adopting races or peoples based on the existing scientific theories on race. In brief, *Dictionary* was supposed to function as a roadmap of sorts for the commission's inquiry, clarifying what kind of races existed "out there" in the world to be studied.

*Dictionary* was ridden with dilemmas and logical contradictions. To distinguish WASPs from southern and eastern Europeans, the commission had to go beyond the larger "white" or "Caucasian" category and devise a more detailed classification scheme that focused on the differences within Europe. The existing scientific consensus on race, which overwhelmingly focused on the distinction between Europeans and non-Europeans, did not provide much support for this move, and the commission was forced to rely on the nascent discussion of racial distinctions within Europe to justify its classification scheme. In the process, the commission inadvertently ventured into what Victoria Hattam has called the "unfixing" of race: To capture the differences among Europeans, the commission undermined the rigid, naturalistic basis of the race concept.[3] Whereas racial distinction between Europeans and non-Europeans relied on supposedly biological traits like skin tone, hair texture, and skull shape, the distinctions within Europe relied on more malleable historical features like language and geography. The introduction of history into the naturalistic race concept triggered a logical contradiction, however: The key feature of race was to essentialize categories to prevent any change in membership or characteristics—what Tukufu Zuberi called "racial reification"—but this historicization opened the path toward racial liberalism, or the understanding that race can change over time.[4] In a sense, as Lodge conjectured, race should be destiny, but the injunction of history made possible for individuals and groups to make their own destiny through their actions. Therefore, the commission had to entertain, at least on the theoretical level, the possibility that racial categories may change over time and that individuals may in a sense choose their own racial category.[5] The commission largely equivocated on this possibility, especially in *Dictionary*, yet this hypothesis provided an important precursor to the development of the concept of ethnicity. It would take decades and many more actors for racial liberalism to fully coalesce, but the foundation of the conceptual emergence was laid out in the commission's fact-finding inquiry.

What follows traces an unorthodox intellectual lineage, connecting different contexts of ideological brokering to document how the paradigm shift in race-thinking came about. The story begins with immigration bureaucrats on Ellis Island in the 1890s; then, we travel to the American colonial administration in the Philippines at the turn of the century, following Daniel Folkmar, the primary author of the *Dictionary*. Lastly, we delve into the murky details of the commission's convoluted scheme of "races or peoples."

## Justifying Races or Peoples

In the opening of its forty-one-volume, twenty-seven-thousand-page report, the commission lays out the overarching classification scheme for its inquiry, titled "Races or Peoples." The commission's proclaimed understanding of race was somewhat different from that of the scientific consensus, which came mainly from Europe at the time (see chapter 1). While the commission did emphasize the saliency of racial categories, it did not subscribe to the natural foundation of these beliefs. As we have seen in Lodge's formulation of race as historical destiny, the commission saw race as something that members of a racial group create for themselves, based on the legacy they inherit from their ancestors. In the onset of the *DCR*, this diversion is made very clear: "The Commission, like the bureau [of Immigration], uses the term 'race' in a broad sense, the distinction being largely a matter of language and geography, rather than one of color or physical characteristics such as determines the various more restricted racial classification in use, the most common of which divides mankind into only five races."[6]

The commission's phrasing "the most common . . . five races" likely refers to a scheme devised by Johann Friedrich Blumenbach, the German founding father of race-thinking who famously divided the human population into "Caucasian, Mongoloid, Negroid, Malay, and American races." As discussed in chapter 1, his key contribution was developing a scientific basis for racial classification: In addition to skin color and hair texture, which were difficult to quantify, he used measurements of skulls to develop what he considered to be reliable categories of race. Many other race-thinkers after him followed his template, conceptualizing race as consisting of essential traits like skull shape and size.[7] However, in the first volume of its report, the commission made clear that the contemporary scholarly consensus of measuring race through skulls was inadequate for its task.

The commission needed a different scheme that went beyond five races, because "for practical or statistical purposes such classification is obviously without value, and it is rarely employed."[8] The commission understood the most pressing matter for its inquiry was the racial status of new immigrants, most from southern and eastern Europe. "Color or physical characteristics" would not be sufficient to distinguish them properly, mainly because they were not visibly different from Anglo-Saxon Whites—at least to the extent that African Americans or Chinese were visibly different from them.[9] On the same page, the Dillingham Commission presented its classification scheme for races or peoples, an alternative to the five races, as follows:

African (black)
Armenian
Bohemian and Moravian
Bulgarian, Servian, and Montenegrin
Chinese
Croatian and Slovenian
Cuban
Dalmatian, Bosnian, and Herzegovinian
Dutch and Flemish
East Indian
English
Finnish
French
German
Greek
Hebrew
Irish
Italian, North
Italian, South
Japanese
Korean
Lithuanian
Magyar
Mexican
Pacific Islander
Polish
Portuguese
Roumanian
Russian
Ruthenian (Russniak)
Scandinavian
Scotch
Slovak
Spanish
Spanish-American
Syrian
Turkish
Welsh
West Indian (except Cuban)
All other peoples[10]

At first glance, the classification looks as if it was based on national or geographical origins. There are, however, several notable features inconsistent with such a rationale for designation. First, the categories were uneven: Some encompassed a wide range of subgroups, while others were surprisingly specific. For instance, "African (black)" lumped together an entire continent, the size of which is in fact much larger than North America. "English" was distinguished from other regions of the British Islands, whereas "French" and "German" did not receive such fine-grained treatment. There were distinctions between "Spanish," "Spanish-American," and "Mexican," presumably to distinguish between people from Spain and the Spanish-speaking population from South and Central America. "Hebrew" stood out as a nonnational category like "African (black)." Most strikingly, the immigrants from Italy were divided into two categories of south and north. In short, these categories were indeed classifying immigrants, but the overall scheme lacked a coherent principle behind it.

In *America Classifies the Immigrants*, Joel Perlmann traces the origin of this particular classification scheme to the Bureau of Immigration in the 1890s.[11] The number of immigrants from southern and eastern Europe surged rapidly in the late nineteenth century, posing a practical challenge for the bureau: Classifying immigrants from the multinational empires of eastern Europe was not as straightforward a task as classifying someone as German or French. In 1899, the bureau devised the aforementioned new scheme based on its experiences of inspecting immigrants arriving on steamships. Rather than focusing on theoretical validity, the classification scheme was designed to assist immigration inspectors in their everyday work. Appearance, language, religion, and a set of simple questions were deployed to sort immigrants into the different categories. Victor Safford (1867–1947), a medical doctor on Ellis Island who devised the races or peoples scheme, reasoned that "people that speak the same language and that have the same religious ties" will "be forced into the same occupations" upon their arrival to the United States, and in order to assess their "industrial and social values," he proposed to classify them based on their language and religion.[12] In other words, language and religion were suggested as proxies to capture the ways in which immigrants grouped themselves, and the bureau did not care to justify the theoretical reason why it chose to use such criteria. All statistical data collected by the bureau followed the races or people scheme, and eventually the Dillingham Commission adopted it to use as the basis for its forty-one-volume report, largely to ensure the compatibility between its own data and that of the bureau. In short, bureaucratic necessity lurked behind the emergence of races or peoples. However, this was only the beginning of the story.

The commissioners learned early on that a classification scheme was not merely a technical issue but also a matter of political and theoretical contestation.[13] Even though they were adopting the scheme out of bureaucratic necessity, they still had to justify their choice to outside audiences. The

Bureau of Immigration was an administrative organization; its primary task was to monitor and control the population inflow, not delve into a theoretical discussion of why the agency operated in a particular way. As long as the officials of the bureau could draw up a table displaying the number of immigrants arriving at Ellis Island, they were fine. The Dillingham Commission was, however, different: It was an investigative commission established to provide scientific grounds on which to design a more effective immigration policy; its legitimacy relied primarily on its insistence that it could produce knowledge about racial distinction, and theoretical as well as empirical validity was a key feature of its work. Plus, race, as we have seen in chapter 1, was a cutting-edge scientific concept, one that was of much interest to both scholars and the public. Hence, the commission had to engage in the difficult task of theoretically justifying the classification scheme of races or peoples, which was initially conceived out of practical necessity by immigration inspectors on Ellis Island. The scheme may not "make perfect sense," but it should be above the level of "anything goes" to ensure the legitimacy of the commission's data collection efforts.

To draft *Dictionary*, the key volume in clarifying the "races or peoples" scheme, the commission hired an expert in "ethnology and anthropology," Dr. Daniel Folkmar. He collaborated with his wife, Dr. Elnora Folkmar, in writing this volume.[14] Because the commission was operating under a hectic schedule, *Dictionary* was being written at the same time that field agents were collecting data using the categories suggested by the races or peoples scheme. In the end, the work that went into *Dictionary* did not exactly guide the inquiry of the commission but served more as a post hoc justification for its classification scheme.[15] Nevertheless, *Dictionary* provides a valuable opportunity for us to witness the challenges faced by the commission members: Caught between the necessity to theoretically justify its classification scheme and the hurried schedule of the project, the commission had to juggle multiple demands in defining what *race* meant in its inquiry. In the process, to ensure further differentiation within the larger "white" or "Caucasian" category, the commission and the Folkmars had to embrace a historical understanding of race as opposed to the rigid, naturalistic Blumenbach tradition represented by the obsession over skull sizes. This embrace marks an important moment in the future grafting of racial liberalism onto racial essentialism, as a new way of thinking about difference emerged from the existing theories of race. To properly make sense of this transition, however, we have to take a detour by way of Daniel Folkmar's professional trajectory—or, more specifically, his work in the Philippines during the American occupation, immediately preceding the commission's inquiry.

## Imperial Origins: The Philippine Commission and the Limits of Essentialism

Born in 1861 in Roxbury, Wisconsin, Daniel Folkmar attended Harvard University and continued his education in several cities in Europe, eventually receiving a doctorate in anthropology from the Sorbonne. Afterward, he taught in universities across the United States, including in the Department of Sociology at the University of Chicago. In 1903, he entered government service by joining the Philippine Commission, the governing body during the American occupation of the islands. David Barrows, chief of the Bureau of the Non-Christian Tribes, hired him for an anthropology project documenting different "types" of Filipinos.[16] After the project, Folkmar subsequently took the position of lieutenant governor of Bontoc Province, in which he acted as a lone American colonial administrator for the Indigenous population in the region. Upon completing his service in the Philippines in 1907, he was recruited by Jeremiah W. Jenks, a Cornell economist on the executive committee of the Dillingham Commission, to work on *Dictionary* as an expert in racial classification and ethnology.[17] Following his stint in the commission, he worked as a special agent for the Census Bureau till his death in 1932.[18]

Folkmar's first job in the Philippines was a work of classic race science à la Blumenbach: Working in the Bilibid prison, the infamous penitentiary built by the Spanish colonial government, Folkmar documented forty-three provincial "types" present among the prisoners, using physical measurements. Working in a small room with a dozen prisoners who doubled as his assistants and subjects, Folkmar faithfully followed in the footsteps of Blumenbach, measuring their heads, taking pictures of them, and making plaster head casts. The resulting monograph, *Album of Philippine Types*, along with the plaster casts, was displayed in the 1904 Louisiana Purchase Exposition in St. Louis.

Folkmar's work was part of a larger exhibition on the world's Indigenous peoples, in which Filipinos took center stage. As representatives of the most recently acquired territory of the United States, Filipinos received much attention from the excited fairgoers. However, as many scholars writing about the racialization of Filipinos point out, the exhibition focused on the supposedly "primitive" aspects of the Philippines in order to highlight the civilizing mission of the American occupation.[19] For this purpose, the Igorot—the Indigenous people of the Luzon region—were specifically hired to be displayed in the fair over more westernized Filipinos, who saw themselves more akin to Spaniards than to the Indigenous population.[20] In essence, Folkmar's job in the Philippines was squarely situated at the

FIGURE 6. Daniel Folkmar working with prisoners at Bilibid prison. Daniel Folkmar Papers, National Anthropological Archives in the records of the Department of Anthropology (Manuscript and Pamphlet File), Smithsonian Institution.

intersection of classic race science and imperial power: Folkmar invoked somatological data to categorize the colonized and justify the colonizers while being supported by the colonial administration.

Contemporary readers may sense a contradiction here. Writing *Dictionary* for the commission, Folkmar relied on language and geography as bases for categorizing races or peoples. Just a few years before, however, he had been immersed in the naturalistic tradition of race-thinking, making plaster casts of prisoners' heads. It seems as though he had made a sudden transition from nature to history, from the biological to the social, as he moved from the Philippines to the metropole of Washington, DC, to work on the Dillingham Commission. What catalyzed this transition? The contradiction only appears as such from our perspective, which takes the separation between the biological and the social as given.[21] As Victoria Hattam has noted in *In the Shadows of Race*, the boundary separating nature and culture, especially concerning race, was murky in the early twentieth century, and many commentators liberally drew from both domains in justifying their concepts regarding group difference.[22]

While the murkiness served as a broader context, there was a more immediate pressure to move away from racial essentialism out of necessity of the American empire. As Julian Go surmises in his work on American racial governance in the Philippines and other colonies, Folkmar's transition closely mirrored the approach adopted by the American colonial administration.[23] Late nineteenth-century American colonialists saw their own colonizing ventures as different from those of other European empires. European empires exercised despotic, exploitative governance over colonies, often resulting in bloody rebellions, one of which in fact gave birth to the United States. In contrast, the young nation's Constitution enshrined the right to challenge despotic ruling, and its governing elites proudly distinguished themselves from European colonialists, who lacked a moral imperative in their overseas ventures. Based on this understanding, American officials saw education and tutelage as their prime objectives in dealing with the Philippines. The Filipinos were not inherently different from Americans in their capability of self-government, the officials proclaimed, especially to assuage the opponents of colonial ventures at home who worried that admission of non-Whites to the nation would undermine its democratic institutions.[24] Colonialists argued that the colonial subjects needed more time and education in uplifting themselves and that the American occupation would guide them in the process. Based on such understanding, the American colonial administration in the Philippines emphasized free elections and public education to instill the values of so-called civilization among Filipinos, especially the political elite. Of course, this rosy portrayal did not match the bloody realities of the occupation itself, as Paul Kramer has noted in his account of the Philippine-American War. In practice, the American colonial state classified the Filipinos into two discreet groups as the "civilized" and the "savages" and attempted to assimilate the former and exterminate the latter.[25] The boundary between the two groups, however, was murky and subject to contestation and interpretation. As katrina quisumbing king has noted with the metaphor of "grammar," this kind of ambiguity in categorization was a key feature of the American empire during the era. Race in the Philippines, or in the American empire more broadly, was more of a flexible framework in making sense of people and their situation than rigid prejudice. While Folkmar was not thinking in these terms, he very much embodied this new grammar of imperial governance, and the technique of governance moved along to the metropole and to the Dillingham Commission as his career progressed.[26]

We can better appreciate Folkmar's evolution as a race-thinker by considering these macro dynamics surrounding him during his stint at the Philippines. While he did not have a bird's-eye view on this broader ideological development, he was reflecting rather seriously about the concept of race as he worked for the Dillingham Commission. He did not necessarily see a contradiction between the biological and the social, but his experience of implementing the race concept on the ground nonetheless sensitized him to the contradictions inherent in racial knowledge production. Folkmar learned that the race-thinking he had absorbed from European universities did not neatly mesh with reality, especially in the Philippines. Hence, he was forced to revise his understanding, an experience that would exactly mirror his work on the commission, as he grappled with the task of categorizing southern and eastern Europeans as a distinctive race from northern and western Europeans. In this light, his evolution as a race-thinker is symptomatic of the work of the Dillingham Commission more broadly: In both instances, the confrontation with the reality of peoples and cultures led to a transformation of racial ideas. And, of course, this confrontation was analogous to the one that American empire-state experienced in its attempt to rule over a diverse set of peoples at home and abroad.

The head-cast project, which was supposed to be the epitome of classical race science, showcased some of this transformation. Under Blumenbach's scheme, Filipinos represented a borderline case, situated somewhere between Mongolians and Malays. They were close to what we would today perceive as Southeast Asians, but there was much influence of the Chinese, according to the nineteenth-century race-thinkers. To complicate things further, the Spanish colonial government had long relied on three distinctive "races" to categorize Filipinos: Christians, non-Christians, and Moros. Christians referred to the coastal elite who had adopted Spanish ways of life and collaborated with the colonial administration; non-Christians referred to the so-called barbaric tribes of the mountainous regions that resisted colonial rule; and Moros referred to the Muslim minority who resided within the colonial jurisdiction but were largely under the political influence of the sultan in neighboring Malaysia.[27] Soon after beginning his project of measuring the heads and bodies of the Bilibid inmates, however, Folkmar witnessed the instability of these categories. As Oscar Compomanes points out, Folkmar's measurements of prisoners did not correspond to these neatly divided categories, and many inmates belonged to multiple categories. While *The Album of the Philippine Types* does not discuss these contradictions, Folkmar's report in his personal archive documents his painstaking efforts to make sense of the illegible.[28] Folkmar's measurements were not what they were supposed to be, according to the existing racial theories, and he did what many scientists would do in their daily work in labs—he checked his measurements and added ad hoc, in-between categories to protect the theories he started with. In the end, Folkmar did what he would do for the Dillingham Commission: He brought in language, geography, and religion in addition to somatological data to define categories that went beyond Christians, non-Christians, and Moros. Through this process, he wound up with forty-three distinctive types of Filipinos. It is telling that he stopped calling these categories "races," instead opting for the generic, less theoretically charged term *type*. In sum, as Folkmar was making plaster casts of prisoners' heads, he could literally see and feel the contradiction posed by racial essentialism—that is, racial categories were not as straightforward and evident in nature as he had learned in the classrooms of Paris.

While this friction between culture and biology begat an intellectual contradiction in the domain of theory and data, Folkmar's experience as lieutenant governor would also challenge how he thought about race—or, more specifically, the people who were racialized. After Folkmar's project in the Bilibid prison, Barrows again tapped him for a lieutenant governor position, this one overseeing the Bontoc region. Although he never published it, Folkmar wrote a memoir of his experience on this job as he was working for the commission on *Dictionary*.[29]

Part travelogue and part reflection, this memoir chronicles how he came to see the racialized in a different light through his engagement with them. To be clear, he did not seem to be cognizant of the broader ideological contours of the American occupation discussed in this chapter. In the beginning, Folkmar confessed that he had a typical perspective of "an imperialist" going into Bontoc, writing that he saw "imperialism and expansion" as "inevitable and natural in the evolution of great nations."[30] This was not surprising, considering his education in Europe during the last decade of the nineteenth century, a circumstance he acknowledges in the memoir. Interestingly, however, Folkmar's experience as governor instilled in him what we may call a proto-ethnographic sensibility, which was somewhat in tune with the mandates of the American colonial authorities. In the preface to the memoir, he surmised that "the spirit of [the] people" of the Philippines "cannot be known except through immersion into the life of a native community. Individuals must be known as we know them in our country. We must know the most minute and trivial details of their life."[31] Sounding more a modern cultural anthropologist than a race-thinker, Folkmar sought to understand the people he governed in their own context by living among them. This uncanny juxtaposition of colonial mindset and ethnographic sympathy cast him perfectly for the role of overseeing the more "primitive" Filipinos who had resisted Western colonizers for centuries: He mused that Barrows chose him as lieutenant governor because he "certainly showed an interest in the people; and the more primitive they were, the better."[32]

The rest of the document does not deviate much from a typical colonial memoir. He traveled through uncharted territory where no Westerners had ever gone before and marveled at its beauty; he formed comradery with the Filipinos he employed, including soldiers; he engaged in a minor scuffle with hostile tribes and directly participated in colonial violence by fighting them off; and he indulged in local cultural practices, including feasts and dance rituals.

In a typical ethnographic fashion, these experiences led him to sympathize with the people he was sent to govern. Folkmar's primary task was to prevent the practice known as "head-hunting." The Igorot maintained a ritualistic form of violence between villages in which an attacker would take the head of the victim as a mark of honor. Taking the head was loosely tied to the coming-of-age ceremony and other important events in Igorot life courses. From the perspective of American colonial administration, however, this local practice was an act of barbarism and thus needed to be stopped. Bontoc Igorot, as Folkmar learned upon arriving at his post, had diverse opinions on this long-standing practice: Some were enthusiastic practitioners, while others were less invested. Folkmar, as a governor, had the responsibility of administrating the legal proceedings for the perpetrators of the violence as they were charged by the colonial government. Because the central administration sent out a touring judge for the provinces and victims' family members served as de facto prosecutors, Folkmar often found himself in a sort of public defender role, which earned him the nickname "defender of Igorrots." Folkmar developed a deep sympathy for the people he was defending, writing that "there were times when this feeling led me to take the Igorrote side against interests of an American . . . against other officials or our good-hearted missionaries."[33] In fact, he seemed to identify more with the Igorot in relation to the legacies of Spanish colonialism: "I heard some fascinating Spanish ladies say in a bantering tone one evening on the hotel veranda to the American ladies of the party that we Americans were savages . . . let them call us savages."[34] In other words, while his job was winning the hearts and minds of those he governed, his own heart opened up to the Igorot as well.

We need not exaggerate the weight of Folkmar's statements. After all, he was living like a king among the Indigenous population he was sent to govern. He had a secretary, a servant, and a cook, on top of the dozens of soldiers who accompanied him as he was visiting villages where head-hunting was prevalent. He wrote of life-threatening moments and lasting connections he built with Filipinos, but realistically these experiences were confined within and made possible by the privilege granted to him by the American colonial administration. What we can glean from his recollection, however, is the fact that the experience exposed him to the limits of racial essentialism. As he confessed, he had "an imperialist" perspective toward the Philippines at the onset. Yet his empirical research as well as his political work sensitized him to the contradictions of racial essentialism: Not all Filipinos were the same, their cultural practice made sense in its context, and, most importantly, the idea of race, as he learned at the universities in the metropole, was not equipped to address the urgent problems of the American colonial administration. In a nutshell, Folkmar felt something other than racial essentialism at the intersection of race and imperialism.[35] It was far from anticolonial resistance but was not squarely within the realm of classic race-thinking, either. Folkmar did not quite understand what it was, but it would follow him all the way to the Washington, DC, as he was tasked to categorize different European "races."

## Juggling Multiple Demands

Folkmar was hired by the Dillingham Commission as a specialist in ethnology and anthropology. The two disciplines were one and the same at the time, but, as we have seen, Folkmar had been exposed to the ethnographic experience that would drive the two apart decades later. We can therefore appreciate the tension between the naturalistic tradition of race-thinking and the more flexible, ethnographically informed approach to race throughout *Dictionary*. To complicate things even further, bureaucratic demands and political considerations also played a role in Folkmar's project with the commission.

In justifying races or peoples, Folkmar began by addressing the commission's core concern: the racial status of new immigrants. "Early in the Commission's investigations among these newer immigrants," Folkmar wrote, "it became apparent that the true racial status of many of them was imperfectly understood even in communities where they were most numerous, and the difficulties encountered in properly classifying the many ethnical names that were employed to designate various races or people suggested the preparation of a volume that would promote a better knowledge of the numerous elements included in the present immigration movement."[36] As shown in the previous passage, conceptual confusions regarding race still lingered in the introduction to this volume of the report: Terms such as *racial status*, *races*, *people*, *ethnical names*, and *numerous elements* were used interchangeably to refer to "six hundred subjects, covering all the important and many obscure branches or divisions of the human family" that *Dictionary* aimed to sort.

In a strange twist of logic, however, *Dictionary* admitted that classification was bound to be arbitrary or more a matter of custom than science. "The sciences of anthropology and ethnology," according to Folkmar's assessment, "are not far enough advanced to be in agreement upon many questions that arise in such a study." It is telling that Folkmar was hired as an expert in these disciplines; in this passage, he confesses that his expertise was insufficient for the task at hand, something that only an insider could utter with confidence. Ironically this humility renders the following statement inevitable: "The use of this classification as the basis for the present work is perhaps entirely justified by the generally prevailing custom in the United States."[37] In his work on the Supreme Court cases about Whiteness, Ian Haney-López shows that courts in the early twentieth century frequently deferred to "common sense" as a foundation for racial categorization.[38] Of course, this move often served as a convenient tool for affirming the existing social hierarchy and attributing Whiteness to the rich and powerful while denying that status to anyone who challenged the system. However, unlike the courts of the same period, the Dillingham Commission could not resort to the naked logic of power or end the discussion by invoking "prevailing custom": Because it was an investigative commission concerned with objectivity and facts, it had to engage in the exercise of defining, and justifying, what "prevailing custom" meant for its classification scheme.

"Prevailing custom" could mean many things, but *Dictionary* decided to privilege the language as the standard to make distinctions among races: "The primary classification of mankind into five grand divisions may be made upon physical or somatological grounds, while the subdivision of these into a multitude of smaller 'races' or peoples is largely upon a linguistic basis."[39] This decision came from practical, rather than theoretical, considerations, such as the fact that the "immigrant inspector or the enumerator in the field" lacked "the training to determine whether that individual is dolichocephalic or brachycephalic in type."[40] Folkmar also emphasized that the classification scheme would coincide better with census data and immigration statistics from other countries.

In short, Folkmar was aware that he was moving away from "races" as discussed and conceptualized by the leading race-thinkers of the time. Just like in the Philippines, he understood that the theories about race produced in the ivory towers of Europe did not matter in the field. Instead, he was focused more on how immigrant inspectors would gather data based on classification and how immigration law and censuses in the United States and other countries would be able to adopt the classification scheme for policy purposes. Language was, according to Folkmar, "the most convenient and natural" way to tell people apart, much more so than other so-called scientific measurements of race, such as skull shape.

Folkmar did not give up entirely on trying to justify "races or peoples" theoretically. Although his discussion of the matter was geared toward attesting to the practicality of the classification scheme, he was aware that it did have some basis in existing literature on ethnology and anthropology. Two tables, presented without much explanation, clarified those grounds, but only to those familiar with the tradition of race-thinking.

The first table, titled "Comparative Classification of Immigrant Races or Peoples," compares the races or peoples scheme with the racial classifications of other theorists. In figure 7, we see the names of the contemporary race-thinkers, such as Brinton and Ripley (see chapter 1), at the top. Although Folkmar does not go into a detailed discussion of these authors, the table conveys an informative argument for readers versed in their work. He was attempting to build a bridge between two conflicting theoretical traditions: Brinton provided a theoretical foundation and explained how the races or peoples scheme came out of the classic tradition of European race theory, which divided men into "five grand divisions"; meanwhile, Ripley's division of Europeans into multiple races spoke to the concern of the Dillingham Commission, which took great interest in the racial status of southern and eastern Europeans. In sum, this table shows how the races or peoples scheme, although originating from the administrative necessity of the Bureau of Immigration, was not entirely a haphazard one.

The second table, titled "Some Classifications of the Grand Division of Mankind" (fig. 8), was Folkmar's attempt to justify his use of language and geography in distinguishing races or peoples. The most important influence here was Joseph Deniker (see chapter 1), whose classification scheme is presented in the middle column. As discussed in chapter 1, Deniker posited that "races" should be based on "somatic character"—meaning physiological traits, such as skin color and skull shape—while "peoples" should "take into account *ethnic characters* (linguistic and sociological), and above all *geographical distribution*."[41] He proceeded to suggest *ethnic groups* as a proper term for the groups classified on the basis of their language and geography. Note that he was suggesting this principle out of a theoretical exigency of classifying population: His scheme included detailed subgroups not only for Europeans but also for non-Europeans, or the "Ethiopian," "American," and "Mongolian" categories. Folkmar chose to overlook these categories while borrowing the principle of language and geography to justify the Bureau of Immigration scheme.

Simply put, in terms of classification scheme, the most pressing issue for the commission was that the traditional understanding of race, based on the notions of "color" and biology, could not provide grounds for distinguishing

Dictionary of Races or Peoples. 5

COMPARATIVE CLASSIFICATION OF IMMIGRANT RACES OR PEOPLES.

| Based on Brinton (cf. Keane). | | | People. | Ripley's races, with other corresponding terms. |
|---|---|---|---|---|
| Race. | Stock. | Group. | | |
| | | | Scandinavian: | |
| | | | Danish | |
| | | | Norwegian | I. TEUTONIC. |
| | | | Swedish | H. Europæus (Lapouge). |
| | | Teutonic | German (N. part) | Nordic (Deniker). |
| | | | Dutch | Dolicho-leptorhine (Kohlmann). |
| | | | English (part) | Germanic (English writers). |
| | | | Flemish | Reihengräber (German writers). |
| | | Lettic | Lithuanian | Kymric (French writers). |
| | | | Scotch (part) | |
| | | Celtic | Irish (part) | |
| | | | Welsh | Part Alpine. |
| | | | Russian | |
| | | | Polish | |
| | | | Czech: | |
| | | | Bohemian | II. ALPINE (OR CELTIC). |
| | | | Moravian | |
| | | | Servian | H. Alpinus (Lapouge). |
| | | | Croatian | Occidental (Deniker). |
| | Aryan | Slavonic | Montenegrin | Disentis (German writers). |
| | | | Slovak | Celto-Slavic (French writers). |
| | | | Slovenian | Lappanoid (Pruner-Bey). |
| Caucasian | | | Ruthenian | Sarmatian (von Hölder). |
| | | | Dalmatian | Arvernian (Beddoe). |
| | | | Herzegovinian | |
| | | | Bosnian | |
| | | Illyric | Albanian | |
| | | Armenic | Armenian | |
| | | | French | Part Alpine. |
| | | | Italian (part) | Part Mediterranean. |
| | | | Roumanian | III. MEDITERRANEAN. |
| | | Italic | Spanish | H. Meridionalis (Lapouge). |
| | | | Spanish-American | Atlanto-Mediterranean and Ibero-Insular (Deniker). |
| | | | Mexican, etc | |
| | | | Portuguese | Iberian (English writers). |
| | | Hellenic | Greek | Ligurian (Italian writers). |
| | | | Hindu | Part Mediterranean. |
| | | Iranic | Gypsy | Part Teutonic. |
| | | Arabic | Arabian | |
| | Semitic | Chaldaic | Hebrew | Part Mediterranean. |
| | | | Syrian | |
| | Caucasic | | Caucasus peoples | Doubtful. |
| | Euskaric | | Basque | |
| | | | Finnish | |
| | | Finnic | Lappish | |
| | | | Magyar | |
| | Sibiric | | Bulgarian (part) | |
| | | Tataric | Turkish, Cossack, etc. | |
| Mongolian | | Japanese | Japanese, Korean | |
| | | Mongolic | Kalmuk | |
| | | | Chinese | |
| | Sinitic | Chinese | East Indian (part, i. e., Indo-Chinese). | |
| | | | Pacific Islander (part). | |
| Malay | | | East Indian (part) | |
| Ethiopian | | | Negro | |
| American (Indian). | | | American Indian | |

FIGURE 7. Table featuring classifications from Brinton and Ripley. *Dictionary*, 5.

southern and eastern Europeans from northern and western Europeans. Under the color scheme, the two groups were all lumped together into an overarching "White" or "European" category. In Deniker's theory, however, Folkmar found the solution to the problem. In "Deniker's remarkable and often misunderstood scheme," Folkmar wrote in the explanatory paragraph at the top of the table, "the larger groups of races recognized by him are more like the grand division of other writers than has been commonly supposed." In this scheme of things, language and geography determined a subset of "larger races," which were defined through physical features. Folkmar did not have to choose between "races" or "peoples" or between physical characteristics and language; instead, he could choose whatever principle of classification seemed necessary for the immigration inspectors and field agents to commence their work.

| Keane (after Linnæus). | Blumenbach. | Deniker. | Huxley. | Flower (cf. Quatrefages). |
|---|---|---|---|---|
| | | 1. Bushman | | |
| | | 2. Negrito | 1. Negroid | |
| | | 3. Negro | | |
| 1. Negro (except 5). | 2. Ethiopian (except 4, 6). | 4. Melanesian | | 1. Ethiopian (except 5) |
| | | 5. Ethiopian (Abyssinian, etc.). | | |
| | | 6. Australian | 2. Australoid (except part of 5). | |
| | | 7. Dravidian | | |
| | | 8. Assyroid | | |
| | | 9. Indo-Afghan | | |
| | | 10. Arab (Semite) | 5. Melanochroid (with part of 5). | |
| | | 11. Berber | | |
| | | 12. Littoral European | | |
| 4. Caucasic (with 5). | 1. Caucasian (except 19, 20). | 13. Ibero-Insular | | 3. Caucasic (with 5). |
| | | 14. Western European | | |
| | | 15. Adriatic | | |
| | | 16. Northern European | 4. Xanthochroid (with part of 27). | |
| | | 17. Eastern European | | |
| | | 18. Aino | | |
| | | 19. Polynesian | | |
| | | 20. Indonesian | | |
| | | 21. South American | | |
| | | 22. North American | | |
| 3. American | 5. American | 23. Central American | | |
| | | 24. Patagonian | 3. Mongoloid (except part of 27). | |
| | | 25. Eskimo | | 2. Mongol. |
| | | 26. Lapp | | |
| 2. Mongol | 3. Mongolian | 27. Ugrian | | |
| | | 28. Turco-Tatar | | |
| | 4. Malay *a* | 29. Mongol (incl. Malay). | | |

FIGURE 8. Table featuring classifications from Blumenbach and Deniker. *Dictionary*, 6.

Much of the choice would depend on the context. The "African (black)" category—defined simultaneously through physical features and geography—in *Dictionary* was sufficient and merited no further specification, because there were rarely any African immigrants arriving on US shores, at least according to the data from the Bureau of Immigration.[42] "Chinese" were all "Chinese," regardless of their linguistic backgrounds,[43] because under the Chinese Exclusion Act there was no need to categorize them as anything other than "aliens ineligible for citizenship." Moreover, there was no need to further discuss the case of "American (Indian)," or the Indigenous population of North America, because they were presumed to be irrelevant to the discussion of immigration. For European immigrants, on the contrary, the classification tree needed to expand to encompass a range of subgroups based on language and geography. In short, while building a patchwork of races or peoples from various scholars, Folkmar was inadvertently articulating the difference between race and ethnicity, highlighting the fact that only Europeans merited ethnic classification on top of racial classification.

To this end, the key to the problem of classifying new immigrants was not having an overarching classification principle for all immigrants but selectively applying different criteria for different groups. While it was sufficient to classify non-Europeans with Blumenbach's color scheme, the "White" category was further broken down through language and geography. For the purposes of the Bureau of Immigration and Dillingham Commission, not only were there different kinds of groups, but there were also different kinds of differences, covering various dimensions of classification. Note also that no outside groups pressured Folkmar to articulate a new principle of classification. It was confusion and contradiction within the races or peoples scheme that triggered the innovation in his classification scheme. While juggling multiple demands—administrative necessity for acquiring data, practicality for inspectors and agents, and theoretical validity for scholars—Folkmar inadvertently paved the way for making a distinction between a biological basis for group identity and a linguistic-geographical one. This distinction would later evolve into the conceptual distinction between race and ethnicity as we understand it today. In a sense, this move tied the knot on the work Folkmar started in the Bilibid prison in the Philippines: Instead of just laying forty-three types on top of the three Spanish race categories, this time Folkmar was able to clarify the relationship between races and peoples and incorporate practicality into the theoretical classification scheme.

The skillful juggling of multiple demands led to unexpected theoretical dilemmas, however: If race can be determined through language and geography, what was to be done with people learning a new language or moving across space? Can they "become" a member of a new race? What's the point of defining race if individuals can freely traverse its boundary? These were questions Folkmar had to address.

## "UNFIXING RACE" AND THE PROBLEM OF LANGUAGE

As was usually the case with race-thinking in general, Folkmar used whatever data he could obtain to rationalize his categories of races or peoples. This data included census data available from the government of the land of origin, with more detailed numbers provided in tables. Regarding races residing in what was perceived as the border area between Asia and Europe (e.g., Turkey, Romania), there was usually a considerable amount of description of physical features, including height and skull shape. If the residential area of "races" did not coincide with geographical boundaries defined by nation-states—usually in eastern Europe, most notably in the case of Magyar in what is now Hungary and nearby areas—*Dictionary* took special care to present a map of the area with racial makeup. In short, *Dictionary* seemed to suggest that the categories of races or peoples factored in every conceivable variable: bodily features, language, geography, culture, and shared political experience constituted the basis of distinction, depending on the circumstances.

In using whatever material he could obtain to justify his scheme, Folkmar was veering closely toward what Victoria Hattam describes as the "unfixing" of race.[44] As stated earlier, the point of calling something race was to essentialize it: Race must be a set of stable, immutable categories that do not change easily. Hence early race-thinkers such as Blumenbach collected skull measurements, which were supposed to be more stable indicators of the underlying racial type of an individual than, say, skin tone or eye color. However, the rise of Lamarckism[45] in the late nineteenth century, according to Hattam, dismantled rigid assumptions about the stability of racial types and opened up the possibility of races being transformed through individuals' experiences. In other words, the foundation of racial science had, at least in some circles, come under scrutiny. Along these lines, Folkmar's scheme also opened the door to the interrogation of racial essentialism by decentering the rigid biological principles of classifications ("five grand divisions of mankind") and complicating them with language, geography, and a host of other factors.

From a practical perspective, the crucial question concerning the stability of races or peoples came down to whether learning a new language could alter how persons were classified. If an immigrant from Poland claimed she was from Germany and spoke fluent German, should immigrant inspectors classify her as a "German" immigrant? A similar question could be raised with respect to the other factors that Folkmar presented in substantiating races or peoples. Most of them could change over time, thereby blurring the boundary between categories and, as a result, endangering the stability of the classification scheme. The dilemma was between flexibility and rigidity: Races or peoples should be flexible enough to account for variations among Europeans but at the same time rigid enough to affirm classification based on the categories.

This dilemma was further discussed in the entry for the English as a race or people. Folkmar considered the challenging question of "Irish and Scotch descent" among the "English": "How long a residence of his ancestry in England entitles him to be called English?"[46] He recognized that the English could serve as an important test case for the whole classification scheme he proposed: Because the English comprised, according to Folkmar, such a self-evident group, the definitions and theories behind this categorization should operate without any contradiction.[47]

His answer is worth quoting at length:

> But how long a residence in England will entitle an Irishman, or a Scotchman, or a French Huguenot, or one of Norman French stock, to be called English if the mother tongue is the test? Evidently, this phrase must be

> interpreted to mean the ancestral or racial language in dealing with a stock which has kept itself quite pure in descent. But since the greater part of the English population of today is of mixed origin, a census may adopt the arbitrary rule that the paternal line only shall determine the race, or, what is evidently more difficult and more scientific, it may name the mixed races as such, or consider the race to be determined by the preponderant element in the mixture.[48]

Clearly, English was not as clear-cut and pure a category as Folkmar had initially imagined. The English race, in fact, was a fusion of multiple other "stocks," such as Scots, the Irish, and even French Huguenots, and not "pure" English. Again, the answer to this dilemma was somewhat "arbitrary": Without any theoretical justification, Folkmar resorted to "paternal line" or yet another determinant, "the preponderant element in the mixture." The meanings of these concepts, however, were not clarified further. On the thorny question of "transition" between different races, Folkmar chose to stick to his "assumption" without theoretical justification: "In the narrow sense, the race of an immigrant is determined by ancestral language, as above indicated. The historical limit which determines the transition from one race into another as thus defined varies with different races. It will be assumed in this article that the English race is practically one thousand years old, since the essential elements composing it were welded before or soon after the Norman invasion."[49]

The final resolution to the dilemma was a hodgepodge of biological rigidity and historical flexibility. The English "race or people" consolidated a thousand years ago, according to Folkmar, and, by definition, English language and geography were determined around such time. Although the exact time frame for the consolidation of each race or people would differ case by case, "one thousand years" represented the careful balance that Folkmar was trying to maintain between racial essentialism and flexibility: flexible enough to classify southern and eastern Europeans as different from other European immigrants but still rigid enough to make the distinctions matter. As Hattam has documented, the move away from the biological conception of race would eventually create theoretical space for the concepts of ethnicity and cultural pluralism in the following decades.[50] Yet none of these developments were foreseen at the inception of the commission's inquiry. Folkmar was trying his best to bring logical consistency to the project of immigrant classification, and he was not engaged in a battle with other actors to control the outcome of the project. Yet the confusion and contradiction within the process led to an unintended consequence—namely, a more flexible perception of difference within the larger European category.

## The Top-Down Impulse Behind the "Ethnic"

Within the immediate scope of the commission's work, a more flexible perception of difference did not matter much. Certainly, it did not lead the commission to understand southern and eastern Europeans in less essentialized terms, and the executive summary did not hesitate to caricaturize them as undesirable races that merited control through restrictive immigration policy, if not blanket exclusion. When we move beyond the commission and extend the timeline, however, we see how the emphasis on the malleability of race provided an important precursor to the development of what we now construe as ethnicity, an important pillar of racial liberalism.

As indicated, the origin story of ethnicity comes with multiple layers. The term *ethnicity* first saw light in 1941, appearing in sociologist W. Lloyd Warner's community stratification study of Newburyport, Massachusetts, according to literary critic Werner Sollors. The concept was employed to designate an additional axis of division within the town in addition to economic class.[51] Drawing on Benedict Anderson's *Imagined Communities*, Sollors charted out how writers and artists of immigrant origin produced shared narratives about the integrity and continuity of a community, thereby cementing the concept of ethnicity as a distinct marker of group identity. In a more analytical vein, sociologists Nathan Glazer and Daniel Moynihan define ethnicity as groupings based on "culture and descent" and list under its umbrella a wide variety of communities ranging from African Americans in the United States to border minorities in China.[52] The authors further articulate the social implication of ethnicity through their discussion of "liberal expectancy," or the belief that ethnicity or distinctions based on culture and descent are destined to disappear in modern society.[53] In this account, Glazer and Moynihan present the prospect of "assimilation," or complete dissolution of distinction through the malleability of ethnicity, as liberal expectancy's core feature.

Nevertheless, it is not difficult to notice the shadow of racial essentialism in these formulations, albeit pitched through the language of culture rather than biology.[54] In *In the Shadows of Race*, Hattam points out that the emphasis on malleability gained its meaning only in relation to that which was not malleable—the concept of race built on an essentialized, naturalized, and ahistorical understanding of difference.[55] Simply put, the unmaking of difference made sense only when a certain kind of difference was designated as beyond such unmaking; hence, racial liberalism presupposes racial essentialism. Hattam traces the juxtaposition between race and ethnicity, or essentialized versus malleable conceptions of difference, to the first decade of the twentieth century, focusing on elite Jewish college students and their quest for identity. Sandwiched between the orthodox upbringing of their immigrant households and the more secular environment in their respective elite East Coast colleges, these students attempted to refashion what it meant to identify as Jewish in a society that essentialized and looked down on Jews. Their answer was to decouple Jewishness from both religion and descent and highlight Jewish literature and philosophy, which were in themselves heavily influenced by the German tradition. In doing so, they wanted to develop a basis of identity that was empowering but not binding—something that would defend them psychologically from the pressures of assimilation but also allow them to avoid overt discrimination. As Daniel Greene points out, it is telling that their leader, Horace Kallen, never connected with Black scholars of the time who were engaged in a similar intellectual pursuit, such as Alan Locke and W. E. B. Du Bois, even though they shared affiliations in elite, WASP-dominated educational institutions such as Harvard. Kallen and his comrades saw their embodied difference from the WASPs as fundamentally different from those embodied by Blacks; the new conception of difference should liberate them from the binding of race, to which African Americans were doomed.[56] In a sense these Jewish students desired freedom to be who they were, but that freedom never encompassed African Americans, who suffered acutely from the most conspicuous forms of discrimination based on race.[57]

The Jewish quest for a new conception of difference was not confined only to the small number of elite students in selective colleges, as Greene further demonstrates.[58] While the 1920s saw the intense wave of the Americanization movement aimed at forcibly squashing any conception of difference outside of WASP domination,[59] the cultural seed of "the ethnic" matured and bloomed once again as descendants of European immigrants came of age through the Great Depression and the World Wars. In the 1930s and 1940s, after the dust settled on the immigration restriction debate through the national quota legislation in 1924, writers and artists of European immigrant origin came along to popularize a concept of cultural difference that could not be subsumed under race.[60] In the 1970s, sociologists, succeeding Glazer and Moynihan, picked up where the writers and artists had left off and explained how such a concept had become prevalent among Whites in the late twentieth century, especially as a response to the emergence of radical social and cultural movements led by non-Whites in the 1960s.[61] In this particular narrative, the story of "ethnic" is presented as a bottom-up story, in which European immigrants and their children have struggled to defend their autonomy against the top-down pressures of race enacted by the WASP-controlled government and its restrictive immigration policies.

Is this story, then, all about how the seed of the ethnic became dormant and survived the roaring 1920s to eventually grow into predominance? Within such a narrative, we are tempted to think of race as bad and ethnicity as good, to portray the origin story of the ethnic as one about European immigrants overcoming stigma and discrimination to proudly claim their heritage. This narrative has been the backbone of racial liberalism—namely, all Americans were once immigrants and should be allowed to celebrate their heritage as they see fit. When John F. Kennedy proclaimed the United States "a nation of immigrants" in 1958, he was alluding to this narrative. And by building on the mythos of European immigrant experience, he presumed that history repeats itself and that the nation will eventually open itself up to descendants of other immigrants as well. Many commentators, all the way to the present, have followed his lead in praising the promise of racial liberalism.[62]

Yet there is still a missing link in this story, notably between the Jewish students' campaign at the turn of the century and immigration restriction of the 1920s. Recent scholarly accounts contradict the progressive inclusion narrative by critically examining its historical implications, especially in relation to the racial order that violently subjugated African Americans and excluded immigrants from Asia and Latin America. Under the rubric of the "ethnicity paradigm," Michael Omi and Howard Winant write, ethnicity in the early twentieth century was exclusively applied to European immigrants while race marked non-European immigrants, distinguishing between assimilable and nonassimilable aliens along the boundary of Whiteness.[63] In a society built on the legacy of slavery, different generations of immigrants utilized the cultural script of ethnicity to their advantage by distancing themselves from African Americans, as Vilna Bashi Treitler forcefully demonstrates in *The Ethnic Project*.[64] In a sense, the ethnic was a key conceptual tool of a White supremacist racial order that treated European immigrants differently from African Americans and other non-European immigrants.

The analysis presented in this chapter builds on this line of reasoning but adds the weight of historical evidence to the argument. Observed closely, the early twentieth-century historiography does provide evidence in line with this argument, and it is no doubt that there was fundamental difference between the ways in which European immigrants were treated compared to non-Europeans.[65] Still, these critical accounts remain largely silent about when and how the concept of ethnicity emerged in the first place and what led to the specific "ethnoracial landscape," which, as Treitler argues, laid grounds for "the ethnic myth."[66] Moreover, by focusing on European immigrants and their social history, even this more qualified account leaves the role of the state—usually the most important initiator of racial formation—out of the picture.

Folkmar's educational and professional trajectory—from the mainland United States to the metropoles of Europe to the Philippines and then back to Washington, DC—provides us some hints to fill this void. Namely, the deadly symbiosis between race and the modern state lies at the foundation of ethnicity. Colonial expansion had already brought challenges to racial knowledge production by demonstrating that traditional ideas about race were too simplistic to provide a foundation of governance, especially within the newly acquired territories in the American empire. Concomitantly, race-thinkers in late nineteenth-century Europe were slowly moving away from an overly rigid and essentialized conception of race, an intellectual move that was soon appropriated by the modern colonial governments, especially in places such as the Philippines. It did not take long for the more flexible concept of difference to find its way to the United States, as we have seen in the case of Folkmar and his attempt to categorize southern and eastern Europeans as undesirable races while invoking language and geography. However, such maneuvering brought the unanticipated consequences of unfixing race: Articulated through the criteria of language and geography, not through skull shapes and sizes, race became less of a God-given destiny and more of a history in the making. As we have seen in the case of the elite Jewish students and races or peoples, a slight change in nuances of definition would provide an important precursor to the emergence of ethnicity in the middle of the twentieth century.

European immigrants and their children grounded their claims of belonging to the United States on the idea of racial liberalism, manifested through the concept of ethnicity. Freed from the binding of undesirable race, their writers and artists of the mid-twentieth century were able to assert distinct cultural identities and establish how they were positively different from WASPs. Moreover, by affirming their difference from mainstream American national identity as cultural and not essential, they implied that those identities could change over time and that as a people, they could in fact "assimilate to the mainstream" through effort.[67] While the Dillingham Commission and Daniel Folkmar expected it would take "one thousand years" for such a transformation, these writers and intellectuals envisioned a much shorter timeline, possibly a generation or two.[68] Both groups, nonetheless, shared the understanding that, culture aside, there were nonchangeable, irreducible differences based on race—namely, those immigrants who were racially different, or not White, existed beyond the possibility of assimilation. In this manner, ethnicity formed a core component of the process I call grafting racial liberalism onto racial essentialism.

[ CHAPTER FOUR ]

# Assimilation

## Dissolving Difference

### From Skulls to Culture

The previous chapter traces the genealogy of ethnicity, from its colonial origins in the Philippines to contradictions around "the English race" in *Dictionary*. This chapter focuses on a complementary concept: assimilation. Whereas the concept of ethnicity captured the kind of difference capable of transforming over time, as expressed through language and geography, the concept of assimilation focused on clarifying *how* such difference could be transformed. Whereas the commission paid some attention to assimilation by collecting data on the lives of immigrants in different locations—main volumes would feature data on English-language acquisition and civic participation—it did not theoretically elaborate on the meaning of the term like it did for ethnicity. However, the commission left a monumental legacy in the development of assimilation theory by sponsoring a research project: Franz Boas's study of head shapes of immigrant children, documented in volume 38 of the *DCR* and titled *Changes in Bodily Form of Descendants of Immigrants* (henceforth *Changes*). Denouncing racial essentialism and explicitly celebrating hybridity, Boas went directly against the main conclusion of the commission by charting out an alternative path that the nation could take by celebrating immigration.

Franz Boas (1858–1942) was a Jewish, German-émigré anthropologist. As a long-time professor at Columbia University, he almost single-handedly orchestrated the discipline's transition from race science to the study of culture, both through his own work and by training a cadre of young anthropologists.

In 1908, Boas was among the experts hired by the Dillingham commission. Supported by the commission's funding, he documented the bodily characteristics, most notably head shapes, of European immigrant children living in New York City. His research assistants from Columbia University, just like the commission's agents we will see in chapters 5 and 6, were dispatched to immigrant neighborhoods to measure the head shapes of children therein. In *Changes*, Boas showed that head shapes—supposedly the most stable indicator of race in the tradition of Blumenbach and Morton (see chapter 1)—changed rapidly once the children were exposed to the American environment. Moreover, regardless of where they came from in Europe, their head shapes converged into a single form as they lived longer in their newfound homeland. The idea that even the most rigid, biological indicator of race, such as head shape, could transform rapidly over time undermined the classical essentialist notion of race as a fixed biological type and provided evidence that European immigrants could transform into something else befitting their new environment. Boas wrote matter-of-factly of what the numbers indicated, but the facts spoke loudly to celebrate the coming of an immigrant nation. And in the process the contradiction in racial knowledge production intensified to the maximum extent: Head shapes—the core component of racial essentialism—became the foundation of racial liberalism that celebrated immigrant hybridity, against the expectations of those involved in the project.

While the executive committee members appreciated Boas's argument, they did not use it in their overall conclusion and recommendation presented in the executive summary. The media showed much interest in the project, perhaps more than any other subsection of the commission's work, yet this was mostly an expression of curiosity about the plasticity of racial types rather than a serious engagement with the study's implications around assimilation and nation building.[1] To be fair, Boas's report pitched its finding in a dry, matter-of-fact manner, not making bold claims but demonstrating how empirical data on head shapes disprove the commonly accepted knowledge about the rigidity of racial types.

When we extend the timeline, however, Boas's study marks an important milestone in the emergence and consolidation of racial liberalism. Up to the early twentieth century, the social sciences, like popular discourse, were under the strong influence of social Darwinism, with a blurred boundary between the biological and social. Based on a deliberate misreading of Darwin's account of evolution, social Darwinism saw the world as an outcome of struggles between individuals, groups, and nations and justified the status quo by invoking nature.[2] As we have seen in chapter 1, this outlook fit perfectly with nineteenth-century race-thinking, in which colonial dynamics were presented as a "natural"—thereby essential and inevitable—law of human affairs. Against this backdrop, as Lee Baker argues in *Anthropology and the Politics of Culture*, social scientists, most notably anthropologists, started to argue for a domain of inquiry independent from nature, which they termed *culture*. This transition was predicated on the criticism of racial essentialism, and Boas provided a template for such criticism in his work for the commission. Boas's students, including Otto Klineberg, Melville Herskovits, and Zora Neale Hurston, as well as Chicago school sociologists such as W. I. Thomas and Robert Park, followed this template to further their criticisms of racial essentialism, and the concept of assimilation represented the frontline of the theoretical warfare against the old guard in academia. Although the decisive outcome of this war at the popular level would not materialize until the demise of Nazi Germany in the 1940s, the academic tide began to turn gradually starting in the 1910s with Boas's work.

By tracing this arc of transformation, encapsulated in the emergence of assimilation as a concept, I chart out how racial liberalism emerged from racial essentialism. Far from revoking the concept of race entirely, racial liberalism complemented racial essentialism by replacing one conception of difference with another, that of culture. While the clash between the two camps was real and consequential, it did not encompass everything that could be said about group differences during the time.[3]

This chapter begins with the state of the concept of assimilation before Boas and discusses in detail the context and content of *Changes*, elaborating on its significance for the development of the theories on culture and assimilation. Then I trace how the concepts traveled, expanded, and transformed by discussing the works of Boas's students and the Chicago school sociologists. I end by charting the limits of these concepts, most evident in the work of Boas's unorthodox disciple, Zora Neale Hurston.

## The Assimilation Concept Before the Dillingham Commission

In the 1900s, the concept of assimilation was slowly gaining attention from sociologists and reformers but had a long way to go in terms of theoretical elaboration. Moreover, the concept was muddled with social Darwinism, and its outlook was very different from what we know today as assimilation theory. Moon-Kie Jung, in his influential paper "The Racial Unconscious of Assimilation Theory," has leveled a devastating and acute criticism of assimilation theory from past to present. The main point of his contention is the theory's inability to directly engage with race—or Blackness, to be precise—even while the notion figures centrally in its objects of inquiry. When we read early twentieth-century assimilation theory, however, this "unconscious" reveals itself front and center, as the concept of assimilation is employed mainly in the context of colonial conquest.[4]

Sarah E. Simons, writing for the *American Journal of Sociology* in 1901, attempted to synthesize the state of assimilation as a concept in the United States.[5] She starts by providing a basic definition of the term, citing European ethnologists and American social scientists: *Assimilation* generally indicated "growing similar" or the "denationalization" of two different races due to contact.[6] Yet Simons points out that the term was used without proper theoretical elaboration: For instance, scholars often used the term without defining other terms central to its meaning, such as *race*, *similar*, *different*, and *contact*, causing confusion. She sought to resolve this ambiguity by taking up the then-popular perspective of social Darwinism. Her first task was to confine the concept of assimilation to concerns about the development of civilization, arguing that "consideration of spontaneous assimilation in groups that have achieved nothing, that have contributed in no way to the world's fund of established knowledge, will not be undertaken." Simons reasons that assimilation is only meaningful in regard to the development of civilization, noting that civilizations emerged "through conquest, and the resulting amalgamation and assimilation of heterogeneous ethnic elements."[7] In other words, assimilation is a process that occurs during a conquest as a mechanism to instill the civilization of the conqueror to the conquered or, in rare cases, vice versa.

Although this way of thinking about assimilation seems absurd from the perspective of mid-twentieth-century assimilation theory or its twenty-first-century variants,[8] we can decipher what Simons meant if we consider the historical backdrop: The nineteenth century was the heyday of European colonialism, when a small number of European powers that had divided and conquered the rest of the world maintained hegemony through ideology as much as through force. With its so-called frontiers disappearing, the United States was on the path to join other European empires in expanding its territory, most notably to Puerto Rico, Hawaii, Guam, and the Philippines. As historians such as Daniel Immerwahr and Eric Love have chronicled, the relationship between race and empire was a pressing concern for American elites who were in the process of reinventing themselves from domestic power brokers to standard-bearers of the imperial world.[9] The expansion of American territory would inevitably bring "democratically unfit" subjects—as non-Whites were deemed—into the community of nation and citizenship; would the founding principles of freedom and equality apply without discrimination to these new subjects? In other words, American elites faced a choice between a unified democratic republic built around an Enlightenment ideal on the one hand and a powerful, expansive empire with an aristocratic racial hierarchy on the other. Of course, the American democratic ideal itself was in fact built on the premise of the racial subjugation of African Americans and the Indigenous peoples of the North American continent as well as non-White immigrants such as Chinese and Mexicans.[10] Nevertheless, in the age of empire, assimilation was understood through the lens of colonialism as a theory of how races could change through contact initiated by morally sanctioned colonial conquests. For instance, President William McKinley in 1898 issued "The Benevolent Assimilation Proclamation" upon acquiring control of the Philippines, promising "the full measure of individual rights and liberties" to the Filipinos as opposed to the despotic colonialism of the Spanish empire.[11] And as such, as we have seen in chapter 3, the mission of the American colonial administration was anthropological as well as political: They had to first determine what kind of people the Filipinos were in order to give them rights and liberties. The work of Daniel Folkmar and others was instrumental in this regard.

In essence, empire may operate on the presumption of racial hierarchy, yet it could not maintain racial essentialism without conditions. In order to annex new territories and bring new peoples into its fold, empire had to make room for the possibility that race could change over time—a key concern for assimilation theory.[12] As we see later in this chapter, this contradiction between racial essentialism and racial liberalism would eventually bring about the scientific disavowal of race itself, at least in the social sciences. And this transition would precede the social disavowal of race as an acceptable account of difference in the 1940s and '50s.

At the onset of this historical development, Sarah Simons presents assimilation as a process that follows military conquest; its outcome was—or, rather, should be—the advancement of civilization. Groups that "have achieved nothing" and "have contributed in no way to the world's fund of established knowledge" lay beyond the horizon of assimilation and were not worthy of scholarly discussion. Most likely Simons is referring to the so-called primitive civilizations of Africa and other colonized continents, as representing barbarianism and degeneration rather than ascendancy of civilization. For Simons, assimilation is a process in which different races submit to a common political order, one that is administered by the conqueror. For assimilation between two races to occur, "race consciousness" of the two groups should somehow converge into one. If that is not the case, "antipathy may be so great as to prevent all union," even if the said civilization has achieved a degree of development. For instance, no one would deny the fact that the Chinese had achieved a considerable level of development in their civilization. Yet, "the Chinese are so utterly out of the sphere of thought of the western man that his non-assimilation to occidental culture seems well-nigh a foregone conclusion. The ideals of the Chinese are diametrically opposed to those of the western man; there are no common culture bonds between the two races." Hence "there is no possibility," Simons rules, "of the formation of fellowship feelings" between those who were too different, such as the Chinese, and hence in those relationships "there can be no assimilation."[13] It is not difficult to hear the echoes of the anti-Chinese mobilization in California between these lines. The Chinese Exclusion Act of 1882 practically ruled out any discussion of assimilation for Chinese immigrants and their children. Under this legal formulation, the solution to the question of assimilation for the Chinese was categorical exclusion enacted through both physical and legal violence.[14]

In other words, Simons had a clear idea about the boundary of assimilation: Races that "have achieved nothing" and are "utterly out of the sphere of thought of the western man"—note that these two designations are distinctive, although they may overlap in some instances—could not be assimilated. In Simons's formulation, the notion of difference easily translated to the notion of inferiority. With races like the Chinese, toward whom "antipathy" was "so great," intermarriage, or "physical assimilation," was also presented as something to avoid. Intermarriage was "the inevitable result" of contact between different races and "plays its part in the process of assimilation," but Simons also argues that assimilation was possible without intermarriage, as evidenced by "the partial assimilation of the negro and the Indian of the United States."[15] This was not desirable because race mixture inherently led to a decline of civilization: "Half-breeds, produced by the mixture of different races, have nowhere attained a high civilization." Simons lists "the Indian half-breed and the mulatto of the United States" as living examples of her theory of civilization decline.[16]

In other words, Simons regarded assimilation as essential in the advancement of civilization through colonial conquest but at the same time wanted to demarcate its limitations. Races deemed "too different" could not be assimilated, and intermarriage, or "physical assimilation," was a misbegotten means of developing civilization. The case of "the partial assimilation of the negro and the Indian of the United States" was invoked to support this point. It is not very clear what she means by "the partial assimilation"—most likely the troubled segregation and exclusion these groups faced in the contemporary United States. However, it was still assimilation—if only "partial"—because they were subjects of the American political order.

In a country where miscegenation was a horrible crime,[17] the theory of race degeneration easily garnered support among elites, and Simons invokes the perceived threat to Whiteness in marking out the boundary of assimilation as a concept. That is, assimilation was a necessary evil in colonial ventures, but, Simons emphasizes, its boundaries should be clearly highlighted lest it lead to the degeneration of Whiteness. Her intentions become clearer when she discusses the pitfalls of assimilation for "white men." "When civilized man on the borders of civilization comes in contact with barbarous or semi-civilized races," Simons claims, "there is modification on both sides."[18] "White men," in their mission of civilizing the world, would inevitably come in contact with "less civilized" races, and the contact would most likely result in their becoming "callous and superstitious and lax in morals." In short, contact and degeneration, along with methods of preventing degeneration, were key components of assimilation theory in the nineteenth century.

This formulation reflected the convoluted politics of gender, race, class, and morality during the time. As Peggy Pascoe documents, the United States boasts a long history of policing interracial marriage in order to maintain the saliency of racial categories in the long term and to ensure the protection of inheritance through family lineage in the short term.[19] In the late nineteenth century, after emancipation, policing focused on purported sexual violence against White women by Black men. As Simons was cautioning against interracial marriage, Ida B. Wells was analyzing the social foundation of such caution by revealing the real reason behind lynchings across the country—namely, the changing power balance between Blacks and Whites.[20] Sociologists Nicola Beisel and Tamara Kay further complicate this account by factoring in immigration in the moral politics of reproduction. Family relations and reproduction lay at the heart of reform campaigns during the early twentieth century because they connected everyday intimate social interactions with the larger dynamics of class reproduction.[21] Simons's caution against interracial marriage and assimilation should be understood in this context—that is, while assimilation was a solution to the problem of immigration, one of its mechanisms, interracial marriage, posed a grave threat to the established understanding of family and sexuality and, therefore, undermined the WASP-led social order. Once again, the idea of race revealed a contradiction, and the prevailing account of racial essentialism was not dynamic enough to address the complicated situation.

In chapter 3, we witnessed Daniel Folkmar at the forefront of the American colonial administration, living out the drama of the so-called White man's burden while making head casts of Filipino prisoners. As we have seen from his unpublished memoir, he oscillated between ethnographic attachment and a savior complex, a murky state of mind in which slow but discernable transformations of race as a concept, documented in *Dictionary*, may have occurred. A few years beforehand, in the pages of the *American*

*Journal of Sociology*, Sarah Simons was providing a theoretical vocabulary to make sense of this trajectory.

Hence, at the beginning of the twentieth century, the concept of assimilation ran into contradictions: If different races were that much *different*, as the nineteenth-century race-thinkers sought to demonstrate, how could they "grow similar"? The question of racial hierarchy logically preceded—and troubled—the question of assimilation: Among "lower races," only those who were redeemable could be the subject of assimilation. However, if there was a clear hierarchy of civilization among different races, and lower races were confined to their lower positions by their limited faculty, either by their natural, inherent characteristics or by God's overall design, how could such races expect to grow at all? A similar argument could be made regarding European races, as we have seen in the previous chapters: How could southern and eastern European races become part of the body politic if their cultural and political characteristics were immutable? Racial essentialism and racial liberalism ran against each other in nineteenth-century colonial ventures as well as in the nation-building project of the twentieth-century immigration debate.

When anthropologist Franz Boas was writing to the Dillingham Commission seeking funding for his research on immigrant assimilation, he was not aware of the fact that his data collection and analysis were the first steps in a long line of historical development that would eventually lead to dethroning racial essentialism in the social sciences. In fact, he pitched his project as a simple exercise of hypothesis testing, an attempt to bear evidence to see whether the well-known theory of racial essentialism could measure up to empirical scrutiny. Yet his data would travel further than anyone, including Boas himself, imagined at the time.[22]

## Baffin Islands: Boas's Ethnographic Encounter with Difference

The history of anthropology rightfully credits Franz Boas for bringing down scientific racism and espousing a universalistic understanding of human nature. Against the nineteenth-century ideas about civilization informed by racial essentialism—Simons's theory is a perfect example—Boas believed in the equal potential of any human groups and argued that any race could achieve what Europeans had achieved if it was provided with enough time and the right opportunities. To Boas, different human groups were not *essentially* different but one and the same in terms of their potential. The observed differences among groups were superficial; their essence—or "faculty," as Boas termed it—was universal. This belief may not surprise us the least bit, but it was a revolutionary statement for a European man in the 1880s. In fact, he was a radical outlier to even entertain the possibility of non-European races being equal to Europeans, and, along with his students, he had to fight throughout his lifetime for the legitimacy of this position. The biographers of Boas generally pinpoint the Arctic expedition he undertook in his twenties as the origin of his universalism.[23]

Born into a wealthy Jewish household in 1858 in Minden, Germany, Boas made up his mind early to become a scientist. Having studied mathematics and physics at a series of German universities—regarded as the best in the world at that time—Boas ultimately settled on geography as his focus. A few years after graduation, in 1883, Boas launched an Artic expedition with funding support from a newspaper. Boas was supposed to write a travelogue for the paper in exchange for the funding. In the nineteenth century, during the heyday of empires, reports from the remote corners of the world were popular material in newspapers and magazines. The young scholar set out to the Baffin Islands near the North Pole for his assignment, hoping to write a tale of a faraway land that would entice the newspaper's readership.

During his expedition, however, Boas faced extreme weather and life-threatening frostbite and was forced to stay in an Inuit village for an extended period (see fig. 9). While being cut off from all outside communication, Boas practiced an archetype of ethnographic immersion: He lived with the Inuit, learned their craft of whale and seal hunting, and participated in the communal life of the village. He even consumed raw seal meat, following the local dietary custom. Ludger Müller-Wille and William Barr argue that these experiences led him to a revelation that all people respond to the challenges of nature in their respective ways and there was no hierarchy among different cultures. The belief in universalism, as the idea was later named, opened him up to the idea of studying different peoples around the world, including the Indigenous tribes of the Pacific coast and Mexico. Of his time with the Inuit, Boas later wrote that he was able to "recognize under the strangest forms of living always again the thinking and feeling human being, who is closer to us in character than we could anticipate after a fleeting impression."[24] Just like Daniel Folkmar, Boas went through an ethnographic rite of passage, sympathizing with and recognizing humanity in his research subjects. However, unlike Folkmar, his sympathies would develop into a full-blown, prolonged theoretical criticism of racial essentialism in the decades to come, complete with a set of theory, data, and methods.

FIGURE 9. Franz Boas in Inuit clothing. Franz Boas Papers, American Philosophical Society.

## Race and Civilization

Instead of directly returning to Germany, Boas spent six months in New York City following his stint in the Baffin Islands. His uncle had migrated to the United States earlier and was operating a successful retail business, and young Boas had a chance to live in a city well known for its vibrant immigrant communities. The German academic job market at the time was tough, and it was even tougher for a young Jewish scholar with idiosyncratic ideas. After defending his habilitation in 1886, Boas decided to try his luck in the United States.

Fast-forward to 1894, Franz Boas was at the lowest point of his academic career—or possibly of his life, according to anthropologist Lee Baker's account.[25] As an ambitious, intellectually fierce scholar with a German PhD, Boas had been looking for a permanent faculty position in the United States for nearly ten years. Having worked with the Inuit in the Baffin Islands and the Indigenous tribes in British Columbia, he had extensive fieldwork experience, contrary to his more established American colleagues, who prioritized armchair theorizing over empirical observation. Yet for a German Jewish immigrant with a thick accent and uncompromising personality, landing a stable job was not an easy matter. He moved from one temporary position to another, taking up short-term curator positions in various museums. During the summer, he worked as a fieldworker for other scholars, taking the transcontinental railroad and procuring artifacts from Indigenous tribes on the West Coast in support of their armchair theorizing.

At this challenging time, he was invited to speak for Section H of the American Association for the Advancement of Science (AAAS), the only national association for anthropologists at the time. Boas put much work into preparing his address. He needed attention from his colleagues, and so he picked the most important and contested topic—"Human Faculty as Determined by Race." This was the first time that he publicly stated his opinion on race. Boas had lived among Inuit and Indigenous tribes of the American continent, developing his own perspective on the existing theories of race and civilization. Yet he was not considered an expert in the area and had not been engaged in the debate that dominated anthropology at the time. He opened his talk by summarizing the existing theories, which amounted to self-congratulation of European civilization as the grand achievement of the White race. European civilization was thought to display a higher degree of development than other civilizations; therefore, the capabilities of the White race must be greater than those of other races. Physical evidence, such as differences in brain size, affirmed these racial differences. In other words, civilization, mental ability, and bodily characteristics formed a core nexus of racial hierarchy—this was the state of contemporary anthropology.[26]

Boas attacked this nexus from multiple angles. His main argument was an elementary expression of what is today known as cultural relativism. Rather than supposing a rigid hierarchy among races, he focused on criticizing the sketchy evidence that buttressed the hierarchy. Boas also pointed out the weak link between physical characteristics and mental ability, citing numerous problems with measurements and data collection. Although

Boas did not deny the hierarchy of civilization altogether, he attempted to sever its ties to racial characteristics, defined according to the physical features and mental ability of a group. In other words, there may be a hierarchy among different civilizations or races; however, Boas reasoned, the existing measurements, such as physical traits and indicators of mental ability, failed to verify such a hierarchy in empirical terms.

The most famous part of Boas's argument for cultural relativism focused on individual variations within racial groups: "The variations inside any single race are such that they overlap the variations in another race so that a number of characteristics may be common to individuals of both races."[27] A contemporary reader would readily recognize this argument, which is recycled every time difference by race becomes a topic of discussion—that variation within race is larger than the variation between races. This was the first time that the argument was articulated. Empirical social sciences were still in their infancy, and anthropology was no exception. Many scholars relied on impressionistic evidence for their arguments, which were strongly influenced by the state of race-thinking at the time (see chapter 1). Equipped with fieldwork experiences, Boas had a more rigorous approach to data. In addition, his German education equipped him with far superior knowledge of statistics than many scholars on the other side of the Atlantic.[28] Utilizing these skill sets, Boas reasoned that racial trait, defined as the average of statistical measurements of the group, could not be associated with the level of development in civilization. Whereas civilizations were bound together in a more or less coherent way, population groups, or races, overlapped greatly in their characteristics, and it would be inaccurate to assume a sharp division between racial groups.

Other arguments relied on an evolutionary framework, overturning the favorite logic of race-thinkers. For Boas, the key was in distinguishing the actual level of development from aptitude for development. Boas claimed that he was not trying to deny the differences in the level of development among different civilizations. He argued, however, that the qualitative differences among civilized societies did not mean that less developed civilizations would not or could not reach their full potential, provided that enough time was given to them. In other words, the contemporary hierarchy of civilization might be a temporary one, and lower-ranked civilizations might possess equal, if not more, aptitude for development as the White civilization on the top. A true evolutionary framework, Boas emphasized, would suppose a longer time frame for the test of potential, as was the case in biological evolution: "If we assume arbitrarily no more than 20,000 years as the age of man, what would it mean that one group of mankind reached the same stage at the age of 20,000 years which was reached by the other at the age of 24,000 years?"[29] As a German-trained PhD with extensive fieldwork experience, Boas saw through the amateur theorizing of American race-thinkers, who often rushed to premature conclusions to rationalize their political convictions and racial prejudice. An accurate understanding of the theory of evolution, as well as attention to empirical data and statistical methods, Boas thought, would correct their misunderstandings.

The most important argument for our purpose, however, comes from his emphasis on assimilation and amalgamation between different civilizations. Boas did not define these terms clearly, as was the case for most of his other concepts. In his usage, however, amalgamation generally denoted a more radical approach to the question of assimilation. Whereas assimilation kept intact the boundary between two groups—think Simons's formulation—amalgamation denoted the breakdown of this boundary, to the extent that the difference between two groups became ineligible. Boas's emphasis on amalgamation broke sharply with most other scholars contemplating the concept of assimilation.

Boas's argument relied on a careful, comprehensive reading of history, not the selective projection of political ideology onto the events of the past, as we have seen in the cases of some race-thinkers (see chapter 1). The hierarchy of civilization assumed the independence of each race and supposed that each race struggled on its own to realize its potential. However, this was, according to Boas, far from what had occurred in history: Many civilizations had been in contact with other civilizations, sharing much of what they developed through trade and communication. In some cases, different civilizations merged into a single entity through assimilation and amalgamation, often resulting in the further development of the involved civilizations. Boas pointed out that the so-called White race of Europe was a result of the amalgamation of multiple groups, the conditions for which were more favorable in Europe than in other regions of the world, largely due to geography.

Again, Boas was a man of his time, and he did not deny racial hierarchy entirely; he conceded that, at least for the time being, Europeans would maintain a higher degree of development than, say, Asians and Africans. Yet his emphasis on the relationship between different races made him push his argument in a direction that challenged the assumptions of the race-thinking of the time. Using the example of the Islamic empires of the Middle Ages, Boas highlighted the applicability of assimilation as a concept: "It is of interest to see in what manner [the Islamic empires] influenced the negro races of the [S]udan. . . . We see that, since that time, large empires were formed and disappeared again in struggles with neighboring states and that a relatively high degree of culture has been attained." This is because "the invaders [Muslims] intermarried with the natives [Sudanese], and the mixed races, some of which are almost purely negro, have risen high above the level of other African negroes."[30]

As was the case in Simons's formulation, military conquest, colonial or otherwise, was an important precondition of assimilation for Boas. The development of civilization following assimilation was also his concern. On the question of intermarriage, however, Boas differed sharply with Simons's theory of race degeneration. He contrasted traffic between races in ancient empires with contemporary European colonization, pointing out that "the whites send only the products of their manufactures and a few of their representatives into the negro country" and the export-only policy would not lead to "[a] real amalgamation between the higher types of the whites and the negroes."[31] In other words, by exporting products and extracting resources without ensuring "real amalgamation" through intermarriage, the contemporary European empires were hampering the potential of colonized nations to civilize. Boas was arguing that the supposed racial hierarchy was a self-realizing prophecy: Europeans were on top because they were blocking everyone else from climbing up the ladder of civilization. Instead, Boas reasoned, Europeans should become one with the colonized through intermarriage, thereby unlocking their potential for development.

From a contemporary standpoint, we can lay many criticisms as to the racialized and gendered nature of Boas's framework. In order to properly situate the novelty of his thesis, however, we have to evaluate his emphasis on assimilation and amalgamation in the context of late nineteenth-century race-thinking. As we have seen in the case of Sarah Simons, the theories of degeneration were very popular, especially among WASP elites who often saw immigration as a threat to the established social and political order of the nation. As we have seen in the case of Agassiz's "revulsion" (chapter 1), the antipathy toward interracial contact and mixture had more of an emotional foundation than a scientific one, even when race-thinkers attempted to amass objective evidence showing the pitfalls of race mixture. In this context, Boas's emphasis on assimilation and amalgamation—which in fact advocated for intermarriage between Whites and those who were deemed not as well developed in their potential for civilization—was considerably out of tune with the mainstream consensus of American society, its implicit affirmation of racial hierarchy notwithstanding.

Although Boas was not preoccupied with either supporting or criticizing the race-thinking of the time, he often chastised pseudoscientific theories of eugenicists when they failed to provide empirical evidence for their bold claims.[32] As an immigrant, a Jew, and, most of all, a person with an uncompromising dedication to scientific empiricism, Boas was not swayed by emotional and moralistic reactions against race mixture. If anything, it was an empirically interesting phenomenon to study.

In *The Half-Blood Indian: An Anthropometric Study* (1894), published the same year as his AAAS address, Boas wrote, "There are few countries in which the effects of intermixture of races and of change of environment upon the physical characteristics of man can be studied as advantageously as in America, where a process of slow amalgamation between three distinctive races is taking place."[33] By "three distinctive races," he meant "native race," "European," and "African." Using his fieldwork among Pacific coast Indigenous tribes as an opportunity to collect data, he observed whether race mixture caused sterility in the following generation. According to the eugenics theories that were widely accepted during the time, racial mixture would lead to the degeneration of "racial stock," resulting in sterilization and regression in the development of mind and body for the following generations.

If these theories were true, Boas would find a decline in birth rate of the Indigenous women who were born out of marriages between White men and Indigenous women ("half-blood Indian"). The evidence he collected did not support these predictions. In fact, "half-blood Indian" women had more children than "pure-blood Indian" women, and their children's head sizes, which were supposed to reflect their level of physical development, revealed no sign of regression. In other words, empirical evidence was not in favor of eugenic theories of degeneration. Although his book focused more on presenting such evidence and disproving existing theories, Boas was beginning to think about a new theoretical framework to address difference among population groups. Assimilation, intermixture, head shape, and the influence of environment—these elements that he encountered in his fieldwork would later inform his project with the Dillingham Commission and eventually provide a foundation for his new theory of race and culture. Using these concepts and variables, Boas would later engage in a lifelong struggle against scientific racism and eventually dethrone racial essentialism by confirming that race was prone to change over time under environmental influence. In other words, what some scholars call the "Boasian revolution" was beginning to take shape in his early fieldwork experiences.[34]

The revolutionary aspects of his theory, however, did not announce themselves in his AAAS address. They were nested in careful analysis of the available evidence on racial difference, most of which proved to be, according to Boas, rather unreliable. His overall conclusion was not a full-blown argument for racial equality but a cautionary remark on the methodology of anthropological research: "When considering psychological evidence, we found that most of it is not a safe guide for our inquiry, because causes and effects are so closely interwoven that it is impossible to separate them in a satisfactory manner, and as we are always liable to interpret as racial character what is only an effect of social surroundings."[35]

## *Changes in Bodily Form of Descendants of Immigrants*

Another decade later, when the Dillingham Commission's inquiry began, Franz Boas was in a very different position from where he had been in 1894: He was a professor of anthropology at Columbia University; he was one of the founding members of the American Anthropological Association; and he had trained a new generation of anthropologists, including Alfred Kroeber and Edward Sapir, who had taken positions in new, emerging institutions of higher education, such as the University of California, Berkeley, and the University of Michigan, and was about to work with the promising next generation, including Margaret Mead, Ruth Benedict, Melville Herskovits, and Zora Neale Hurston. Although he did not have much time to do fieldwork himself, he had been orchestrating multiple projects in and out of the United States; he was also involved in the movement that founded the National Association for the Advancement of Colored People and was corresponding with an emerging cadre of Black intellectuals, including W. E. B. Du Bois. Most important, he was regarded as a leading figure in the emerging discipline of anthropology.[36]

It was in this context that Boas came to contact Jeremiah W. Jenks, a Cornell economist who had a prominent role in the Dillingham Commission (see chapter 5). Boas first pitched his idea to Jenks in the form of a research proposal, hoping that the commission would provide the necessary funds for his data collection. Citing the contemporary shift in the composition of immigrants from "the tall, blond northwestern type of Europe" to "the east, central, and south European types," Boas stated that his goal in the proposed investigation was to test for "the marvelous power of amalgamation that our nation has exhibited for so long a time." In other words, he proposed to assess the degree to which European immigrants "amalgamate" when they migrate to the United States and, if so, how. To measure changes in racial type, he would collect data on head measurements and color of hair and eyes from various immigrant groups.[37]

After Boas's passionate plea and reporting of preliminary findings, the commission finally granted the necessary funding and permission to proceed with the project.[38] The resulting report, *Changes*, became one of the most cited volumes in the entire forty-one-volume collection. As he proposed, Boas demonstrated that physical features of racial types were far from stable; exposure to a new environment would lead to assimilation of physical features, resulting in the convergence of characteristics in the children of immigrants, and he was "compelled to conclude that when these features of the body change, the whole bodily and mental make-up of the immigrants may change."[39]

This rather bold statement relied much on his use of head measurements. In fact, he did not find too much evidence of assimilation in color of hair and eyes. Anthropologists and biologists of the time had yet to fully rediscover the Mendelian theory of inheritance, and Boas did not have the theoretical tools to make sense of his categorical data on eyes and hair. Head shape, however, was a different story. Head form, according to Boas and other race-thinkers of the time, "had always been considered one of the most stable and permanent characteristics of human races,"[40] and the cephalic ("cephalix") index—defined as the ratio of the maximum width of a head divided by the maximum length—provided a reliable means to compare differences in head forms across different races. Drawing from the large body of previous research on head forms in Europe, Boas observed the effect of environment, measured by the length of stay in the United States, on the cephalic index. The key question was whether living in a new environment would lead to changes in head shapes. In other words, would immigrants remain a distinctive and different race after they had spent time in the United States, or would they readily transform into something else? Was race really essential, as Lodge had argued with his "one thousand years" logic (see chapter 1)? The answers to these questions were presented through a series of graphs and diagrams (see figs. 10 and 11).

Previous research from Europe indicated that "Hebrews" (i.e., eastern European Jews) were farthest apart from "Sicilians" (i.e., Italians from the island of Sicily) in terms of their racial type. The differences in their respective cephalic indexes were greater than any other two groups within Europe. Whereas Hebrews had the highest cephalic index, representing their "round heads," Sicilians had the lowest cephalic index, representing their "long heads." But as seen in figure 10, children born after their mothers had immigrated to the United States displayed more similar cephalic indexes (see point 2); as point 3 shows, the convergence became greater when the mothers had stayed on American soil longer before giving birth. As noted in figure 11, "in this country both approach a uniform type, as far as the roundness of the head is concerned."[41] In other words, head shape, or the cephalic index, was far from being a stable measure of a racial type; rather, just like other bodily characteristics like height and weight, it was a product of environment. Therefore, Boas implied, race was, after all, a product of environment, and there was no essential, unchanging trait that

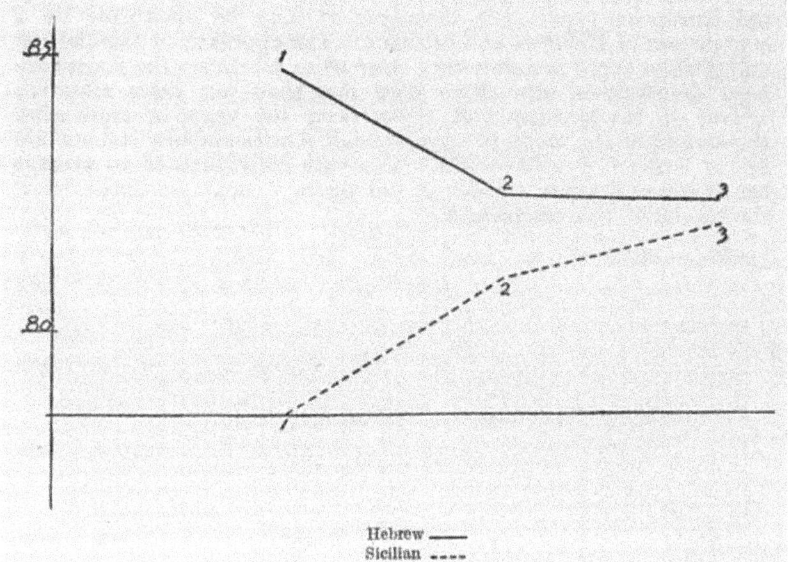

FIG. 2.—Comparison of head form of Hebrews and Sicilians, arranged according to time elapsed between birth and immigration.

FIGURE 10. Cephalic indexes of "Hebrew" and "Sicilian" children of immigrants. Boas, *Changes*, 8.

would confine immigrants to a fixed type. In other words, race was not a destiny—a new environment will lead to a new head shape, one that is determined less by the past and more by the present moment. After making this decisive argument, Boas went on to fill almost all of the remaining 550 pages of the report with figures and tables, addressing and discarding most, if not all, alternative explanations for the results.[42]

The tone of his argument was conspicuously at odds with the Dillingham Commission's report as a whole. The commission's focus was to classify and count immigrants to distinguish desirable immigrants from undesirable ones. To this end, the commission presented an "avalanche of printed numbers"[43] that filled the forty one volumes of the report. Boas brought about another avalanche, but one that was rushing in a different direction: His 550-page report, peppered with technical terms and sophisticated graphs and tables, demonstrated that even the cephalic index, supposedly the most stable feature of racial type, went through considerable transformation under the influence of a new environment—and within just a single generation. Hence, Boas implied, the racial categories that the commission was attempting to essentialize were far from reliable—in fact, Boas was carefully, but boldly, claiming that "a new American type" of race was emerging out of immigration. Boas used all the tools available to the race-thinkers of the

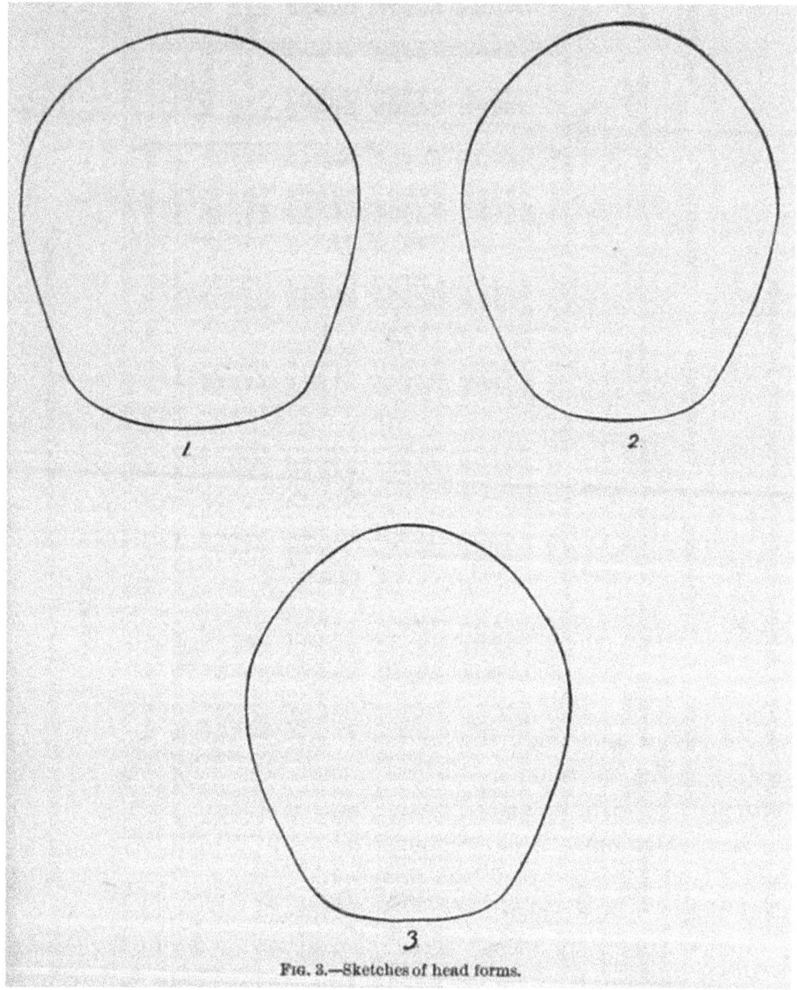


FIGURE 11. Sketches of head forms: (1) "Hebrews," (2) "Sicilians," and (3) American-born children. Boas, *Changes*, 9.

nineteenth century to amplify the contradiction within the enterprise of scientific racism: Empirical evidence did not support racial essentialism, and if race was so fuzzy a concept, was there a point in using the concept at all?

## Assimilation and Racial Liberalism

As we saw in his AAAS address of 1894, Boas had been interested in the assimilation and amalgamation of races for some time. Unlike his colleagues who accepted eugenic theories of race degeneration, Boas saw contact between races as a key mechanism in the development of civilization. Nevertheless, he never formally defined what he meant by assimilation. Several commentators acknowledged that Boas did not clearly define his most important theoretical concepts, such as culture and folklore.[44] Instead, he liberally used them in different contexts, always putting empirical data ahead of conceptual precision. In this regard, Boas's scientific template fit into that of the commission: The "avalanche of printed numbers" stood in for precise definitions and theorizing, and, consequently, it was not clear whether all the data collected belonged under the same heading.

However, Boas's theoretical inclination was slightly different from that of other theorists of assimilation, such as Sarah Simons, although he did not fully lay out how he differed from them. In his writings on African Americans, Jews, and Indigenous peoples in contemporary American society, Boas strictly adhered to a definition of assimilation as interracial marriage or race mixture: Assimilation to Boas meant "becoming indistinguishable" in physical attributes, to the point where marginalized groups could pass without being noticed as such by other members of the society. In this regard he was more of a physical anthropologist than a cultural one—a fundamental irony since he virtually founded the latter field. Writing for the *Yale Review* in 1921, Boas opined that the supposed "Negro question" would not disappear "until the negro blood has been so much diluted that it will no longer be recognized just as anti-Semitism will not disappear until the last vestige of the Jew as a Jew had disappeared."[45] Prominent scholars of this "Negro question" during the time, such as Robert Park, Booker T. Washington, and W. E. B. Du Bois, largely avoided the topic of interracial marriage, expecting public backlash. With the idiosyncratic sensibility of an immigrant, Boas charged on toward this seemingly inevitable conclusion with scientific conviction.[46] In a sense, he was not far from classic race-thinkers of the nineteenth century, who spoke for the European empires. In Sarah Simons's framework, colonial conquest would lead to the dissolution of race consciousness; in the Boasian scheme, intermixture would lead to physical absorption of the smaller group into the larger one. In both cases, we still see the traces of racial hierarchy and imagery of conquest by the strong over the weak.

In *Changes*, however, we see a radically different usage of the assimilation concept. In Boas's work with the Dillingham Commission, assimilation was defined as "growing alike" not through intermixture but through common environmental influence and adaptation. It is striking that Boas's analysis did not feature comparison of immigrant groups with "Americans," which was the most prevalent comparison across the forty-one volumes of the *DCR*. To Boas, "Americans" were not a predefined group whose lifestyle and culture should be protected from immigrants, as the executive summary of the commission supposed, but an outcome of the process through which immigrants were assimilating in a new environment. In other words, head shape number 3 in figure 11 was "American," as defined by his empirical data, and against this hard-edged empiricism, the romantic ideology of racial essentialism had no place to stand. Men like Lodge and Roosevelt dreamed of a shared destiny for the American people, defined through blood and history; to Boas, being American meant sharing a similar shape of head, nothing more, nothing less.

The Boasian concept of assimilation did not have to do with immigrants conforming to some preconfigured notion of Americans; rather, it denoted the process of their transformation and adaptation in a new environment, almost in a biological fashion: As plants and animals evolve when transplanted to a new environment, European immigrants evolved in the American setting, resulting in "a new type." Writing for *Science* in the year he was working on the report, Boas proclaimed that "the phenomenon of mixture presented in the United States is unique" and "that a similar intermixture has never occurred before in the world's history; and that our nation is destined to become what some writers choose to term a 'mongrel' nation."[47] Again, contrary to progressive reformers and race-thinkers, he used the word *mongrel* not in demeaning sense; he used it in a strictly biological manner to indicate the mixture and evolution of organisms. Assimilation was, in this case, a process that led to the formation of this "mongrel nation" and its unique racial type. Against those who argued that southern and eastern European immigrants were undesirable and too different to be assimilated into American society, Boas presented evidence showing that they were in fact transforming into "a new American type" in the new environment, just as the previous generation of immigrants had. And the American type itself was a product of this process.

## The Boasian Revolution, Chicago Sociology, and the Concept of Culture

Although his concept of assimilation was ambiguous and potentially conflicted, Boas opened up a new theoretical ground in *Changes* by doing away with the most profound contradiction within the concept. As we saw in Sarah Simons's synthesis, the outcome of assimilation had always been tied to the development of civilization and maintenance of the established racial hierarchy. Boas did retain some features of this perspective, especially when he was writing about the disappearance of marginalized groups through dilution of their "blood." As we have seen in his 1894 address, however, he did provide a ground to argue for the equality of all races; even if other races did not *appear* equal, there was a possibility that they would rise to a level equal to that of the European civilization and the "white race," sometimes through their own effort and other times through intermixture and diffusion of culture. The question of capacity for development was no longer a problem for the concept of assimilation; the focus was on *process* and, in some cases—such as in the case of Boas's work in the Dillingham Commission—an unexpected new outcome that could emerge out of the process.

The impact of Boas and his students on anthropology is often characterized as paradigm-shifting, and some commentators have dubbed the disciplinary transition circa the 1910s as "the Boasian Revolution."[48] By centering the concept of culture and embracing ethnographic fieldwork, among other things, Boas and his students laid the foundation of anthropology as we perceive the discipline today. Furthermore, as Charles King documents in his collective biography *Gods of the Upper Air*, their work formulated a new framework through which group difference was understood in the United States: By replacing race with culture and introducing relativism, Boas and his students put forward more egalitarian appraisals of different ways of life. Those who had been deemed different became objects of tolerance and appreciation, not contempt and exclusion. In short, racial liberalism found its boldest scientific expression in the Boasian school.

Scholars find much congruence between the core ideas of Boasian anthropology and the Chicago school of sociology.[49] Both schools brought about paradigm shifts in their respective disciplines, leaving lasting legacies in both theory and the institutional structure of the professions. Archival evidence suggests that the congruence was actually more of a direct influence than mere coincidence.[50] W. I. Thomas, a member of the earlier generation of Chicago school sociologists, had invited Boas to the University of Chicago for a lecture in 1907. After the visit, Thomas continued to write to Boas occasionally, expressing his intellectual admiration and asking permission to include a portion of *The Mind of Primitive Man* in *Source Book for Social Origins*, an edited volume used as a textbook in the Department of Sociology at the University of Chicago.[51] As George Stocking noted, Boas was central to the foundation of the Chicago school: "The debt is further evident in 1912—the year after *The Mind of Primitive Man* appeared in the book form—when Thomas buttressed his assertion of human equipotentiality with quotations from Boas. But most of all, the debt leaps out unacknowledged page after page of Thomas's writing, which parallels Boas's at numerous points."[52]

Simply put, the most important contribution of Chicago sociology—the race-relations cycle, assimilation, culture, and spatial model of different groups living together in urban environments—relied on the Boasian understanding of human potential: To interrogate group dynamics and social change, one should be able to assume equal potential for all groups to develop through interaction with each other before delving into how specifically they would interact. Race-thinking, including eugenics, argued that this was neither possible nor desirable, for groups were too different to interact with each other. Boas argued otherwise and provided a theoretical starting point for the Chicago school to build its intellectual enterprise. For Boas, difference was not something to avoid, exclude, or discriminate against but a precious object to be captured and theorized through empirical observation.

Hence, it is not surprising to find Boas's influence in Robert E. Park's (1864–1944) canonical work on assimilation. Writing for the *American Journal of Sociology* in 1913, Park provided two definitions of the concept, focusing on individual freedom and group-level takeover, respectively: "Historically [assimilation] has had two distinct significations. . . . There is a process that goes on in society by which individuals spontaneously acquire one another's language, characteristic attitudes, habits, and modes of behavior. There is also a process by which individuals and groups of individuals are taken over and incorporated into larger groups." The key dimension he added to the Boasian formulation, however, was to bring in the concept of nation. "The modern Italian, Frenchman, and German is a composite of broken fragments of several different racial groups," and "interbreeding has broken up the ancient stocks, and interaction and imitation have created new national types." In other words, assimilation has led to the formation of nations, either through individuals voluntarily taking up other ways of life or one group dominating and forcing their ways of life on the other. Whereas Boas presented "American types" as an open-ended entity in the making, Park saw the end point of assimilation in more definitive terms. The outcome of assimilation was, Park emphasized, "definite uniformities in language, manners, and formal behavior" found in nations.[53]

The last phrase, "uniformities in language, manners and formal behavior," was clearly Park's own addition to Boasian thinking. As an anthropologist with fieldwork experience in various places, Boas never believed that any manifestation of culture could be "uniform" or coherent. In fact, his early works on Kwakiutl language taught him that endless variations and diffusion of the variations were essential characteristics of any given culture or social group. Even when he was suggesting the notion of a new American type, he was open to the possibility of further change of such type—again, assimilation was more of a process than a fixed outcome for Boas. For Park, on the contrary, the emphasis was on outcome: Whereas Boas was interested in the fact that immigrants were transforming themselves, Park asked what they were transforming into. Like Simons, who was interested in the development of civilization, Park was interested in the formation of coherent national identity. In short, Boas's theories of the transformative potential of immigrants to forge a new identity became a nationalist narrative through which diverse groups of people came to embody a preexisting American characteristic.

While Park and other sociologists were advancing a nationalist narrative through the concept of assimilation, Boas's students seized on his method and theory rather than appropriating the concept itself. For these protégés, *Changes* became a template of sorts to intellectually move away from racial essentialism and embrace and explore the elusive concept of culture. The most obvious example of this development would be Otto Klineberg's (1899–1992) work on racial differences in intelligence. Klineberg was a psychologist by training and technically not a student of Boas. But he came into Boas's orbit during his time as a junior scholar at Columbia University and went on to apply the framework presented in *Changes* to the question of intelligence. In *Negro Intelligence and Selective Migration* (1935), Klineberg rebukes the existing research on racial difference in intelligence by foregrounding environmental influence. As numerous scholars have pointed out, modern intelligence testing emerged during World War I at the intersection of eugenic theories and a directive to single out recruits deemed "unfit" for duties. From its inception, various testing modules as well as the notion of a unified, quantifiable measure of innate mental ability retained racial bias, especially against African Americans and southern and eastern European immigrants.[54] Intelligence was in many ways the perfect measure of race for race-thinkers: More than skin color or even head shapes, which were prone to change, a number representing power of reasoning embodied what race was supposed to be about—a natural and essential trait that would set one group apart from another.[55] Using similar rhetoric to Boas in *Changes*, Klineberg criticizes this reified understanding by demonstrating how intelligence scores transformed rather easily in different environments. Comparing the test scores of African Americans in the North and in the South, he was able to prove that northern Blacks who originated from the South displayed a vast improvement in their intelligence test scores in a relatively short period of time. Using a graph that recalled Boas's cephalic index trends (see fig. 10), Klineberg also showed that, regardless of their origins, African Americans living in New York City displayed an upward convergence of intelligence scores over time. In other words, just like head shapes, innate mental ability transformed rather easily in a new environment, and, once again, race proved to be less essential than what race-thinkers made it out to be. Given the right environment, as Boas had surmised decades earlier, people of any race could develop their potential in the future, regardless of their actual level of development at the time. Klineberg stops short of using the concept of assimilation, but he does document the eventual convergence of intelligence scores of different groups. Directly addressing the question of education and environment, Klineberg went on to pass the torch of racial liberalism into the mid-century struggle for racial integration, serving as an expert witness in the case *Brown v. Board of Education* (1954) in favor of desegregation.

The lineage was a bit more complicated in the case of Melville Herskovits (1895–1963), who was Boas's student and is well known for building the Anthropology Department of Northwestern University as well as its African studies program. Herskovits in many ways embodied the world Boas was imagining in *Changes*. Born in 1895 in a small town in Ohio, Herskovits grew up in a Jewish household in which religious customs were respected but not forced. He characterized his personal background as more midwestern than Jewish, although he did dabble in rabbinical studies as a college student before enlisting to fight in World War I.[56] Under the influence of Boas at Columbia, Herskovits conducted studies on bodily measurements of African Americans in the early 1920s, replicating the data collection procedure and theoretical framework presented in *Changes*. The result was published as *The American Negro* (1928).[57]

Combining Boas's insights in *Changes* and in the study of the "half-blooded Indian," Herskovits set out to understand the physical status of the "American Negro" by closely examining the ancestry of his respondents. Herskovits argued that contemporary African Americans were, from a genealogical standpoint, not a "pure" but a "mixed" racial group, with many White and "Indian" ancestries featured in their family trees. This, according to contemporary theories of race mixture, was supposed to make them unstable—meaning that their physical characteristics should display high variability. However, Herskovits's data indicated that African Americans showed low variability in physical traits, attesting to the stability of their type. In other words, the existing theories based on nineteenth-century race-thinking could not explain the current makeup of African Americans, who were mixed in genealogy but stable in physical traits.

We can easily sense the echo of Boas's emphasis on the hybridity of "American type" in Herskovits's characterization of African Americans. Hybridity was not a negative trait to avoid; rather, it was a precondition for any racial group. And, by extension, both Boas and Herskovits implied, there was not much essential about the configuration of race as a concept: The dynamics of assimilation, amalgamation, or interracial mixture—however one chooses to name it—were bound to change racial makeup constantly, and such processes would lead to the formation of a new group. We can thus only tentatively contend with race as we apprehend it at a given point of time, be it American or African American. Whereas Boas's American type was looking into the future, Herskovits's work effectively showed that hybridity was a necessary dimension of any race at any point, starting with the paradigmatic case of African Americans.

Later in his career, Herskovits took his findings from *The American Negro* in an interesting direction. As noted, there was a paradox at the heart of this work: African Americans were a mixed group by ancestry, yet they appeared to be relatively homogeneous in their physical characteristics. On what basis should we call them a "race" or "group"? In an early iteration of the social constructionist approach, Herskovits reasoned that African Americans appeared to be a coherent group not because of their shared biological traits but because of the social dynamics surrounding them. In further articulating the basis of group identity, Herskovits zeroed in on culture, defined as the surviving influence of artistic and religious traditions from a group's origin, which meant Africa for African Americans. In *The Myth of the Negro Past* (1941), which established him as the authoritative figure in African studies, Herskovits documented how African diasporic communities across the Americas retained African influences in religion, art, and everyday social interaction. Once again, this was a rebuke of contemporary race-thinkers who presented African Americans as a "childlike" people devoid of history, culture, and tradition. In fact, according to Herskovits, members of the African diaspora were the people who successfully defended their culture against the ordeals of slavery, forced migration, and resulting cultural annihilation. For pan-Africanists such as W. E. B. Du Bois and Marcus Garvey, this was a welcome message that affirmed the resiliency and cohesion of African American communities across the Atlantic. For others who were concerned about the contemporary plight of America's most visible minority group, however, culture was a double-edged sword. Franklin E. Frazier, a Black sociologist who conducted studies of Black families in Chicago, exemplified such a reaction in his review for *Nation* in 1942. Because of Herskovits's overemphasis on cultural tradition from Africa, "spontaneous responses, imagination, and the acquisition of new habits and attitudes are ruled out of the Negro's efforts to adapt his behavior to American civilization." Herskovits's focus on "African patterns of thought," according to Frazier, implied "that even more fundamental barriers exist between blacks and whites than are generally recognized."[58]

Within three decades of Boas's study of immigrant children, the tables had turned in the debate regarding race. Boas and Herskovits had dethroned nineteenth-century race-thinking by critiquing its focus on physiology and purity. In Herskovits's search for an alternative to biology, however, the elusive concept of culture—presented as the tenacious influence of a mythical past from a faraway place—lent itself to another form of essentialism. Racial essentialism, as Frazier acutely sensed, was being replaced with cultural essentialism. African Americans were still bound by the notion of their group identity, and even though the basis of the bind shifted from biology to culture, their shackles remained intact. We can see the obvious contrast with the trajectory of ethnicity (see chapter 3) for European immigrants, through which they became free of the bind represented by the concept of race. Under the ethnicity paradigm, as authors such as Vilna Bashi Treitler, Michael Omi, and Howard Winant have critically theorized, immigrant background was a source of inspiration; meanwhile African culture was both a protection and limitation at the same time.[59] As anthropologist Lee Baker has aptly phrased, the cultural politics of race was replaced by the racial politics of culture.[60]

## Beyond Comparison: Hurston's Ethnography of Southern Black Folklore

Last but not least, there is another intriguing twist in the theoretical genealogy that connects race to culture. It belongs to Zora Neale Hurston (1891–1960) and her anthropological work on southern Black folklore, the most unlikely offspring of the Boasian revolution.[61] Born in 1891 and raised in one of the first all-Black towns to be incorporated, Eatonville, Florida, Hurston was educated at Howard University and Barnard College. As the first African American student to attend Barnard, Hurston came into the orbit of Boas and his students at Columbia, including Herskovits, Margaret Mead, and Ruth Benedict. Hurston had a connection to *Changes* when she worked as a research assistant for Herskovits's project for *The American Negro*. Her task was to collect bodily measurements of Harlem residents by recruiting them off the street, just like Boas's assistants had done for his project with the Dillingham Commission a few years earlier. For this job, she took an anthropometry course and was trained in specific measuring techniques, including that for the cephalic index. Langston Hughes, a leader of the Harlem Renaissance, wrote that "almost nobody else could stop the average Harlemite on Lenox Avenue and measure his head with a strange-looking anthropological device and not get bawled out for the attempt, except Zora, who used to stop anyone whose head looked interesting, and measure it."[62]

When it was time to do her own work of anthropology, however, Hurston charted a different path. With the blessing of Boas, Hurston drove down to all-Black towns in Florida in search of African American folklore. She mainly listened to and documented the stories of people, without attempting to theorize anything general from the data she collected. In fact, her project resembled those of Boas's early days, when he was traveling up and down the Pacific coast to record language in and collect artifacts from Indigenous communities. The result was a collection of tales, songs, and bits of wisdom that were familiar to Hurston, who had grown up in the setting, but entirely foreign to the academic audience in New York.

Meanwhile, the Boasian criticisms of nineteenth-century racial essentialism proceeded by way of comparison: Assessing various combinations, either through statistics or ethnography, Boas and his students showcased convergence between different races. This promise of convergence formed the core of the assimilation concept and, in turn, racial liberalism. That is, racial groups may appear different, but those manifestations of difference are far from essential and prone to transformation under environmental influence; furthermore, they will eventually become indistinguishable. To escape the bind of race, one has to forgo group identity and become something else—a hybrid (Boas) or a patriot (Park). Otherwise, one clings to the past by way of tradition (Herskovits). In any case, difference should disappear in order to make way for newfound freedom within one's adopted culture. Such were the pathways to freedom provided to the racialized in the world imagined through racial liberalism.

Hurston's fieldwork, and her subsequent literary writings, escaped this model entirely and presented a line of flight out of these choices. She never compared African Americans to Whites. The African American tradition of folklore was, she implied, meaningful, beautiful, and valuable in its own right. She did not address the question of equality or the humanity of African Americans, for the answer was too evident to her. The more pressing question was what they thought and how they lived their lives in the aftermath of slavery and under the Jim Crow regime of the South. In *Mules and Men*, Hurston portrays a world illegible to outsiders, built from humor, satire, and the fantasies of African American working people. She writes of their parties, food, and plays as well as the petty and not-so-petty grievances that sometimes ended in knife fights. Rich with tales of "Old Messa" and "John the negro," Hurston's stories channeled the voices of people who had never figured into the grand discussion of race and its social implications. "In an assimilationist era, when black intellectuals stressed the similarities between the races," her biographer Robert Hemeney writes, "Hurston proudly affirmed the cultural differences." Hurston "believed that an esthetically oriented black subculture provided a striking contrast to the imaginative wasteland of white society."[63] In the end, Hurston parted ways with the assimilationist paradigm by affirming the difference represented by race, not trying to do away with it.

Her infamous objection to *Brown v. Board of Education* can be interpreted somewhat differently in this context. In her letter to the editor to *Orlando Sentinel* in 1955, Hurston elaborated on her distaste for racial integration. Again, she changed the terms of the debate from equality to something else: "The whole matter revolves around the self-respect for my people." Out of that self-respect, she asked, "How much satisfaction can I get from a court order for somebody to associate with me who does not wish me near them?" She praised the quality of Black schools in Florida and argued that Black children would be better served if more government attention was paid to their schools, not racial integration per se. She invoked the case of Indigenous tribes, or "Indians," to make her case: "There is no whine in Indian . . . he fought . . . valiantly for his lands . . . it is inconceivable of an Indian to seek forcible association with anyone." Idiosyncratic as it may seem, this argument makes more sense from the purview of her anthropological intuitions. She rightfully saw through the criticisms of racial essentialism and perceived the new bind that the concept of culture represented. If she dwelled on the question of comparison and equality, she would not escape the charge of *whine*—the term she attributed to much of the mainstream civil rights movement. Echoing the Black Power movements that would emerge decades later, Hurston spoke of pride and self-determination for her own people. Her rebuke of racial integration marked an end to the lineage that started with the Dillingham Commission and *Changes*: Hybridity, nationalism, and cultural essentialism had emerged in the void left by racial essentialism; Hurston added the bastard child of racial pride and self-determination to this list. By doing so, she gestured toward ways to move beyond racial liberalism.

[ CHAPTER FIVE ]

# Reinterpreting the Facts

## Women and Immigrants Talk Back

In the preceding chapters, I document how racial ideas were professed and contested in the Dillingham Commission's inquiry and beyond. While centering the people directly involved in the project, such as Daniel Folkmar and Franz Boas, we have seen how the state-led fact-finding attempt affected their respective intellectual trajectories and, by extension, those who came into their orbits. A common thread runs through these trajectories: The concept of race transformed from the straightforward, direct assurance of WASP supremacy (i.e., Lodge's idea of race and nation; see chapter 1) to a multifaceted, dynamic configuration consisting of different components. Chapters 3 and 4 show how newly formulated concepts of ethnicity, culture, and assimilation stemmed from this transformation. Together, these concepts provided a foundation for racial liberalism, or the belief that the figure of the racialized migrant could one day become a part of the national body politic through effort. This was seemingly a different way of conceptualizing population difference, one that was in contrast to racial essentialism, which surmised that the racialized other will remain so indefinitely. More pointedly, assimilation was presented as an alternative to exclusion in solving the immigration problem.

This chapter moves away from broader intellectual transformations and zooms in on the micro process that enabled such transformation—namely, on the role of the facts and the different interpretations people interested in immigration generated from them. As seen in the executive summary, the Dillingham Commission officially reaffirmed the standard restrictionist ideology, and it did what it could to present the encounter between the state and the facts in a way that supports this conclusion. This did not mean that the entire organization was devoted to the restrictionist agenda, and those who worked on the frontlines of data collection sometimes delivered facts that did not squarely support racial essentialism. While these unruly facts received less attention from the commission—especially in its executive summary and policy recommendations—pro-immigrant actors outside the commission used the same set of facts to counter the restrictionist ideology and racial essentialism that undergirded such ideology.

This opposition was not merely a repetition of the immigration debate that had been going on for decades. While the familiar characters engaged with each other on the same issue, as Mary Poovey observed in the context of political debates in early modern Britain, this time facts effectively anchored the exchange, defining the boundary of acceptable, legitimate discourse. The warring factions had a common ground around which to stage their respective arguments. Moreover, the existence of the commission's data forced dialogues across the boundaries of class, gender, and political ideology, and new discursive networks emerged through these dialogues. Importantly, traditionally excluded groups such as women reformers and immigrant intellectuals actively utilized facts to participate in these networks. As we have seen in previous chapters, the conceptual innovations associated with racial liberalism were buttressed by these newly formed networks, as the elitist, exclusive ideology of WASP supremacy evolved into the configuration of ethnicity, assimilation, and culture. Both American social sciences and immigration policymaking were deeply impacted by this transition.

In the following, I present episodes of the unruly facts being interpreted and reinterpreted by a diverse set of actors. I start with those who first encountered facts on the ground—the field agents hired by the commission—and move on to the experts who had some control over the interpretation of those facts. I then address how women reformers and immigrant intellectuals outside the commission reinterpreted the facts to counter restrictionist ideology. In the process, I sketch out the discursive infrastructure on which the consolidation of racial liberalism was possible.

## Field Agents Report Back

As briefly discussed in chapter 2, the Dillingham Commission's inquiry was a wide-reaching operation, with more than three hundred people on its payroll. While existing works on the commission have largely focused on the high-ranking members, such as the experts with academic credentials and the politicians on the executive committee, recent scholarship has also paid attention to midlevel staffers.[1] In the following, I highlight the work of the staff members who were witnessing the encounter between the state and facts on the ground—namely, those who were hired to conduct surveys and ethnographic observations in immigrant settlements across the country. The Dillingham Commission referred to them as field agents.

Jeremiah Jenks (1856–1929) and William Jett Lauck (1879–1949), two economists who had worked on other Progressive Era investigative commissions, spearheaded the commission's data collection activity as designated experts.[2] Their project, titled "Immigrants in Industries," would feature the data collected from various industrial towns throughout the country, covering a wide range of trades in specific locales, from coal mines on the East Coast to meatpacking plants in the Midwest. Their reports on these industries would constitute sixteen of the forty-one volumes of the *DCR*. Their perspective on immigration and the so-called new immigrants was not as obvious as someone like Lodge's: As social scientists, they preferred to let the data speak rather than putting forward an ideology. Unlike Edward Ross, they had no proven record of ranting against immigrants. But their design for inquiry hints at their overall theoretical framework in thinking about immigration. Just like race-thinkers before them, they employed "races or peoples" to classify immigrants and collected data based on this classification scheme to compare groups with each other (see fig. 12). Although they did not seem to stress any preconceived notions about desirability of specific groups, this framework would easily lead to a hierarchy of different groups.

Jenks and Lauck drew up a very detailed master plan to guide their project.[3] They began by stressing the importance of the population count according to races or peoples because that data would serve as the foundation for all other inquires. They also noted other topics for data collection, such as geography of the site, its history of immigration, its occupational characteristics, assimilation, and the social and civic lives of immigrants. There were sections concerning racial hierarchy, such as "employer preference of immigrants," for which field agents were instructed to ask which races or peoples were the most preferred by employers; also featured were "racial displacements," for which agents had to decide whether new immigrants were displacing old immigrants or native-born American workers and, if so, why. These two topics were clearly designed to single out southern and eastern Europeans as undesirable races who were taking away jobs from more preferred American workers. In collecting such information, the commission was hoping to obtain data that would support the common restrictionist narrative of new immigrants taking jobs from native-born American workers.

However, when the field agents of the commission, equipped with these plans, took to their respective research sites, they encountered all kinds of other information that did not neatly fit into the restrictionist narrative. The field agents, who did not have a clear sense of the overall design of the commission's inquiry, wrote back faithfully about what they had

I. C. 79.

THE UNITED STATES IMMIGRATION COMMISSION, WASHINGTON, D. C.

CHECK OR PAY No. ______

1. What is your name? ______
2. Where do you live (street and number)? ______
3. Mark the race to which you belong with a cross (thus X):

| | | | |
|---|---|---|---|
| ___American, white. | ___Finnish. | ___Lithuanian. | ___Russian. |
| ___American, negro. | ___French-Canadian. | ___Magyar. | ___Ruthenian. |
| ___Bohemian. | ___German. | ___Montenegrin. | ___Scotch. |
| ___Bulgarian. | ___Greek. | ___Moravian. | ___Servian. |
| ___Croatian. | ___Hebrew. | ___Norwegian. | ___Slovak. |
| ___Danish. | ___Irish. | ___Polish. | ___Slovenian. |
| ___Dutch. | ___Italian (north). | ___Portuguese. | ___Swedish. |
| ___English. | ___Italian (south). | ___Roumanian. | ___Syrian. |

If of any other race, write name of race here ______

4. Occupation (what work do you do)? ______
5. What do you earn per day? ______ 6. What do you earn per week? ______
7. What work did you do before coming to the U. S.? ______

PLEASE ANSWER QUESTIONS ON BOTH SIDES OF THIS SLIP.

FIGURE 12. A sample survey used by field agents of the commission. W. Jett Lauck Papers, Albert and Shirely Small Special Collections Library, the University of Virginia.

seen and heard in the field.[4] Without adhering to the restrictionist agenda, these agents were strictly following the guidelines of scientific methodology that they had learned in their schooling and thereby generating the unruly facts that were not expected or desired by those who had initiated the inquiry.

## IMPOSSIBLE CLASSIFICATION

On the very first page of the report on a Pennsylvania mining town, an agent wrote about the difficulty of applying the races or peoples scheme in the actual process of data collection. “It has been impossible,” the agent confessed, “to secure accurate information as to the number of each race employed in the plant.” Even men who were “above the ordinary” in terms of their intelligence and experience in the industry felt “at sea when attempting to classify [immigrants] by races.” Immigrants from eastern Europe were generally lumped together as “Slavish” by foremen asked to classify them. Tasked with hiring workers, the foremen were “looking for results,” and “no questions [were] asked as to his race.” The theoretical validity of the races or peoples scheme did not matter much on the job. The foremen hired workers who could produce results; the workers’ races mattered less than the fact that they were able-bodied men who could do the job.[5]

In a report on a steel factory town in Pennsylvania, another agent expressed his skepticism about using the commission's classification scheme to collect data: "Your agent has exhausted every means to ascertain the number of each race, when first employed, but this is absolutely impossible." Again, just as in the previous case of the mining town, the agent could obtain only a "statement of old employers, who hired the majority of these men" and from it could gather merely that "a few years ago all of these foreigners were called Slavs or Hunns." More precise classification by races or people was impossible; therefore, any earnest attempt to collect statistics according to the provided categories was bound to be "utterly impossible." The agent was able to compel the employers to "venture an opinion" on the races of workers, "only by associating one incident with another." In other words, the agent had to make his interviewees conform to the commission's terms—often against their own wills. To be clear, not all field agents reported difficulties in applying the commission's classification scheme. However, none made a full use of races or peoples either, simply because not all groups were present in the towns they were studying.[6] In most cases they went along with local classifications, such as Slavs for all immigrants from eastern Europe, neglecting the commission's original design.

## IMPOSSIBLE HIERARCHY

In addition, the questions designed to obtain information that confirmed a racial hierarchy—"employer preference of immigrants"—yielded many unexpected results. For instance, in the steel factory mentioned, "the officials of this Company prefer these recent immigrants in the following order, viz: Slovacs, Poles, and Magyars," while the employers saw "very little difference in the other races." Moreover, "the Slovac is considered the most intelligent and in the opinion of those who come in daily contact with him, he will advance more rapidly than the others." The agent dutifully continued to convey all the information obtained, despite its decreasing relevance to employer preferences based on performance in the workplace: "Many of this race have purchased homes, which is always interpreted as making for a better citizenship, and a permanent force from which to secure laborers."

The question of employer preference was designed to establish a hierarchy between old immigrants and new immigrants and also a racial hierarchy within the latter group. In this answer there is no mention of the old immigrants, so it is not clear which groups were preferred between the old and new immigrants. The rank order of various eastern European groups somehow confirmed the commission's intentions, but the information about home purchases was not in line with the restrictionist agenda—especially the fact that Slovacs, who were supposed to be an undesirable race, were ranked as highly desirable workers and homeowners. According to the popular restrictionist argument, these new immigrants were supposed to have come to the United States to work for money without any intention to settle permanently, and their supposed transience was the reason why they were causing social problems; however, the commission's own inquiry often revealed that they were putting down roots and buying homes for their families, showing that in fact new immigrants were not so undesirable after all.

"South Italians" were, under the restrictionist agenda, generally regarded as an undesirable immigrant group. However, the commission's data had different things to say about Italians' standing: "In one mining establishment," according to the commission, "the South Italian miners were said to be the most industrious of all the races employed, and they were reported to work more steadily than either Russians or the natives." Of course, not all stereotypes were proven wrong, and the South Italians reportedly "consumed a large quantity of whisky and beer." Still, they "were less given to intoxication than the natives" and displayed "a greater tendency toward sobriety than any of the other employees." Even their supposed "inability to use English was said to have had no effect whatever upon the efficiency" of their work in the mine. The Italians were "said to take a greater interest in their homes than was shown by the natives. They cultivate gardens around them and in other ways try to make them attractive."[7]

Again, South Italians during this period were stigmatized with every possible negative immigrant stereotype: Restrictionists argued that they were lazy, politically suspect, and immoral; they were also caricatured to drink heavily and commit crimes when they were drunk.[8] But the data from the field proved otherwise: They were not only better workers and more temperate drinkers but also more invested in homeownership and improvement than natives.

Sometimes the hierarchy question solicited discourse rather than a clear answer because the interviewees had a much more nuanced understanding of the subject. The employers often added in their own agenda in answering the question. In a report about a sugar refining company in Philadelphia, for example, one foreman had devised a very sophisticated racial hierarchy of his own.

> Mr. Peterson ranks the races about as follows when compared with each other and with Americans:
>
> (a) Efficiency—German, Polish, American, Irish.
> (b) Progress—German, American, Irish, Polish.

(c) Adaptability—German, American, Irish, Polish.
(d) Tractability—German, Polish, American, Irish.
(e) Industriousness—German, Polish, American, Irish.

> Your agent thinks Mr. Peterson is probably German himself.[9]

The implication of the last sentence was obviously that the interviewee, Mr. Peterson, was biased toward Germans. Even without Germans, the other three groups do not form a clear, one-dimensional hierarchy. Detailed as it was, Mr. Peterson's hierarchy did not single out southern and eastern Europeans as undesirable groups. Instead, it showed that racial hierarchy was bound to be multidimensional, relative, and, most importantly, biased. There was no hint of irony or sarcasm in this agent's faithful reporting, yet the information itself exposed the vulnerability of the commission's project and displayed the uselessness of attempts to confirm a racial hierarchy.

Unfortunately, Lauck's papers do not feature any of the letters he or Jenks wrote to agents as responses to these reports. By tracing the paper trail to the final reports, however, we can indirectly infer how the commission dealt with the challenges created by the empirical data. Of course, the most obvious way to deal with these issues was to quietly shelve the field reports and then selectively incorporate the data in a way that supported the hierarchy between old immigrants and new immigrants. Certainly, strange omissions of this sort occurred throughout the report, and some of the reports quoted here did not appear in the final version of the volumes, based on my review of all volumes. The summary volume represented the boundary between southern and eastern Europeans and northern and western Europeans as undoubtedly bright and affirmed the strict hierarchy between the two groups. Based on these (erroneous) interpretations of the data collected, the commission recommended exclusion of southern and eastern Europeans and suggested the literacy test as a scientifically informed policy measure for immigration control.[10]

The executive committee was aware of the discrepancy between the commission's overall conclusion and the vast amount of data collected. As Robert Zeidel carefully describes, the last days of the commission were a hectic affair, with time and funding running out while the executive committee faced Congress and a public eager for the results from the massive four-year operation. The pressure compelled the executive committee members to adopt a firm policy position of recommending literacy tests, for which Lodge and his restrictionist allies had long been advocating.[11] However, William Bennet, the pro-immigrant representative from the Bronx, objected, arguing that "no logical argument . . . based on the report" supported such a recommendation. While he could not overturn the overall restrictionist sentiment within the executive committee, Bennet did leave his mark in the executive summary by authoring "Views of the Minority," a single-page note attached to the end of the forty-eight-page introduction. In this note, Bennet alluded to discrepancies like the one discussed here, noting that the commission's data showed "immigrants are not criminal, pauper, insane, or seekers of charity."[12] As Katherine Benton-Cohen observes, "Bennet's dissent was the only window most observers had on the internal inconsistencies, differences of opinion and equivocal evidence in the reports."[13]

However, there were people who peeked into the window left open by Bennet. Some of the challenges featured in the reports by field agents survived, especially in the main body of the *DCR*. Across the thirty-eight volumes—excluding the first two volumes intended as the executive summary and the index volume that never got published—there were numerous tables and ethnographic accounts contradicting the overall conclusion of the Dillingham Commission. The restrictionists were satisfied with the executive summary and did not bother to take a closer look. They relied on the commission's facts—or, more precisely, the legitimacy conferred by those facts—to support their argument, without actually paying attention to the totality of those facts. On the other hand, the experts who oversaw the inquiry, Jenks and Lauck, published a separate academic monograph addressing some of the omissions and contradictions discussed in this section. However, pro-immigrant intellectuals and organizations would use the data collected by the commission to refute its findings and, in turn, argue that immigrants were not much different from nonimmigrants. In the following section, I present how interpretations and reinterpretations of the commission's facts enabled a dialogue across the boundary of class, gender, and immigration status, thereby building the foundation on which the grafting of racial liberalism onto racial essentialism became possible.

## "Unprejudiced Spirit" of *The Immigration Problem* (1911)

Following the *DCR*'s publication, many authors referenced its findings in their work. In many cases the reference was brief—they either cited the conclusion presented in the executive summary or selectively referred to a specific set of data to support their argument about immigrants.

Edward Ross, perhaps the most well-known and respected restrictionist academic of the time, referred to the *DCR* several times in his influential pamphlet *The Old World in the New: The Significance of Past and Present Immigration to the American People* (1914). Bridging racial essentialism and empirical data, Ross reasoned that new immigrants were unfit for the American nation. In his polemic, the Dillingham Commission's findings were affirmatively referenced as providing empirical evidence for the supposedly undesirable characteristics of contemporary immigrants. Invoking his famous theory of race suicide, Ross concluded by doubling down on the incompatibility between "American blood" and "immigrant blood." He also added a dose of antisemitism by arguing, baselessly, that the Dillingham Commission was a product of Jewish control over immigration policy.[14]

On the opposite side of the political spectrum lies *Old World Traits Transplanted* (1921) by W. I. Thomas of the Chicago school. Arguing that the Americanization of immigrants was a necessary condition for democracy, Thomas attempted to humanize much-maligned new immigrants by presenting their life stories, drawing heavily on intimate ethnographic accounts such as diaries and letters. In the process, Thomas also selectively referred to the commission's data in order to illuminate the broader context of his ethnographic evidence while not discussing the commission's overall conclusion or recommendations. Somewhat ironically, both sides of the immigration debate were able to find something useful in the commission's data because it procured so much material.

The Dillingham Commission, or at least the experts who participated in its data collection efforts, nominally embraced this open-access approach, explicitly inviting others to examine the facts on their own. In the immediate aftermath of the Dillingham Commission's inquiry, Jenks and Lauck published *The Immigration Problem*, an academic monograph that relied extensively on data from the Dillingham Commission. In the preface, Jenks and Lauck make clear how they approached their inquiry: "The writers are not advocates, but interpreters of facts . . . until about the time the [commission's] investigation was completed, they had not formulated in their own minds any definite policy which they believed the Government should follow." It is hard to take their words at face value, especially in light of the field agents' report previously discussed. But this stance compelled them to invite anyone who disagreed with the commission to "examine carefully the data in an unprejudiced spirit before he condemns the conclusions" because the data would enable a "careful student [to] reach an independent judgment."[15] But such a statement did not mean that they had no opinion of their own. In fact, they had a clear stance on immigration and felt that they were "justified in giving facts on their authority" because they "worked four years directly upon this investigation."[16] And that opinion, as we will see, did not range too far from the usual restrictionist talking points, although it was differentiated from the ideology of WASP supremacy professed by the likes of Lodge.

Jenks and Lauck started their book by mentioning the "standard of civilization" in judging immigrants, thereby siding with nineteenth-century race-thinkers (see chapter 1), but the main body of the monograph remains surprisingly faithful to the data, even more so than the *DCR* itself. In fact, while the *DCR* glossed over many of the contradictions in the data collection, Jenks and Lauck made note of them even when the data did not firmly support their restrictionist argument. At one point, they wrote, "It is impossible to show whether or not the totality of crime has been increased by immigrants."[17] Elsewhere, discussing the data relating to various social problems, they concluded that "there is no serious danger to be apprehended immediately from the social defects of the immigrants."[18] Jenks and Lauck even faithfully summarized Boas's findings and expressed excitement for the implication of his thinking on theories of race.[19]

Instead of racial reasoning, Jenks and Lauck effectively hinged their argument on the economic competition caused by immigrants—namely, that immigration suppressed wages and worsened working conditions for American workers. The two economists emphasized that their argument against immigration did not originate from race prejudice, which they found baseless and irrational; instead, they highlighted the industrial conditions, for both employers and workers, in which the cons of continuing immigration outweighed the pros. They acknowledged that immigrant labor played an important role in the industrial expansion of the nation. Yet, they argued, "complete saturation" had happened, and it was no longer desirable to have a continuing stream of labor pouring into the country.[20] Therefore, the United States as a nation should control the inflow of immigrants, particularly those who happened to originate from southern and eastern Europe. In other words, Jenks and Lauck's restrictionist position was presented as an inevitable, instrumental response to changing economic conditions, not an irrational obsession over the changing makeup of the nation.

However, Jenks and Lauck saved their race-thinking for another occasion. While the *DCR* presented European immigration in the East and Asian immigration in the West as two different phenomena occurring in two distinctive locations far away from each other, Jenks and Lauck saw the connection between them. In discussing Asian immigration, they first made clear that their position differed from anti-Asian agitators on the West Coast, whom they regarded as motivated by race prejudice and ignorance. In fact, based on the great civilizations in China and Japan, Jenks and Lauck reasoned that "Orientals" were not inferior to Whites and labeled anyone who dared to argue so as awfully misinformed about the world history.[21]

In addition, Jenks and Lauck acknowledged the positive facts about Japanese immigrants (see chapter 6): "They seem desirous to learn western ways and methods, and externally, at any rate, they conform to the customs of the time. They make very earnest effort to learn English; they take up the studies the Americans have in their schools; they adopt American dress . . . and a considerable number of them are professing Christians." However, "in spite of this external assimilation they, nevertheless, beyond doubt, maintain their race characteristics to a greater degree than do most of the European races."[22] This seemingly objective fact was a problem because "the presence of these races in large numbers on the coast doubtless prevents the migration from eastern cities of white immigrants."[23] In their view, the industrial cities of the East Coast had reached the point of "complete saturation" in terms of immigrants, while the West still had room to accommodate them. The only problem was that the room was occupied by Asian immigrants. Therefore, they expected that "Italians and Portuguese in considerable numbers [would] come directly from their home countries for work along the Pacific Coast"[24] if some form of exclusion against Asian immigrants were applied. In other words, the economic solution to European immigration on the East Coast necessitated the race-based exclusion of Asian immigrants on the West Coast.[25]

Jenks and Lauck ended the book affirming the potential of "new immigrants" by way of contrast to immigrants from Asia: "In spite of the criticism of the immigrant from Southern and Eastern Europe, there is every reason to believe that they are much more easily assimilated than are the Asiatics, and that in a comparatively short time they will become available as part of the general labor supply and prove to be, both as laborers and as citizens, more satisfactory than the Asiatics."[26] In *The Immigration Problem*, what was alluded to in the *DCR* was made explicit: There was a vision for a new racial order, one that effectively divided White and non-White immigrants and invited the former to assimilate while excluding the latter. Considering the developments detailed in the preceding chapters, *The Immigration Problem* felt like a directive, one that provided a blueprint for the policy development that transpired in the decades after the commission's inquiry. Through quotas for Europeans and exclusion of Asians, as well as violent social control imposed on African Americans and Latinos, the racial order centering Whiteness was gradually realized in the 1920s and 1930s. This is not to say that Jenks and Lauck were driven by a predetermined racial ideology. In fact, they put stock in the facts they collected with the help of field agents, even ones that were inconvenient for them, such that the ideology of WASP supremacy collided with their "unprejudiced spirit" over facts. The pressure of this dissonance pushed Jenks and Lauck away from the original restrictionist ideas and into an elusive racial blueprint centering on Whiteness, still in its nascent formation. It would take other people to make vivid this new vision.

## Reinterpreting the Facts: Women and Immigrants Talk Back

### MASSACHUSETTS COMMISSION ON IMMIGRATION

Although it started as a political compromise, the Dillingham Commission's inquiry was a much-anticipated project, especially for those who were interested in immigration. Regardless of the commission's evident ideological leanings, the model of scientifically informed, fact-based governance appealed to many policymakers and citizens. As a response, several state and city governments launched a similar inquiry, explicitly branding it under the auspice of an immigration commission. These inquiries not only modeled themselves after the Dillingham Commission but also drew from its findings to address the issues about immigrants in their specific locale—mostly the large cities on the East Coast.

While these local commissions shared with their federal counterpart the dedication to facts, they emerged from a very different political context. The major industrial cities on the East Coast had been receiving immigrants for generations, starting in the mid-nineteenth century, and many of these immigrants had a strong influence on local politics by way of their concentration in urban centers. New York, Boston, and Philadelphia were prime examples of such cities. Because of the difference in political context, these commissions were made up of people who differed from the executive committee of the Dillingham Commission, and they, in turn, hired a different set of experts to conduct fact-finding.

Pro-immigrant activists, many of whom were women, participated actively in these inquiries, and they put forward a very different argument using the same facts generated by the Dillingham Commission. These women activists did not deny the supposed undesirability of new immigrants; it was true that many of them were living in poor conditions. However, these reports argued that the government should actively intervene in those conditions to make them more desirable, instead of excluding them from the nation. Embodying the spirit of the Progressive movement, these local commissions highlighted education and welfare as keys to a more robust community of citizenship. In advancing this argument through the Dillingham Commission's facts, they provided a counterpoint to the restrictionist argument focusing on federal-level exclusion. The most notable example of this type of commission was in Massachusetts.

From its organizational structure to the style of reasoning in the report, the Massachusetts Commission on Immigration followed the template established by the Dillingham Commission. The state legislature tasked the governor to appoint the executive committee, which featured prominent members of the state legislature and the head of the chamber of commerce. The committee also featured a notable academic with expert knowledge on immigration, Professor Emily G. Balch of Wellesley College.[27] The committee subsequently hired an executive secretary, who was charged with conducting the investigation: Grace Abbott (1878–1939), the younger sister of Edith Abbott (1876–1957).[28] The investigation itself also followed the formula of the Dillingham Commission, focusing on subjects such as crime, welfare, employment, and education, combining statistical data and ethnographic accounts. In the process, the report relied much on the Dillingham Commission's data, citing and duly acknowledging the contribution of the federal investigation.

It is important to note the social background of Grace Abbott, especially in terms of her shared institutional affiliations with male experts like Jenks and Lauck but not with WASP elites like Dillingham and Lodge.[29] Grace came from a well-to-do family in Nebraska, where her father was a lawyer and a member of the state legislature. Her mother, remarkably for a woman during the time, had graduated from college and worked as a schoolteacher. Edith recalled the sisters' upbringing as "a prairie childhood," a decidedly more down-to-earth experience compared to those of men like Lodge, who retained a somewhat exaggerated sense of self-importance.[30] Both sisters were attracted to higher education and social justice activism early on, but their gender allowed only limited options to pursue these dreams. Among such options was the University of Chicago, a rare co-ed institution at the time. In fact, Edith went to graduate school in Chicago at the same time as Lauck, under the same advisor, before joining Hull House alongside her sister.[31] Grace was first recruited to the immigrant-serving organization as a secretary to reformer Jane Addams to help her manage the newly established Immigrant Protective League. She quickly took prominent positions in the organization by demonstrating her skills as a leader. Both Grace and Edith resided in Hull House and worked with other reformers.

Hull House was an ethnographic site, not unlike Folkmar's Philippines, from which the Abbott sisters could see with their own eyes "how the other half lived," to borrow the phrase made famous by contemporary photojournalist Jacob Riis. Hull House provided classes to immigrants on a wide variety of subjects, including English, American citizenship, and marketable crafts. Immigrants and their children regularly dropped by its large living room to seek advice for their daily problems.[32] Progressive and socialist activists from overseas, some of them exiles from czarist Russia, visited and discussed politics at the communal dining table. On the official side, the resident reformers worked with the city government to address the chronic health and sanitation issues of the neighborhood. They also collaborated with Chicago school sociologists, supplying much of the raw data that would lead to the school's classic works on urban sociology.[33] In 1908, Grace published an article in the *American Journal of Sociology* titled "The Chicago Employment Agency and the Immigrant Worker" that was based on these activities.[34] All this experience shaped Grace's understanding of contemporary immigration—namely, that immigrants were no different from nonimmigrants and social conditions were the prime force that structured both groups' lives. By the time she was being considered for a position in the Massachusetts Commission, Grace was a firm believer in the humanity of immigrants, new and old alike.

The Massachusetts Commission had a very different goal from that of the Dillingham Commission. Instead of singling out southern and eastern Europeans as undesirable races, the Massachusetts Commission attempted to understand the social context that forced immigrants into those undesirable circumstances. In its resolve to establish the commission, the Massachusetts legislature stated that the fact-finding inquiry should assist in "the enactment of such laws as will bring non-English speaking foreigners, resident or transient, into sympathetic relation with American institutions and customs."[35] In other words, instead of demonstrating the necessity of excluding immigrants, the investigation attempted to facilitate the assimilation of immigrants. While citing the Dillingham Commission's data, the Massachusetts Commission critically examined every aspect of it, highlighting many discrepancies. By doing so, the Massachusetts Commission refuted many of the Dillingham Commission's findings.

At first glance, the most compelling feature of the *Report of the Commission on Immigration on the Problem of Immigration in Massachusetts* (*MCR*) is its use of photography. Whereas the *DCR* generally refrained from using visuals and opted to mainly present tables featuring numerical data, the *MCR* included a number of striking photographs to convey what immigrant lives looked like during the time.[36] The very first page of the report, even before the title, features an image of workers taken in a construction camp near Boston (fig. 13). Related to the discussion of housing conditions in the main body of the report, this picture provided readers with a vivid portrayal of what it was like to be a new immigrant. As the picture shows, the conditions were far from nice, and the men look tired. This image stood in a striking contrast to a photo in the section on evening schools for immigrants (fig. 14).

The caption for the evening schools photo explains that this picture was taken in an evening school class for Greek immigrants, featuring students of all ages. The students were all dressed up, with their hair neatly styled. The caption further notes that the students included "the educated and those

FIGURE 13. Immigrants in a construction camp. *MCR*, i.

FIGURE 14. Immigrants in an evening school. *MCR*, 128.

unable to read and write in any language." In this picture, immigrant men appear eager and energetic, full of passion for education.

The contrast between these two images clearly conveyed the overall argument of the *MCR*—that the immigrants were undesirable only because their social conditions were, and that government intervention by way of education and welfare could help them become better American citizens. Led by Lodge, the restrictionists had long advocated for literacy tests for immigrants, as reflected in the Dillingham Commission's final recommendation. In this context, the picture showcasing an evening class for illiterate immigrants delivered an unspoken yet strong rebuke of the restrictionist agenda. In a manner that recalled the discussion in *Dictionary* (see chapter 3), the *MCR* showed how illiterate migrants could learn to read and write and would become less undesirable over time, given the right opportunity and adequate support.

The criticisms of the Dillingham Commission's argument continued in the main body of the report. For instance, the *MCR*'s section on immigrant employment allocated many pages to refuting the displacement thesis put forward by the Dillingham Commission. According to the Dillingham Commission's conclusions, southern and eastern Europeans were taking jobs previously held by American workers, and this takeover was undermining "the American standard of living" by driving down the wages of low-skilled manual labor.[37] However, the Massachusetts Commission, using the Dillingham Commission's data, showed that this was an unsubstantiated claim. In fact, American workers had moved to better-paying jobs, and it was unusual for "employers to engage recent immigrants at wages actually lower than those prevailing at the time of their employment."[38] In a striking tone that anticipated the apparent biases of the German foreman in the previous section, the report noted that any attempts to rank employees by their efficiency would be "an expression of individual preference or prejudice rather than a business judgment"; defying the stereotype of immigrant labor as unskilled, it also added that "in the textile industry, where weaving is the most important and the most skilled work, the Polish and Lithuanian women are being used as weavers in increasingly large numbers."[39] In other words, through a close, critical reading of the *DCR*, the Massachusetts Commission debunked the findings of the federal investigation: Immigrant workers were not driving down wages; if anything, they were being paid less than their skill level and efficiency merited.

On the matter of crime, the *MCR* provided a nuanced account of what was reported as crime by police. The *DCR* data showed that immigrants committed less violent crimes and their run-ins with law enforcement concentrated on "drunkenness." On this issue, "often an objectionable habit or custom which the immigrant brings with him is allowed to become much more serious here," the *MCR* argued, "because of American indifference or lack of understanding." Apparently, police officers told the Massachusetts Commission that the "Poles would not give us any trouble if it weren't for their weddings." Oftentimes the weddings led to "drunkenness disorder" because American liquor was stronger and the Polish population in the United States was largely composed of young people. Instead of engaging in fearmongering based on stereotypes, the *MCR* recommended "co-operation between the church and the civil authority" to regulate these cultural gatherings. This line of reasoning was applied to other topics, such as welfare and education: A close scrutiny of the Dillingham Commission data by the Massachusetts Commission revealed that immigrants were less likely to be on welfare than their native-born counterparts, and many of their children attended American schools; when they did not, it was because the municipal governments did not invest enough in the public education system. Through these analyses, the Massachusetts Commission effectively revealed that immigrants were not separate, undesirable races to be feared and restricted but people temporarily struggling in an unfamiliar land. In other words, the *MCR* provided a different overarching framework of interpreting the Dillingham Commission's data based on racial liberalism, in which immigrants were not racially essentialized but merited sympathy and intervention to improve their social positions, so they could eventually develop "sympathetic relations with American institution and customs."

The *MCR* also discussed extensively the dangers of "white slavery"—young immigrant girls becoming victims of human trafficking and prostitution, due to their vulnerability.[40] However, in these pages, the *MCR*'s professed racial liberalism hovered closely to racial essentialism, showcasing the shared roots of the two sets of ideas in the desire to "define and rule" immigrants.[41] The report allocated many pages to the stories of young immigrant girls being picked up by suspect persons at the train station to be delivered directly into the clutches of pimps and gangsters in cities' red-light districts. In another vein, the survey of housing conditions addressed issues of safety and sanitation, but the *MCR* highlighted gender as the topic of utmost importance. Due to overcrowding, many young girls were housed under the same roof with young men who were not their immediate family members, and, according to the *MCR*, this was one of the most serious issues that immigrant communities faced. The *MCR* recommended intervention by the state as a solution to this urgent matter, by way of increased policing of pimps and gangs as well as more focused enforcement of housing regulations to uphold morality.

In addressing such issues within the domain of "moral concerns," however, the *MCR* echoed essentialist ideas, positing immigrant women as innocent, vulnerable victims in a dangerous urban environment. Conversely, the *MCR* portrayed men—or immigrant men in particular—as predators driven by their uncontrollable desire. In a sense, this perspective was only a few degrees removed from the likes of "race suicide" by Edward Ross, in which immigrants were imagined as reproducing irresistibly to supplant WASPs by outstripping their birthrate. In both accounts, immigrants were imagined as animal-like figures onto which American intellectuals projected their obsessions about sexuality. While human trafficking and coerced prostitution certainly existed during this time, it is debatable whether they were the most serious issues for immigrant communities. The focus on the sexual and reproductive behavior of immigrants revealed more about the American psyche than the immigrants themselves.

As many scholars of the early twentieth-century reform movements have argued, the sympathetic concern for immigrants went hand in hand with an urge to discipline their "immoral" ways of life.[42] The living arrangements and sexual practices of immigrants were certainly a "concern" for women like Edith and Grace Abbott. The moralistic, condescending undertone is clear in the following passage describing immigrant men's conditions: "With the men in the non-family groups the most serious difficulty is their general forlornness," because they "do not touch the outside world . . . they work long hours for low wages and are open to every temptation." The *MCR* warned that "abnormal vice develops dangerously among them." That is why mere enforcement of housing regulations was not enough, and "something more is necessary" to "meet the social needs of this group of young foreign men and women."[43] In short, instead of the *DCR*'s racial vision, the *MCR* presented a moral vision for immigrants, and in both cases the government was the medium through which a particular social order would be realized. And, of course, the two seemingly contradictory sentiments espoused by racial liberalism—benevolent sympathy and overbearing discipline—were connected at their roots through the desire to define and rule immigrants.

Against the "vice" of immigrant sexuality, racial essentialism proscribed exclusion while racial liberalism promoted active policing. We can better appreciate these two different approaches through the lens of racial governance, enacted by the racial state.[44] Many theorists of the racial state have argued that the state employs two contrasting modes of governance, approximately termed exclusion and inclusion, in its handling of population.[45] While racial others are labeled as such and excluded from the body politic, people who belong are disciplined into a proper mold befitting the nation. We see this dynamic in the Dillingham Commission and the Massachusetts

Commission: While the former excluded undesirable races, the latter inscribed how such groups could become desirable through social support and moral policing. And these seemingly contrasting but ultimately complementing modes of racial governance shared their foundation in the Dillingham Commission's data.

In projecting social needs on immigrants—"something more is necessary"—the *MCR* did not clearly define what "something" could be but occasionally alluded to "feelings" of belonging as a possible candidate. Discussing the naturalization ceremony, the *MCR* reported that many immigrants participating in the occasion "are shocked at the informality of the present procedure, and the whole thing seems to them to have been made coarse and cheap." The *MCR* envisioned that "appreciation of the responsibilities of citizenship would be increased if some sort of impressive ceremony were used when the final papers are granted." This is because "old-world people accustomed to dignified official procedure" could only be "taught to feel that they are entering upon a new period of their lives" through spectacular ceremonies.[46] In a condescending tone that is similar to the assimilation theory of the Chicago school of sociology (see chapter 4), the *MCR* pondered over engineering feelings of belonging among immigrants, possibly through a lavish ceremony that reminded them of their old homes under despotic rulers.

Although the Massachusetts Commission did not comment on the subject in an explicit manner, it is telling that the commission largely avoided using the concept of race in its report. Instead, the term *immigrants* was used to denote the commonality shared by both old and new immigrants, and the data supporting such commonality was presented to counter the Dillingham Commission's emphasis on race. In other words, whereas the Dillingham Commission focused on dividing up the larger category of Whiteness into smaller races, the Massachusetts Commission and pro-immigrant activists were trying to patch up those divisions, interrogating their empirical legitimacy and implying that all immigrants share a common humanity. By doing so, the *MCR* presented a different vision for the nation—one that was not concerned about race and hierarchy but focused on morality and a collective sense of belonging. Nonetheless, in both cases, immigrants were treated as objects on the receiving end of knowledge production and social engineering.

## ISAAC HOURWICH AND A SOCIALIST CRITIQUE

In addition to the Massachusetts Commission, Isaac Hourwich (1860–1924),[47] an economist working for the US Census Bureau, published a monograph refuting the Dillingham Commission's findings. *Immigration and Labor: The Economic Aspects of European Immigration to the United States* (1912) was an impressive work, to say the least: In a whopping 544 pages, Hourwich engages in the formidable task of deconstructing the almost entire forty-one-volume corpus of the Dillingham Commission, displaying his mastery of statistics and government-produced data. The fact that he wrote the book as the Dillingham Commission was still analyzing its data was even more remarkable.[48]

Isaac Hourwich's life trajectory was that of a stereotypical immigrant radical, except for the fact that he once worked for the federal government of the United States. Born to a middle-class family in Lithuania, Isaac Hourwich studied mathematics at the University of St. Petersburg. After his involvement with socialists, which led to a five-year exile in Siberia, Hourwich moved to New York City and earned a doctorate degree in economics from Columbia University. He published numerous important articles in academic journals; worked for various federal agencies, including the Census Bureau; and maintained an active presence in socialist and Zionist circles in both the United States and Russia. The American Jewish Committee, which sought to produce a counterargument to the Dillingham Commission's findings, recruited Hourwich to produce a monograph even before the inquiry was finished.[49] Based on his prior experience as an activist and statistician, he brought a dose of contemporary Marxism to the conversation: He wanted to cut through the muddled debate on immigration with scientific criticism and unveil the material base of the problem—that is, labor and its economic condition.

Hourwich begins his book by addressing Jenks and Lauck's thesis—namely, that immigration was primarily about economic concerns, not racial ones.[50] The *DCR*'s "conclusion has determined the scope of the present book," Hourwich writes, and he set out to treat "immigration solely as an economic question."[51] He acknowledged the Dillingham Commission's openness toward data, professed in Jenks and Lauck's book, but also pointed out that "there are few people who will go beyond the conclusion of the Commission and undertake the task of examining the evidence, presumably stored up in its voluminous report."[52] Of course, Hourwich was such a person.

Whereas the Massachusetts Commission focused on highlighting the obvious contradictions between data and conclusion in the *DCR*, Hourwich often reengineered the raw data itself, producing a different set of comparisons that overturned the commission's findings. The key was not comparing immigrant groups of different races in the same year to see which race stood out, as the Dillingham Commission had attempted; instead, Hourwich factored in the years of residence for each immigrant group and showed that the contemporary southern and eastern Europeans were moving along a trajectory not too different from the northern and western European immigrants of a few decades ago. To this end, Hourwich presented not just a snapshot but trends over time of various indicators to demonstrate the trajectory of different immigrant groups. Faithfully following the basic principles of statistical analysis—"finding the right comparison"—Hourwich conducted a sophisticated table-by-table analysis of the commission's data. In fact, his techniques were often much more advanced than the plain two-way cross tables filling the majority of the forty-one-volume, twenty-seven-thousand-page *DCR*.[53]

After an exhaustive review of the Dillingham Commission's data, Hourwich concludes that "the immigration commission, after a study of the earnings of more than half a million employees in mines and manufacture, has discovered no evidence that immigrants have been hired for less than the prevailing rates of wages."[54] Brushing aside restrictionist agitation by noting that "every complaint" against immigrants "was but an echo of complaints which were made at an earlier day against the new immigration from Ireland, Germany, and even from England," Hourwich rules that the Dillingham Commission's analysis was fundamentally misguided.[55] As far as statistics are concerned, the classification by race was at the heart of the problem because it "inevitably led to the slitting up of all statistical data into minute groups unfair for any generalizations."[56] Much like the Massachusetts Commission, Hourwich argued that "splitting up" was not a valid way to study immigrants. Speaking from a purely economic perspective, Hourwich emphasized that all immigrants, regardless of their race, were just workers with different skill levels and preferences.

"There is," Hourwich concludes, "consequently no specific 'immigration problem'" but "a general labor problem, which comprises many special problems, such as organization of labor, reduction of hours of labor, child labor, unemployment, prevention of work-accidents, etc."[57] His proposed solution was not immigration restriction but a classic socialist proposal: labor unions. Active union organizing among immigrant and nonimmigrants workers would naturally lead to better economic conditions for all workers and thereby ameliorate many social problems. On this point, Hourwich also criticizes the *DCR* for supposing unionization as "a sign of [immigrants'] assimilation" and "that the foreigner merely imitates the ways of the native [unions]." In fact, "the membership of most of the labor organizations has from their inception been very largely foreign-born."[58] Logically speaking, Hourwich suggests, if one was really concerned about the "American standards of living" and the plight of workers, as some restrictionists claimed, one should propose to accept more immigrants, not less, so they could contribute to labor organizing. He ends his 544-pages monograph by comparing immigration restriction to ill-conceived populist ideas of the past, such as the free silver movement.[59]

## Cross-Cutting Networks Leading to New Ideas

Throughout the 1910s and onward, the commission's data was taken up on many occasions. As many scholars have documented, this period coincided with the rise of American social sciences: moving away from reliance on Europe, the United States was emerging as a field of intellectual innovation, with social sciences at the forefront. Race was at the crossroads of this transformation as well. Whereas eugenics contributed much to the public understanding of race and heredity, professional social scientists were increasingly moving away from racial essentialism, and culture was emerging as an alternative framework.[60] As chapter 4 discusses, Franz Boas and W. I. Thomas were major proponents of this transition in their respective disciplines of anthropology and sociology. The reform tradition, represented by figures such as Jane Addams and organizations like the Massachusetts Commission on Immigration, also played a role in the process. Together, networks connecting educated professionals across government, business, and academia were emerging, and such networks were fueling the expansion of the federal government's policymaking capacities.[61]

The Dillingham Commission's data made a critical contribution to this larger trend by providing the infrastructure for a forum in which scholars of different opinions and backgrounds could engage in an evenhanded academic debate about immigration.[62] Experts on the commission, such as Jenks and Lauck, explicitly called for such debate, even while the transition to culture and assimilation was at odds with their vision of race, immigration, and national identity. Although the powerful executive committee members of the commission such as Lodge and Dillingham saw support for racial essentialism and immigration restriction in the commission's data, others saw a more liberal vision of nationhood, in which immigrants could assimilate to mainstream society over time.[63] Isaac Hourwich and Grace Abbott represent those tendencies. Although their origin was different from men like Lodge and Dillingham in terms of gender, class, and immigration status, their social worlds overlapped in the emerging institutions of higher education and policymaking circles of the federal government. While they had opposing perspectives on race and immigration, they still engaged in an academic debate with each other based on facts, in the process effectively formulating a discursive network that traversed the boundaries of class, gender, and immigration status. The assimilation debate in the ensuing decades occurred through this network, and its formation can be traced back to the facts that the Dillingham Commission produced at the turn of the century.

In writing about consolidation of "scientism" in American social sciences in the 1920s, Dorothy Ross notes the concept's appeal: "The children of immigrants . . . may have found the universalism, impersonality, and discipline of science attractive, for it could erase invidious ethnic difference as well as structure their experience of rapid social change."[64] We can put forward a similar argument for the prototype of scientism in the 1910s—namely, that of the fact-based discussions around immigration. People from different backgrounds came together amid chaotic social change and discussed immigration, mediated by facts collected by the government. These exchanges would contribute to the grafting of racial liberalism onto the long-standing tradition of racial essentialism.

[ CHAPTER SIX ]

# Japanese Immigrants and Insurmountable Difference

## One Data Set, Two Interpretations

Yamato Ichihashi (1878–1963) was a Japanese immigrant who worked as a special agent for the Dillingham Commission (see fig. 15). He collected statistical and ethnographic data for volumes 23, 24, and 25 of the *DCR*, collectively titled *Japanese and Other Immigrant Races in the Pacific Coast and Rocky Mountain States* (henceforth the *Pacific Coast Reports*).[1] The Dillingham Commission offered him the first job he took after graduating from Stanford University. Just like many other highly educated non-Whites of the time, Japanese immigrants and their children faced severe discrimination in the labor market and could not pursue white-collar jobs for which they were qualified. Thus, it is not surprising that Ichihashi took great pride in working for the United States federal government: The opportunity represented not just his acceptance in American society but also a hope for all Japanese immigrants, a hope that empirical data based on thoughtful observation would lead to mutual understanding and respect between the Japanese and Americans. More than seventy years later, Ichihashi's son, Woodrow, still remembered his father beaming with pride when he showed the Immigration Commission badge to his little son.[2]

Following his stint with the Dillingham Commission, Ichihashi went on to receive a PhD from Harvard University and eventually became the first tenured professor of Asian ancestry in the Department of History at Stanford University. The Dillingham Commission was a crucial turning point in his career. His dissertation as well as his most well-known work, *Japanese in the United States* (1932), was based on the data he collected for the commission. His use of the data, however, differed very much from that of the commission. Ichihashi argued that the data proved Japanese immigrants were more desirable as potential citizens than any other immigrant group—including not only the Chinese and Mexicans but also southern and eastern European immigrants, such as Italians, Greeks, and Poles.[3]

FIGURE 15. Yamato Ichihashi. Stanford Historical Photograph Collection (SC1071 BP 3381), Department of Special Collections and University Archives, Stanford University Libraries.

Based on the facts he collected for the commission, Ichihashi criticized the naturalization ban against Asian immigrants. The Naturalization Act of 1790 stipulated that only "aliens" who were "free white persons" could become US citizens through naturalization, if they met residency and other requirements. This ban effectively barred any non-White immigrants from obtaining American citizenship, regardless of how long they resided in the country's territory.[4] In Ichihashi's view, this ban failed to take recent data showing the so-called desirability of Japanese immigrants into account and therefore should be revised.

The commission, on the other hand, had different ideas about the same set of data. As Katherine Benton-Cohen has argued, Japan and Japanese immigration figured centrally in the legislative sequence leading up to the Immigration Act of 1907, which launched the commission (see chapter 2), and there was much interest in the data Ichihashi collected.[5] The restrictionists on the West Coast had been a staunch supporter of Theodore Roosevelt and his government, and the concern about "yellow peril" and the rise of Japan in the Pacific had a nationwide appeal. In a sense, the Dillingham Commission faced a genuine opportunity to intervene in the raging debate about Asian immigration by providing data on an unprecedented scale, the scope of which included all the West Coast states as well as Arizona and New Mexico. However, this initial interest did not translate to heightened focus in the final report. Most of the executive summary concerned southern and eastern European immigration and, in terms of policy recommendations, did not provide any new ideas, reaffirming the existing restrictions against Asian immigrants—the Chinese Exclusion Act of 1882 and the Gentlemen's Agreement of 1907.[6] The commission did not seem to be interested in what Ichihashi found through his data collection efforts. In a sense, the data was just lying there, tucked in the later volumes, waiting for someone to hear its voice.

The commission and Ichihashi had the same set of data, collected by Ichihashi and other Japanese students who worked as special agents. Two parties, however, differed radically on how the data should be interpreted and used. This chapter traces how these diverging interpretations emerged from the data and, more importantly, how in the process Japanese immigrants came to occupy a special place in the dominant racial order, one that was radically different from other European immigrants and native-born White Americans.

Like southern and eastern European immigrants, Japanese immigrants defied easy categorization because at least some commentators—Japanese immigrants themselves as well as their allies (see chapter 7)—saw them as fundamentally different from Chinese and other Asian immigrants. Ichihashi presented them as the epitome of desirability, a non-White group that should be accepted into the White body politic by way of their positive traits; the commission, on the contrary, saw them as not necessarily undesirable but deemed them to be "too different" to be included in the national community.[7] Ichihashi's lone advocacy for Japanese immigrants aside, this was the position eventually adopted by US immigration policy. As opposed to other European immigrants, whose difference was assumed to subside over time through assimilation, the difference embodied by the Japanese immigrants was deemed essential in the sense that it would not transform under any condition. Prior chapters traced how anti-immigrant mobilization unexpectedly gave birth to racial liberalism, represented by the triad of ethnicity, assimilation, and culture. This chapter documents the implicit principle that undergirded this development: the continuing significance of racial essentialism, represented through the boundary demarcating Whiteness. In this vein, Japanese immigrants were the exception that proved the rule of racial liberalism.

In sum, the Japanese case presented a contradiction in racial knowledge production. Of course, this was not taken as a serious issue because the executive committee members, as well as the public, were not much interested in revising their understanding of Asian immigration. As Ian Haney-López has shown in *White by Law*, Whiteness during the early twentieth century was a self-evident truth, defined by power and privilege and not through positive character. To the absolute majority of White Americans during the time, the boundary demarcating Whites and Asians was crystal clear, and no amount of data or effort could make it less so.[8] The case of Japanese immigrants, however, presents to us an intriguing thought exercise: What if someone had faithfully followed through with the promise of data? What if someone stood by the unruly facts and let them speak freely, instead of subjugating them under a political agenda? Could there have been a different configuration of racial order regarding Whiteness? The Dillingham Commission had at its disposal a seed of an alternative racial order, one in which desirability and Whiteness were decoupled from each other to allow for all immigrants to become Americans over time. Under this vision, racial liberalism, represented by the conceptual triad of ethnicity, culture, and assimilation, would apply to all immigrants regardless of their race, doing away with racial essentialism for good. Entertaining this hypothetical scenario leads us to reckon with the limits of racial liberalism—namely, that the ostensibly novel way of thinking about difference kept intact the most tenacious aspects of racial essentialism, with the former functioning as a protective belt around the latter. By examining Ichihashi's life and work, we can appreciate lost opportunities and interrupted trajectories underlying this process and obtain a more comprehensive picture of how we arrived at our present.

This chapter consists of two sections. First, I discuss the contents of the *Pacific Coast Reports* in detail, showing how Japanese immigrants were rendered both desirable and unfit for citizenship at the same time. I highlight the instances in which the commission employed different standards from those applied to southern and eastern Europeans as a strategy for characterizing Japanese immigrants as "unassimilable" aliens not belonging to the nation. By changing the standard against which different groups were evaluated, the commission created two dimensions of hierarchy to be applied in defining national belonging. The second section focuses on Ichihashi's efforts to use the commission's data in favor of Japanese immigrants. Unlike the inroads made by the pro-immigrant intellectuals and activists we see in other chapters, this effort would ultimately fail in gaining support from the US elite and public, and Japanese immigrants would remain "aliens ineligible for citizenship" until 1952. Defying the hopes of people like Ichihashi, Japanese immigrants and their children, many of whom were US citizens, would face an unprecedented ordeal of mass incarceration during World War II. I conclude the chapter by discussing how Japanese immigrants serve as an archetype of differences that cannot be overcome, as opposed to the differences of southern and eastern European immigrants, which were posited as surmountable through the concept of assimilation. In the end, this chapter explains the ways in which racial liberalism was still confined by racial essentialism.

## On the West Coast, a Different World of Immigration

Out of the forty-one volumes that compose the *DCR*, only three focused on the West Coast: Volumes 23, 24, and 25 focused on California, Oregon, and Washington as well as Colorado and Utah, with occasional mentions of the data from Idaho and Wyoming. In many aspects, these reports were different from other volumes. As opposed to other volumes focusing on the East Coast, South, and Midwest, these volumes highlighted the regional characteristics of the West, such as relative underdevelopment of manufacturing, reliance on agriculture, and chronic labor shortages in both cities and rural farming communities. The immigrant groups that received attention were different as well. In the table of contents for the *Pacific Coast Reports*, the commission presented a list of the major groups that needed empirical study. Here, rather than making fine distinctions among the European races as it had done in the other volumes, the commission settled with the umbrella category of "European and Canadian Immigrants" and did not bother to probe into differences within that vast category, although it did use terms such as Italians, Greeks, and Poles in the main body of the report. In other words, the differences among Europeans were in this instance not a priority for the commission. Instead, page after page was devoted to the groups that rarely appeared in the other volumes: Chinese, Japanese, "East Indians," and Mexicans.[9]

The three volumes of the *Pacific Coast Reports* amounted to approximately 2,100 pages and resembled other volumes in their subject matter and style. When examined closely, however, the *Pacific Coast Reports* reveal several critical differences. First, the concept of displacement—immigrant workers competing with and eventually replacing American workers—does not receive much attention, at least compared to the volumes that focused on the East Coast and Midwest. The Dillingham Commission was especially interested in the immigration history of industrial towns and allocated many pages to discuss whether and how the inflow of immigrant workers, mostly from southern and eastern Europe, had driven out American workers. In the *Pacific Coast Reports*, however, the concern about displacement, at least of American workers, was much less salient: There were not too many American workers to replace in the first place; instead, different immigrant groups arrived at different times and replaced each other to meet the fluctuating labor needs of the frontier.

For instance, under the section heading "Race Change," a report on the vineyards of Sonoma Valley brushed aside concerns about displacement: "The white race were never very numerous as grape pickers," and "the Chinese, from the beginning of the industry, predominated as pickers until they were largely replaced by Japanese. The Japanese now outnumber all other grape pickers about three to one." Of course, this transition had been propelled by the Chinese Exclusion Act of 1882. In addition to the Japanese, a few remaining Chinese and a small number of recently arrived "East Indians" worked as pickers in vineyards.[10] On the other hand, skilled labor, such as winemakers, had always been predominantly White. Racial division of labor was very much visible, but displacement did not occur because no "American workers" wanted the jobs held by Chinese, Japanese, South Asian, and Mexican workers.

Therefore, a typical report on a West Coast town would start with a mention of the Chinese, and sometimes Mexicans, who were at the bottom of the occupation hierarchy. The Exclusion Act brought a torrent of symbolic and physical threats to Chinese workers from local government and White workers, and many chose to voluntarily return home.[11] The remaining workers were growing old without being replenished by young immigrants. In many communities, Japanese immigrants began to fill this gap, starting around the 1880s. On the other hand, European immigrants, such as the Irish, Poles, and Italians, were trickling in from the East Coast, working in many industries alongside Japanese, Mexican, and aging Chinese workers. However, the European workers seldom stayed in unskilled jobs for more than two or three years—they moved around to improve their lot, and many opted for factory jobs in cities that provided higher wages and better job security. The labor demands of agriculture and railroad construction—still the most important industries in California and other western states—had been met mainly by the Chinese, and the Japanese were filling the gap left by the Chinese. In short, certain sectors created a free-for-all labor market in which a variety of immigrant groups were competing with each other for more jobs, better working conditions, and higher wages. The concept of displacement was ill-equipped to explain this complicated intersection of race and labor, and those who worked on the *Pacific Coast Reports* were fully aware of the fact.

Still, whenever possible, the Dillingham Commission attempted to retain a clear line separating the old immigrants from new immigrants, arguing that the difference between these two groups was just as marked on the West Coast as it was on the East. In discussing the workers employed in railroad construction, for example, the commission found that "social and political considerations all indicate that there exist two fairly distinct race groups, on the one hand the natives, north Europeans and Canadians, and on the other, the south and east Europeans, the Mexicans, and the Japanese." Instead of highlighting this larger divide, the commission focused more on how Mexicans and Japanese laborers stood out from other European immigrants. They were "chiefly employed at common labor, where mobility of labor is an advantage and where no educational qualifications obtain." Japanese and Mexican workers were employed in "gangs," which, as the commission asserted, removed them from "association with the natives and hence hinder[ed] the development of a civic interest among them and a desire for American citizenship."[12]

As a part of the larger *Immigrants in Industry* reports, the *Pacific Coast Reports* focused mainly on labor and not on the social and political aspects of immigrant lives. Other reports from the East Coast and Midwest paid considerable attention to how immigrants were living, presumably to assess the possibility of their eventual assimilation. On the West Coast, however, there was not much to discuss in terms of assimilation. Many of the immigrants were seasonal workers, and their housing often consisted of simple makeshift huts in which they would stay only while their seasonal jobs lasted. In many towns, there was no institutional infrastructure that catered to these immigrants, unlike in some eastern towns, where unions, schools, welfare offices, and police all actively interacted with immigrants in one way or another. Therefore, while the *Pacific Coast Reports* contained some discussion about assimilation, including English-language proficiency and citizenship acquisition, topics such as immigrants' crime rate and use of government aid rarely received attention. In the railroad construction industry, turnover was extremely high, and in farming communities, there were rapid changes among tenant farmers, day workers, and even farm owners. While a fraction of family-owned farms featured small-scale farming, the agriculture sector in general was characterized by large-scale operations that, due to the ongoing need of cheap, seasonal labor, saw the waxing and waning of different groups. In other volumes, the commission would have lamented such a state of affairs; conversely, in the *Pacific Coast Reports*, discussions about the social and political consequences of immigration were much more descriptive than normative.

Elsewhere, but for a very limited number of communities, the reports presented a radically different outlook on immigration and industry, in which racial distinctions existed but a hierarchy of racial groups seemed to be absent. In one mining town in Wyoming, "all races [were] on an equal footing."[13] In addition to Whites, Chinese and Japanese miners were "eligible to union membership and the relations engendered by the association which such membership entail[ed] [were] almost fraternal. Japanese and Chinese [wore] their union buttons with pride and [were] given the same treatment as other races." Given the widespread agitation against "oriental" labor in the West, and the fact that almost always unions were the main agitator, this small community, where "the races mingle[d] freely both at work and in their social life," was a notable exception.[14] In similar mining communities on the East Coast, by contrast, which were described in other volumes, there was always a strict racial hierarchy, and groups were segregated without much interaction between them: Native-born Whites (or "Americans," as they were often referred to) were on top, southern and eastern Europeans were in the middle, and Black workers were at the bottom. At least in a limited number of communities in the West, this racial triad was replaced by a "fraternal" bond among all kinds of workers, although the Chinese and Japanese occupied the bottom positions held by Blacks in the East.

In summary, the *Pacific Coast Reports* presented a multifaceted description of the social world on the West Coast and, unlike other volumes, did not dwell much on the friction between American workers and immigrant workers or the conflict between old immigrants and new immigrants. And perhaps because of this softening of the social divide, the findings from the *Pacific Coast Reports* were much less consequential in the overall summary and had a limited impact on the Dillingham Commission's overall conclusion and recommendations. However, these facts showcase that the reality was indeed much more complicated than the racial ideology upheld by immigration restrictionists indicated. Regardless of whether they were highlighted, these unruly facts remained there to be discovered and mobilized. As we saw in the cases of pro-immigrant advocates (see chapter 5), some of those mobilizations were highly consequential in the long term. Others were less so, as we see with the life of Yamato Ichihashi. But together all of these realized and unrealized possibilities constitute the particular trajectory through which we have arrived at our current understanding of race and ethnicity.

In the policy recommendation featured in the executive summary of the *DCR*, only three simple points pertain to the findings of the *Pacific Coast Reports*. The commission argued that the Chinese Exclusion Act should stand; the Gentlemen's Agreement, which prevented Japanese and Korean workers from entering the country, should also stand, as long as it remained an effective means of controlling immigration from the Far East. The only new recommendation was that the US government should consult with the British government to prevent further migration from the British India.[15] Perhaps in the *Pacific Coast Reports*, the Dillingham Commission was the most faithful to its founding principle—conducting a fact-finding inquiry and nothing more, nothing less.

## Japanese Immigrants: "Ambitious and Progressive"

As with other fact-finding activities of the commission, however, the empirical reality of Japanese immigration on the West Coast did not always substantiate the commission's preconceived notion of racial hierarchy. This is most evident in the sections dedicated to Japanese immigrants, featured in volume 23.

A dilemma arose from findings that suggested Japanese immigrants on the West Coast were "too good": They embodied almost all the positive characteristics attributed to desirable immigrants, except that they were not White. According to the Dillingham Commission's data, they were hard workers, many of them intended on settling down permanently as farmers, they dressed in Western-style clothing and tried hard to learn and speak English, they did not commit crimes and stayed away from drinking and gambling, they desired to get married and raise families, and they were willing to endure hard times in order to move up the socioeconomic ladder. Discussing the general quality and character of Japanese workers in agriculture, the commission wrote, "For several years the Japanese were favorably received and praised for their industry, quickness, adaptability, and eagerness to learn American ways."[16]

In other words, they possessed all the traits that the commission described as "progressive." The concept meant many things in this era—the Progressive Era—but in the context of the Dillingham Commission, it meant that certain "progressive" immigrant groups were rapidly moving in a positive direction, improving their so-called desirability; for instance, Italian and Polish workers were often regarded as not progressive because, according to the Dillingham Commission and popular stereotypes, they had no intention of settling down in the United States and often worked in nonskilled temporary jobs, only to spend all their weekly wages on their weekend drinking rituals. These workers often associated only among themselves, usually in their ethnic enclaves, which, again, according to the Dillingham Commission, were hotbeds of crime and immoral behavior. German immigrants, on the contrary, often saved money, bought a patch of land, and made the transition from being unskilled workers to independent farmers. By doing so, they moved out of the ethnic enclaves and blended in with other Americans. Civic and cultural adaptation—naturalization, being interested in community affairs, speaking English, and adopting American customs—naturally followed. Throughout all the other volumes of the *DCR*, being progressive was equated with old immigrants and their desirability; southern and eastern European immigrants were not progressive because they stuck to their ways and could not adapt to their new environment.

Within this framework, the *Pacific Coast Reports* showed Japanese immigrants to be much more progressive than Chinese or Mexican workers and possibly more so than southern and eastern European workers. A basic summary of statistical data on English-language acquisition showed that "among those who had been in the United States less than five years the Japanese and Koreans show relatively great progress." And the Japanese who had been in the United States for more than five years "showed more progress than other races except the North Europeans."[17] Japanese "progress" was underscored through comparison with other non-White groups who worked in similar positions, such as seasonal farmwork: "The slow progress of the Chinese and Mexicans in this regard stands in striking contrast to the rapidity with which the Japanese have acquired our language, especially since these races have always been employed in much the same kind of seasonal work and have lived under much the same conditions."[18] In other words, while working side by side with the Chinese and Mexicans, Japanese immigrants picked up English much more rapidly and, perhaps as a consequence, were more successful in moving upward. To account for this difference, the commission reverted to cultural stereotypes: "The Chinese have always been self-satisfied and have looked back toward their old civilization as the only culture worth the while. The Mexican laborers, on the other hand, are notoriously indolent and unprogressive in all matters of education and culture, and evince little desire to learn to speak English."[19] The common trope of orientalism—that the "Orientals" tend to cling to their old culture while refusing to accept modernity—applied to the Chinese but not to the Japanese. Ironically, the Dillingham Commission was making claims that were in sync with Japanese ideologues who preached the supposed distinctiveness of Japan from other Asian countries (see chapter 2): The stereotypes about the "Orientals" somehow did not apply to the Japanese, whose superiority was manifested by its empire engaged in European-style colonialism over other countries in Asia.

As historian Eiichiro Azuma has documented in *Between Two Empires: Race, History, and Transnationalism in Japanese America*, this was not very different from how the Japanese immigrants understood themselves—as decisively different from other non-White groups, such as the Chinese, Mexicans, or Filipinos. When the Dillingham Commission wrote that "the Japanese compare favorably with the households of north European immigrants," it was confirming the longtime aspirations of Japanese immigrants themselves.[20]

The progressive qualities of Japanese immigrants were elaborated in discussions of their economic mobility—progressing from seasonal farmwork to tenant farming and eventually owning small farms. Like Chinese workers before them, many Japanese immigrants started as seasonal workers, supplanting White workers through their willingness to accept harsh conditions and longer working hours for lower pay. "Reliable white persons have found it easy to secure more remunerative and agreeable employment," the Dillingham Commission observed, "while Japanese, being more regular in their work, more willing to work long hours, and more easily secured when needed, have been preferred by the employers to the less desirable class of white persons available." Unlike southern and eastern European immigrants discussed in other volumes, employers found the Japanese "more satisfactory at the rate of wages they are paid than the white men available for work as common laborers at the wages they command in the industry."[21]

At the same time, the Dillingham Commission recognized that the Japanese were ambitious to leave the lowest strata of labor market and climb the socioeconomic ladder: "The members of this race do not like to work for wages, are ambitious, and desire to establish themselves as business men or as independent producers, as most of them were in their native land . . . furthermore, the Japanese are venturesome."[22] Unlike Chinese and Mexican farmworkers, who seemed to have no aim other than getting seasonal work for immediate economic gain, according to the commission, the Japanese actually had long-term plans of becoming independent farmers themselves. The section on tenant farming details how the Japanese were achieving their goals: Using strong ethnic networks, they put together money saved and provided funds to individuals who were buying land or leasing farms to engage in tenant farming. Typically, such arrangements would entail high risks for the tenant. The lessee would often be charged with the price of using the tools and seed, paid directly to the lessor, and would be forced to work in the most undesirable plot in the whole farm. After the harvest, the owner would take a fixed amount from the returns, relegating all the risks ranging from weather conditions to fluctuating crop prices to the tenant. In a sense, tenant farming was a gamble—one could hope for large returns in good years, yet if things went wrong, one would lose the investment in addition to the value of one's labor.

Remarkably, according to the Dillingham Commission, many Japanese immigrants emerged as winners in this gamble, eventually buying high-quality farmlands in areas such as San Jose, the Central Valley, and along the Sacramento River. Once established, these farmers hired newly arriving Japanese workers as seasonal laborers, so the cycle of upward mobility among the Japanese continued. In addition, the settled Japanese farmers married, often by bringing women from Japan—the infamous "picture brides" story partially originated from this practice[23]—and had children. Even in cities, Japanese immigrants made rapid progress as small business owners, catering to both White and Japanese clientele, and San Francisco and Seattle developed clusters of Japanese businesses throughout the city.[24]

In many aspects, Japanese immigrants were the embodiment of the immigrant success story, which the Dillingham Commission supposedly cherished. The commission found that unlike most southern and eastern Europeans, or the Chinese workers a generation before them, Japanese immigrants did not come into the United States merely for economic gain. Instead, they were motivated, self-sustaining individuals who seemed to value everything that was American: English language, family, hard work, and independent living through the ownership of farms or small businesses. Japanese immigrants perfectly fit into the criteria of being desirable, except for the fact that they were not White. In a sense, the Japanese immigrants presented a conundrum in racial knowledge production: Desirability and Whiteness did not exactly overlap, and the fact begged for an explanation.

## "Differing So Greatly"

The commission's answer to this conundrum was to refine the criteria, or "move the goal post," as the contemporary discussion of race and standards of evaluation has termed this practice. Simply put, once Japanese immigrants turned out to meet the standard of desirability, they were subjected to further scrutiny with a different set of standards, one that would surely fail them.

After explaining these positive traits, the commission pointed out that all those seemingly positive traits made the Japanese a target of prejudice and discrimination. As much as employers praised the Japanese for being industrious and ambitious, the Dillingham Commission found, they condemned the Japanese for their self-interest. Everywhere they go, "the Japanese . . . [were] condemned by every economic class." This is because "the economic interests of all classes are believed to be adversely affected by the presence of or by the methods pursued by the Japanese." Workers resented the Japanese for their willingness to take on difficult jobs for low wages and their tendency to put up with the worst living conditions. Farm owners, who increasingly relied on Japanese workers, were beginning to see that unlike the Chinese workers, the new seasonal laborers were not as docile: "The recently established custom of taking a smoking and resting period of from five to fifteen minutes when they finish weeding or cultivating a row of celery has grown out of this independent spirit due to their control of the labor situation."[25] The Japanese were acceptable as long as they filled the void left by the Chinese but "were not as satisfactory laborers as the Chinese." Japanese ambitions were at once admirable and noisome because "they are more progressive and desirous of rising above the wage relation; they are ambitious to enter other lines of work besides the lowest kind of farm labor; they have come to make more frequent demands for higher wages and better living conditions than the Chinese."[26] In short, the Japanese were less likely to accept the status quo, and employers did not like their rebelliousness.

The resentment quickly escalated into moral condemnation of their "methods": The Japanese immigrants working as grape pickers, the commission reported, were "careless in their work and dishonest." "In their zeal to make large earnings . . . they make great haste while picking . . . they do not pick the grapes properly, wasting some and leaving others unpicked upon." Employers argued that "the Chinese and Indians stand in strong contrast to the Japanese in this regard."[27] Similar accusations were leveled at Japanese tenant farmers as well. Whereas the Chinese tenant farmers were "entirely honest in all contractual relations" and "[did] not abandon their leases," the Japanese tenant farmers' "standing . . . [was] much lower." Oftentimes they would abandon the leased land, leading the farm owners to seek out other tenant farmers within a single harvest cycle. This led landowners to often require Japanese tenants to pay their rents in advance.[28]

This resentment led to isolation and alienation from local communities. While they were in some respects model immigrants who embodied the progressive ideal, the Japanese were categorically barred from obtaining American citizenship, since the Naturalization Act of 1790 limited naturalization rights only to "free white persons."[29] With the exception of children who were born on American soil, the Japanese remained alien subjects while working on their farms and raising their families, regardless of how many years they had resided in the United States or how progressive they were.

Ironically, the Dillingham Commission saw much promise in Japanese immigrants' potential for civic engagement, even more so than for European groups who could obtain citizenship shortly after meeting residency and other requirements. In a report on a farming community in Sacramento County, the commission reported on whether and what kind of newspapers the immigrant residents subscribed to in their homes. Reading newspapers, the commission reasoned, displayed "to what extent these farmers have been assimilated" and testified to "their standards of living." Italian and Portuguese farmers, it turned out, displayed disappointing results in this respect: Only half of the Italians and 20 percent of the Portuguese farmers subscribed to any newspaper at all. The Japanese, on the other hand, were very impressive: "Of 128 [Japanese] families . . . only 18 subscribed for no paper at all." In addition, "two-thirds of them subscribed for two or more," whereas other groups rarely went beyond one newspaper. To be fair, almost all of these farmers subscribed to the papers printed in their language. For instance, the Italian farmers' readership was confined to "a small paper published in Stockton, or [another paper] published by Italians in San Francisco." Although an absolute majority of the Japanese read Japanese-language newspapers (103 out of 110), some of them subscribed to an English-language newspaper as well.[30] By all measures, it appeared that the Japanese farmers in this village in Sacramento County were closer to the ideal of an independent, informed, and self-sufficient citizenry than Italian and Portuguese farmers were.

However, there was a key difference between the Japanese and other immigrant groups, if not American society more generally. Although the Dillingham Commission found that "the Japanese are greatly interested in political matters, are intelligent, quick to absorb new ideas, and progressive," there was something elusive about them—for instance, the fact that they "have been accustomed to a somewhat different form of government and have exhibited a strength of feeling for a loyalty to their country and its Government and the Mikado, seldom, if ever, found among other people."[31] In other words, the Japanese were exceptional, in both a positive and negative sense: "The Japanese have a comparatively small percentage of illiterates among them, are intelligent and eager to learn of American institutions, make fairly rapid progress in learning to speak English, and unusually good progress in learning to read and write it. They have not proved to be burdensome to the community because of pauperism or crime." This was an exceptional quality for a recent immigrant group, as shown throughout the *DCR*. At the same time, however, "the Japanese, like the Chinese, are regarded as differing so greatly from the white races that they have lived in but as not integral part of the community. A strong public opinion has segregated them, if not in their work, in the other details of their living, and practically forbids, when not expressed in law, marriage between them and persons of the white race."[32] As a response, Japanese immigrants shunned community life as well: "The race antipathy [against the Japanese] has done much to cause and to perpetuate the clannishness of the Japanese immigrants."[33] This mutual avoidance led to the fact that the Japanese "process of assimilation has not been proceeded far, save in the learning of English and in the adoption of American clothes and some American business methods. . . . The associations between the Japanese and white race are limited, and, with few exceptions, not upon the basis of equality."[34]

In short, the character traits that made the Japanese "desirable" in the first place also rendered them as "differing so greatly" from American social norms, removed from community life, even among other immigrants more generally. The tradition of assimilation theory in sociology has long treated this cultural difference as temporary, something that would naturally diminish as immigrants move upward and come into increased contact with mainstream society.[35] The Dillingham Commission, however, was already presenting evidence against the theory of wholesale assimilation a good half century before its heyday: In discussing the success of Japanese business owners in Seattle, the commission found that "a few Japanese businessmen find a place in the social life of the city. But here, as elsewhere, and for the same reasons of racial, language, and institutional differences and brief and more or less temporary residence, the Japanese are farther removed from normal American life than any European immigrant race."[36] Even successful business owners had to endure strong prejudice, to the extent that the everyday operation of their business activity became a focus for anti-Japanese sentiment.

In response, a couple of Japanese laundry owners in Seattle came up with the ingenious idea of putting White faces on their businesses in order to avoid prejudice. "Two of the Japanese laundries employ white collectors," the commission explained, "[to] secure some white patrons who do not know that the laundries are conducted by Asiatics." As we have already seen, the Japanese immigrants displayed a range of characteristics associated with being desirable, except for having the appearance of Whites, regardless of how the notion was defined. In an ironic attempt to reduce the social distance between themselves and the majority White residents, these two savvy business owners employed White employees to interact with their customers, while they managed the operations of their laundromats behind the scenes of social interaction. As the commission immediately added after noting this practice, however, most of the patronage secured by the Japanese laundromats was to be accounted for on economic grounds: "Their prices were generally lower than those charged by their white competitors."[37] In other words, their success and desirability were confined to the economic domain, while in social respects the Japanese immigrants remained ever-distant, inscrutable aliens whose differences could not be comprehended by the so-called American mind. As many scholars of Asian Americans in the late twentieth century have noted, the mismatch between economic mobility and civic alienation was the key feature defining the Japanese immigrants described in the Dillingham Commission.[38]

In summary, Japanese immigrants were in a double bind: The traits that made them progressive and desirable simultaneously made them "diff[er] so greatly" because they did not fit into the stereotype of the compliant immigrant worker, which, according to the employers interviewed by commission agents, the Chinese workers had been so successful in fulfilling. If anything, the commission officially maintained a neutral stance toward this finding: It did acknowledge that the predicament of the Japanese immigrant largely originated from the prejudice held by native-born Whites. At the same time, the commission clearly did not tout the Japanese as a "model minority" as some commentators would do after World War II; the Japanese remained an exceptional case in the hierarchy of race and desirability,[39] but not to the extent that endangered the entire worldview the commission envisioned. Therefore, the commission decided to remain in the realm of facts, faithfully report what they found, and recommend that the existing restrictions against Asian immigrants, including the Japanese, should be maintained. The commission moved on to contend with other matters of interest to restrictionists, such as the fate of southern and eastern European immigrants. In the case of the Japanese, the unruly facts were left to stand—largely, because they were unlikely to be consequential.

## Japanese Immigrants in Context: Ichihashi as a "Schoolboy"

Yamato Ichihashi, the Japanese student who collected data for the commission, did not move on. In fact, much of his academic career was devoted to building on his work with the Dillingham Commission. Ichihashi used the commission's unruly facts, as well as the additional data he collected throughout the decades following the commission's inquiry, to advocate for the naturalization rights of Japanese immigrants.

This was surely a radical cause in early twentieth-century America, which had limited naturalization rights to "free white persons" for more than a century. Yet as Ian Haney-López has documented, challenges to the ban never ceased and reached their peak with a series of high-profile Supreme Court cases in the early twentieth century, including *Ozawa v. United States* (1922) and *Thind v. United States* (1923).[40] Takao Ozawa was a successful businessman from Hawaii who graduated from the University of California, Berkeley. He challenged the naturalization ban on the grounds that he embodied American culture as much as any other White man and that his fair skin deemed him White even though he acknowledged that he was a member of "the Japanese race." The Supreme Court rejected his argument by asserting that Whiteness had less to do with the color of one's skin or cultural assimilation and more with being a member of the Caucasian race. However, just a year later, the court provided a very different rationale in rejecting the challenge posed by an Indian immigrant, Bhagat Sing Thind. Thind argued that contemporary race-thinking considered Indians a branch of the "Aryan race," thereby classing people like himself as a member of the Caucasian race. While the court did acknowledge that on scientific grounds, Indians and Europeans shared a common ancestry to some degree, it rejected Thind's challenge by noting that Whiteness was more than just a scientific concept: "It may be true that the blond Scandinavian and the brown Hindu have a common ancestor in the dim reaches of antiquity, but the average man knows perfectly well that there are unmistakable and profound difference between them today."[41] In other words, Whiteness was to be defined by "the average man" through his common sense. While the set of rulings may have quelled the legal challenges for a time, the logic of the Supreme Court persuaded no one, and Ichihashi sought a different venue to challenge its defense of Whiteness: social science and facts.

To properly contextualize the debate about naturalization rights for Japanese immigrants, we need to first understand why Japanese immigrants believed they were different from other Asian immigrants, most notably the Chinese workers who had arrived in the United States before them. This belief had at least some factual basis.

Sociologists Min Zhou and Jennifer Lee have suggested a theory of "hyper-selection" to explain the relatively high rate of upward mobility among post-1965 Asian immigrants: Those from Korea, China, Taiwan, and India were much more educated than immigrants from other countries, and this relative advantage in education level accounts for much of their subsequent economic and educational mobility. In other words, although they looked like they "started from the bottom," so to speak, like all other immigrants, some of the post-1965 Asian immigrants in fact were a few steps above others in their human capital.[42]

We can apply the same explanation to the case of Japanese immigrants around the turn of the twentieth century. Unlike Chinese immigrants, who hailed from the poverty-stricken farm villages of Taishan with a basic level of schooling, if any,[43] Japanese immigrants arrived with the experience of a modern education system. The Meiji Restoration of 1868 led to an unprecedented level of social upheaval in Japan: As the island nation opened itself up to Western powers and embarked on the so-called modernization of its society and culture, many Japanese were forced to reckon with a new way of life. Those in the middle strata of the traditional status system were most impacted: Landowning small farmers and samurais, the backbones of the feudal society of the Edo period, were left to fend for themselves in free-market capitalism, in which land and money were increasingly concentrated in the hands of the few. To sons born after the Meiji Restoration in such families, it was clear that they could not follow in the footsteps of their fathers when envisioning their lives. Modern agricultural technology made it impossible for small landowning farmers to compete with large corporations. The Meiji government prohibited civilians from carrying swords, rendering samurais socially obsolete. Young lower-middle-class Japanese men understood clearly that they needed to take risks and do something to survive in the winner-takes-all world of unfettered capitalism and imperialism.

Many of these men received up to a high school education and garnered some understanding of the world beyond Japan, along with an exposure to the English language. Migration to the United States provided a perfect opportunity to imagine a different life: They wanted to work and study in the United States to survive and even succeed in a rapidly changing world. While these Japanese immigrants came to fill the gap in the labor market left by aging Chinese workers, they came with a different mindset, at least according to some of them. Rather than focusing on saving money to return home quickly, as the Chinese workers had done a generation ago, Japanese immigrants aspired to improve their socioeconomic position and settle in the United States: They wanted to earn money, but at the same time they looked for opportunities to pursue education.[44]

By all accounts, Yamato Ichihashi's early life perfectly encapsulated this tendency among Japanese immigrants. A son of a small farmer from Nagoya, Ichihashi landed at San Francisco in 1894 as a sixteen-year-old.[45] He put himself through high school and community college, most likely working as domestic help in an affluent San Francisco household. Eventually he received his bachelor's and master's degrees in economics from Stanford University, followed by a PhD in history from Harvard University. Afterward, Ichihashi became a tenured faculty member in the Department of History at Stanford University, a clearly impressive achievement in an era that granted hardly any professional opportunities for non-Whites.

Ichihashi did not leave many records about his early life, especially from the time before he entered Stanford, but we can indirectly infer that he was a domestic worker. During the early twentieth century, many Japanese students who came to study in the United States worked in White households, especially in San Francisco, in exchange for room and board. Ichihashi, in his later writings as a Stanford professor, described the ambitions and tribulations of these "schoolboys" with intimate detail, praising their "progressive spirit."[46] However, there was a reason that domestic work was left for young Asian male immigrants on the West Coast: It was an emasculating occupation. Male domestic servants worked near and under the direction of housewives and thus were seen as "boys" regardless of their actual age. The cartoon strip shown in figure 16 portrays the realities of schoolboys during the era.

This comic strip is based on the personal experience of the artist, Henry Kiyama, who arrived in San Francisco from Japan in 1904 as a teenager.[47] In the comic strip, the schoolboy is sent to an American household to do menial chores, such as peeling onions and potatoes. Even though he had received good grades in English back in school, he could not understand what the lady of the house was telling him. Nevertheless, the schoolboy was content that he was making much more than he would have in Japan as a town hall clerk. Many of Kiyama's comic strips end with dark comedy like that shown in this one, in which the main protagonist is told to "go home" by others, usually White, native-born Americans. The narrative reflects how Japanese schoolboys, including Ichihashi, faced an intense pressure, to say the least: They had to work and study while facing racial discrimination and exclusion. "Going home" was not an act chosen from nostalgia but a sign of failure, proof that they had been rejected by American society.

Perhaps the adversity led to their unique consciousness: Japanese immigrants saw themselves as ambitious and progressive people capable of overcoming barriers through effort and mutual support. Influenced by the nationalist ideology espoused by the Japanese Empire, they saw themselves as representing their nation's ascent on the global stage. Just like the way Lodge and Roosevelt imagined Anglo-Saxons (see chapter 1), Japanese immigrants saw their individual trajectory as embodying the historical trajectory of their people, the only non-Western nation to be on par with Western superpowers through late modernization.[48] More pointedly, they

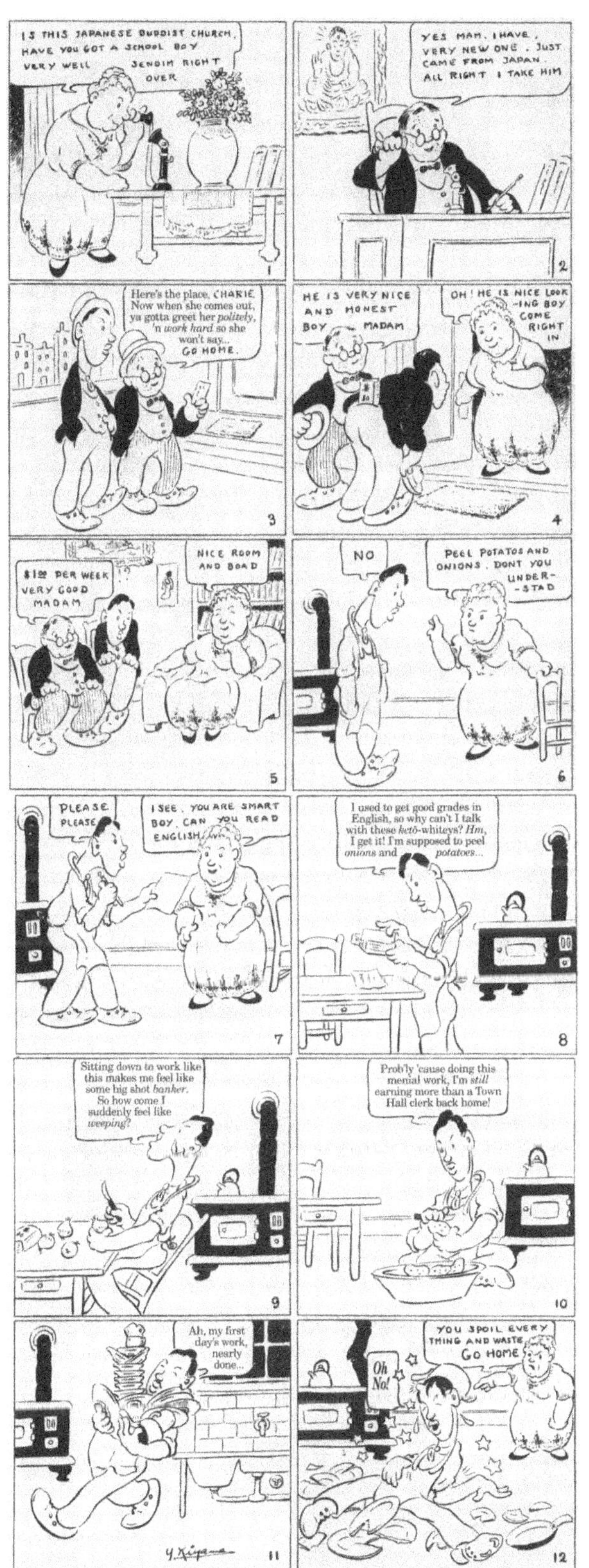


FIGURE 16. "Schoolboys." Kiyma, *Four Immigrants Manga*.

maintained that they were, for these reasons, different from other immigrants, especially Chinese workers. In fact, in 1905, the Japanese Empire had emerged victorious in its war against Russia, the first-ever victory by a non-White nation in the modern era of imperialism. As such, Japanese immigrants did not want to be treated the same as people from the so-called backward nation of China. Early twentieth-century Japanese immigrants did everything they could to distance themselves from Chinese and other Asian immigrants, a tendency Azuma terms "de-sinofication."[49]

While most White Americans did not distinguish between Japanese and Chinese, many White elites in the early twentieth century maintained a certain fascination with the former and a strong contempt for the latter. In fact, when faced with the San Francisco Japanese schoolchildren crisis in 1906 (see chapter 2), President Theodore Roosevelt himself advocated for an exception to the law of Asian exclusion, hinting at his support for the naturalization rights of the Japanese in his congressional address, in which he praised the "decency of character" found in many Japanese immigrants.[50] Such inclusion, Roosevelt argued, would further US interests in the Pacific as well as fortify the position of Japanese immigrants within the mainland United States, ultimately benefiting all those involved. Theodore Roosevelt himself participated in weekly sessions of martial arts in the White House, facilitated by an instructor from Japan.[51] Perhaps because of this personal relationship, he could see their supposed "decency of character."

David Starr Jordan (1851–1931), an ichthyologist and the president of Stanford University at the turn of the century, was an avid advocate for eugenics and a racial theory of human differences.[52] At the same time, he was fascinated by Japan and its people and served as a lifelong supporter and mentor for Ichihashi. Jordan's infatuation began with his fieldwork in the country in 1900. As a student of Louis Agassiz (see chapter 1), he was deeply invested in botany and ichthyology and conducted a number of research trips to collect fish that no one had ever studied. This led him to Japan, a secluded island nation not very well known to Westerners. During the trip, he was greatly impressed by Japanese scientists who displayed sophisticated understanding of the nation's fauna and flora.[53] The impression affected his vision for Stanford as well: Jordan was mindful of the new university's location and fully embraced the institution's potential to build ties across the Pacific. He saw it as the place where newly emerging trans-Pacific elites could be educated, somewhat akin to the manner in which the Ivy League universities educated elites who exemplified the ideal mix of classic European high culture and vibrant American spirit.

As a biologist, he adhered to then-popular ideas of eugenics and social Darwinism; at the same time, he was a Japanophile who held Japanese people and culture in high esteem, characterizing them as "in full harmony with the nations of Europe." He even attempted to expand contemporary racial theory to label Japanese as Caucasians, arguing that the people of the islands originated farther west and had no connection to "Mongolian" races such as the Chinese and Koreans.[54] The Japanophile university president paid special attention to Japanese students at Stanford as well, inviting them to a dinner at his house annually and visiting their dorms in person.[55] During a time when male Chinese and Japanese immigrants worked as cooks and maids for faculty members in their campus housing, these gestures defied social conventions and bestowed an aura of legitimacy to the small group of Japanese students on the campus. In these more liberal encounters, Jordan quickly noticed Ichihashi, the leader of the group, and throughout Ichihashi's career he would serve as an invaluable professional reference and mentor.

As a first step of a lifelong sponsorship, Jordan recommended Ichihashi to the PhD program in economics at Harvard upon his graduation from Stanford. After completing his work with the Dillingham Commission for a couple of years, Ichihashi moved to Cambridge, Massachusetts, to embark on his doctoral work. His dissertation was chaired by none other than William Z. Ripley, whose theories about racial difference among Europeans formed the backbone of the Dillingham Commission's inquiry (see chapter 1); Fredric Jackson Turner, who developed the frontier thesis (1893), also served as a committee member.[56] In 1913, Ichihashi wrote and submitted a dissertation that focused on Japanese immigrants in California, using the data he had collected for the Dillingham Commission. Interestingly, even at the time of filing his dissertation, he "[had] not read a page of those intensive and doubtless most impartial studies"—the *Dillingham Commission Reports*—because it "had not been accessible" to him, although the reports were published in 1911. However, he was confident in the data and analysis featured in the dissertation, because he had been "the chief instrument in gathering the data" while visiting various places such as the "fishery at Monterey, sugar beet industry in Salinas, vineyards of Fresno and potato and asparagus field in Stockton."[57] After finishing his dissertation, Ichihashi returned to Stanford at the urging of Jordan and eventually rose to the rank of a tenured, full professor in the Department of History.[58]

In many ways Ichihashi represented what he advocated for: an ambitious, "progressive" Japanese immigrant who was willing to settle and move upward in American society. His effort and talent outmatched those of his competitors, as seen from his unlikely ascent through American higher education. Yet he was still deemed "unassimilable" and banned from naturalizing as a citizen of the United States, even after he had spent more than four decades living in the country while building a remarkable career. The contrast between race and ethnicity as insurmountable and redeemable difference, respectively, manifested in his life trajectory: He did everything he could to overcome his racial identity as a non-White person and carve out a space for himself, but he was still haunted by the essentialized conception of difference, which categorized him as someone who should "go home." In the following section, I narrate how these tensions played out in his life and how his advocacy for the rights of Japanese immigrants met a tragic end in the mass incarceration of Japanese Americans during World War II. Taken together, his life and work demonstrate how racial liberalism complemented—rather than dismantled—the reign of racial essentialism by championing White immigrants over non-White ones.

## *Japanese in the United States* (1932): Advocating for Racial Accommodation

In 1932, at the height of his academic career and almost two decades after receiving his PhD, Ichihashi finally finished revising his dissertation and published it as *Japanese in the United States*. In addition to the data he and three other Japanese students had collected for the Dillingham Commission, he conducted additional fieldwork in California and engaged in an extensive analysis of immigration restriction movements during the 1910s and 1920s. Following faithfully the Dillingham Commission's mantra, Ichihashi aimed to "have his readers draw their own conclusions [regarding Japanese immigrants] so long as they judge by facts and not by hearsay."[59]

However, Ichihashi had mixed feelings about the *Pacific Coast Reports* and the Dillingham Commission more generally. As he notes in the acknowledgments of his dissertation, he initially expressed great pride in having worked in a federally funded scientific project. However, after the publication of the *DCR* and experiencing intense anti-immigrant sentiments in the 1910s and early 1920s, during which the push for immigration restriction gradually overpowered pro-immigrant forces in every corner of American society, Ichihashi found himself at odds with the Dillingham Commission. In the introduction to *Japanese in the United States*, he laid out the trajectory of the book as well as his professional life: "The writer has been a resident of the United States for nearly thirty years, mostly in California; he has been through thick and thin in everything pertaining to the Japanese residents and has a good deal of first-hand information. His academic interest in the subject began some twenty years ago . . . as an agent of the United States Immigration Commission of 1908–1910 . . . since then it has been his desire to improve his study for publication." Throughout the book, Ichihashi quoted extensively from the *Pacific Coast Reports* and used its data—which he himself had collected—to provide "an impartial presentation of facts relating to [Japanese immigrants]."[60]

Although he did not engage in a direct, overt criticism of the Dillingham Commission, his feelings about the organization became clear when he discussed its findings, specifically those on the "Alaska boys," the Japanese immigrants working in salmon canneries in Alaska. Unlike in other places, such as rural California, in Alaska the Japanese were portrayed as "the worst" compared to other groups in the *DCR*. Ichihashi pointed out that "the Commission's agents failed to secure data concerning the other races [besides Japanese]" and confessed that he had not known "the information was to be used in a comparative way." In other words, when he was working for the commission, he had taken the commission's inquiry at face value, perhaps revealing his own naive perspective as a recent college graduate: He had thought the commission was sincerely interested in finding facts about Japanese immigrants in the United States and had not pondered the possibility that the information would be used to compare groups with each other and place them along a scale of desirability. Criticizing the commission's bias, Ichihashi himself expressed a rather universalistic view concerning all immigrants regardless of their "race": "However, such a treatment of data on Japanese men does not make their case any worse; they are bad enough. Perhaps it should be remarked that Chinese are notorious gamblers, Filipinos are famous brawlers, and Koreans drink just as well as Japanese. As a matter of fact, the vices here mentioned are by no means confined to the Japanese; they are human vices common to certain classes of all races of mankind. In truth, the picture of Japanese laborers can well represent the conditions of the labor force in the industry." In making this argument, he was following in the footsteps of the advocates of southern and eastern Europeans we saw in chapter 5.[61]

To be fair, his intention was to rationalize the supposed bad behavior of this group of Japanese immigrants. But in doing so he revealed the contradiction in the Dillingham Commission's project as a whole: The commission wanted to build a racial hierarchy out of the data, yet the fieldwork results yielded information about the social conditions of immigrants, not their racial characteristics. As the commission piled on additional data to make the hierarchy reliable and robust, the contradiction in racial knowledge production became even more evident. In any case, Ichihashi did not have control over how his data would be used, and he did not appreciate the way it was used. In *Japanese in the United States*, he put the data into perspective—that is, his perspective, which he presumed to be not only more informed but also more objective—while attempting to provide a more accurate portrayal of the immigrant group he studied, of which he was a member.

In the process, he laid bare the supposed contradiction embodied by Japanese immigrants, of being "progressive" and "differing so greatly" at the same time. The only way to overcome this contradiction, he argued, would be to do away with the race clause in the naturalization law and open up the pathway for citizenship for Japanese immigrants so that they could fully participate in the social and political life of the nation. To this end, Ichihashi highlighted the positive findings from the *Pacific Coast Reports* while providing explanations for the negative ones. In doing so, he liberally and flexibly mobilized both racial and cultural explanations to vindicate Japanese immigrants. Unfortunately, Ichihashi also supported his argument by condemning other immigrant groups, especially the Chinese.

The American public, according to Ichihashi, made a mistake in extending anti-Chinese sentiment to the Japanese. In fact, these two groups were very different, although the latter had taken on the jobs of the former. When exposed to the harsh working conditions in the United States, "the Japanese, being more intelligent and sensitive to these conditions than the Chinese coolies, naturally reacted more vigorously; they did not consider themselves coolies, a fact which had been recognized from the very beginning of their coming by the contract agreements, public or private."[62] In other words, as opposed to the Chinese "coolies" who were tricked into hard physical labor and trapped by their slavelike labor contracts, the Japanese were free men who had chosen to come to work in the United States. Therefore, they refused the service of White middlemen—managers who often bridged the relationship between day laborers and employers, especially in the case of the Chinese and Mexicans—and preferred to work with Japanese bosses, many of whom were chosen by the workers themselves. Through these labor gang bosses, according to Ichihashi, the Japanese workers more forcefully conveyed what they wanted to employers, often demanding higher wages and better working conditions. If anything, Ichihashi argued, this should be evidence that the Japanese merited democratic citizenship more than other immigrants, for they had a propensity for freedom of expression and self-government.

In addition to their supposed high intelligence, Ichihashi emphasized the fact that the Japanese immigrants in the United Staets were a highly selective group of people, anticipating recent arguments about the selectivity of Asian immigrants in the United States.[63] Citing the data from the *Pacific Coast Reports*, "The Japanese immigrants," wrote Ichihashi, "exhibited a satisfactory average with respect to money in their possession, ability to read and write, and degree of intelligence and ambition."[64] Perhaps the last part—intelligence and ambition—was his own idiosyncratic theory without the support of concrete facts, but he offered both his own and others' "firsthand experience" to corroborate his argument.

In addition to touting the exceptional character of the Japanese immigrants, Ichihashi also strove to fend off some of the criticisms leveled against them. The most common charge was that they were "untractable"—namely, that the Japanese were hard to deal with as laborers, as opposed to the Chinese workers before them, who were easy to control. Ichihashi drew on the classic American ideal of self-determination to defend Japanese immigrants. "No fair-minded American can justly condemn" the Japanese, he wrote, "although this virtuous moving on has been persistently interpreted as a vice when practiced by the Japanese." Taking a somewhat condescending and ironic tone—after all, Ichihashi, an alien excluded from citizenship, was appealing to American values of freedom and equality—Ichihashi urged Americans to be true to their own values: "It may be painful, but we must admit that the progressive spirit of Japanese immigrants has to be tolerated, so long as it is considered a virtue in America, a land of opportunity and of self-made men and women." Perhaps from firsthand experience, Ichihashi understood "why Japanese immigrants are nervous, restless, ambitious, and unstable as compared with the passive Chinese": mainly because they were so keen on moving forward and upward. He brushed off the criticism of being "untractable" by reminding the reader of "the common complaint of housewives, still dreaming of old-fashioned servants no longer to be had, that their Japanese servants are often too intellectual and philosophical."[65]

Another common complaint against Japanese immigrants was that they worked in groups of so-called labor gangs under Japanese bosses that drove off American workers by working for low wages. Ichihashi explained that "labor gangs" were in fact communitarian organizations, and the majority of "gang bosses," who were often criticized for exploiting their fellow countrymen, were actually "businesslike, trustworthy, and decent in treating their employers and the men." He contrasted them with White labor gang bosses who largely oversaw Mexicans. Whereas White bosses merely exploited Mexican workers for profit, Japanese bosses were a part of the community and looked out for the well-being of their men. He cited the strong ethnic community as the main reason why Japanese immigrants were so successful in moving up in the occupational hierarchy of the West Coast.

By the same token, the assertion that Japanese workers were driving out American workers was, according to Ichihashi, false. Contrary to popular perception, "aside from the aging Chinese there were none to be driven." Ichihashi also criticized employers' preference for Chinese workers: "Many an employer expressed preference for the Chinese, but this must be understood as largely psychological; they wanted the Chinese because they were not to be had. In the same way, employers now expressed preference for the Japanese to Mexicans, Filipinos, etc., because Japanese have largely disappeared as farm hands."[66] In short, Ichihashi had a firm sociological understanding of the labor market in the West Coast: Successive inflow of immigrant groups led to what appeared to be racial displacement; in fact, race had nothing to do with the trend—different groups might occupy the position of manual workers at different times, yet the structure of the labor market would not change fundamentally. Therefore, Ichihashi maintained, blaming the Japanese—or, for that matter, any group at all—would be unfair.

After he responded to various criticisms, mostly related to the labor market positions of Japanese immigrants, Ichihashi went on to tackle the most damaging of them all: their supposed lack of capacity for assimilation. As we have seen in the *Pacific Coast Reports*, the Japanese, along with the Chinese and Mexicans, were often deemed too different in race and culture to warrant any possibility of assimilation. Ichihashi begged to differ. Regarding racial difference, he argued that this was not an issue, because, at least among "Mongolians," Japanese were racially closest to Americans. Echoing Boas's argument (see chapter 4), Ichihashi first established that both Americans and Japanese are "hybridized stock[s]," meaning that there were various elements within the racial groupings. Citing a French craniologist, Ichihashi noted that "there is scarcely a race which has not contributed to make the Japanese nation—the Caucasian, the Mongolian, the Malay, and even in the south, a slight tinge of Negrito from the islands of the Pacific." In other words, the Japanese were not that simple—they were both Caucasian and Mongolian at the same time, with some elements of "Negrito" as well. Here he was faithfully following in the footsteps laid out by his mentor, David Starr Jordan, who had hinted at the presence of "Caucasian blood" among the Japanese.

In fact, according to Ichihashi, if we look at the facial features of the Japanese population in Japan, "Greek, Roman, Jewish noses are well represented, as well as very flat and broad ones." Even in terms of language—the Dillingham Commission's favorite marker of distinction—Japanese stood out as a singular group: "A common notion in the West [is] that Japanese and Chinese are allied tongues; in reality they are as far apart as English is from Hittite." As any attempt to group Chinese workers with Japanese workers was mistaken, so was the presumed linguistic affinity between the two countries. Instead, "linguistically Japanese remains a solitary orphan."[67] In other words, Japanese were a racially unique group. Whether they would be able to assimilate with Americans, Ichihashi reasoned, was an empirical question. And Ichihashi was advocating for a chance to test different hypotheses by opening the path toward naturalization for Japanese immigrants.

## The Return of Essentialism and Ichihashi's Silence

The relationship between Japan and the United States gradually worsened in the three decades after the Dillingham Commission released its report, as Japan pursued an aggressive expansion policy in Asia. The position of Japanese immigrants, as well as that of Ichihashi, also became more precarious in the 1930s and onward. As a renowned expert on all things Japan, Ichihashi actively engaged in public speaking and writing, advocating for the Japanese perspective. Although he himself was a liberal, after the fascist takeover of the Japanese government, he had little choice other than to act as its de facto representative, justifying the empire's warmongering. Not too surprisingly, Ichihashi became isolated from his campus and public life, as well as from the Japanese government, which suspected that he had become too close to Americans. In the late 1930s, his position as a spokesperson for each of the countries, the position in which he once took great pride, was not welcome on either side of the Pacific.

In 1942, three months after the attack on Pearl Harbor, the US government apprehended Ichihashi along with another 120,000 Japanese immigrants and their children. Ichihashi and his family members were sent to the Tule Lake concentration camp, remembered for its harsh conditions and fierce political infighting among the incarcerated. He would spend the next three years there, collecting data on and keeping a diary about the everyday life of internees to one day write about the experience. The staff at Tule Lake regarded him as "really disloyal" and labeled him "essentially a fascist . . . far more dangerous than any other individual in the community." Of course, this was because he publicly spoke against the Wartime Relocation Authority; meanwhile, other confined Japanese Americans respected him as "a learned gentleman." However, at the same time, the same report notes that he answered "yes" to the infamous loyalty question 28, pledging unqualified allegiance to the United States and disavowing that for the Japanese emperor.[68] As he had written in his dissertation, "having been through thick and thin of the life in the United States," Ichihashi as a result became increasingly bitter and withdrawn from the world, rarely speaking to anyone, including his immediate family members.

Ironically, as Ichihashi was fading from the public spotlight, the United States as a nation finally came to terms with Japan and the kind of difference it supposedly represented. The wartime propaganda had depicted Japan and the Japanese in a very different light than the Germans. The Japanese were described as an entirely different kind of people than those from European countries and were often depicted as demons or monkeys beyond human empathy. Nisei, the US-born Japanese, were also seen through this lens, as maintaining a supernatural connection to their homeland and thus suspected of disloyalty and treason. As Eric Muller chronicles in *The American Inquisition*, they were consequently subjected to an unprecedented, unconstitutional ordeal of loyalty tests to prove their belonging to their own country.

The ultimate irony is that the American victory over Japan ushered in more tolerance of Japanese Americans, putting an end to the ordeal. In this context, Ichihashi's lifelong mission of explaining Japan and the Japanese was completed by a White female anthropologist, with help from a Japanese American. Ruth Benedict (1887–1948), the effective heir to Boas's throne in cultural anthropology, wrote *The Chrysanthemum and the Sword* (1946) as a part of her wartime service for the Department of Defense. Sensing imminent victory in the Pacific, the Department of Defense needed a plan to properly occupy and govern Japan afterward. The foremost challenge was to accurately understand the country and its people, which had been reduced to absurd caricatures through wartime propaganda. Benedict, working with many other social scientists for the department, was tasked to write a report that would explain the Japanese character to decision-makers in military and government. Without learning the language or ever visiting the country, Benedict primarily relied on literature and ethnographic accounts by others to produce a comprehensive analysis of the nation's culture. Benedict also recruited Robert Hashima from one of the concentration camps as a so-called native informant to guide her through the secondary sources. Together they would present Japanese culture as logically coherent yet fundamentally different from American culture.

C. Douglas Lummis has written a most detailed appreciation of Benedict's book as well as Hashima's role in the overall project.[69] Born in the United States, Hashima was educated in Japanese secondary schools during the 1930s and later returned to the States as an adult—the trajectory typically embodied by those known as kibei in the Japanese American community. According to Lummis, Hashima simultaneously resisted and absorbed the ideological content of Japan's militaristic education, developing his own ethnographic understanding of the empire and its people. Although he did not necessarily identify with the perspective, he saw Japan through the lens of its fascist leaders as a warrior country bound by hierarchy, shame, and unconditional loyalty to the emperor. It was this lens that he provided to

Benedict. Whenever Benedict was confused about her secondary sources, she would ask for Hashima's interpretations of them, and Hashima would provide insights from his own ethnographic excursion to the country during his formative years, thereby helping formulate the core ideas of *The Chrysanthemum and the Sword.*

The book's core contentions present a dramatic contrast to those of Ichihashi's work: Whereas Ichihashi presents Japanese immigrants as better than other immigrants as well as Americans, subjecting all groups to universal standards, Benedict treats Japan and its people as an exception, portraying them as fundamentally different and bound by special habits of mind not comparable to any other. Therefore, as the argument went, Americans should understand and deal with Japan on its own terms, not compare it with other countries or their own. Here we see the ultimate solution to the insurmountable difference that Japanese immigrants represented in the Dillingham Commission: Japan—and, by extension, Japanese immigrants in the United States—was to be understood and appreciated on its own terms. Embracing the premise of fundamental cultural difference, the US occupational government faithfully heeded the anthropologist's advice and kept intact most Japanese institutions and customs, including the culturally significant role of the emperor. Once again, as we have seen in the case of African Americans and cultural anthropology (see chapter 4), racial essentialism returned through the guise of racial liberalism, or the concept of culture, to consolidate the boundary of Whiteness and American national identity.

In the coming decades, Japan was to revamp its demolished industrial economy and become the foremost security partner of the United States against the threat of communism in Asia. Interestingly enough, *The Chrysanthemum and the Sword*, translated in Japanese, was a massive hit in postwar Japan and played a crucial role as the former empire set out to search its soul after its devastating defeat. Discussing the role played by Hashima in the process, Asian American critic Karen Yamashita muses that Benedict's book "[occupied] a people with their own fiction." According to Yamashita, "an investigation of culture might predict human reactions and outcomes," and "Benedict was hired to predict and therefore, to occupy, the future."[70] We might add that the Benedict's fiction replaced the future Ichihashi imagined, the future he wanted to bring about through his advocacy based on the commission's unruly facts. In Ichihashi's future, Japanese immigrants stood alongside Whites as a respected member of the US body politic, having met the benchmarks of citizenship and belonging. In Benedict's future, Japan was a faraway island country forever bound by its exotic culture.

Meanwhile, in the United States, the Immigration Act of 1952 finally did away with the naturalization ban for Asian immigrants, including the

Japanese. This was Ichihashi's dream coming true. Asian immigrants, regardless of their race and national origins, could become American citizens. However, Ichihashi chose not to naturalize; he did not choose to return to Japan after the war, as some Japanese immigrants did, either. Released from Tule Lake, he returned to his former residence on the Stanford campus and resumed his duties as a professor. Yet he did not publish anything and did not give any public speeches. He chose to fade away into obscurity, slowly and quietly, and die as a stateless person in the land that he had lived in for more than seventy years.

In 1966, three years after Ichihashi's death, Berkeley sociologist William Pettersen published an article titled "Success Story, Japanese-American Style" in the *New York Times*.[71] This article again put Japanese immigrants at the center of attention as an exceptional, "model minority," thereby perpetuating the familiar stereotype of being "desirable" and "differing greatly" at the same time.[72]

## Conclusion: Insurmountable Difference

Japanese immigrants were very much an exceptional group in the Dillingham Commission's inquiry. In fact, they were the only non-White immigrant group that displayed all the so-called desirable qualities the commission put forth. According to the commission's data, they were educated, diligent workers who strove to settle in the United States and start families. Whereas the Chicago school sociologists worried about European immigrants and their "old world traits transplanted"—to borrow the title of the book by W. I. Thomas, Robert Park, and Herbert Miller—the Japanese were eager to give up their old ways and adopt American customs. And they were highly successful in their occupations, be they farming, manual work, or small business ownership. Although these qualities supposedly made them qualify as the sort of desirable immigrants that the Dillingham Commission prized, they were categorically barred from naturalization because of their non-Whiteness. Despite—or perhaps because of—their being so desirable, Japanese immigrants faced intense resentment and discrimination from all other groups, native-born Americans and immigrants alike.

Japanese immigrants represented a contradiction within the commission's scheme of racial hierarchy and desirability of immigrants—namely, that Whiteness and desirability did not correspond perfectly, especially in the case of Japanese immigrants. The solution for this contradiction was to invent another standard against which to evaluate Japanese immigrants. Unlike other immigrants, they were not evaluated on the basis of criminal propensities, reliance on government aid, ability to speak English, or economic prosperity. They were evaluated instead on the basis of their civic and political participation, areas from which they were excluded because of restrictive naturalization laws and racial resentment, as the Dillingham Commission acknowledged. In a contest for citizenship and belonging, in which various immigrant groups competed against each other, the finish line was constantly moving for Japanese immigrants. In fact, due to the naturalization ban, they were not even allowed on the field to run in the first place.

This formulation of different assessment criteria completed the circle of racial ideas espoused by the Dillingham Commission: Not all immigrant groups were evaluated in the same manner; instead, the standard with which to gauge the distance from the Anglo-Saxon, Protestant core of the nation changed according to the group being evaluated. In the case of European immigrants, the criteria for desirability had to do with the moral politics of the Progressive Era, entailing concerns about crime, welfare, economic productivity, and English-language acquisition. With time and effort, it was expected that these immigrant groups would improve on these areas. On the contrary, in the case of Japanese immigrants, the measure of successful assimilation was engagement in civic life, for which they had no hope of improving their conditions because of naturalization laws. Ichihashi's idiosyncratic but passionate definitional argument for Japanese Whiteness notwithstanding, the Dillingham Commission made it clear that the Japanese did not belong in the nation because of their "differing so greatly." In other words, Japanese immigrants were the exception to racial liberalism that proved the rule of racial essentialism and Whiteness.

The case of Japanese immigrants provides a useful opportunity to contemplate the path not taken by the commission: It could have discarded the idea of Whiteness altogether and focused on the moral politics of desirability, upending the association between race and nation once and for all. Although this was not politically plausible, it was intellectually possible as laid out in Ichihashi's passionate defense for his people. In that case, racial liberalism would have realized its full potential by dissolving the concept of race altogether, at least in matters related to immigration. In the end, however, Ichihashi's advocacy was met with silence: The commission—and, by extension, US immigration laws—maintained different criteria for European and non-European immigrants. These interpretive skirmishes show that unruly facts altered the internal dynamics of racial ideas but did not abolish the idea of race at large. The grafting of racial liberalism onto the mantle of racial essentialism was maintained on this ground, as Whiteness excluded non-White immigrants from the body politic even while the triad of ethnicity, culture, and assimilation was deployed to facilitate the integration of European immigrants.

[ CHAPTER SEVEN ]

# The Strange Career of National Quotas

## Direct Consequences of the Dillingham Commission

The preceding chapters have documented ideas, networks, and debates that emerged from the Dillingham Commission's inquiry. The commission produced facts about immigrants, and, based on those facts, scholars, policymakers, and activists began to discuss the so-called immigration problem. Even though these parties differed widely on the nature of and solution to the problem, they nevertheless centered the commissions' facts in their discussion. Transformations and innovations in racial ideas occurred on this terrain: The ideology of WASP supremacy that animated the commission's inquiry, as well as the reified, undifferentiated understanding of race undergirding the ideology, gave way to a multilayered, dynamic collection of ideas about peoplehood and nation, and the ever-expanding networks surrounding the commission's facts fueled the evolution. Ethnicity, assimilation, culture, and, finally, race—these crucial concepts, employed to account for distinction and belonging, emerged in this period, along with a renewed understanding of what kind of nation the United States should be. I describe this process as the grafting of racial liberalism onto racial essentialism and point to the conceptual framework of race and ethnicity as the outcome of such a transformation.

To be clear, the Dillingham Commission did not singlehandedly bring about this societal-level transformation. It is more accurate to understand the Dillingham Commission as encapsulating and providing a foundation for these changes: encapsulating because the organization encompassed seeds of different ideas that would evolve later into meaningful social forces; providing a foundation because the power and legitimacy granted by the American state rendered its work significant, regardless of where one stood on the immigration debate. However, participants in the Dillingham Commission were not aware of these implications. In fact, the emergence and consolidation of these ideas and networks were decades in the making, all the way up to the mid-twentieth century, and their impact can only be seen retrospectively through observing the magnitude of change over a long period. Perhaps a geological analogy will suffice. People living on continents do not feel their movements, yet tectonic plates shift gradually and continually to make an entirely new map. Albeit on a much smaller scale, I have tried to describe this kind of shift in the ideas surrounding peoplehood in the early twentieth-century United States by centering the figure of the racialized immigrant and facts.

This does not indicate that the Dillingham Commission had no immediate consequences. The existing historiography mostly situates the commission within broader trends of the early twentieth century, in which the rising tide of the restrictionist movement secured a victory over pro-immigrant forces to bring about immigration restriction.[1] The Johnson-Reed Act of 1924, also known as the National Origins Quotas Act, is often hailed as a victory for restrictionists, through which the United States legally manifested its "architecture of race," as historian Mae Ngai has dubbed the legislation.[2] By distributing different quotas for different European-origin groups and excluding Asians all together, even while tacitly keeping the southern border open to allow for the seasonal migration of Mexican agricultural workers, the Johnson-Reed Act built an enduring system of migration control that shaped the demographics as well as the self-perception of the nation. That is, Europeans were invited to assimilate, and non-Whites (mostly Asians) were categorically excluded, while Mexicans (and others from Central and South America) were tolerated as a source of labor. With the continuing subjugation of African Americans through racial violence and Jim Crow segregation, the United States effectively became a nation for and by White people.

I do not dispute this reading of history. Anti-immigrant forces, armed with the concept of race, won and imposed their agenda through a law that was in force over four decades. The often-neglected question, however, is how the idea of race actually manifested itself—that is, found a practical and legible expression of its ideology. The Dillingham Commission's inquiry shows that it takes a great deal of persistent effort to materialize racial ideology and that the process is fraught with confusion and contradiction. This demand is even more intense in immigration policy, in which racial ideology requires not just logical consistency and empirical validity but also practical implementation. As Daniel Folkmar emphasized in *Dictionary*, immigration officials should be able to effectively exclude and include immigrants based on their race, and the racial ideas behind the policy should be more consistent and practical than "anything goes."[3] This chapter documents how the Dillingham Commission's inquiry served as experimental ground from which new policy ideas emerged, one of which would compose the most important pillar of the Johnson-Reed Act. Against the narrative that emphasizes the victory of restrictionists and increasing dominance of eugenics in policymaking, I highlight that the push for quotas encompassed inclusive as well as exclusive stances about immigration and therefore was not the preferred option for restrictionists.[4] Furthermore, I also show that the categorical exclusion of Asians in the 1924 act—an important but often-neglected feature of the law—can also be traced back to the commission.

In the following, I start by highlighting the immediate legislative consequences of the Dillingham Commission: the literacy test and the Emergency Quota Act of 1921. I also explain how the quota idea survived in the period between the commission's inquiry and its eventual implementation in the early 1920s, by being reappropriated as an inclusive measure against the categorical exclusion of Asians. I conclude by discussing the fateful moment that sealed the design of the 1924 act, a drama featuring Henry Cabot Lodge that sheds light on how the diverging lines originating from the commission finally converged into policy design.

## From Literacy Tests to Quotas

The commission's choice recommendation for immigration policy was literacy tests for immigrants—a prospective immigrant should be able to read and write in their native language in order to enter the United States. The proposal was not a novel idea. As early as the 1840s, lawmakers in Massachusetts and Connecticut, two states with high volumes of Irish migration, considered the idea of using literacy as a prerequisite for franchise. After the Civil War, opponents of African American voting rights often invoked similar proposals.[5] In other words, literacy tests had long been instruments of exclusion that drew a line based on race, class, and immigration trajectory, albeit not as clearly as some of its advocates preferred, for in theory anyone could learn to read and write both in their native language as well as in English (see fig. 17).

Related to immigration policy, Henry Cabot Lodge, as a first-time congressman in the House, introduced the test initially in 1891. Since then, the test became the prized goal for the restrictionist lobby. Lodge and his restrictionist allies, including the IRL, had engaged in numerous attempts to pass laws containing the test requirement, only to encounter entrenched opposition in Congress and the executive branch. Even when restrictionists were able to thwart the staunch opposition, the law was vetoed by presidents several times, starting as early as 1897.[6]

The original 1907 act that created the Dillingham Commission had the same literacy test provision from the 1890s. However, the commission, whose establishment supplanted the literacy test requirement in the final act, was supposed to collect data to provide a foundation for scientifically informed immigration policy. The restrictionists hoped that its operation would legitimize their preferred means of exclusion. In the executive summary of its report, the commission seemed to respond to this expectation by highlighting and essentializing the divide between old immigrants and new immigrants: "The new immigration as a class is far less intelligent than the old, approximately one-third of all those over 14 years of age when admitted being illiterate. Racially they are for the most part essentially unlike the British, German, and other peoples who came during the period prior to 1880."[7] Although, as we have seen in the previous chapters, the actual data from the field did not warrant

FIGURE 17. A cartoon depicting the literacy test. Library of Congress.

such a clear-cut division, the Dillingham Commission firmly stood by this restrictionist ideology. The new immigrants were different and less desirable races or peoples, and the United States needed a means to weed them out. In the last section of the executive summary, the commission provided a series of policy ideas for immigration restriction, with literacy tests at the top of the list: "(a) the exclusion of those unable to read or write in some language."

In 1913, in the wake of the Dillingham Commission's policy recommendations, the restrictionists once again managed to pass the Literacy Test Bill, only to face another defeat with a veto from President William Howard Taft. The Senate, led by Lodge and Dillingham, swiftly overrode the veto, yet the House failed to follow suit by a margin of merely two votes.[8] Restrictionists had to wait another four years, until the end of World War I, to push one more time. Buoyed by the red scare following the Russian Revolution and the imagined threat of radical foreigners importing political violence to the country, Congress in 1917 successfully overrode the veto by President Woodrow Wilson to restrict immigration. Finally, the literacy test was implemented as the official immigration policy of the nation, and restrictionists saw the 1917 law as the culmination of their efforts that dated back to the early 1890s.

As it turned out, historical circumstances outpaced this sorting mechanism, and the exclusionary measure, which had taken thirty years to become law, did not stand for long. In the 1890s and 1900s, a significant divide existed between the industrial nations of western Europe and the less developed, largely agricultural nations of southern and eastern Europe. Compulsory general education, a hallmark of industrial capitalism and modern state formation, was a novel institution, and southern and eastern European countries lacked the capacity to educate their population in basic skills such as reading and writing. The literacy test proposal was designed to exploit this divide, to exclude immigrants from rural areas of so-called backward nations without singling out certain nationalities that restrictionists abhorred. By the time the proposal was implemented in 1917, however, this divide had largely disappeared, with many of the "backward" nations catching up with their developed neighbors in compulsory general education. When the Immigration Naturalization Service started to examine the literacy of incoming immigrants after World War I, it became clear that the test had a minimal impact on the overall flow of immigrants from southern and eastern Europe.[9] The restrictionists had to go back to their policy playbook to come up with a different idea to curb immigration. National quotas were their answer.

## NATIONAL QUOTAS

Historian Mae Ngai highlights the role of the Census Bureau and its quota board chairman, Dr. Joseph A. Hill, who also worked as a high-ranking staff member on the Dillingham Commission, in shaping national origin quota restrictions.[10] As an expert in census and demographic data, Hill did much to make possible the implementation of national origin quotas: Drawing on his experience with population data, he devised a means with which to ascertain national origins of the US population based on the census, which would in turn serve as the basis for immigration quotas. Although Hill, as a statistician, did protest the absurdity of the hypotheses embedded in the calculation, in the end he faithfully came through with a table of specific numbers for each nationality. In short, Joseph Hill did much of the work in terms of practically implementing the racial ideology behind the quota act.

The idea of using numerical quotas, however, did not originate from his work. In fact, the quotas emerged out of the Dillingham Commission's inquiry as a backup plan for the literacy test. Son-Thierry Ly and Patrick Weil have traced the development of the quota system from the Dillingham Commission to its implementation in the 1920s, highlighting how different factions of restrictionists, including Dillingham, Lodge, and others, engaged in a legislative struggle to push forward their preferred means of restriction.[11] However, Ly and Weil do not discuss how exactly the quota idea emerged out of the commission's inquiry. In the recommendation section on the executive summary, right below the literacy test proposal, was another possible policy idea for restriction: "(b) The limitation of the number of each race arriving each year to a certain percentage of the average of that race arriving during a given period of years."[12] While the literacy test, proposal (a), was a given from the beginning, considering Lodge and all the restrictionist lobbying that influenced the commission, the quotas, proposal (b), were truly a new invention emerging from the fact-finding operation. Its language carried the hallmark of the Dillingham Commission—its obsession with defining "race" and counting by category. Still, the formula—the "percentage of the average of that race arriving during a given period of years"—was somewhat different from the national origin quotas of the 1920s: In the actual law, the quotas were distributed to each national origin group according to the number of group members already residing in the United States. In the commission's recommendation, the quotas were tied to the number of arrivals. But the idea's most critical feature, "percentages"—setting a number cap for prospective immigrants based on the number of immigrants of the same category—first saw light in the Dillingham Commission's recommendation. With literacy tests, categorical distinction was central, as one is either literate or not, with the former being desirable and the latter not; with the quotas, numbers, and the demographic calculation and tabulations undergirding those numbers, were the core component of racial ideology. This concept was a crucial breakthrough, and its implementation, while time-consuming, was merely a matter of detail.

The idea of using percentages by race but not race per se (i.e., categorically denying entry to the entirety of a certain group) was developed by William W. Husband (1871–1942), the executive secretary of the commission. Born in 1871 in East Highgate, Vermont, to an Irish immigrant father, Husband experienced rapid social mobility throughout his life. After a stint as a postmaster and journalist in Vermont, he joined the office of Senator Dillingham as a staff member and moved to Washington, DC. The executive secretary position of the commission was a turning point in his career. On the job, he was able to connect with many politicians and scholars and claim himself to be an expert on immigration policy. In 1921, he was appointed commissioner-general of immigration and oversaw the implementation of the national quotas. Even after his work in immigration, he continued to work in the federal government by serving as an assistant secretary of labor until his retirement.[13] His life trajectory thus mirrored that of the nation during the turn of the century: He moved from a rural farming community to an industrial metropolis, starting his career in "the state of courts and parties" but in the end retiring from a powerful federal bureaucracy backed by social science knowledge production.[14] Tellingly, immigration was the linchpin holding together his different positions across various organizations within the orbit of federal government.

In an unpublished personal memorandum, Husband claimed that he was the one who originally came up with the idea of national origin quotas, circa 1913.[15] Husband's well-organized personal paper collection documents the daily ordeals of his job during the four years of the Dillingham Commission's inquiry: He had to gather busy executive members in one place for regular committee meetings; he had to correspond with independent investigators, like Franz Boas, many of whom had their own questions and misgivings about the commission; he had to oversee the staff at the commission's Washington, DC, headquarters, making decisions about their hiring and salary;[16] and when there was trouble with other federal agencies, he had the responsibility of sorting things out. And, in the process, he was able to connect with other middle-level bureaucrats, such as Isaac Hourwich, over their shared experience with empirical data. As

Robert Zeidel describes, the last days of the commission were a hectic affair, in which twenty-seven thousand pages of empirical data were rushed to print to meet the deadline imposed by Congress. One can only imagine the intensity of the work Husband, as the last line of defense against various political pressures and a multitude of issues around data collection, did in the final stretch.[17]

In 1941, Husband wrote a memo detailing the exact moment in which he came up with the idea of national origin quotas. "One evening in the spring of 1913, probably April," he recalled, "my brother-in-law . . . [and I] were discussing the immigration problem before a wood fire in the house on Highland Place, Washington." The literacy bill was going through another round of debate in Congress in 1913, which would end in a failure to override the presidential veto by two votes in the House. With inside knowledge from working in the commission for four years, Husband most likely would have been talking to his brother-in-law about what he expected to come out of the debate. The idea for quotas based on the number of arrivals was already available, as shown in the recommendation (b).

While talking, Husband had a moment of epiphany: "It suddenly occurred to me that some percentage system based on the foreign-born population of the United States might afford a means of accomplishing what was desired, which admittedly was to cut down the great influx of aliens from Southern and Eastern Europe." The system was especially appealing because it provided "the desired solution of the troublesome problem without a logical suggestion of discrimination among the various nationalities concerned."[18] He immediately went up to his study to write down his idea. In the following days, he was able to calculate the exact number of immigrants allocated to each nation, based on the data that he had on hand.[19]

Husband took his idea to his boss, Senator Dillingham, and after a few weeks the two men distributed a press release. The national origin quota proposal officially saw light on June 2, 1913. Restrictionists responded in a lukewarm manner; they were still caught up with the idea of literacy tests, for which they had been advocating for over two decades, and were unsure of the new idea. Nonetheless, Dillingham proposed a bill for quotas in 1913, even though it received virtually no support from either restrictionists or their opponents. The quota proposal died without receiving much attention. In the debate over the literacy test in 1917, Dillingham again brought up quotas, although he confessed that he himself was not fully committed to the idea.[20] Restrictionists would come back to the idea in 1921, only after the literacy test had proven to be ineffective in excluding southern and eastern Europeans (see fig. 18).

FIGURE 18. A cartoon depicting the national origins quota bill. Library of Congress.

## Detour: Gulick's Advocacy for Japanese Immigrants Through Quotas

During the eight-year period between its origin in 1913 and comeback in 1921, the national origin quota proposal took an interesting detour. Although the idea was initially rejected by restrictionists over the literacy test, Sydney Gulick, a pro-immigrant activist, continued to advocate for it in order to further his goal of supporting Japanese immigrants and maintaining a good diplomatic relationship between Japan and the United States. The important difference of Gulick's proposal from Husband's was its focus on universalism: Quotas would apply to all countries regardless of race, even to formerly excluded ones such as China. Gulick framed the idea as an antidote to race-based categorical exclusion, prompting Ly and Weil to characterize the major as "anti-racist."[21] The emphasis on national origin was justified because the higher number of conationals already residing in the United States implied an ease of assimilation for newcomers—or so argued Gulick. The quota proposal thus combined the goals of immigration control and assimilation, without entering the thorny territory of race and racial discrimination. Therefore, while the proposal was first circulated within restrictionist circles, the idea appealed to antirestrictionists as well.

Sydney Gulick (1860–1945) started his career as a missionary in Japan but assumed the role of what would later be categorized as a lobbyist upon his return to the United States. Born in a generational missionary family, Gulick grew up envisioning living a life of gospel in remote corners of the world. After graduating from Dartmouth College, Gulick and his wife sailed in 1888 to the city of Kumamoto on the island of Kyushu, Japan. While Kumamoto was close to the early treaty port of Nagasaki and featured a long history of Christian missionary work and community, it was still a remote city far away from the metropolis of Tokyo. Unlike many other missionaries, Gulick retained a keen intellectual inclination as well as a sort of ethnographic sensibility toward his surroundings: Rather than forcing his faith upon others, he wanted to first understand Japan and its people to meet them where they were. He studied the Japanese language, known to be notoriously difficult for missionaries, and became fluent in both speaking and reading in a mere five years. He routinely read periodicals and academic works written in Japanese and gave his sermons in the language. He criticized most of the English-language writing on the island country as misguided, authored by tourists who did not understand the language and therefore did not obtain access beyond the superficial, orientalist imagination. During his fifteen-year mission, he made himself an expert on Japan, writing and publishing several perceptive monographs about the country and his experience. Recognized by both American missionaries and Japanese scholars, he was employed as a permanent faculty member at the prestigious Doshisha University in Kyoto.

His life took a sudden turn when a health issue forced him and his family back to the United States in 1913. Witnessing firsthand anti-Japanese mobilization in California, Gulick took on the responsibility of educating the public, much like Yamato Ichihashi had done with his academic work. His esteemed position within the network of missionaries and Japanese scholars quickly established him as a key figure in the discussion of all matters relating to Japan. Gulick's *The American Japanese Problem*, published in 1914, made a case for Japanese immigrants, arguing that, just like other immigrants before them, they too would make excellent Americans with their hard work and zeal for everything American. He dispelled many of the common misunderstandings and stereotypes about Japanese immigrants by drawing on both academic literature and his experience of living in Japan for more than fifteen years. In addition, he patiently explained the increasing influence of Japan in Asia, perceptively noting the fact that the newly emerging empire was indeed very conscious about its perceived image on the world-stage. The United States, according to Gulick, had much to gain in terms of diplomatic relation by not discriminating against Japanese immigrants, whose ordeal Japan and its public regarded as a national humiliation. Notably, he also cited Franz Boas's work in the Dillingham Commission, boldly stating that "if, as Neo-Lamarckians hold, the character thus acquired is inherited, then there will be progressive evolution from the Japanese to the English race."[22] While he did not cite Ichihashi's work, he effectively conveyed the same argument from the perspective of an American. While Ichihashi's passionate plea was largely ignored, Gulick gained access to the halls of power, presenting his case numerous times in Congress and meeting with powerful policymakers.

Most importantly, however, he put forward the national origin quotas as a universal and positive solution to the "oriental problem"—if not to the "immigration problem" as a whole. His quota scheme would treat all immigrants seemingly fairly because there were no country-specific measures such as those given in the Chinese Exclusion Act or the Gentlemen's Agreement. Gulick emphasized assimilation by basing his 5 percent quotas on the numbers of naturalized citizens from each country, instead of just residents. That is, the base for quotas would come from the number of immigrants settled into the United States who voluntarily took up the American citizenship, as opposed to the number of all immigrants, which included a sizeable number of workers who were in the country for a limited time. Of course, complementing this design would be naturalization rights for all immigrants regardless of their race, in addition to the establishment of a federal bureau that would assist in the process. Turning restrictionists' thinking upside down, Gulick's proposal imagined quotas as a control mechanism of entry and assimilation for all immigrants regardless of origin. He noted that he prepared this idea without knowledge of Husband's idea.[23] Regardless, his proposal gained some traction, and he remained the most important speaker for Japan and Japanese immigrants for decades, all the way up to the Johnson-Reed Act of 1924 and beyond.

The fact that Husband and Gulick came up with practically the same idea at the same time without mutual influence shows that the quota proposal was a plausible idea for anyone thinking seriously about the immigration problem: Immigration had to be checked in some form, and race as a concept would not do the job; the elements of the social science tool kit, on the other hand—the census numbers and the concept of assimilation—were readily available for those willing to look beyond the ideology of WASP supremacy and racial essentialism. Whereas Husband approached the issue from a bureaucratic perspective, Gulick added a dose of Christian moralism, with an emphasis on universalism and the eventual assimilation of much-maligned Japanese immigrants. Hence, as Ly and Weil note, it is not surprising that the idea received only lukewarm responses from restrictionists until 1921: Racial essentialism was not yet ready to yield, albeit partially, to racial liberalism in dealing with the "immigration problem," at least in terms of policy.[24]

The national origin quota proposal finally received support from restrictionists in 1921 after they witnessed the ineffectiveness of the literacy test and began looking for an alternative. As numerous scholars have observed, the enthusiastic support from eugenicists was crucial in the legislative process, although the idea's origin did not have much to do with eugenics.[25] More specifically, Harry Laughlin, the director of the Eugenics Records Office at the Cold Springs Harbor Laboratory, was appointed as the "Expert Eugenical Agent" of the congressional immigration committee and testified extensively on the supposed biological benefits of the quota system.[26] Subsequently, eugenicists were also influential in the calculation of the exact quotas, including the decision to use the census results from 1890 as the baseline. Because the 1890 census featured a higher proportion of WASPs, such a decision would adversely affect the quotas for southern and eastern European countries, compared to using the 1910 census. Furthermore, the quota board made the decision to exclude all "Negro" and "Indian" populations from the calculation, thereby firmly specifying the boundary of Whiteness for immigration policy.[27] Joseph Hill's computations were carried out on top of these preconditions. Eventually, the national origin quotas became the most consequential immigration policy for the United States, effectively controlling immigration from the 1920s to 1965, when the Hart-Cellar Act finally struck down the system and opened the gates for a new wave of immigration to the country.[28]

## The Middle-Level Managers and Race Making

In his study of middle-level federal bureaucrats in the early twentieth century, Daniel Carpenter posits that they were crucial actors who facilitated the expansion of federal administrative capacity through innovations in governance.[29] More precisely, because middle-level managers were organizationally located between political appointees at the top and frontline administrative staff on the ground, they were exposed to both the overall goals and everyday workings of agencies, putting them in "the best position to experiment, learn, and innovate." "Administrative learning," Carpenter writes, "is a form of active experimentation, or learning by doing. An agency that manages numerous programs and offices is, in a sense, conducting a number of experiments."[30] The role of William Husband, the executive secretary of the Dillingham Commission, exemplifies this argument. While Husband hadn't administered policy programs on a small scale like Carpenter's officials, he had overseen many different inquiries on race and immigration, and every little issue from these inquiries—ranging from esoteric debates on race-thinking to challenges in data collection efforts—went by his desk.

His moment of epiphany, then, can be understood as a case of administrative learning, or "learning by doing," amid confusion and contradiction in the commission's project. Unlike Lodge, who did not have to do the work of applying his theory of race to empirical data, Husband was well positioned to witness the gap between racial ideology and the reality of immigration on the ground. While overseeing the everyday operations of the commission for four years, he was best able to see the fact that the clear-cut division between races or people did not work in reality. He was also in touch with people like Isaac Hourwich, who had a very different interpretation of the same data. Lodge and his restrictionist friends made decisions in their own insulated world, with their racial ideology protected by the privileges of class, power, and pedigree. They could profess their vision for the world and hire other people to care about thorny issues like logical consistency and empirical validity. Husband was in a very different position. He was the kind of person hired to deal with the issues, and as such he needed to learn and experiment. Unlike his bosses, he had no power and privilege to shield himself from reality. It is not surprising, then, following Carpenter's argument, that he became a source of innovation in immigration policy.

After his stint in the commission, Husband had numerous chances to articulate his perspective on race and immigration, which was heavily influenced by his experience managing the data collection efforts. For instance, speaking before the Republican Club of New York in 1913, Husband delivered a nuanced argument markedly different from the standard restrictionist talking points. While acknowledging "alien criminality" as "a serious problem," Husband emphasized that "when the elements of age, sex, occupations and surroundings are considered it does not appear that the immigrant is relatively more criminal than the native," echoing the argument advanced by Hourwich.[31] In another address given in 1915, Husband made clear that he was "not among those who believes very strongly in the inherent superiority of Western European peoples over the rest of mankind," confessing that through his work on the Dillingham Commission, he had "seen something of these new immigrant peoples," and "the more [he] see[s] of them the stronger is [his] conviction that they are fundamentally good."[32] In other words, seeing the data on new immigrants made him less convinced of the restrictionist arguments focusing on their supposed undesirability. His idea of circumventing the direct use of race at an individual level by using national percentages was compatible with this recognition. Note that this was not forced on him through political contestations around the Dillingham Commission. Rather, the recognition became possible because of the confusion and contradictions in the commission's racial project, which exposed Husband to the unruly facts that defied the racial essentialism of immigration restrictionists.

What does this episode teach us about the state and race making? Scholars have long worked to separate the personified ideological intent—racism—from the actual process of enacting state policies based on race. In discussing the "banality of evil," Hannah Arendt writes about how indifferent individuals embedded in a powerful system of bureaucracy within a totalitarian state become the main agent of race making.[33] In the post–civil rights era, Eduardo Bonilla-Silva points out that there are no openly racist individuals behind policies that reproduce racial inequality and domination.[34] In a recent work, Hana Brown documents how institutional context affects implementation of race through her analysis of the enforcement of the Indian Child Welfare Act (1978).[35] All these works point to the impersonal workings of the state as the main agent in race making—that is, the racial state is not racist, at least in the everyday, personified sense of the term that centers on individual-level prejudice; rather, the state engages in the mundane work of "defining and ruling" the population it governs without much animosity, and this fact makes it even more lethal and effective.[36]

Husband and bureaucrats like him are crucial linchpins that hold together this apparatus, all the more so because they are not deeply attached to any racial ideology. Unlike race-thinkers (see chapter 1), race to them is not an object of fascination or strong attachment; rather, it is a cumbersome concept that makes their everyday work tricky. As we have seen in the case of Husband, because of their more practical approach to race, these middle-level bureaucrats embedded in race making have room to experiment and innovate. Timothy Mitchell, along with other theorists, presents the state as a loose set of diverse institutions barely separated from civil society, only traceable through its effect.[37] If we are still able to categorize some of its effects under the concept of the racial state, following David Theo Goldberg, it is because of actors like Husband.[38] They bring much-needed elasticity to the whole apparatus and by holding together ideology, bureaucracy, and objects of governance through their innovative engagement with reality. This account, while in line with the "racism without racists" thesis, presents a different line of inquiry, one that focuses on the conflicting tendencies within the racial state. This line of inquiry begs the crucial question of how the racial state maintains its power to be racial while seemingly encompassing contradictory tendencies within it. My account of the grafting of racial liberalism onto racial essentialism in the early twentieth century presents one possible answer to this question.

## The Last Hurrah: Lodge on Enforcing Whiteness

As discussed previously, quotas would reemerge as an alternative to literacy tests after it became clear that the tests were not a useful means of restriction. In 1921, the new generation of restrictionists, led by Albert Johnson, a Republication senator from Washington, were a different breed from those of Lodge and Dillingham. Whereas old-school restrictionists were motivated by the patrician concerns of New England elites, Johnson and his followers cut their xenophobic teeth on the anti-Asian populist movements on the West Coast. There were many background factors that accelerated radical tendencies within the restrictionist movement as it advanced on new fronts. The Great Migration of African Americans from the South prompted race riots in major northern cities; World War I brought disillusionment about international cooperation, which led to isolationism; and, most importantly, the Russian Revolution fueled the fear of anything radical and foreign. Whereas the old restrictionists saw immigrants as a social problem, the new regarded them as an existential threat, something that needed to be eliminated at all costs. Going beyond the social sciences and empirical evidence, they gravitated toward more direct expressions of their racial ideology, as represented by figures such as Madison Grant and the Ku Klux Klan. Even while the mainstay of social scientists was moving away from racial essentialism (see chapter 4), public opinion and political discourse were increasingly moving toward it with the appeal of eugenics. Against this backdrop, Johnson proposed a two-year total moratorium on all immigration, hoping for a permanent exclusion of all immigrants.[39]

Obviously, this was more wishful thinking than reality, as pro-immigrant forces still exercised considerable influence on policymaking. Populist-leaning House proposals were repeatedly defeated in the Senate, as foreign policy concerns and business interests held sway in the upper chamber. Hence any blanket exclusion, temporary or not, was not a viable option. Consequently, restrictionists turned to the Dillingham quotas, originally proposed in 1912 by Husband to lukewarm reception. In addition to Dillingham's bill, Gulick's relentless lobbying on behalf of Japan kept the quota proposal alive throughout the 1910s, and the corresponding bill was put forward by Senator Thomas Sterling (R-SD) as a competitor to Dillingham's. The key difference was the issue of race—that of Asian immigrants, to be precise: While Dillingham's quotas retained exclusionary measures toward Asian immigrants (i.e., the Chinese Exclusion Act, the Gentlemen's Agreement with Japan, and the Asiatic Barred Zone), the Sterling bill would do away with these measures and allocate quotas to all groups regardless of their race. In addition, the bill would provide the pathway toward naturalization for groups previously ineligible, just as Gulick had argued. While the so-called universal policy would go nowhere with the restrictionists in the House, the three-way competition between different means of immigration control—between the Dillingham quotas, Gulick's universal quotas, and Johnson's moratorium—would force Johnson and his allies to begrudgingly accept the compromise of the Dillingham quotas, although they reduced the percentage of admission from 5 to 3 percent. The Emergency Quota Act of 1921 was passed and immediately demonstrated its effectiveness by reducing immigration.

In 1924, the quota act was about to expire, and the long-standing legislative debate on immigration was finally about to reach its conclusion. With the overwhelming majority in both the House and Senate supporting some form of a comprehensive immigration restriction, Congress was looking for a permanent policy solution. The quota proposal, which had been in place for three years and proved its effectiveness, was a clear front-runner. Lining up the support of eugenicists, restrictionists doubled down on the necessity of immigration restriction, upping the stakes by employing the language of biology.[40] If immigration was left unchecked, they argued, the United States as a nation would experience a disaster due to the corruption of its blood. While presented as science, as David FitzGerald and David Cook-Martin have argued, eugenics clearly brought renewed pathos to the debate on the future of the body politic.[41]

During the debate, however, there were a few other pathways for lawmakers to move forward with restriction. With Johnson absent from Washington, DC, while he campaigned for the Republican presidential nomination, the restrictionist camp began to show signs of division, especially on the issue of Japanese immigrants. Because of diplomatic concerns, several senators, including David Reed, a Republication senator from Pennsylvania and the sponsor of the 1924 act, hinted that restrictionists might be open to the idea of a Japanese quota. With Japan's rapid ascension in the Far East, according to their argument, it would be wise to avoid unnecessarily offending the emerging empire. They argued for a pragmatic compromise by way of recognizing its place among other European nations, and symbolic allocation of quotas would serve the purpose. The specific number admitted would vary by calculation method, but in most cases Japan would be allotted approximately one hundred, a symbolic gesture in the context of overall immigration flow. Hence including Japan in the quota scheme, instead of subjecting its immigrants to the humiliating racial exclusion clause, would make sense for national interest.

Another point of contention was around the amendment recognizing the Gentlemen's Agreement of 1907. The Dillingham quota bill had left Japan in limbo, between nations excluded by the Asiatic Barred Zone and European countries with quotas. That is, Japan was initially not subjected to the Asiatic Barred Zone, and Congress instead handled the immigration control between the United States and Japan with the Gentlemen's Agreement. As discussed in chapters 2 and 6, the name of the treaty said a lot: As opposed to a country like China, which fell below the international standard for meriting administrative attention and respect, Japan was regarded as a "gentleman" of sorts and was expected to regulate its own people. In practice, the Japanese government agreed to curb working-class male migrants, while those who did not belong to this category, including so-called picture brides and students, were free to enter the United States.

As Ichihashi's generation of early Japanese immigrants settled and found their footing along the West Coast, they began to form families. Children of Japanese immigrants born on US soil and thus natural-born American citizens by way of the Fourteenth Amendment, were growing up as a unique group of non-White Americans who were also not Black. While subjected to discrimination and civic exclusion, Japanese immigrants, as Ichihashi described, made remarkable strides forward in farming and commerce, within only a generation's time. Their US-born children were being educated at places like the University of California and Stanford, but their professional aspirations were stymied by persistent exclusion from the professional sectors. The best job they could get upon graduation was working as a journalist for a Japanese-language newspaper. As the Ozawa Supreme Court ruling of 1922 once again confirmed, the boundary between Whites and Japanese was strongly enforced, and the so-called most desirable immigrants and their children still faced an uphill battle in American society.[42] Restrictionists zeroed in on their case because Japanese immigrants represented a threat to the established racial order: As Ichihashi argued, they were too "ambitious" and wanted more than they were supposed to. They needed to be put in their proper place and face categorical exclusion just like the Chinese before them.

Against this backdrop, the Senate considered three options for Asian immigrants under the quota scheme. Gulick's universal policy was a no-go from the beginning, as it would eliminate all forms of racial distinction in immigration policy. On the opposite side was the categorical exclusion of all "aliens ineligible for citizenship," as proposed by Johnson and restrictionists. At the midpoint was the status quo of recognizing the exceptional nature of Japanese immigrants under the Gentlemen's Agreement. Sensing the inevitable restrictionist victory, some senators as well as the executive branch sought a defensive compromise, recognizing the Gentlemen's Agreement with a last-minute amendment to the Johnson bill. It amounted to a few words in the bill that would provide diplomatic cover for President Calvin Coolidge in dealings with the Japanese government, which had already expressed discomfort with America's treatment of its people on the West Coast. Given the risk for diplomatic insult, Secretary of State Charles Hughes communicated through back channels with Japan and sought the empire's understanding. At Hughes's request, Ambassador Masano Hanihara even wrote a letter in support of the Gentlemen's Agreement, explaining how the Japanese government would continue to restrict the movement of its subjects from the other side of the Pacific. Hughes promptly shared the letter with the Senate, hoping that doing so would seal the deal on the amendment.

Henry Cabot Lodge, at seventy-four years old, was facing the twilight of his career. Dillingham died in 1923 after seeing his quota proposal pass in Congress, even if only as a temporary measure. As a senior statesman with an illustrious career behind him and lingering health issues, Lodge mostly listened to his younger colleagues debating immigration, albeit in different terms from his times. Lucky for him, the new restrictionists were fighting and winning the battle of immigration restriction, his lifelong goal. At the same time, as someone who had built his career on championing US interests on the world-stage, Lodge was expected to green-light the amendment on the Gentlemen's Agreement. In fact, as chapter 2 details, he was an instrumental figure in putting together the agreement in the first place, having, alongside Teddy Roosevelt, brokered the deal between the San Francisco school board and the Japanese government in 1907 in the so-called Japanese schoolchildren crisis. In short, throughout his entire career Lodge walked a fine line between diplomatic consideration and domestic racial concerns, and if there was anyone who would support the amendment, it would be the senior senator from Massachusetts.

Surprisingly, however, Lodge engaged in a sudden but consequential action at the last moment.[43] As soon as the Senate began to debate the immigration bill and proposed amendment on April 14, 1924, Lodge proposed to move the discussion to a secretive executive session. When the senators emerged from behind closed doors some fifty minutes later, many were fuming, with the winds decidedly shifting against the amendment. In a recap of the conversation, Lodge questioned the Japanese ambassador's letter—or, more precisely, a specific choice of words in it. In the long-winded letter, Hanihara detailed how the Gentlemen's Agreement came about and explained Japan's sincere commitment in enforcing its terms, even addressing some of the restrictionist concerns about loopholes in the current regime. In concluding the letter, Hanihara expressed his concerns about wholesale Japanese exclusion, noting that he had written the letter "very candidly and in a most friendly spirit." Such an extreme measure would bring "grave consequences" in "otherwise happy and mutually advantageous relations between our two countries." Lodge zeroed in on "grave consequences," arguing that the Japanese ambassador was making a "veiled threat."[44] "The United States," Lodge expounded, "can not legislate by the exercise by any other country of veiled threats." To Lodge, the amendment, if passed, would "assum[e] the dignity of a precedent": That is, giving in to this kind of veiled threat would set an example for the future, something he was determined to avoid at all costs.[45]

With this single intervention, the tide of discussion turned decisively. The amendment became not a symbol of a practical compromise but a matter of principle—whether or not the United States would succumb to a foreign power's veiled threat—issued by a non-White race of all things. The jingoistic framing worked effectively on most senators, leading even the initial supporters of the amendment to reverse their position and enthusiastically support Japanese exclusion. The question then became one not of diplomacy but of sovereign right, the right to enforce the boundary of citizenship along the racial line of Whiteness. This boundary, according to Lodge and allied senators, was one that should not be breached for practical calculations, for it could not, in their view, be separated from the principle on which the United States as a nation-state was standing. More pointedly, one senator clearly articulated the implications of making exceptions for Japan and Japanese immigrants: "When you open the door to a country on a quota basis, you open the door to that country to ask all the things that other countries which have a quota basis ask and receive at our hands."[46] In other words, a one-hundred-person quota for Japan was not just about one hundred Japanese immigrants arriving on Western shores. It was a sign that the Japanese were to be considered on equal footing with other European nations, and this admission would eventually open up the path to other rights such as naturalization and land ownership.

Over seventy years, Lodge had lived a life of ruling over other people, and based on the experience he likely knew when to draw the line and settle the question of hierarchy, both internationally and racially. Perhaps that was the reason why he came down strongly against the Japanese exception for seemingly no reason.[47] The amendment recognizing the Gentlemen's Agreement was defeated with a vote of 76–2. In subsequent weeks, the Johnson-Reed Act of 1924 was passed with quotas for European and categorical exclusion for Asians, including the Japanese.

This would be Lodge's final moment in the legislative spotlight. He died in November of the same year, in a hospital bed overlooking Back Bay in his cherished hometown of Boston. With his death and the Johnson-Reed Act of 1924, the trajectory of racial ideas extending out from the Dillingham Commission converged: As racial liberalism was grafted onto racial essentialism, the boundary of Whiteness kept complete transformation in check, rearticulating race as the most important principle in defining national identity of the United States.

## Coda: National Quotas as a Hybrid, Contingent Outcome of Knowledge Production

What was the legislative consequence of the commission? A ready-made answer to this question would be literacy tests, which the commission recommended and, in a way, helped write into law in 1917. From this vantage point, the commission's inquiry appears to be a predetermined exercise, one that restrictionists controlled entirely to justify their preferred means of restriction. In this chapter, I have argued otherwise: The focus on knowledge production reveals how confusion and contradictions within data collection efforts led to the unintended transformation of racial ideas and, by extension, policy proposals aimed at realizing those ideas. Moving the focus to the longer arc of immigration policymaking in the early twentieth century, I have shown that the national quotas—or, more precisely, the racial order manifested through the Johnson-Reed Act of 1924—was the true consequence of the commission.

This is not merely a historical revision through the discovery of new archival evidence. In fact, a few commentators have already recognized the connection between the Dillingham Commission and quotas.[48] Rather, my analysis provides a novel take on how we conceptualize an "outcome" when it comes to race and its legislative and social manifestations. As seen in the case of Husband, the quota idea was an ambiguous product. The idea emerged as a practical solution to the tension between the ideology of WASP racial supremacy and facts on the ground—out of the grueling, day-to-day work of middle-level bureaucrats sandwiched between unruly facts and various forces they could not control. The trajectory of quotas through the 1910s demonstrated the idea's hybrid character: While restrictionists initially showed lukewarm responses, a pro-immigrant activist saw it as a way to circumvent racial discrimination, especially in the case of Japanese immigrants. Meanwhile, eugenicists provided crucial support for their version of the idea, pushing it across the finish line in 1921 and 1924. The design of the policy itself came out of the highly volatile, contingent space of knowledge production in the Dillingham Commission. However, the volatility and hybrid character were kept in check by Lodge's last-minute action in the Senate, which preserved Japanese exclusion and retained the idea of race as a clear-cut, insurmountable difference.

What does this somewhat convoluted trajectory of national quotas say about the causal importance of the Dillingham Commission? To be clear, I do not argue that the commission caused immigration restriction or the Johnson-Reed Act, in the sense that the absence of its inquiry would have led to the absence of immigration restriction. That would be an overstatement, as broader social circumstances were pushing the United States to some form of comprehensive restriction that differed from the patchwork of exclusions from the nineteenth century. The crucial questions, however, are what *form* the restriction would take and how that form would structure the demographics as well as the identity of the nation. In this light, the commission provided a crucial space for innovative racial thinking to occur, and those innovations resulted in the specific ways the racial ideology of restrictionists manifested, albeit in a manner that was not foreseen by anyone involved. The particular form of restriction was viable only because it was hybrid. Knowledge production opened up the racial ideology of WASP supremacy and grafted elements of racial liberalism onto its body to formulate a more flexible and heterogeneous manifestation of race. I am hesitant to call it a success for any party because it was not intended by anyone invested in the issue, yet I can call the result highly consequential, as it shaped the way we thought about race in the twentieth century and, by some measure, how we think of it in the twenty-first as well.

This point highlights a tension in the theory of race making—that the outcome of a clash between different ideologies and the particular form that outcome takes in implementation do not always align with the original creators' intentions. Scholars often rush to confirm a decisive outcome (e.g., restrictionists won) and neglect how the outcome manifested (e.g., national quotas for Europeans and categorical exclusion of Asians) and with what implications. The earlier focus on eugenics in the 1920s is an obvious example of such a tendency. Perhaps more so than in other domains, the power of race as an idea lies in the details, for the details are what structure bodies and relations to construct a racial order. The exclusive focus on eugenics and the victory of restrictionists obscures the fact that their victory was a contingent, highly unstable outcome of prolonged struggles. By highlighting diverging lines connecting the Dillingham Commission and the exclusionary laws in the 1920s, this chapter has attempted to underscore the underlying vulnerability beneath immigration restriction and its "architecture of race."[49] That is, as opposed to being an omnipotent figure, the racial state exercises racial governance in a much more unstable and contingent way than we usually imagine, and oftentimes its racial effect becomes manifest only in retrospect. And knowledge production and the unruly facts were central to such contingency. This chapter has provided one example of this concept in action.

[ CONCLUSION ]

# The Limits of Racial Liberalism

In 1943, Ruth Benedict, then a Columbia professor and the heir apparent to Franz Boas, published a pamphlet intended for wide circulation. With Benedict's lucid writing and cartoon illustrations, *The Races of Mankind* presented the gist of Boasian thinking on race in an accessible format. The argument of this forty-three-page booklet stands in sharp contrast to the racial essentialism of immigration restrictionists in the early twentieth century. According to Benedict and her coauthor, Gene Weltfish,[1] humankind shares a single biological origin (fig. 19), and apparent differences among them could be understood not in terms of race but through the lens of culture. In a manner reminiscent to Daniel Folkmar's in *Dictionary*, the authors also stressed the fact that anyone could learn any language, thereby asserting the flexibility of culture over biology (fig. 20). Once again, just like Boas in his study of cephalic index, the authors presented numerical data from intelligence testing to demonstrate the primacy of environment over race (fig. 21). Most notably, they also emphasized the importance of social context over innate traits, noting that anyone could become anything with the right opportunity and support (fig. 22). Put together, these arguments portrayed a world full of diversity and harmony, free from prejudice and ripe with possibility for all people. In other words, it was the world imagined through the lens of racial liberalism.

Such a world provided a firm rebuttal to the hierarchical racial vision of Nazi Germany, in which all peoples were placed in a one-dimensional hierarchy and the master race of Aryans stood on top. Benedict was fighting the war on the intellectual front by attacking the worldview of Nazis: Race was not a destiny, and although human diversity existed, the fate of such diversity depended on our own making. Describing the United States as a nation that featured every race around the world, Benedict urged the country to "clean its own house" and "stand unashamed before the Nazis" in order to "get ready for a better twenty-first century."[2] As a part of wartime propaganda, millions of copies of *The Races of Mankind* were distributed in both

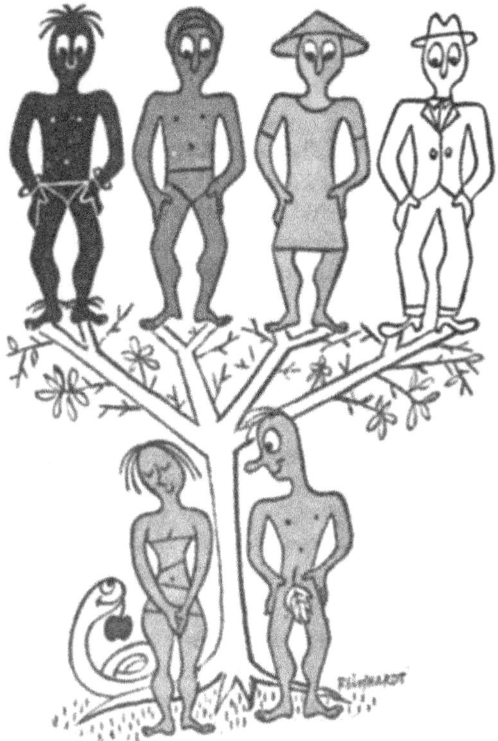

THE PEOPLES OF THE EARTH ARE ONE FAMILY.

FIGURE 19. The single origin of humankind. Benedict and Weltfish, *Races of Mankind*, 4.

the United States and Europe, among soldiers as well as defense industry workers. The Allied forces also used the pamphlet in their denazification efforts in Europe after the war.

When Henry Cabot Lodge disavowed any capacity for change among southern and eastern European immigrants in his 1896 Senate address—according to Lodge, "argument had no effect" on their racially predetermined character—he marked one extreme of the debate on race and national belonging. He took a firmly essentialist stance by arguing that the United States was a nation founded and dominated by WASPs and would remain such, because race was a destiny and thus impossible to change. This conviction initiated the immigration debate and eventually brought forth immigration restriction, encapsulated in the Johnson-Reed Act of 1924. Lodge and his friends won the political battle, at least in the short run.

A less spectacular but perhaps more consequential force coalesced in opposition to this current, namely, the consolidation of racial liberalism, or

**Anyone can learn any language.**

FIGURE 20. Learning language. Benedict and Weltfish, *Races of Mankind*, 17.

**Median Scores on A.E.F. Intelligence Tests**

| | |
|---|---|
| ***Southern Whites:*** | |
| Mississippi | 41.25 |
| Kentucky | 41.50 |
| Arkansas | 41.55 |
| ***Northern Negroes:*** | |
| New York | 45.02 |
| Illinois | 47.35 |
| Ohio | 49.50 |

FIGURE 21. Comparison of intelligence test scores between Northern Blacks and Southern Whites. Benedict and Weltfish, *Races of Mankind*, 15.

a belief that individuals could overcome their race through effort. *The Races of Mankind* may have been only forty-three pages, but it built on the decades of scientific research and intellectual tug-of-war around race initiated by Boas and carried on by his students. Many of these students were women or people from immigrant backgrounds. Roughly fifty years after Lodge's

**With better home, school, medical care, Johnny could have been Jimmy.**

FIGURE 22. The importance of environment. Benedict and Weltfish, *Races of Mankind*, 14.

address in the Senate, the US government was distributing *The Races of Mankind*, firmly stating that race was not a destiny and "Johnny could have been Jimmy" depending on social context.

The preceding chapters of this book have aimed to document the undercurrents that made this development possible. The analysis focuses on the unintended consequences of racial knowledge production, or how a state-sponsored inquiry produced unruly facts around which racial liberalism consolidated. In the beginning of the century, racial essentialism was the mainstay of race-thinking among scholars and the public, while notable exceptions such as W. E. B. Du Bois and Franz Boas were beginning to challenge its dominance. Congress launched the Dillingham Commission against this backdrop, hoping that a state-sponsored empirical inquiry on a massive scale would bring scientific legitimacy to immigration policy. Immigration restrictionists stood firmly by their racial essentialism and saw southern and eastern Europeans as undesirable races. They hoped that facts and an "avalanche of numbers" generated by the commission would boost the legitimacy of their racial ideology.[3] However, the result modified their expectations, and the outcome of knowledge production took off on its own trajectory. The unruly facts that emerged from the Dillingham Commission's inquiry became a fulcrum around which racial liberalism consolidated. That is, a careful consideration of the racial status of southern and eastern Europeans suggested that they were undoubtedly White and that their supposed difference was less essential than previously thought, especially compared to non-White immigrants. Moreover, facts on the ground showed that southern and eastern Europeans were not too different from other immigrants or native-born Americans. While the commission in its conclusion stuck to racial essentialism and dubbed them undesirable races, women and immigrants, who were previously excluded from the discussion of immigration, seized on the unruly facts presented in the main volumes to make their case for immigrant assimilation. The stories of people like Franz Boas, Grace Abbott, Isaac Hourwich, and, to a lesser degree, William Husband exemplify this movement. Throughout the decades following the commission's inquiry, we see the tide of race-thinking changing its course: Race ceased to be destiny for European immigrants, while it continued to exert its grip on non-Whites. The Johnson-Reed Act of 1924, cultural relativism in anthropology, assimilation theory in sociology, and the so-called invention of ethnicity in literature, as it has been dubbed by Werner Sollors, can be understood as partial manifestations of this broader transformation.[4]

At the same time, racial liberalism did not completely displace racial essentialism through scientific appeal, as Benedict had hoped with *The Races of Mankind*. The US government needed to distribute millions of copies of the pamphlet to dispel the myth of race among its employees and the general public, and its laws and policies still carried the legacies of racial essentialism in many areas. Rampant racial violence in the 1920s and 1930s—lynching, the Ku Klux Klan, and the border patrol, to mention a few incarnations—also testifies that racial essentialism still retained much influence even while racial liberalism was consolidating as a new way of thinking about population difference. I do not mean to argue that racial liberalism replaced racial essentialism. My contention, on the contrary, is that racial liberalism was grafted onto the existing strain of racial essentialism to formulate a more dynamic and flexible system of categorizing and governing peoples. Simply put, there emerged two different kinds of population differences under the larger rubric of race, one essential and the other not so essential. As I discuss in chapter 7, the Johnson-Reed Act of 1924 reflected such a "reworking" of race, to borrow the term coined by Moon-Kie Jung.[5]

The distinction between nonassimilable aliens and assimilable immigrants, or non-White and White peoples, mapped onto the two-tiered system of racial categorization, otherwise known as race and ethnicity. The former came to be associated with prejudice, violence, and inequality; the latter, with pride, culture, and community.[6] Through this binary, we dream of a world in which the former disappears and the latter flourishes, and our analytical attention as social scientists has focused on why the former seems to haunt us to this day.[7] My account of the early twentieth-century immigration debate challenges this binary. Race and ethnicity are historically constructed categories, and as such they form parts of the larger machinery through which the American state defined, classified, and governed different groups of people.[8] They cannot be understood apart from the context of their historical construction, and the unruly facts uncovered by the Dillingham Commission lie at the heart of that construction.

The analysis the preceding chapters have presented provides important qualifications to the extant sociological knowledge on race and immigration history in the United States—to how it affected the dynamics of race making, the origins of race and ethnicity, and the role of the state in racial governance, respectively.

First, on the dynamics of race making.[9] Many of the existing theories of race making prioritize political contestations: In many accounts, there are two competing forces in the process—the categorizers who seek to impose a racial ideology and the categorized who fight back against the attempt. Michael Omi and Howard Winant's racial formation theory best exemplifies this trend through its reliance on Gramsci's metaphors of "war of maneuver" and "war of position."[10] From this perspective, race making is a contest, in which the institutions in the state and civil society become a battlefield for racial hegemony. Each side knows what it wants, and it does what it can to mobilize forces and win the battle so it can shape the resulting racial order as it pleases. Oftentimes this perspective presents race making as a series of heroic battles between racists and antiracists. While actual analyses in many instances feature nuances and layers, the framework itself poses a danger of resorting to the simple myth of good versus evil.

The case of the Dillingham Commission challenges this framework by invoking the contingency inherent in racial knowledge production and highlighting its unintended consequences. The metaphor of contest supposes clearly defined goals and coordinated actions taken up in pursuit of those goals. But too often race makers do not understand the dynamic realities underlying differences among people, as seen in the case of immigration restrictionists, who had only a vague idea about southern and eastern Europeans that was propelled by racial essentialism. As the preceding chapters demonstrate repeatedly, unruly facts did not support their agenda but opened up a contingent space in which projected ideologies and intentions were ultimately refracted through the demands of logic and evidence. In this open space there emerged a new set of networks, experts, activists, and bureaucrats, some of whom did not share the ideology and social background of the restrictionists. To be clear, there was a "war of position" going on between the restrictionists and supporters of immigrants, most notably in Congress, but the Dillingham Commission's inquiry, once began, was beyond the control of either side. And the resulting unruly facts proved to be more consequential in deciding the enduring legacy of the commission because they became the focal point around which racial liberalism consolidated. Although in hindsight the restrictionists appear to have prevailed by presenting southern and eastern Europeans as undesirable, thereby confirming their allegiance to racial essentialism, the enduring legacies of the commission—the grafting of racial liberalism onto racial essentialism, most visible in the concept of ethnicity and the Johnson-Reed Act of 1924—was something that they did not intentionally manage.

This understanding calls for scholars of race making to appreciate contingency and pay more attention to the outcomes that seem tangential—but are ultimately consequential—to the process. Put differently, there may be a payoff in focusing on the long-term broader consequences over immediately noticeable victories and defeats. In the early twentieth century, restrictionists thought they had won the battle over immigration, yet the larger current was drifting in a different direction, one that outstripped the imagination of all those involved. The framework of contest often leads us to an all-or-nothing, winner-takes-all mindset, which, in terms of race, can result in a fatalistic understanding of historical developments. Indeed, the twentieth century, within this framework, does not provide us with much to hope for, as despite the decline of scientific racism and the victories of the civil rights movement, other insidious forms of racial governance, including, but not limited to, colorblind racism, mass incarceration, and the "deportation machine," have emerged.[11]

The stories of racial knowledge production and its failures provide interesting food for thought, if not a silver lining in the otherwise dark clouds of never-ending repressions. Namely, race is a fundamentally misguided attempt to justify inequality based on group difference, and efforts to garner legitimacy on behalf of the idea will always result in failures and unintended consequences. Therefore, the system of racial governance is inherently vulnerable, even without the heroic challenges from the racialized, because the system is built on a contradiction. In other words, race is bound to fail, and one form of repression—however violent and cruel it may be—will eventually have to give way to another, with noises and troubles inevitably following. The process may not be entirely to our liking and may not develop into freedom or liberation in a traditional sense, but we can take circumspect hope in the fact that, at any given point in time, the system of racial governance is far from stable and is always fraught with contradictions.

In *Seeing Like a State*, James Scott highlights the role of contingency and failures in state-led high modernist interventions in the twentieth century.[12] In his analysis, both nature and humans prove to be too diverse and unpredictable to be tamed by the simplifying schemes of the state, and what appears to be an initial success almost always produces a backlash in the form of ecological disasters or social abandonment. The most ambitious projects of state intervention, ranging from German forestry to Brazilian urban planning to land reforms in Southeast Asia, all met their eventual demise, regardless of how much material resources and human genius were tapped in their development. Race, I argue, provides perhaps the best example of these failures and unintended consequences because of the inherent contradictions within the idea. Human beings are too diverse to be classed into a few hierarchical categories; even maintaining the simplest divide of "us" versus "them" results in myriad challenges, with the boundary shifting and blurring all the time.[13] The story of racial knowledge production in the early twentieth century teaches us that even the most consequential acts of race making are not free from contingency and unintended consequences.

Second, on the origin of race and ethnicity. The analysis presented in this book enriches and broadens the discussion on how the concept of ethnicity originated. In many introduction-level sociology courses, we teach students to differentiate between race and ethnicity, as the former concerns biology and the latter focuses on culture. We also teach them that race has a dubious biological basis and is a socially constructed notion, just like ethnicity. As confused students often ask us, this does not tell us much about whether and how race and ethnicity are distinguished from each other. Nor does it enlighten us on why socially constructed notions exercise so much power over how we see differences between peoples.

Without a full-blown historical account, our understanding of these crucial sociological concepts remains elusive. The analysis featured in this book brings such an account. Sociology as a discipline has long been limited by the reliance on what Omi and Winant term "the ethnicity paradigm": Rather than taking it as an explanandum, sociologists have often taken ethnicity as an explanans, without factoring in the process through which the concept gained appeal. By doing so, sociologists have—sometimes enthusiastically, and other times unwittingly—played an accomplice to what Mae Ngai calls "the telos of immigrant settlement, assimilation, and citizenship": We have sometimes parroted a linear narrative mapping out the sequence of immigrant trajectory, one in which ethnic difference is gradually superseded by national belonging, often over generations, although we do acknowledge barriers and detours in the process.[14] The problems with this framework are numerous, but the most glaring oversight is its inability to properly question and conceptualize race as anything other than a temporary hurdle to the ideal of the unified, nonsegmented nation.[15] Instead, sociologists have focused on tracing the trajectory of ethnicity as it is embodied and negotiated by people while largely neglecting its conceptual origin and application in governance, especially in relation to race. In so doing we do not properly question the enabler of the telos—the American state—while we overanalyze where immigrants and their children are located within the narratives of assimilation, integration, incorporation, or national belonging, whatever we choose to call it.[16]

Scholars are pushing back against this tradition by highlighting how the race-ethnicity pair spearheaded the American state's attempt to define and rule different peoples: In the early and mid-twentieth-century United States, ethnicity was exclusively applied to European immigrants while race marked the boundary of Whiteness, distinguishing between assimilable and nonassimilable aliens.[17] In a society built on the legacy of slavery, different generations of immigrants utilized the cultural script of ethnicity to their advantage by distancing themselves from African Americans. Yet these accounts do not exactly pinpoint when and how the concept of ethnicity emerged, and what led to the specific "ethnoracial landscape" on which "the ethnic myth" was possible, as Vilna Bashi Treitler informs us.[18]

Existing accounts hint at Jewish elite college students and the Menorah Society as playing a significant role in the formation of ethnicity at the turn of the twentieth century.[19] As Daniel Greene tells us, these Jewish students were at the crossroads of past and future. They grew up hearing from their parents the stories of pogroms in eastern European farming villages and, though less in intensity, certainly experienced everyday discrimination and social closure while growing up in American society. As some of them ventured out from their segregated immigrant neighborhoods to storied elite colleges, hitherto reserved for WASP men like Lodge,[20] they were forced to embark on a journey of self-discovery and definition. These students wanted to claim their standing in American society not by assimilating but by asserting a distinctive Jewish cultural identity.[21] They saw themselves as neither Black nor White, unlocatable along the two axes of the American racial order.[22] Horace Kallen's articulation of pluralism emerged in this context, arguing for a novel form of difference embodied by upwardly mobile American-born children of Jewish immigrants. As recipients of largely secular educations, they oriented the newly defined Jewish identity away from religion and toward the German enlightenment tradition, in which secular German Jews played an important part, and literature became a focal point of self-expression.[23]

In the 1930s and '40s, after the dust settled on the immigration debate with the Johnson-Reed Act of 1924, writers and artists of European immigrant origin came along to fashion a concept of cultural difference that could not be subsumed under race.[24] Many of them were not Jewish, but the Menorah Society's literary inclinations had a universal appeal to children of

European immigrants who experienced stigma and the pressure of assimilation. Sociologists, most notably those of the Chicago school, operated against this backdrop, documenting the trajectory of this group as they moved through American society. A later generation of scholars extended the framework to the postwar period and through the civil rights movement. They explained how ethnicity resurged as Whites responded to the emergence of the radical social and cultural movements led by non-Whites in the 1960s.[25] They also tested the concept against post-1965 immigrants and their children from Asia, Africa, and Latin America to examine how they fit into the American racial order defined by the two axes of Black and White.[26] Yet there is a missing link in this story, notably between Jewish college students at the end of the nineteenth century and "ethnic" writers of the 1930s and 1940s.

My account of the Dillingham Commission shows that the missing link is the state and its quest for a legitimate mode of population governance, or what Mahmood Mamdani has conceptualized as a technology of "define and rule."[27] Before Jewish students coined the concept of ethnicity, the American state had initiated, but not fully completed, the sequence of events that would usher in a new way of defining difference and ruling over people who were deemed so. As we have seen in the case of Folkmar, the seed of racial liberalism dates to the American colonial government in the Philippines and its encounters with the Indigenous population of the islands. The challenges of governing a diverse population in a faraway place brought sharp relief to the limits of racial essentialism, and the concurrent development in late nineteenth-century race-thinking—what Victoria Hattam has called the "unfixing" of race—provided a starting point in the quest for a new system of racial governance. In the Dillingham Commission, the state faced a similar challenge regarding immigrants. While the more flexible conception of race was useful in singling out southern and eastern Europeans, this move also led to the logical conclusion that they may be able to improve their "undesirable" status to become better American citizens. In other words, the necessity in governance was a key catalyst in bringing in an unexpected set of ideas and people to the discussion of difference. In this context, the simple binary understanding of race as a top-down imperative and ethnicity as a bottom-up initiative proved to be analytically limited.[28]

In the case of European immigrants, this transformation provided a discursive space for them to assert their inclusion in the American nation. As we have seen in the preceding chapters, already in the 1910s and 1920s the tide was turning in some corners of academia, as racial liberalism was grafted onto racial essentialism. It was on this foundation that the writers and artists of the mid-twentieth century were able to recognize the distinct cultural identities of European immigrants and their children. Moreover, by affirming their difference from American national identity as cultural and not essential, they implied that those identities could change over time and that they could in fact "assimilate to the mainstream" through effort.[29] While the Dillingham Commission and Daniel Folkmar expected it would take "one thousand years" for such a transformation to occur, these writers and intellectuals envisioned a much shorter timeline, possibly a generation or two.[30]

Both groups, nonetheless, shared the understanding that, culture aside, there were unalterable, irreducible differences based on race. Namely, those immigrants who were racially different, or not White, existed beyond the possibility of assimilation. The conceptual distinction between race and ethnicity, or unassimilable aliens and assimilable aliens, was an unintended byproduct of the Dillingham Commission's encounter with facts on the ground. The national quota legislation, which specified numbers of admissible immigrants from European nations and categorically excluded those from Asia, was an institutional manifestation of that distinction.[31] Meanwhile "the ethnic project," "the invention of ethnicity," and, ultimately, "assimilation"[32] had only become possible on these shifting grounds.[33] Of course, it would take decades and a series of major historical events—World War I, the Great Depression, and the New Deal come to mind—for the children of European immigrants to identify with and mobilize under ethnic identity. But the concept of assimilation goes all the way back to the Dillingham Commission, to the unruly facts it provided and the ensuing consolidation of racial liberalism around them. In this light, as Katherine Benton-Cohen has already pointed out, the Johnson-Reed Act appears not only as the most "racist" immigration policy in the history of the United States but also as an ingenious, yet unforeseen, innovation in racial governance, in which southern and eastern Europeans were promised a possibility of gradual inclusion to the body politic at the expense of unfettered migration.[34] In a nutshell, the full historical analysis tells us that ethnicity is an inseparable part of the American racial order and its analytical usage should be considered in relation to race, as scholars have argued over the years.[35] My account adds the weight of detailed historical evidence to this argument, while urging sociologists to break free from the telos of assimilation and eventual belonging to the American nation.

Lastly, we turn to the state. We can read the preceding chapters as chronicling how the American state engaged in racial "self-invention and self-reflection" at the margins of its institutional infrastructure in the course of its attempt to define, classify, and govern people who were deemed different.[36] Lodge and his racial essentialism reigned supreme on the surface, at least up to the passing of the Johnson-Reed Act and his death in 1924. At the margins of the American state, however, there were less noticeable but meaningful experiments happening, starting with Folkmar's work in the Philippines, Boas's cephalic index project, Ichihashi's lone advocacy for Japanese immigrants, and so on. These centrifugal forces were still connected to racial essentialism and its proponents through the unruly facts that the Dillingham Commission procured. By providing resources and legitimacy to the fact-finding inquiry, the state was effectively investing in a new wave of racial ideas, without apprehending what it was doing.

As mentioned, discussion of the state during this period has highlighted how, at many levels, the governing institution assisted attempts at wholesale racialization and permitted, and sometimes directly exercised, physical violence against the racialized.[37] I posit that this reading of historical development is not necessarily inaccurate but one dimensional. While the center of political power and ideological legitimacy was busy demonizing undesirable races, at the margins different groups of actors were inventing the future, inadvertently consolidating and bringing forth racial liberalism. By arguing that some among the undesirable races were capable of improving themselves, these advocates initially quarreled with powerful actors over the primacy of racial essentialism. In the end, however, racial liberalism proved to be more suitable for the changing times, with a more flexible population classification system ensuring a more effective system of governance.

Granted, much of this development has been analyzed by theorists of the racial state, in terms of how the state employed contradictory ideas to enforce a system of governance on population.[38] These scholars are correct in pointing out the continuity between race and ethnicity, or how different labels, such as minorities or migrants, function not just as analytical categories but also as governing principles as the state defines, classifies, and rules over people.[39] My analysis differs in that it highlights unruly facts that function as intermediaries of these contradictory trends and ultimately spur innovations in governance without purposeful coordination. Put simply, there was no mastermind behind the retooling of racial governance in the early twentieth century and no coherent social force behind the "ethnic myth." The state is not a uniform actor, and many actors within its orbit operate largely independently, with a diverse set of goals.[40] Needless to say, it is difficult to line up these heterogeneous actors to accomplish a task, especially when the task involves something like inventing a new system of population governance. But the unruly facts, in an ironic fashion, made possible this task: Different actors encountered each other through the notion of facts and engaged in debates because they delegated authority to things beyond their control—facts, in this case. This analysis pushes us to move beyond the common caricature of the state as a Leviathan, an omnipotent figure with multiple hands that forces an outcome it desires. The racial state of unruly facts looks like an insecure, confused giant, possessing power but fumbling in its actions. Ironically, however, the contingency and indeterminacy generated by the unruly facts created a negotiated field for moving forward. The racial state, in the end, humbly and cunningly opened itself to reflexive self-criticism, and its ultimate efficacy stemmed from the act. Racial liberalism represents this efficacy.[41]

Fast-forward to the late 1960s. The civil rights movement exposed to broad daylight the violent manifestations of race in the Jim Crow South, leading to legal victories for racial integration. The Johnson-Reed Act was abolished and replaced with the Hart-Cellar Act, and racial and national exclusion was no longer central to American immigration policy. For the first time in US history, *race* and *racism* became dirty words—regardless of their true feelings, both elites and the public sought to avoid being labeled with the terms. The short-term political victory of restrictionists in the 1920s notwithstanding, facts, social scientists, and reformers claimed ultimate victory in the national debate about race, immigration, and national belonging, and as John F. Kennedy proudly proclaimed, the United States became "a nation of immigrants." It seemed that racial liberalism was finally victorious, and science and facts prevailed over prejudice.

However, sweet victories came with bitter disillusionment. Approximately twenty-five years after *The Races of Man* was published, racial liberalism began to witness its limits. Formal equality without tangible economic progress led African Americans to take to the streets in a series of urban riots across the nation. Capitalizing on the fear of conservative and moderate Whites, Richard Nixon took the White House with the slogan of law and order, which was a way of invoking the figure of the Black criminal without directly referring to race.[42] As numerous scholars have argued, the old Jim Crow gave way to the new Jim Crow, with de facto segregation, mass incarceration, and "colorblind racism."[43] In immigration policy, as Mae Ngai observes, the 1965 act brought "both greater inclusion and greater exclusions": While the new regime opened the door for immigrants from Asia, the focus on "territoriality, border control, and abstract categories of status . . . naturalized the construction of 'illegal aliens' . . . as Mexican."[44] By the early 1970s, most Americans agreed—or pretended to agree—that all races were equal and that racism was bad, just as Ruth Benedict had preached, but in real life they clung to an essentialized understanding of those who broke the nation's law and threatened its community. Academics and politicians did not invoke the scientific concept of race as much as they used to, but everyone was aware who the racial others were. It is telling that the oldest of racial categories, from Blumenbach's color scheme, "black" and "brown," came back to haunt this renewed configuration of race.

Against this backdrop, Margaret Mead and James Baldwin sat down with each other in the summer of 1970 to engage in a wide-ranging conversation that revolved around race and the current state of the nation. They both dreamed of a nation freed from the bind of race. But they hailed from different corners of American society and thus dreamed differently. The conversation between the two, in an eerie, poetic manner, showcases both the contours and limits of racial liberalism.

Born in 1901, Mead was the youngest among Boas's students and as such became an unofficial torchbearer of the Boasian school after the sudden death of Benedict in 1948. In *Coming of Age in Samoa* (1928), Mead showed how sensitive, deeply intimate notions such as sexuality and morality could vary in different societies, thereby effectively advocating for relativism and tolerance. As the most influential anthropologist and public intellectual of her generation, Mead championed the causes of the peoples and places perceived as different and inferior, including women, youth, immigrants, and African Americans, throughout the 1950s and 1960s.

Born in 1924 in Harlem, in the wake of Johnson-Reed Act, Baldwin largely taught himself to write, rising to prominence with fiery, unapologetic commentaries on race in the United States. Openly expressing his dissatisfaction with racial discrimination in the nation, he sought refuge in Paris during his younger years while continuing to write for American audiences. In 1957, he returned to the United States and became one of the most prominent literary voices for the civil rights movement during the 1960s.

Mead and Baldwin represented different strains of thought challenging racial domination in American society—the former based on racial liberalism of the early twentieth century, the latter emerging from the Black freedom struggle. Both agreed that the existing system of racial domination was unjust and needed to be transformed; neither believed in the hierarchy of peoples and cultures, and both opposed discrimination based on this hierarchy. Most importantly, both agreed that the United States needed to do more to address the question of race.

*A Rap in Race* (1971) documents their seven-and-a-half-hour conversation in book format. Discussing urban riots after the Civil Rights Act, Baldwin argued that the White American public could not understand "all of these people stealing TV sets and looking like savages," given "all the symbols and tokens of progress" in the 1960s. Under the guise of racial liberalism, White

Americans "conclude . . . that if those people on the South Side washed themselves and straightened up they could all be Harry Belafonte." Underlying this belief is a broader ideological underpinning: "There is nothing wrong with the system, so the American thinks; there is something wrong with the people." After all, European immigrants, once despised, successfully became Americans through effort. Why not African Americans? This is "the most dangerous delusion of all," Baldwin explains, "because it exacerbates the rage of the people trapped in the ghettos. They know why they are there, even if America doesn't."[45] Here we see a stark contrast to Ruth Benedict's claim of "Johnny could be Jimmy." Race may not be destiny, but that does not free "Jimmy" from his social circumstances. Racial liberalism, without equality in socioeconomic conditions, becomes indistinguishable from racial essentialism, because the outcome is still the same. Only this time more blame is placed on people because they were, in the myth of American meritocracy, given the opportunities to improve their lot but failed.

Although Baldwin and Mead agree that race should not be a factor in the society and that the racialized should be treated better, they situate themselves in fundamentally different positions in relation to the American state. Mead is invested in the American state's power to realize its promise of equality and freedom and believes in progress over time for all races. On the contrary, Baldwin sees the American state at the heart of the problem, and without fundamental changes in political institutions, race would never disappear as an issue. Here we are reminded of the Chicago school's turn toward nationalism in assimilation theory as well as Yamato Ichihashi's tragic quest for national belonging. In the end, as David Theo Goldberg presents in *The Racial State*, the state employs diverse sets of racial ideas, including racial essentialism and racial liberalism, to maintain its racial dominance.[46] Baldwin is alluding to this feature in his dialogue with Mead, who is an unabashedly proud American invested in the narrative of progress championed by racial liberalism. Racial liberalism, in Baldwin's understanding, is not necessarily different from racial essentialism when it comes to the question of the state: There will always be *some* racialized people left behind in the pathway to freedom and equality, and the state was at the heart of this selection process. As Orlando Patterson poignantly articulates in *Slavery and Social Death*, freedom in the United States has historically hinged on other people's binding—the historical fact that Mead did not, and could not, understand.[47] That is why Baldwin argues that "the future doesn't exist" for people like him under the American state.[48]

Mead tries to bring Baldwin into her territory by invoking the core tenet of racial liberalism—facts. Regardless of where they see each other headed, Mead pleads, they should be able to agree on where they stand in order to formulate a foundation for discussion and, possibly, collective action. She wants Baldwin to agree on facts, to which Baldwin replies, "I do not care what the pursuant facts are. I cannot afford to care." As he sees it, there is critical difference in how people like himself and people like Mead see facts.

> BALDWIN: "The difference is that you, generically, historically, write the facts which I am expected to believe. The difference is that you, historically, generically, have betrayed me so often and lied to me so long that no number of facts according to you will even convince me."
>
> MEAD: "If that's so, the world is doomed. If we can't reach a point where everybody in this world can understand facts. . . . See that's it."[49]

Throughout this book, we have witnessed how bureaucrats, intellectuals, and activists of different backgrounds came together around facts to formulate a new way of thinking about race. In a sense they engaged in a project of "racial worldmaking," to borrow the phrase from literary scholar Mark Jerng.[50] In addition to critiquing racial essentialism, they formulated a hypothetical historical narrative in which the racialized overcome their deficiencies to stand on equal footing with Whites, exemplified by the figure of European immigrants. This was indeed a dynamic vision of hope, change, and progress, presented as an antidote to the retrograde world upheld by racial essentialism. Mead's teachers and colleagues designed this new world and, as its designers, were its core inhabitants. Baldwin's were not, although they did try to invite themselves in. We remember the efforts of people like Zora Neale Hurston and Yamato Ichihashi in the Dillingham Commission's orbit, as well as those of early African American social scientists such as W. E. B. Du Bois, as told by Aldon Morris.[51] But the mainstay of racial liberalism broke sharply from these figures by not questioning the relationship between Whiteness and the American nation. It makes sense that Mead believes in facts and conversation. In stark contrast, Baldwin speaks on behalf of the people who did not get to write facts, the people who were betrayed, lied to, and denied entry to the world of racial liberalism.

Now fast-forward to the twenty-first century. We are living in another period of "unsettled times," to borrow the phrase of sociologist Ann Swidler, in terms of how race is articulated. Maybe "unhinged times" is more fitting, considering recent political rhetoric.[52] In addition to the infamous "Mexicans are rapists" speech from 2015, Donald Trump delivered another memorable line in 2024 during his third presidential run. In a debate televised to more than 67 million viewers nationwide, Trump stated that Haitian immigrants in Springfield, Ohio, were abducting and eating their neighbors' dogs and cats. Obviously, this was another instance of baseless demagoguery aimed at fearmongering, and journalists, politicians, local officials, and residents of Springfield all rushed to debunk this claim, showing that there was no factual basis to it.

Somewhat surprisingly, the Trump campaign did not defend the facticity of this outrageous utterance, however limited. The campaign did not supply distorted statistics or a made-up anecdote, as it had done in 2016 in response to the backlash to Trump's statements about immigrant crime. Instead, the campaign followed up with a series of AI-generated memes on its Instagram account, showing cats rallying for Trump as their protector. The memes circulated widely within the corner of the internet populated by Trump supporters, and no one was held accountable for the false claim. On the other hand, elementary schools in Springfield received multiple bomb threats and had to close for days.

This was not a sudden development. In 2015, in order to refute Trump's claims on immigrants, the National Academy of Science gathered prominent social scientists to collect facts and present analysis. The resulting report, *The Integration of Immigrants in American Society*, examined various topics such as education, language acquisition, occupation, poverty, and residential integration and concluded that immigrants were integrating into American society without too much trouble. More specifically, scholars found strong evidence of progress through generations: Immigrants may start from less-than-ideal positions at the time of arrival, but their children and grandchildren rapidly close the gap with the native-born population over time, to eventually become "indistinguishable" from "the mainstream," to use the phrasing from assimilation theory.[53] More pointedly, the report directly addressed the issue of crime and showed that immigrant populations have lower crime rates than the native-born population. In other words, immigrants were not criminals, at least no more so than their native-born counterparts.

The problem, as we know, is that the other side did not yield when it was presented with facts. In 2015, there was at least an attempt at dialogue, as opponents of immigrants sought out the victims of immigrant crime to use their personal experience to counter the more comprehensive statistical analysis. It was not an even exchange, but it was at least some engagement. In 2024, however, memes and laughter took over, indicating that the immigration debate was never a debate to begin with—it was the telling of a dark fantasy aimed to stoke fear and mobilize support.

I wrote this book in the context of this political and epistemological crisis. To be clear, this book does not offer a catchall solution to our dilemmas. I do not intend to portray the Dillingham Commission and the early twentieth century as "good times" during which facts dismantled racial ideology and social scientists prevailed over prejudiced politicians and the public. My goal in telling this story is to show the limits of the epistemological framework promulgated by racial liberalism and, hopefully, inspire scholars to imagine beyond its limits. In sociology and other related disciplines, we are trained to believe in facts and motivated to challenge prejudice so we can humanize the figure of the racialized immigrant and thereby intervene in policy controlling her life. In this light, ethnicity, culture, and assimilation in the early twentieth century provided an alternative to racial essentialism and freed immigrants from their race to pursue belonging in the American nation. My account, however, demonstrates clearly that the pathway laid out by these concepts was engineered by the state through the work of the experts it supported in order to sustain and buttress the system of racial governance, although the process itself was a contingent outcome stemming from knowledge production. The emphasis should be on *contingent*: Rather than presenting history as the expression of a mastermind working to update and reinforce White supremacy, I highlight the vulnerable and slippery nature of race as an idea and how its reworking via racial liberalism granted some flexibility to preserve the entire system. The unruly facts were the key catalyst enabling this process.

In our times, facts have lost their appeal, and, consequently, the nexus of racial liberalism and racial essentialism is reaching its breaking point. While we, social scientists, cling to our data to dispel the myth of race, racial essentialism is once again taking hold among the public. I am by no means arguing that we drop the task of educating the public and policymakers by dispelling the myth of racial essentialism with our facts. At the same time, social scientists may benefit from thinking beyond just facts. Racial liberalism was one way in which people's desire for freedom materialized. It does not have to be the only way. Either consciously or unconsciously, social scientists tend to cling to the heydays of our disciplines in the early twentieth century, in which facts and expanding networks around the American state brought forth a new model of racial governance. My account of the period, however, teaches us that the period was more of an exception than a norm and that the new world created by facts was confined to a selected few. As Baldwin proclaims, there were those who did not write facts, those who were left behind, betrayed, and lied to. Perhaps they can provide us with an inspiration for a new approach.

In *Seeing Like a State*, James Scott has gifted us with the concept of legibility. The Dillingham Commission's operation was an example in which the contingent politics of legibility were on full display—a case in which challenges to legibility had the potential to alter ideology and the means of governance.[54] But what about the politics of *illegibility*? Or, more precisely, how can we bridge the legible and illegible to imagine immigrants beyond "the telos of settlement, assimilation, and citizenship"[55] imposed by racial liberalism?

I envision two directions toward which scholarship on race and immigration can strive.

First, as I have hinted at throughout this book, we can focus less on the plight of the racialized and more on how race becomes a vehicle for the state's attempt to define and rule different populations. This includes breaking down the boundary between various categories imposed on the population, such as immigrant, refugee, and minority. The focus should be not on the difference between these categories but on how supposed difference within populations becomes consolidated into these categories, which come with their respective sets of legal, administrative, social, and cultural dynamics.[56] Only then can we understand race not as an exception to the rule of an increasingly global and diversified society but as a governing principle that undergirds such diversity.[57] The modern state has for centuries governed groups by categorizing them and treating them differently, regardless of labels attached to them. Race can be a conceptual window through which we examine this history.

Second, we can present a richer, more robust account of immigrant lives, one that is not subsumed by "the telos of settlement, assimilation, and citizenship." It is a worthwhile effort to show, based on solid facts, that immigrants do not commit crime at higher rates than nonimmigrants. However, such analysis alone inevitably flattens out the figure of the immigrant as either committing crime or not committing crime. Needless to say, there are many aspects of immigrant life that have nothing to do with crime—or any other indicators of integration to American society, for that matter. In criticizing the genre of "immigrant literature," literary scholar Glenda Carpio has argued that the empathy incited by the story of hardship and suffering often prevents readers from critically examining their own complicity in such suffering.[58] In such reading, empathy, she further argues, borders on condescension and blinds the readers from the structural conditions that enable such suffering as well as their own standpoint from which empathy extends. While the direct comparison of literature and social science is not feasible, I believe this criticism merits a consideration in sociologists' approach to race and immigration as well. Namely, when we rush to report that immigrants do not commit crime and do not eat neighbors' pets, what questions are we not asking? Are we not reducing the immigrant to a character in the world of racial liberalism, in which she marches bravely through prejudice and discrimination toward full integration, possibly only reached during her children's generation? Critical reflections on these questions, I believe, will lead us to produce a more comprehensive and empirically accurate account of immigrant lives.

In this regard, I see two non-White researchers situated at the margin of the Dillingham Commission's orbit as providing inspirations, imperfect as they were in their efforts. They both worked with the tools at their disposal to ask the questions others associated with the commission did not dare to ask—that of Whiteness and Blackness, respectively.

Yamato Ichihashi, as a native informant turned researcher, dedicated his career to explaining Japanese immigrants to White policymakers and the public. In the process, he rendered the illegible Japanese immigrants legible by presenting them as embodying an ideal of desirability. However, his vision exceeded that of the state, and he saw and reported too much—to the extent that the information presented revealed a contradiction in racial liberalism. That is, Japanese immigrants had already traveled the path of eventual progress laid out by racial liberalism, only to discover that, at the end of the road, full acceptance was impossible due to their being non-White. In a sense, Ichihashi's faithful following of racial liberalism exposed its foremost contradiction around Whiteness.

On the contrary, Zora Neale Hurston procured illegible information that went far beyond the epistemological framework of racial liberalism. Hurston's Black people were not miserable, nor were they getting any "better," that is, moving toward eventual assimilation or integration. They just lived their lives, and their "culture" was presented not as an explanation of difference but as a testament of their being. There was no framework for assessing their place, no myth to dispel through facts, and no destination to reach in the future. Instead, in the stories Hurston collected, facts intertwine with dreams to open up a new dimension of what it means to be Black beyond White people's contempt and pity.[59] In her account, race finally ceased to be a framework for understanding the lives of the racialized.

Ichihashi and Hurston also dreamed of freedom from race but in a way that was incompatible with racial liberalism. Looking ahead on the pathway of racial progress, Ichihashi arrived at the destination too fast, discovering its forbidden secrets; Hurston got off the pathway altogether and drifted into uncharted territories. Although their dreams of freedom were neglected and cut short during their lifetimes, their trajectories point to the world beyond racial liberalism. Perhaps in that world we can escape the stalemate of myth versus facts in the immigration debate.

# Acknowledgments

I wrote this book in the decade between 2015 and 2025, when immigration once again became the most contested issue in American society. As an immigrant, student, researcher, writer, and teacher, I have experienced a myriad of emotions throughout the decade: excitement and enthusiasm on better days, but fear, astonishment, and despair on many other days. A host of supporters and fellow travelers stayed by my side during those days and helped me get through this book. We live in the age of inflated rhetoric in academia and routinely call each other "rock star" and "genius" as compliments. I am certainly neither and was only able to produce this book because of those who held my hand throughout the process. Congruent with this book's theme, I would like to celebrate the collective enterprise of knowledge production, the beautiful codependent community of curious individuals who cannot help asking questions even at considerable personal cost and sacrifice.

Research for this book began during my doctoral work in the Sociology Department at the University of California, Berkeley. Hence the first order of appreciation belongs to my teachers there.

I still remember vividly receiving an email from Ann Swidler fifteen years ago, titled "Berkeley!" My life certainly changed from that day on, and I embarked on the lifelong journey of being a professional scholar. Throughout my years in graduate school and beyond, Ann has been a source of invaluable advice, especially when I was facing important intellectual and professional choices. When I was contemplating starting this project, which was a radical shift in my intellectual trajectory up to that point, she simply told me to "try it out for a week" to see if I liked it. There was no discussion of repercussions or risks—only the question of intellectual curiosity. I could not have amassed the courage to dive into uncharted territory by myself without her encouragement, and for that I am grateful.

Cybelle Fox has taught me many things, but I will forever remember her patience and kindness. She took a somewhat unruly student under her wing when I did not know what I was doing. She sat through hours of conversations in which I thought aloud the ideas for this book. Of course, 90 percent of what I told her ended up being shot down by either me, her, or other commentators, but those conversations kept this project moving forward. She taught me to be thorough and relentless in scholarship but also simply to be a kind human. I hope to express my appreciation for her by being equally patient with all the unruly students who will come my way.

As I make progress in my academic career, I find myself increasingly asking the question: What would Taeku Lee do in this situation? Such was his imprint on my identity as a scholar. I had the good fortune of shadowing him on multiple research projects and in the process was able to learn the art of decision making, both in academia and life. It is through the example of his work and life that I got to understand what it means to strive for meaningful things with humility. I hope to return the favor by making good decisions throughout my career.

Other teachers also provided support throughout various stages of my graduate career. Irene Bloemraad has shaped how I think about immigration, and she cheered me on even when I felt like I was going in circles. Mara Loveman inspired much of the theoretical framework of my dissertation and provided me with a renewed sense of intellectual excitement in the later years of graduate training. Marion Fourcade was and continues to be a source of inspiration. Cristina Mora, Chris Miller, and Armando Lara-Millán have helped me grow intellectually and professionally. Brian Powers believed in me from the beginning and generously shared his insights and wisdom throughout the process. Neil Fligstein provided crucial help at the final stage of this project.

Last but not least, Michael Omi offered much guidance as I developed the theoretical argument of this book. When I was totally lost, he suggested that I criticize his theory—or more precisely, carefully build my argument against his work to clearly formulate my theoretical intervention. That was a crucial turning point of this project, and I am grateful for his openness. His intellectual generosity should be something that each of us should aspire to.

I moved 9,000 kilometers—that is, some 6,600 miles—across the Pacific to start my doctoral work. On the first evening after I landed at the San Francisco airport, as the long summer day in Berkeley succumbed to darkness, I realized that I knew no one within a thousand-mile radius of me. It was a terrifying feeling. But over the years, my friends from the graduate school eased my fear and made me feel at home. As we often reminisce when we meet at conferences, the 2010s in the Bay Area were the best time of our lives, even though we were stressed out about work and personal finances. I often imagine going back in time to enjoy once more those long walks, coffee chats, and passionate discussions that made us who we are today.

In no particular order, Carlos Bustamante, Carter Koppelman, Alyssa Newman, Yang Lor, Herbert Docena, Gowri Vijayakumar, Louise Ly, Kristen Nelson, Rebecca Elliott, Beth Pearson, Katy Fox-Hodess, Peter Ekman, Kate Maich, Fithawee Tzeggai, Kristen Nelson, Benjamin Shestakofsky, Jonah Brundage, Jessica Schirmer, Christian Olmos, Andy Cheng, and Jeffrey Weng sustained me throughout my time in Berkeley. The members of the Interdisciplinary Immigration Workshop—Alicia Sheares, Isabel García, Dani Carrillo, Andy Chang, Christian Phillips, Jae Yeon Kim, and Brendan Shanahan—read and commented on many chapters of my dissertation. The Korean family made up of Keun Bok Lee, Esther Cho, Joohyun Park, Paul Chung, and HongJune Park was a lifeline, especially when things did not go as I expected. The members of Sociologists of Color and Allies (SoCA) have done some remarkable work in the department, and I hope we continue to make an impact both in and out of the profession.

After I arrived at Dartmouth, my colleagues in the Sociology Department welcomed me with open arms and supported me in everything I did. Deborah King and Misagh Parsa provided much-needed institutional wisdom. Marc Dixon, as the department chair, gently helped me chart out my trajectory in a new environment. Emily Walton, always a good friend, read a portion of this book and provided comments. Kathryn Lively, Kim Rogers, Janice McCabe, Jason Houle, Brooke Harrington, Greg Sharp, Kristen Smith, Rebecca Johnson, and Michele Tine continue to be the best colleagues one can hope for. Junior faculty writing group members Casey Stockstill, Shonta' Allen, and Smriti Upadhyay remind me that we are in this together.

Special thanks go out to my Dartmouth faculty mentors. John Campbell read the entire manuscript and provided crucial insights. I learned from John how to professionally engage with scholarly ideas. Matt Garcia also read all of the manuscript, and he urged me to speak directly about what is happening in our times. The ideas in the conclusion owe much to his advice. Matt Delmont has also lent crucial institutional support when I needed it.

The participants of the Mellon Faculty Fellows group were the first to see and respond to some of the material presented in this book. Israel Reyes, Richard Wright, and Mingwei Huang patiently combed through the first iteration of chapter 3 and asked sharp questions. Richard's reflection on his career also provided an inspiration for the conclusion.

Beyond Dartmouth, I am greatly indebted to the scholars who studied the Dillingham Commission. Once I thought I was a hopeless student interested in a topic about which no one cared. The warm embrace of Robert Zeidel, Joel Perlmann, and Katherine Benton-Cohen made me realize that I was not alone. I thank them for sharing their work and encouraging me to take baby steps. Notably, Katherine Benton-Cohen took time and effort to point out all the errors and lapses in my argument. I am especially thankful for her generosity over the years.

Ann Morning came all the way to Hanover, New Hampshire, to attend the book workshop. Her input on the introduction as well as other parts of this book proved to be crucial. Hana Brown provided insightful comments on the theoretical implication of my analysis and encouraged me to say what I wanted to say. Jaeeun Kim, katrina quisumbing king, Anna Skarpelis, Leslie Hinkson, and Roger Waldinger have also read parts of the book over the years and provided productive suggestions. Lastly, Moon-Kie Jung saw what no one else saw in this book and helped me sharpen my edge without sacrificing my distinctive style of thought. Thanks to him I now firmly believe that every obscure reference and phrase in one's writing has a reader somewhere in the world.

I am especially indebted to Mary Grover, my editor, for making this work legible. Without her careful attention, I could not have found a path out of the treacherous process of writing and re-writing. Elizabeth Branch Dyson initially saw the potential in my manuscript and allowed me to be myself through the publication process. Mollie McFee helped with the logistics of publishing.

Family matters most. My parents, Tae Jung Kim and Kyunghee Yang, have been an anchor in my life. I am more like them than they recognize. I thank my mother-in-law, Soonhwa Kim, for her support and prayers. My sister, Sunmee Kim, was an invisible companion of my journey as she herself worked toward her own sociology PhD and book publication. May and June deserve special thanks for keeping me awake through the long nights of reading and writing.

My child, Siwon, arrived at the halfway point of the journey. I do hope that he gets to live in a world where none of the things I discuss in my book is remotely relevant for his life. I do understand that my time with him in this world is finite, and hope that I can help fill his youth with happy memories.

Although I have mentioned many names, and all of them deserve my gratitude, none do more than Sujin Eom. It was only after I met her that I began to take myself and my career seriously. More than anything, her presence made me cherish every single day throughout my time in graduate school and beyond. As my life took me to unexpected places, she kept me grounded and provided a place to call home. I look forward to the day when we get to reminisce about all the adventures we've had together.

Parts of the argument and evidence presented in this book have been published in *Theory and Society* and *Qualitative Sociology*, among others.

# Appendix

## The Titles of the *Dillingham Commission Reports*

1. Volumes 1–2: *Abstracts of Reports of the Immigration Commission, with Conclusions and Recommendations and Views of the Minority.*[1]
2. Volume 3: *Statistical Review of Immigration, 1820–1910. Distribution of Immigrants, 1850–1900.*
3. Volume 4: *Emigration Conditions in Europe.*
4. Volume 5: *Dictionary of Races or People.*
5. Volumes 6–7: *Bituminous Coal Mining.*
6. Volumes 8–9: *Iron and Steel Manufacturing.*
7. Volume 10: *Cotton Goods Manufacturing in the North Atlantic States; Woolen and Worsted Goods Manufacturing.*
8. Volume 11: *Silk Goods and Manufacturing and Dyeing; Clothing Manufacturing; Collar, Cuff, and Shirt Manufacturing.*
9. Volume 12: *Leather Manufacturing; Boot and Shoe Manufacturing; Glove Manufacturing.*
10. Volume 13: *Slaughtering and Meat Packing.*
11. Volume 14: *Glass Manufacturing; Agricultural Implement and Vehicle Manufacturing.*
12. Volume 15: *Cigar and Tobacco Manufacturing; Furniture Manufacturing; Sugar Refining.*
13. Volume 16: *Copper Mining and Smelting; Iron Ore Mining; Anthracite Coal Mining; Oil Refining.*
14. Volumes 17–18: *Diversified Industries.*
15. Volumes 19–20: *Summary Report on Immigrants in Manufacturing and Mining.*
16. Volumes 21–22: *Recent Immigrants in Agriculture.*

1. The titles of the volumes were obtained from the opening pages of volume 1. Volume 42, which was supposed to include an index, was planned but never printed.

17. Volumes 23–25: *Japanese and Other Immigrant Races in the Pacific Coast and Rocky Mountain States.*
18. Volumes 26–27: *Immigrants in Cities: A Study of the Population of Selected Districts in New York, Chicago, Philadelphia, Boston, Cleveland, Buffalo, and Milwaukee.*
19. Volume 28: *Occupations of the First and Second Generations of Immigrants in the United States; Fecundity of Immigrant Women.*
20. Volumes 29–33: *The Children of Immigrants in Schools.*
21. Volumes 34–35: *Immigrants as Charity Seekers.*
22. Volume 36: *Immigration and Crime.*
23. Volume 37: *Steerage Conditions, Importation and Harboring of Women for Immoral Purposes, Immigrant Homes and Aid Societies, Immigrant Banks.*
24. Volume 38: *Changes in Bodily Form of Descendants of Immigrants*: (Final Report).
25. Volume 39: *Immigration Legislation.*
26. Volume 40: *The Immigration Situation in other Countries: Canada, Australia, New Zealand, Argentina, Brazil.*
27. Volume 41: *Statements and Recommendations Submitted by Societies and Organizations Interested in the Subject of Immigration.*

# Notes

## INTRODUCTION

1. Under the first Trump administration, the United States Citizenship and Immigration Service deleted all mentions of "a nation of immigrants" from its mission statement. Instead, the new mission statement foregrounded "protecting Americans, securing the homeland, and honoring our values" as the agency's core mission. The Biden administration once again overhauled it to include "America's promise as a nation of welcome and possibility with fairness, integrity, and respect for all we serve." In 2025, both mission statements were deleted from the agency's website, replaced by a terse description of "What We Do": "USCIS is the federal agency that oversees the lawful immigration to the United States. We are a component of the Department of Homeland Security." https://www.uscis.gov/about-us/mission-and-core-values/what-we-do.

2. My use of the term *race* follows that of Michael Omi and Howard Winant in *Racial Formation*. Rather than a scientific concept, race is a primarily historical construction, the meaning of which is always embedded in the contemporary social struggles for domination. In the modern era, race relied heavily on the authority of natural science—more specifically, biology—and invoked the purported natural divisions in humankind for its intellectual and political legitimacy. As Omi and Winant point out, however, the concept of race has always been political and encompassed the violent process of "sorting out the bodies" (78) to distinguish "us" from "them," often through the capacity of nation-states. In their attacks against immigrants, both the early twentieth-century immigration restrictionists and Trump repeat these centuries-old rhetorical tropes. Therefore, I refer to them as "racializing"—attributing race to the existing social relations—immigrants.

3. Swidler, "Culture in Action."

4. I define the immigration restrictionists as the broad coalition of intellectuals, politicians, and activists who were concerned about the impact of immigration at the turn of the twentieth century. Although they differ in specifics, all of them believed that there should be government intervention aimed at controlling, if not altogether stopping, the inflow of immigrants—southern and eastern Europeans in particular. "Nativists" denote an elusive coalition based on a political ideology, which itself is hard to pin down. Their animosity toward immigrants was motivated by various factors, such as racial and religious prejudice, economic self-interest, and

environmental concerns (see Higham, *Strangers in the Land*). The diversity in their ideological inclinations and social background makes it difficult to conceptualize them as a coherent group, especially across different time periods. For instance, the Boston Brahmins saw themselves as antithetical to the Know-Nothings of the 1850s, in both social background and ideology (see chapter 1). On the other hand, I use "immigration restrictionists" to refer to those who shared a policy goal—controlling immigration through the actions of the federal government—regardless of their ideology, specifically in the context of the late nineteenth century.

5. Benton-Cohen, *Inventing the Immigration Problem.*

6. Henceforth I refer to the reports as the *Dillingham Commission Reports* (*DCR*).

7. For a contemporary discussion, see Jiménez, *The Other Side of Assimilation*; Jiménez and Horowitz, "When White Is Just Alright"; and Waters and Jiménez, "Assessing Immigrant Assimilation."

8. Guess, Nyhan, and Reifler, "Exposure to Untrustworthy Websites"; Jerit and Zhao, "Political Misinformation"; J. Allen et al., "Evaluating the Fake News Problem"; Rao and Greve, "Plot Thickens"; Green, Fielding, and Brownson, "More on Fake News"; M. Kim et al., "When Truth Trumps Facts." Many of these works focus on the psychological and social basis of faulty reasoning, such as confirmation bias and "echo chambers." The scholars in science and technology studies, on the contrary, have understood such seemingly external factors not as anomalies but as essential preconditions for facts and scientific inference. See Ludwik Fleck, *Genesis and Development*, for the earliest incarnation of this argument.

9. Some commentators have correctly pointed out the parochial nature of the term *race* and proposed "ethnicity" as the more general concept for comparative social scientific analysis of peoplehood across time and space. See Cornell and Hartmann, *Ethnicity and Race*; Wimmer, "Race-Centrism"; Winant, "Race"; Bonilla-Silva, "Essential Social Fact of Race"; and Loveman, "Is 'Race' Essential?" More recently, Ann Morning and Marcello Maneri, in *Ugly Word*, proposed the term "descent-based difference" to eschew some of the common misunderstandings associated with race, while José Itzigsohn and Karida Brown, in *The Sociology of W. E. B. Du Bois*, submitted "racialized modernity" as the central object of inquiry for sociology. On the other hand, both Mustafa Emirbayer and Matthew Desmond (*Racial Order*) and Loic Wacquant (*Racial Domination*) respectively attempted a synthesis under the overarching concept of race while incorporating diverse branches of theories ranging from pragmatism to Gaston Bachelard's epistemology. While there is much to appreciate in these scholarly exchanges, this book prioritizes "race" on the following grounds. First, in the early twentieth century, race was the most important theoretical vocabulary through which the immigration debate was conducted. As I show in chapter 1, the term encompassed many things but, at the same time, carried a specific set of meanings when used in certain contexts. It is simply convenient and more accurate to use *race* as an overarching term in describing and analyzing the immigration debate in the early twentieth century than using *ethnicity*, a technical term used by a handful of ethnologists during the time. Second, my aim is to understand how the debate contributed to our understanding of race (and ethnicity) in the twenty-first century; therefore, it is pertinent to foreground the concept. That is, our contemporary understanding of the term was forged through the confusions and contestations we witness throughout the book, and my goal is to faithfully trace these processes, not present a more theoretically informed terminology.

Loic Wacquant and Pierre Bourdieu (*Invitation to Reflexive Sociology*) warned against the conflation of "folk" and "scientific" categories; race is certainly a folk category, but my task in this book is to understand how this folk category became a widely accepted framework, despite its inherent contradictions, inaccuracies, and inconsistencies. In a sense this book is a historical explanation of how we came to cling to the concept, not an investigation into whether the concept is theoretically valid or not.

10. My use of racial liberalism is informed by David Theo Goldberg's discussion of "naturalism" and "historicism" within the modern racial state (*Racial State*, 44–45). "Naturalism" regards racial others as "being naturally incapable of development and historical progress," whereas "historicism" sees them as currently inferior to, but capable of eventual progress toward and parity with, Whites. I revise these two terms as "racial essentialism" and "racial liberalism," respectively, to denote major intersecting currents of racial ideas in the late nineteenth and early twentieth centuries. For racial essentialism, I decided to forgo the use of nature because the concept of race often spilled over to the domains deemed not nature, leading to seemingly contradictory terms such "historic race" (see chapter 1). For racial liberalism, I am explicitly connecting "historicism" and its emphasis on eventual progress to mid-twentieth-century political ideology associated with the early civil rights movement focusing on desegregation (see Guinier, "From Racial Liberalism to Racial Literacy," for its mid-century genealogy; see Crenshaw, "Race Liberalism," for contemporary relevance; see Schickler, "New Deal Liberalism," for relation to New Deal liberalism; and see Brilliant, "Reimagining Racial Liberalism," for a different perspective focusing on multiracial coalitions in California). My use of racial liberalism comes close to Darda's (*Strange Career*, 11) formulation: "the antithesis of segregation, a construction that shut out race radicalisms and bred a host of other binaries—exclusion versus inclusion, biological racism versus cultural difference, racial essentialism versus environmental 'root causes'—that made reform look like the revolution radicals had foreseen" (see also Murakawa, *First Civil Right*). In making this connection, I highlight that racial liberalism's focus on desegregation actually has its origins in the early twentieth-century immigration debate—pro-immigrant advocacy and its emphasis on assimilation, to be precise. In terms of immigration, my use of the two terms maps onto, though not exactly, Rogers Smith's discussion of "ascriptive" and "civic" nationalisms in *Civic Ideals* as well as Roth, Stee, and Regla-Vargas's contrast between "essentialism" and "constructivism" in "Conceptualization of Race." Compared to "constructivism," my use of racial liberalism is more historically specific, with an emphasis on gradual progress of the racialized, the idea that emerged in the early twentieth century and rose to prominence in the postwar period. In other words, racial liberalism is more of a narrative with a specific temporal component while "constructivism" is an analytical stance. See Jerng, *Racial Worldmaking*. Lastly, my use of racial liberalism is distinct from Charles Mills's usage in *Racial Contract*, which focuses on criticizing the neglect of race in social contract theory and liberal political philosophy more generally.

11. In analyzing the early social sciences' understanding of Black psyche, Daryl Scott devised in *Contempt and Pity* the terms *contempt* and *pity* as two attitudinal companions to essentialist and liberal understand of race, respectively. I apply his framework to the figure of the racialized immigrant.

12. Lew-Williams, *Chinese Must Go*. Historian Arthur Link defines the Progressive movement as "the popular effort, which began convulsively in the 1890s and waxed and

waned afterward to our own time, to insure the survival of democracy in the United States by the enlargement of governmental power to control and offset the power of private economic groups over the nation's institutions and life" ("What Happened," 834–37). Of course, these movements had various concerns and constituents and did not display much consistency. The Progressive reform movement in immigration focused on assisting and assimilating European immigrants in big cities like Chicago. The heyday of these movements, approximately from the 1890s to the 1920s, is called the Progressive Era.

13. There is a lingering debate on how Mexicans, or immigrants from Central and South America more broadly, fit in the Black-White divide. For a comprehensive discussion focusing on the early twentieth century, see Fox and Guglielmo, "Defining America's Racial Boundaries."

14. Benton-Cohen, *Inventing the Immigration Problem*. See Ngai, *Impossible Subjects*, for the importance of this historical juncture.

15. Skowronek, *Building a New American State*; Frymer, *Building an American Empire*; Jung and Kwon, "Theorizing the US Racial State."

16. My approach shares affinity with Robert Merton's ("Three Fragments") notion of "strategic research materials" as well as Bruno Latour's (*Science in Action*) actor network theory.

17. This caricature is more often found in works surveying the immigration policy development of the early twentieth century. Oscar Handlin's seminal assessment of the commission (*Race and Nationality*) has had a strong influence on these characterizations. See Tichenor, *Dividing Lines*, 42, and Zolberg, *Nation by Design*, 232–33, for examples. The works that engage with the commission in more detail—such as Benton-Cohen, *Inventing the Immigration Problem*; Zeidel, *Immigrants, Progressives, and Exclusion Politics*; and Perlmann, *Americans Classify the Immigrant*—provide a more nuanced perspective.

18. Throughout the book, I generally refrain from using the term *racist*, other than in parenthesis to invoke the conventional meaning of the adjective. *Racism* and its derivative, *racist*, became popular after Ruth Benedict made them core themes in her 1943 wartime pamphlet *The Races of Mankind* (see also the conclusion to this book). Early twentieth-century commentators generally eschewed the term—if they were not entirely ignorant of it—and relied on "race prejudice" to convey a similar, but not entirely identical, meaning. Labeling an entity or person in the early twentieth century as "racist" comes with little analytical benefit, as almost everything and everyone during the period, even those who pushed back against *racism*, would qualify as racist under our contemporary sensibilities. Rather than focusing on whether an entity is racist or not, I pay more attention to where such entity is located within the spectrum of racial ideas available during the period. I am indebted to Katherine Benton-Cohen (*Inventing the Immigration Problem*) for this perspective. In a similar vein, Lee Baker (*Anthropology*) proposed *racialist* as an alternative term.

19. I follow the lead of Benton-Cohen (*Inventing the Immigration Problem*) on this point.

20. Brown and Jones, "Rethinking Panethnicity"; Romero, "Crossing"; Treitler, "Social Agency"; Sáenz and Douglas, "Call for Racialization." See also Jung, "Racial Unconscious," for a comprehensive critique. The theory of segmented assimilation may

be the most conspicuous example of such cross-fertilization (Portes and Zhou, "New Second Generation"; Portes and Rumbaut, *Immigrant America*; Portes and Rumbaut, *Legacies*). Omi and Winant, in *Racial Formation*, as well as Vilna Bashi Treitler, in *Ethnic Project*, argue that the figure of the immigrant, or its narrative form, "immigrant analogy," functions as an alibi for the plight of African Americans. That is, the narrative of immigrants overcoming hardships indirectly blames African Americans for not doing the same. See Hattam, *In the Shadow of Race*, for a related discussion focusing on ethnicity. In her works on Asian racialization and anti-Blackness, "Racial Triangulation of Asian Americans" and *Asian Americans in an Anti-Black World*, Claire Jean Kim has also demonstrated that this dynamic has been central to the formulation and maintenance of the racial order in the United States.

21. Roth, *Race Migrations*; Jones, "They Are There with Us." Works on Latino migration have also relied on the framework of race and racialization in explaining heightened administrative surveillance around Latino migrant workers (Chavez, *Latino Threat*; Golash-Boza, *Deported*). Aristide Zolberg, in *Nation by Design*, and David FitzGerald and David Cook-Martin, in *Culling the Masses*, also address this gap by centering race in their historical studies of American immigration policy.

22. Treitler, "Social Agency"; Treitler, *Ethnic Project*; Omi and Winant, *Racial Formation*. See Blauner, "Internal Colonialism," for an early iteration of this idea. See Wacquant, *Racial Domination*, for an extended critique.

23. Mamdani, *Define and Rule*. See also Sharma, *Home Rule*; and Goldberg, *Racial State*. My approach shares an affinity with the postcolonial perspective on the American state, which problematizes national boundaries and places so-called domestic minorities and immigrants on a unified analytical spectrum as colonial subjects (Blauner, "Internal Colonialism"; Go, "Thinking Against Empire"; see Hammer and Itzigsohn, "Rethinking Historical Sociology," for a review). In *Enduring Empire*, katrina quisumbing king provides a detailed account of how the American empire employed this divide in its engagement with the Philippines by simultaneously rendering Filipinos as both overseas colonial subjects and domestic minorities. As she points out, connecting these two different definitions were the continuing legal and physical violence against the racial other.

24. See also endnote 9 in this chapter.

25. Gossett, *Race*; Painter, *History of White People*.

26. Morning, *Nature of Race*; Omi and Winant, *Racial Formation*; Jung, *Reworking Race*.

27. See Shiao et al., "Genomic Challenges"; Fujimura et al., "Clines Without Classes." See also Roth and Ivemark, "Genetic Options"; Roth and Yaylacı, "Genetic Options and Constraints."

28. Zuberi, *Thicker Than Blood*.

29. From this perspective, "scientific racism" can be understood as a particularly effective manifestation of such legitimacy. The literature on symbolic power of the state recognizes the crucial role played by modern-nation states in this process (Loveman, "Modern State"; Bourdieu, *On the State*; Goldberg, *Racial State*).

30. Hochschild and Powell, "Racial Reorganization"; Anderson, *American Census*; Nobles, *Shades of Citizenship*; Schor, *Counting Americans*; Prewitt, *What Is Your*

*Race?*; Fox, *Three Worlds of Relief*; Katznelson, *When Affirmative Action Was White*; Lieberman, *Shifting the Color Line*; Quadagno, *Color of Welfare*; Mandelberg, *Race Card.*

31. Emigh, Riley, and Ahmed, *Changes in Censuses.*

32. Mora, *Making Hispanics*; Rodríguez-Muñiz, *Figures of the Future.*

33. Pascoe, *What Comes Naturally*, 140–42. The proposal initially defined anyone with more than 1/64 of Indigenous "blood" as "colored," practically classifying anyone with any known Indigenous heritage as non-White. The revised law included the so-called Pocahontas rule, recognizing only those with more than 1/16 of Indigenous "blood" as "colored." More interestingly, members of Indigenous tribes, whose ancestry placed them on both sides of this divide, had defied this system by registering themselves as "white."

34. With a different topic but in a similar analysis, Ian Hacking writes of "sticky" objects of knowledge production in *Social Construction of What?*

35. Omi and Winant, *Racial Formation*, 104.

36. In their campaign speeches, Donald Trump and his surrogates would read the names of people murdered by undocumented immigrants. They could have just argued that all undocumented immigrants are criminals without evidence, but they chose to supplement the faulty claim with corroborating information. Of course, such information is misleading, to say the least, but it is important to note that they needed to have *something* on which to base their accusation. Critics counterargued, citing representativeness of the named individuals' crimes and other forms of validity checks (e.g., that said incidents take up less than 0.01 percent of all murders, the native-born population has a higher murder rate, etc.), adding further pressure to the task of justifying race. In reality, a family member of a victim undermined this rhetorical strategy by revealing that Trump never spoke to the family, contrary to his claims. See "Trump Said He Spoke to Murder Victim's Family. The Victim's Sister Said It Never Happened," *Washington Post*, April 2, 2024.

37. Faust, *Scared Circle.* See also Skarpelis, "Horror Vacui," for an example from Nazi Germany.

38. Morning, "Does Genomics Challenge." The sociological criticism against genetic determinism generally takes this line of reasoning. The proponents of "genetic race" usually respond with a dose of pragmatism (e.g., racial categories are based not on an essential notion of race but on inductive data patterns), but this argument is not too far from that of racial essentialism in the early twentieth century, especially that held by eugenicists.

39. Jasanoff, *States of Knowledge.*

40. Schaffer and Shapin, *Leviathan and the Air-Pump*, 332.

41. Merton, "Unanticipated Consequences."

42. Muhammad, *Condemnation of Blackness*; C. Muller, "Northward Migration"; Bonilla-Silva, *Racism Without Racists*; Alexander, *New Jim Crow.* Naomi Murakawa, in *First Civil Right*, explicitly connects 1940s liberal advocacy with the rise of mass incarceration after the 1960s.

43. Poovey, *History of Modern Fact*; Frankel, *States of Inquiry.*

44. Lipsky, *Street-Level Bureaucracy.*

45. See Vaughan, *Challenger Launch Decision*, for an example of a contemporary investigative commission beyond the Progressive Era; see also Poovey, *History of Modern Fact.*

46. Mitchell, "Limits of the State," 78.

47. Frankel, *States of Inquiry*, 4–10. In *On the State*, Pierre Bourdieu saw commissions as core parts of the apparatus that exercise symbolic power: "Public commissions are stagings, operations that consist in staging a set of people who have to play out a kind of public drama" that lead to "a new definition of a problem constituted as public" (25–26).

48. Frankel, *States of Inquiry*, 8–9.

49. Frankel, *States of Inquiry*, 3; see also Hacking, *Social Construction of What?*; Hacking, "Making Up People."

50. Frankel, *States of Inquiry*, 10. See Canaday, *Straight State*, for an example focusing on sexuality.

51. D. King and Smith, "Racial Orders." Omi and Winant, in *Racial Formation*, make a nearly identical point while highlighting the state-society relationship over institutional configurations.

52. Poovey, *History of Modern Fact*; see also Schaffer and Shapin, *Leviathan and the Air-Pump.*

53. Frankel, *States of Inquiry*, 21.

54. Wiebe, *Search for Order.*

55. Skowronek, *Building a New American State*; Carpenter, *Forging of Bureaucratic Autonomy.*

56. D. Ross, *Origin of American Social Science.*

57. Turner, "Significance of the Frontier."

58. Frymer, *Building an American Empire*; Love, *Race over Empire.*

59. Griswold, "Agrarian Democracy"; see also Roy, *American Dark Age.*

60. Higham, *Strangers in the Land.*

61. E. Ross, *Old World in the New.*

62. Benton-Cohen, *Inventing the Immigration Problem.*

63. L. Gordon, *Moral Property of Women.*

64. Tichenor, *Dividing Lines*, 122; see also Spiro, *Defending the Master Race.*

65. E. Lee, *At America's Gates*; Lew-Williams, *Chinese Must Go.*

66. Pascoe, *What Comes Naturally*, 94–95.

67. Dunbar-Ortiz, *Not "A Nation of Immigrants."* See also Blackhawk, *Rediscovery of America*, 223. For both African Americans and "Indians," there was an element of racial liberalism in their racialization. There was a conscious effort, often led by Black leaders like Booker T. Washington, for "racial uplift," which emphasized African Americans' potential to better their material and mental conditions through concerted community effort (see also chapter 1). Native Americans were also given a chance to assimilate into White society by accepting a modern, nontribal way of life, although doing so meant

the effective erasure of Native people and culture. These strains of racial liberalisms are different from the one I highlight in this book in two aspects. First, they were more similar to reform campaigns focused on community than intellectual efforts to tackle racial essentialism. Second, they did not consist of a boundary-crossing network of the sort I describe in later chapters. Therefore, they did not effectively challenge the dominance of racial essentialism in both academia and society in general. See Baker, *Anthropology*, for an analysis of these movements focusing on racial uplift.

68. Guterl, *Color of Race*; Roediger, *Working Toward Whiteness*; Kolchin, "Whiteness Studies."

69. Jacobson, *Whiteness*. There is a long, convoluted history of defining Whiteness in legal terms (Haney-López, *White by Law*). As Cybelle Fox and Thomas A. Guglielmo in "Defining America's Racial Boundaries" have shown, however, the legal Whiteness of southern and eastern Europeans was seldom in doubt, especially as compared to Blacks, Asians, and Mexicans. Their status in relation to WASPs, however, was a different question.

70. Morris, *Scholar Denied*; Stocking, *Race, Culture, and Evolution*; Baker, *Anthropology*.

71. Swidler, "Culture in Action."

72. Benton-Cohen, *Inventing the Immigration Problem*.

73. Handlin, *Race and Nationality*, 104.

74. Tichenor, *Dividing Lines*, 42. FitzGerald and Cook-Martin make a brief reference to the commission, citing its emphasis on Mexican immigrants as laborers rather than citizens (*Culling the Masses*, 13).

75. Higham, *Strangers in the Land*, 189.

76. D. King, *Making Americans*, 50–84.

77. Zolberg, *Nation by Design*, 232–38. To be fair, all the scholars cited here had a broader focus, and the commission takes up less than a chapter in their respective monographs.

78. Zeidel, *Immigrants, Progressives, and Exclusion Politics*.

79. Perlmann, *Americans Classify the Immigrant*.

80. Benton-Cohen, *Inventing the Immigration Problem*.

81. Jung, *Reworking Race*.

82. Alba and Nee, *Remaking the American Mainstream*; M. Gordon, *Assimilation in American Life*; Zeigler-McPherson, *Americanization in the States*.

83. Kevles, *In the Name of Eugenics*; FitzGerald and Cook-Martin, *Culling the Masses*.

84. As I detail in the following chapters, the rise of cultural anthropology and the Chicago school of sociology epitomize these developments. Hattam, *In the Shadow of Race*; Yu, *Thinking Orientals*.

85. Omi and Winant, *Racial Formation*; Treitler, *Ethnic Project*; Hattam, *In the Shadow of Race*; Sollors, *Invention of Ethnicity*.

86. Zeidel, *Immigrants, Progressives, and Exclusion Politics*; Perlmann, *Americans Classify the Immigrant*; Benton-Cohen, *Inventing the Immigration Problem*. Benton-Cohen's comprehensive biography has been especially useful in discovering often-neglected sources.

87. Emigh, "The Power of Negative Thinking."

88. Foucault, *Discipline and Punish*, 81.

89. Foucault, *Security, Territory, Population*, 117.

90. Foucault's genealogy, David Garland writes, starts from "quite concrete and specific critical observations about the present, and, more particularly, about the analyst's object of study as it is constructed and experienced in the present. These genealogies begin with a certain puzzlement or discomfiture about practices or institutions that others take for granted" ("What Is a 'History of the Present,'" 379).

91. Hacking, "Making Up People," 107; Omi and Winant, *Racial Formation*, 104.

92. Du Bois, *Dusk of Dawn*, 67. I thank the anonymous reviewer for suggesting this quote.

93. Clemens, "Towards a Historicized Sociology"; Pacewicz, "What Can You Do"; Hirschman and Reed, "Formation Stories."

94. Emigh, "The Power of Negative Thinking"; Stoler, *Along the Archival Grain*; Lala-Milán, Sargent, and Kim, "Theorizing with Archives"; Ginzburg, *Clues, Myths, and the Historical Method*; Koselleck, *Practice of Conceptual History*.

95. The concerns about generalization and selection undergird such criticism. While I cannot engage in a full discussion of these concerns here, suffice it to point out that such criticisms are more useful in discussing a research object in relation to other comparable objects within a common frame of reference. However, there are research objects that establish the epistemological possibility of seeing others as comparable, thereby conditioning the possibility of generalization. One may argue that those objects are constitutional in the sense that they define what is thinkable and sayable—including the concerns about generalization and selection—within a particular domain of intellectual inquiry. In these instances, the concerns about generalization and selection are irrelevant because such concerns are conditional on the analysis of the said research objects. In *Model Cases*, Monica Krause demonstrates that the French Revolution as a research object establishes the very possibility of thinking about revolutions; furthermore, the Russian Revolution establishes the possibility of thinking about revolutions beyond liberal-bourgeois political activity. Lastly, the Haitian revolution further expands the epistemological domain to allow for consideration of political possibilities that exceed the limits of "racialized modernity" (Itzigsohn and Brown, *Sociology of W. E. B. Du Bois*; Go and Watson, "Anticolonial Nationalism"; Hammer and White, "Toward a Sociology of Colonial Subjectivity"). In these cases, generalization and selection become an issue only after the establishment of epistemological possibility of thinking about these cases, respectively. While the case of the Dillingham Commission and the racial ideas in the early twentieth century are not as dramatic as these events, they did establish the possibility of our contemporary thinking about race and ethnicity. In terms of how Foucault's method fits into this discussion, see Agamben, *Signature of All Things*, particularly on the concept of "series."

96. Merton, "Three Fragments."

97. In *The Challenger Launch Decision*, Diane Vaughan emphasizes the importance of avoiding the presentist bias in understanding the decision-making process in organizations. To explain why the *Challenger* accident happened, Vaughan assembles archival documents and interviews to trace the thought processes of those who had

been in positions to stop the launch but had not done so. The key issue is that Vaughan, as well as her readers, are fully aware of the tragic outcome, whereas the actors at NASA had been totally unaware of it before the tragedy struck. Warning against post hoc theorizing of the unthinkable, Vaughan emphasizes the necessity of putting ourselves in historical actors' shoes: What seems obvious to us now was not obvious to them, and only by prioritizing their perspective, and the social circumstances under which the perspective was created and reinforced, can we understand how an unlikely event happens. Of course, this process of understanding is distinct from attributing (or not attributing) moral and legal responsibility to the actors for their decisions. In our case of racial ideas, I would add that analytically parsing out the dynamics and implications of racial ideas is a separate task from condemning them and that the conflation of the two leads to an ineffective criticism of racial domination. See Benton-Cohen, *Inventing the Immigration Problem*, and Baker, *Anthropology*, for similar approaches to racial ideas in the early twentieth century. See also quisumbing king, *Enduring Empire*.

## CHAPTER ONE

1. Zuberi, *Thicker Than Blood*, 34; see also Omi and Winant, *Racial Formation*.

2. Hannah Arendt uses the term in a similar manner in *The Origins of Totalitarianism*.

3. The genetic account suggests categorical human differences originate from distributions of gene chromosomes, presumably through evolutionary processes and migration patterns dating back to prehistoric times. See Shiao et al., "Genomic Challenges," as well as Morning, *Nature of Race*; Morning "Does Genomics Challenge"; Roth and Yaylacı, "Genetic Options and Constraints"; and Duster, *Backdoor to Eugenics*.

4. Itzigsohn and Brown, *Sociology of W. E. B. Du Bois*, 15.

5. Brace, *"Race" Is a Four-Letter Word*.

6. One can presumably make an argument that a rudimentary form of racial liberalism prevailed in the premodern era, preceding racial essentialism.

7. Lie, *Modern Peoplehood*, 89–91.

8. Gossett, *Race*, 35.

9. Lie, *Modern Peoplehood*.

10. Gossett, *Race*, 37.

11. Painter, *History of White People*, 75.

12. Painter, *History of White People*, 82–84.

13. Quoted in Painter, *History of White People*, 82.

14. Bophal, "Beautiful Skull."

15. Painter (*History of White People*, 84) argues that the relative scarcity of Caucasian skulls, especially of the female variety, contributed to this special appreciation. The supply of non-Caucasian skulls, while never enough, was relatively abundant due to colonial expansion and massacres occurring outside the Europe continent. The invasion by Russia of Central Asia yielded Blumenbach's Georgian skull, hence the origin of the term "Caucasian."

16. Along with Linnaeus and other early naturalists, Blumenbach is generally known as not attributing a *hierarchy* to his racial classification scheme, focusing more on *category*, the other core component of race-thinking. In fact, as Gossett points out, he often criticized those who brought the prejudice of ethnocentrism into the scientific enterprise of racial classification scheme, claiming that "if a toad could speak . . . and were asked which was the loveliest creature upon God's earth, it would say simpering, that modesty forbade it to give a real opinion on that point" (*Race*, 39). "At the time when the negroes and the savages were still considered as half animals," one of his admirers argued in a memoir published after his death, "Blumenbach raised his voice, and showed that their psychical qualities were not inferior to those of the European, that even amongst the latter themselves the greatest possible differences existed, and that opportunity alone was wanting for the development of their higher faculties" (Marx, "Life of Blumenbach," 9).

However, Blumenbach did maintain a racial hierarchy of his own. Faithfully following the book of Genesis, he maintained that all humanity originated from the first couple, Adam and Eve, who just happened to be of Caucasian race. After their fall from Eden, the skin color of their descendants gradually darkened to yellow, red, brown, and black as they adapted to different climates in different continents around the world. Known as the "degenerative hypothesis," this narrative of decline was initially proposed to explain varieties of skin color in the global population while staying within the boundaries of the biblical doctrine of the time. Yet this hypothesis of degeneration from Whiteness became a key recurring theme for future generations of race-thinkers, who associated the presence of non-Whites with the decline of White, European civilization.

17. Fabian, *Skull Collectors*, 23–26.

18. Shapin, "Phrenological Knowledge"; Cooter, *Cultural Meaning*. As James Poskett (*Materials of the Mind*) argues, the circulation of skulls, tools, and periodicals of phrenology reached not only European metropoles but also remote places like China and Australia, forming the early foundation of the global scientific community to come. This preexisting network of circulation partially explains the appeal of racial ideas in places outside Europe in the nineteenth and early twentieth centuries.

19. Fabian, *Skull Collectors*, 31.

20. Gossett, *Race*, 74.

21. Stanton, *Leopard's Spots*, 35.

22. See Stocking, *Race, Culture, and Evolution*, for a full account of polygenism during this period. Morton, in fact, had a lively exchange with John Bachman, a minister from South Carolina who owned slaves. If different races were indeed different species, "mulattoes," or children from interracial marriage, should not exist or at least should be infertile, as observed in the interbreeding of different animal species. Based on his observation in the South, Bachman argued that this was not the case, with "mulatto" families reproducing themselves over generations. As we see in chapter 5, Franz Boas provided empirical evidence of this argument with data from "Indians" and "half-breeds."

At the same time, Bachman's defense of monogenism did not indicate his support for racial equality. He cited the biblical tale of cursed Ham, Noah's third son, as an ancestor of "Negros," and also noted that "in intellectual power the African is an inferior variety of our species . . . he is incapable of self-government." His defense of slavery was more paternalistic, as White Christians helping their Black brothers and guiding them to their rightful position in society. The debate around polygenism was eventually settled with the advent of Darwin and his idea of evolution, who firmly asserted a single biological origin for humankind. Of course, Darwin's theories came with another set of debates as well as its own variety of race-thinking, social Darwinism (Gossett, *Race*, 62–63, 67).

23. Gossett, *Race*, 64–65.

24. Horsman, *Josiah Nott of Mobile*.

25. Horsman, *Josiah Nott of Mobile*, 81.

26. See Stocking, *Race, Culture, and Evolution*, for a more detailed history of the American School of Ethnology.

27. Stocking, *Race, Culture, and Evolution*.

28. Arendt, *Origins of Totalitarianism*, 170–75.

29. Ironically, Gobineau was a true pessimist who despised any attempt to intervene in contemporary politics. Except for his short stint with Parisian royalists in his twenties, he refrained from any kind of political organizing, firmly believing in the inevitability of the fall of Western civilization. Steven Kale ("Gobineau, Racism, and Legitimism") has argued that this stance stems from the irreversible defeat of the French nobility in the nineteenth century.

30. It should be noted that Gobineau was looking at successes and failures of civilizations from the perspective of "the white race."

31. Biddiss, *Father of Racist Ideology*, 120–21.

32. Gobineau, *Essay*, v.

33. Irmscher, *Louis Agassiz*, 241.

34. Machado, "Nineteenth-Century Scientific Travel."

35. Frankel, *States of Inquiry*, 223; see also Guyatt, *Bind Us Apart*. Agassiz was staging a careful balancing act between his political affiliation to the North and his scientific allegiance to polygenism. In a way, this stance anticipated the "separate but equal" doctrine by condemning contact between different races while acknowledging their formal equality. As we see in chapter 4, this "visceral revulsion" to race mixture would survive the Progressive Era and influence not only the American eugenicists but also social scientists of the early twentieth century, such as Robert E. Park of the Chicago school.

36. As David Livingstone (*Nathaniel Southgate Shaler*) has noted, there was a logical contradiction in Shaler's position: Only Whites could assist African Americans in achieving a civilization, yet extended contact would lead to degeneration of not only Whites but all the races involved. In the early twentieth century, this paradox of "white men's burden" weighed heavily on the minds of reform-minded race-thinkers who did not categorically deny non-White potential for equality. If contact meant improvement and degeneration at the same time, what should they do as reform-minded Christians firmly believing in the universality of humankind?

37. Somewhat ironically, Shaler as a private individual remained "a reluctant nativist" who "remained a bit touchy, for example, about Brahmin exclusiveness, and while welcome in Boston homes, he never felt quite at one with the society of

which he had become a part" mainly because of the fact that he was from Kentucky. He was one of the rare Harvard faculty members who would open up their homes to the students of Russian Jewish background (Livingstone, *Nathaniel Southgate Shaler*, 132). Moreover, W. E. B. Du Bois, in his autobiography, listed Shaler as one of the few professors who actively supported him, recalling an incident in which "Shaler, invited a Southerner, who objected to sitting by me, out of his class" (Du Bois, *Dusk of Dawn*, 19). These anecdotes confirm that race as a social force is distinctive from prejudice at an individual level.

38. See Louis Menand's acclaimed origin story of pragmatism, *The Metaphysical Club*, for another perspective on these men. Although Menand does not foreground race and Reconstruction, they were the core concerns of the New England elites who saw themselves as moral and political leaders of the nation.

39. Hochschild, *Strangers in Their Own Land*.

40. Higham, *Strangers in the Land*.

41. Yokota (*Unbecoming British*) has portrayed the antebellum United States as a postcolonial nation haunted by identity crisis and insecurity, suffering from an inferiority complex with Europe. The heady cultural and intellectual admiration continued until the late nineteenth century, and we can see its effect on Agassiz's rapid rise and acceptance as "the professor." That is, his European origin added credibility to his status as an esteemed scientist. In addition, many of the Boston Brahmins spent summers and studied for years in Europe, usually in Germany, often pursuing doctoral degrees. Both Henry Cabot Lodge and Theodore Roosevelt spent a considerable amount of time in Germany during their formative years and, in the process, were deeply influenced by German romanticism.

42. Livingstone, *Nathaniel Southgate Shaler*, 137.

43. Livingstone, *Nathaniel Southgate Shaler*, 131.

44. Foner, *Reconstruction*; Du Bois, *Black Reconstruction*.

45. Roy, *American Dark Age*.

46. Born as a slave, Washington worked in various industries before graduating from the Hampton Institute, an industrial school for Blacks located in Virginia. Later he founded the Tuskegee Institute and emerged as the most prominent Black leader in the early twentieth century. Washington and W. E. B. Du Bois later had a lively debate around the best course of action for the Black community, and Du Bois criticized him sharply for forgoing the political pursuit of civil rights. While Washington publicly defended his position, he privately concurred with Du Bois's emphasis on politics. Robert Park of the Chicago school worked under his tutelage at Tuskegee earlier in his career during his thirties. See Moore, *Booker T. Washington*.

47. Baker, *Anthropology*.

48. They are referring to the Know-Nothing Party and the Chinese exclusion movement, respectively.

49. Solomon, *Ancestors and Immigrants*, 105.

50. Tichenor, *Dividing Lines*.

51. Solomon, *Ancestors and Immigrants*, and Higham, *Strangers in the Land*, provide a general overview on the IRL, while Spiro, in *Defending the Master Race*, tells the

stories of the individual members of the league. In addition to these works, I also draw on the original archival sources from IRL papers at Houghton Library, Harvard University.

52. Solomon, *Ancestors and Immigrants*, 110.

53. "Replies to Immigration Restriction League Circular Letter (1904)," Immigration Restriction League (U.S.) Records, 1893–1921; circular letters; replies to circular letters: 1904–1905, MS Am 2245, folder 1049a, Houghton Library, Harvard University.

54. The exclusive societies functioned as a model for Lodge's thinking of immigration control: "The Porcellian stood at the summit of Harvard's elaborate and rigid social hierarchy, which began to sort students from the moment the new freshmen arrived in Cambridge. By sophomore year, the class was officially divided into the social elect and the outsiders by the venerable Institute of 1770, which identified the one hundred members of the class most fit for 'society'" (Karabel, *Chosen*, 15). Theodore Roosevelt also belonged to the club, along with many other male members of his extended family.

55. The two men's friendship began early, when they were both young politicians in the Republican Party, and lasted throughout their lifetimes despite changes to their respective political positions. Roosevelt revered Lodge—who was eight years his senior and had passed through the same exclusive social circles of Harvard, the Porcellian, and the mentorship of Henry Adams—and asked for his advice in important matters. Teddy's sudden ascension to the White House in 1901 provided Lodge with enormous political clout. "While Roosevelt was President, Lodge was probably in and out of the White House as often as he was in and out of his home on Massachusetts Avenue" (Garraty, *Henry Cabot Lodge*, 223).

56. Lodge, *Early Memories*, 19. Lodge repeats the same exact episode later when discussing his experience of playing youth sports (86). He uses a contemporary slang, "muckers," with quotations, to refer to immigrant boys. Throughout the book, he passingly remarks on the newcomers to Boston in a disparaging manner but seldom with direct labels of race or national origin. Interestingly, his grandfather warned Lodge about his obsession with pedigree, telling him, "My boy, we do not talk about family in this country. It is enough for you to know that your grandfather is an honest man" (42). Apparently, the lesson did not register.

57. Garraty, *Henry Cabot Lodge*, 226. The Boston Brahmins were generally antagonistic toward the new generation of industrial capitalists, many of whom were based in New York City. In addition to differences in lifestyles, the two elite groups clashed in terms of their economic foundation: Whereas the Boston Brahmins traditionally relied on trade and commerce with Europe, industrial capitalists opened factories to replace European imports, and their factories were the main reason the new immigrants were flocking to American cities. Of course, this conflict of interest was often expressed through the language of morality and culture, all of which the new immigrants, and sometimes their employers, supposedly lacked (Solomon, *Ancestors and Immigrants*).

58. Solomon, *Ancestors and Immigrants*, 115–16.

59. Lodge, "Restriction of Immigration."

60. Much has been written about the racial status of early Irish immigrants (Ignatiev, *How the Irish Became White*; Roediger, *Wages of Whiteness*; Roediger, *Working Toward Whiteness*; Jacobson, *Whiteness*). In Lodge's case, both theoretical and practical necessity undergirded the inclusion of the Irish in the "fit" group: The Irish, Lodge argued, had been dominated by the British for long enough to warrant their assimilation and subjugation into the Teutonic tradition. In addition, perhaps more importantly, Irish immigrants and their organizations in Boston and Massachusetts were his core constituents.

61. Hattam, *In the Shadow of Race*, 23; Stocking, *Race, Culture, and Evolution.*

62. Hacking, "Avalanche of Printed Numbers"; Porter, *Trust in Numbers*; Muhammad, *Condemnation of Blackness.*

63. F. Walker, "Restriction of Immigration." See Benton-Cohen, *Inventing the Immigration Problem*, for further implication of this argument.

64. Benton-Cohen, *Inventing the Immigration Problem.*

65. The incident known as the "Ross affair" was actually triggered by his speech targeting Japanese, not Chinese, immigrants. Regardless, Jane Stanford, the widow of Leland Stanford, was not willing to tolerate the maverick young professor who did not seem to respect his employer. Ross was forced to resign and subsequently moved to the University of Nebraska and then to the University of Wisconsin, where he oversaw the founding of its esteemed sociology department. The Ross affair invoked wide-ranging opposition from progressive intellectuals across the country, leading to debates about academic freedom and protection of tenure and eventually to the foundation of the American Association of University Professors. On the other hand, Ross continued to maintain hostility toward Japanese immigrants in later life, all the way to the 1940s. As a prominent public intellectual and active supporter of the American Civil Liberties Union, he was not afraid to speak out against injustice, including early incarnations of red scare. Yet he did not participate in the organization's challenge against the Japanese internment in 1943, confessing in a personal letter that it was the only issue that he could not bring himself to side with the ACLU on. He did not specify the reason. I discuss these events more in detail in Ross's presidential biography on the American Sociological Association website (Sunmin Kim, "Edward Alsworth Ross," American Sociological Association, last updated March 18, 2024, https://www.asanet.org/edward-a-ross/).

66. Tichenor, *Dividing Lines.*

67. See Baker, *Anthropology*, chap. 3, for his role in early American anthropology.

68. Deniker, *Races of Man*, 280 (italics in the original text).

69. Kevles, *In the Name of Eugenics.*

70. Both Galton and Pearson used the term *race* to denote the differences between geniuses and laypeople. In other words, race was more about class position and ability than skin color and other traits associated with descent.

71. Kevles, *In the Name of Eugenics*, 1.

72. MacKenzie, *Statistics in Britain*; Xie, "Franz Boas and Statistics"; Porter, *Trust in Numbers.*

73. Kevles, *In the Name of Eugenics*, 28.

74. In this light, recent attempts to refashion race as a practical, data-driven category of analysis are not different from eugenics in its analytical strategy.

75. Kevles, *In the Name of Eugenics*, 64.

76. Davenport, *Heredity in Relation to Eugenics*, 216, 218, 221; quoted in Kevles, *In the Name of Eugenics*, 47.

77. Kevles, *In the Name of Eugenics*, 51.

78. Kevles, *In the Name of Eugenics*, 51.

79. FitzGerald and Cook-Martin, *Culling the Masses*.

80. For a more detailed account of how the bill came to pass, see chapter 2.

81. Dyer, *Theodore Roosevelt*, 3.

82. Shaler believed that among the different branches of "the American race," "the frontier men" from Kentucky, his home state, displayed the best quality (*Autobiography*). Being a faithful student, Roosevelt affirmed his professor's claims by championing Kentucky men on various occasions as a proud example of the American race full of the frontier spirit.

83. Wimmer, "Herder's Heritage."

84. In this aspect, Roosevelt's race-thinking had an affinity with those who attempted to conceptualize the collective trajectories of non-White races as struggles against dominance and subjugation. See Dawson, *Behind the Mule*, for the discussion of "linked fate" among African Americans. Donna Jones in *Racial Discourse* shows that very different thinkers, such as Roosevelt and Marcus Garvey, espoused their own version of the idea, and this trend can be traced back to the French life philosophy of the early twentieth century, namely Henri Bergson's work.

85. Hawley, *Theodore Roosevelt*, 64.

86. On this note, he had a special obsession about Japanese culture and the empire's ability to become a major superpower in the struggle for global hegemony. See chapter 6 for a more detailed account on how Roosevelt saw Japan, the Japanese, and Japanese immigrants in the United States.

## CHAPTER TWO

1. I borrow the term *strange bedfellows* from Tichenor, *Dividing Lines*. This chapter relies heavily on his account of the legislative politics in the early twentieth century as well Benton-Cohen's biographies of the commission members in *Inventing the Immigration Problem*.

2. Tichenor, *Dividing Lines*, 46–49.

3. Tichenor, *Dividing Lines*, 67.

4. E. Lee, *At America's Gates*; Lew-Williams, *Chinese Must Go*.

5. Benton-Cohen, *Inventing the Immigration Problem*.

6. Tichenor, *Dividing Lines*.

7. As noted in chapter 1, Lodge and restrictionists were not advocating for categorical exclusion of southern and eastern European immigrants. They did not necessarily argue that all southern and eastern Europeans were undesirable; rather,

they maintained that a higher number of people among them belonged to that category and argued that a literacy test—implemented across all groups—could effectively prevent the undesirable component of any group from entering the country. In other words, their policy proposal for immigration restriction was thoroughly rationalized by statistical thinking about race, although their motivations might have been rooted in categorical, essentialist understandings of race and nation. See chapter 1 for more details.

8. See the biography of Dillingham later in this chapter for a description of his "moderate" restrictionist stance.

9. Tichenor, *Dividing Lines*, 124.

10. William Howard Taft, then the secretary of state, sat down for a meeting with Katsura Tarō, the prime minister of Japan, in 1905. The two powerful men discussed matters related to the other countries in the Pacific. The presumption was that United States was willing to overlook Japanese aggressions in the Far East, including the occupation of Taiwan and the Korean peninsula, as long as Japan recognized American control of the Philippines. Although the Taft–Katsura agreement was never formal, it was widely understood as a sign that the United States recognized Japan as an equal partner in international affairs. See Esthus, *Theodore Roosevelt*, for the complicated diplomatic history behind the meeting.

11. Azuma, *Between Two Empires*.

12. E. Lee, *At America's Gates*; Lew-Williams, *Chinese Must Go*.

13. For instance, in May 1905, sixty-seven trade unions, led by the otherwise progressive San Francisco Building Trades Council, launched the Japanese and Korean Exclusion League, an organization focused on restricting immigration from Japan and Korea. With enthusiastic support from local media, such as the *San Francisco Chronicle*, and local politicians, the organization actively lobbied for discrimination and restriction against all Asian immigrants (Bailey, *Theodore Roosevelt*, 28–45).

14. Benton-Cohen, *Inventing the Immigration Problem*, 46–47.

15. Love, *Race over Empire*. See also quisumbing king, *Enduring Empire*. The classic example of this dilemma is seen in the American occupation of the Philippines (Kramer, *Blood of Government*) and ensuing ambiguous racial position of Filipinos under the US welfare bureaucracy.

16. Zeidel, *Immigrants, Progressives, and Exclusion Politics*, 41.

17. Zeidel, *Immigrants, Progressives, and Exclusion Politics*, 26.

18. Lund, "Vermont Nativism."

19. Valentine, *Report of the Commissioner*, cited in Lund, "Vermont Nativism," 6–8.

20. See Benton-Cohen, *Inventing the Immigration Problem*, for further details on the so-called distribution scheme in other regions, including the South.

21. Lund, "Vermont Nativism," 12.

22. P.9, "Address of Mr. Heflin, of Alabama," in *John L. Burnett: Memorial Address Delivered in the House of Representatives and the Senate of the United States, Sixty-Sixth Congress*, House Document No. 1021 (Government Printing Office, 1922). The biographical details were obtained from the memorial addresses as well as from Jon

Sedlaczek, "John Lawson Burnett," *Encyclopedia of Alabama*, last updated July 7, 2023, http://www.encyclopediaofalabama.org/article/h-3645.

23. Cong. Rec., 59th Cong., 1st Sess. (9192).

24. Cong. Rec., 59th Cong., 1st Sess. (9192).

25. P.41, in *John L. Burnett.*

26. P.12, in *John L. Burnett.*

27. Zeidel, *Immigrants, Progressives, and Exclusion Politics*, 44–45; see also McKeown, *Melancholy Order*; Torpey, *Invention of the Passport*, for a broader perspective on passport.

28. The legislative aftermath of the Dillingham Commission is discussed in detail in chapter 7.

29. The biographical details draw from the materials found in William Stiles Bennet Papers, Special Collections, State University of New York.

30. Eyal, *The Disenchantment of the Orient*; Eyal, "Sociology of Expertise"; Eyal and Buchholz, "Sociology of Intervention."

31. William Wheeler, a businessman from San Francisco, was an exception.

32. Some of the papers in the collection of William Husband, the executive secretary of the commission, pertain to the matters of personnel, including hiring procedure and salary.

33. See Benton-Cohen, *Inventing the Immigration Problem*, for the role of women in the Dillingham Commission.

34. Tichenor, *Dividing Lines*, and Handlin, *Race and Nationality*, are examples of such perceptions.

35. Benton-Cohen, *Inventing the Immigration Problem.*

## CHAPTER THREE

1. Zuberi, *Thicker Than Blood.*

2. As reviewed in chapter 1, few race-thinking categorization systems exceeded five divisions (e.g., Blumenbach's five-color scheme). This is probably because the logical contradictions associated with categorization increase exponentially as more groups are added. Furthermore, additional categories make it more challenging to present an intuitive hierarchy. As this chapter reveals, ethnicity addresses these problems by building a two-stage classification system.

3. Hattam, *In the Shadow of Race.*

4. Zuberi, *Thicker Than Blood.*

5. In this sense, the commission anticipated "ethnic options" many decades before the idea became popular (Waters, *Ethnic Options*).

6. *DCR*, 1:17.

7. Painter, *History of White People*, 66–85.

8. *DCR*, 1:17.

9. Of course, the "visible" difference is also a product of social and historical construction. In the United States, the so-called eyeball test, or what Omi and Winant

call the "ocular" dimension of race, begets its validity from the history of segregation and migration control (*Racial Formation*). See Obasogie, *Blinded by Sight*, for an extended engagement with the (in)visibility of race.

10. *DCR*, 1:17.

11. Perlmann, *Americans Classify the Immigrant*.

12. Perlmann, *Americans Classify the Immigrant*, 22–23.

13. Bowker and Starr, *Sorting Things Out*.

14. Elnora Folkmar was also a medical doctor. Later in her life she actively participated in the suffrage movement as well as in the eugenics movement (Benton-Cohen, *Inventing the Immigration Problem*, 120).

15. See Benton-Cohen, *Inventing the Immigration Problem*, 14.

16. David Barrows's career spanned the military, politics, anthropology, and the American colonial administration. After his stint in the Philippines, he served as president of the University of California system. His namesake building on the Berkeley campus was renamed in 2020 amid protests focusing on his track record of violence in the Philippines.

17. Jeremiah's brother Albert worked on the Philippine Commission as an anthropologist. See Benton-Cohen, *Inventing the Immigration Problem*.

18. Biographical information obtained from Daniel Folkmar Photographs of Philippine People, circa 1903–1907, NAA Photo Lot 105, National Anthropological Archives.

19. President McKinley expressed this mission poignantly in his proclamation about "benevolent assimilation" (*Executive Order*). See Go and Foster, *American Colonial State*, for the uniqueness of the American approach to the Philippines. Simply put, American policymakers found the Philippines' geographic location strategically useful but its non-White population undesirable. To "civilize" the latter, the Philippine Commission was tasked with developing the capacity for self-government among Filipinos, and the non-Christian tribes proved to be the major challenge to this goal. When the Bureau of Non-Christian Tribes was established, the anthropological research was officially conflated with the political mission. In this light, the work of the Philippine Commission dovetails with that of the Dillingham Commission as it combined knowledge production and governance as the institutional body dealt with the question of the other. See Love, *Race over Empire*, and Immerman, *Empire for Liberty*, on the racial dilemma of the American occupation of the Philippines.

20. Kramer, *Blood of Government*, 426; Rydell, *All the World's a Fair*.

21. Latour, *We Have Never Been Modern*.

22. Hattam, *In the Shadow of Race*.

23. Go and Foster, *American Colonial State*; Go, "'Racism' and Colonialism."

24. Love, *Race over Empire*. These critics often relied on the analogy of the South and the enfranchisement of formerly enslaved people during Reconstruction.

25. Kramer, *Blood of Government*. Julian Go, in "'Racism' and Colonialism," reports that US soldiers referred to the Filipinos—the ones they were fighting against—as "niggers." Their opponents were most likely Indigenous people in remote areas, not so-called civilized colonial elites in coastal cities.

26. quisumbing king, *Enduring Empire.*

27. Kramer, *Blood of Government.*

28. Camponanes, "Images of Filipino Racialization"; Folkmar, *Untitled Manuscript*, ca. 1907, box 66, Daniel Folkmar Papers, the National Anthropological Archives in the records of the Department of Anthropology (Manuscript and Pamphlet File), Smithsonian Institution.

29. Folkmar, *Untitled Manuscript.* The preface was signed in 1907, but the manuscript shows the signs of continued editing afterward. Folkmar makes a several references to "my current work in the federal government"—likely that of the Dillingham Commission—throughout.

30. Folkmar, *Untitled Manuscript*, 15:5.

31. Folkmar, *Untitled Manuscript*, preface.

32. Folkmar, *Untitled Manuscript*, 19:30–31.

33. Folkmar, *Untitled Manuscript*, 15:5.

34. Folkmar, *Untitled Manuscript*, 22:40.

35. A rudimentary form of racial liberalism was evident in the broader ideological contours of American imperialism more generally, while Folkmar did not necessarily understand its full implications. Hellen Tilley, in *Africa as a Living Laboratory*, advances a similar argument in the context of European colonialism and medical knowledge circulation in Africa. I am indebted to Ann Swidler for this reference.

36. *Dictionary*, 1.

37. *Dictionary*, 5.

38. Haney-López, *White by Law*; Pascoe, *What Comes Naturally.*

39. *Dictionary*, 3–4.

40. *Dictionary*, 4.

41. Deniker, *Races of Man*, 280 (italics in the original text)

42. From 1899 to 1910, the total number of immigrants in the African (black) category was 33,630—less than 0.4 percent of the total number of immigrants (9,555,673) during the period (*DCR*, 1:97). If Folkmar was faithful to Deniker's scheme, the African (black) category should have a subset, likely consisting of "Bushman," "Negrito," "Negro," "Melanesian," and "Ethiopian." These subcategories appear nowhere in the commission's main volumes. Instead, the Dillingham Commission used both "negro" and "black" to refer to African Americans, not immigrants in the African (black) category.

43. As an empire with a long history of subjugating and assimilating minority groups, China and the concept of "Chinese" also presents an interesting case for challenges associated with racial and ethnic classification schemes. See Mullaney, *Coming to Terms*, for the ways through which the Chinese Communist Party in the 1940s dealt with these challenges.

44. Hattam, *In the Shadow of Race.*

45. Before the theory of natural selection and Mendelian genetics were widely accepted, Jean-Baptiste Lamarck was an authoritative source on how an organism came into its current form. According to Lamarck, acquired characteristics could transform

organisms, and those transformations were inheritable. Inspired by his theory of gradual biological change, some race scholars questioned whether racial categories were transformable over time and whether individuals can be classified into a different race, depending on the environmental context (Hattam, *In the Shadow of Race*).

46. *Dictionary*, 54.

47. English culture and tradition held an important place in the minds of WASP elites, such as Lodge (see Solomon, *Ancestors and Immigrants*).

48. *Dictionary*, 54.

49. *Dictionary*, 54–55.

50. Sollors, *Invention of Ethnicity*. Vilna Bashi Treitler, in *Ethnic Project*, correctly points out that this development occurred at the expense of African Americans.

51. Sollors, *Invention of Ethnicity*; Warner and Lung, *Modern Community*.

52. Glazer and Moynihan, *Beyond Melting Pot*, 4. See Brubaker, Loveman, and Stamatov, "Ethnicity as Cognition"; Wimmer, *Ethnic Boundary Making*; and Lamont and Molnar, "Study of Boundaries," for the modern-day iterations of this concept.

53. Glazer and Moynihan, *Beyond Melting Pot*, 7. The authors recognized the limits of "liberal expectancy" by showcasing how five different groups in New York City retained distinctive features through the early and middle decades of the twentieth century.

54. Sollors readily admitted that by 1941 race "had assumed too many charged connotations by its fascist use" and ethnicity was "more unambiguously defined against the fascist trajectory from racist stereotypes to genocide" (*Invention of Ethnicity*, 14–15).

55. Hattam, *In the Shadow of Race*.

56. Greene, *Jewish Origin*.

57. See Patterson's classic account of freedom and slavery in *Slavery and Social Death*.

58. Greene, *Jewish Origin*.

59. Ziegler-McPherson, *Americanization in the States*.

60. Sollors, *Invention of Ethnicity*.

61. Alba, *Ethnic Identity*; Waters, *Ethnic Options*.

62. Perlmann, *Italians Then, Mexicans Now*; Alba and Nee, *Remaking the American Mainstream*.

63. Omi and Winant, *Racial Formation*.

64. Treitler, *Ethnic Project*.

65. Fox and Guglielmo, "Defining America's Racial Boundaries."

66. Treitler, *Ethnic Project*, 9.

67. Alba and Nee, *Remaking the American Mainstream*; Baker, *Anthropology*.

68. Franz Boas's study in the Dillingham Commission exemplifies this argument. See Benton-Cohen, *Inventing the Immigration Problem*, as well as chapter 4 of this book.

## CHAPTER FOUR

1. "Changes in Human Types," *New York Times*, December 18, 1909.

2. Stocking, *Race, Culture, and Evolution*.

3. Gould, *The Mismeasure of Man*; Baker, *Anthropology*; Anderson, *From Boas to Black Power*; King, *God of the Upper Air*.

4. Jung, "Racial Unconscious."

5. While American sociology in its founding was a male-dominated field, just like any other social domain during the time, the early issues of the *American Journal of Sociology* featured articles from notable women reformers, such as Jane Addams and Frances Kellor. These authors wrote about pressing issues of the time, including poverty, labor regulation, and child welfare, while male scholars tended to focus more on abstract and grandiose subjects like theory and history. Sarah Simons's paper was one of the rare discussions of race and immigration.

6. S. Simons, "Social Assimilation," 790–91.

7. S. Simons, "Social Assimilation," 793.

8. Gordon, *Assimilation in American Life*; Alba and Nee, *Remaking the American Mainstream*.

9. Immerwahr, *How to Hide an Empire*; Love, *Race over Empire*.

10. Guyatt, *Bind Us Apart*.

11. McKinley, *Executive Order*.

12. See also quisumbing king, *Enduring Empire*.

13. S. Simons, "Social Assimilation," 799.

14. Lew-Williams, *Chinese Must Go*.

15. S. Simons, "Social Assimilation," 801; see also Baker, *Anthropology*, and Ramírez, *Assimilation*, for assimilation of African Americans and Indigenous peoples.

16. S. Simons, "Social Assimilation," 802. Note that Simons was carefully treading on a contradiction: The United States, emerging from slavery and settler colonialism, featured many instances of race mixture represented by "half-breeds" and "mulattos"; yet the nation seemingly reached a high level of civilization. Simons elided this contradiction by implicitly placing these individuals outside the scope of the national body politic, as exceptional cases that merited no analysis other than contempt.

17. Pascoe, *What Comes Naturally*.

18. S. Simons, "Social Assimilation," 804.

19. Pascoe, *What Comes Naturally*.

20. S. Allen, "Black Feminist Roots."

21. Beisel and Kay, "Abortion, Race, and Gender"; L. Gordon, *Moral Property of Women*.

22. See Benton-Cohen, *Inventing the Immigration Problem*, for a detailed account of how Boas came to participate in the commission.

23. Müller-Wille and Barr, *Franz Boas*.

24. Müller-Wille and Bar, *Franz Boas*, 143.

25. Baker, *Anthropology*.

26. Boas, "Human Faculty," 222–23.

27. Boas, "Human Faculty," 227.

28. Xie, "Franz Boas and Statistics." While pioneers such as Frances Galton and Karl Pearson began to develop linear regression, statistics remained at a rudimentary level during the late nineteenth century, and American social scientists remained unaware of these developments. On the contrary, as a scholar of European origin, Boas kept up with this cutting-edge trend. Daniel J. Kevles, in *In the Name of Eugenics*, documents how eugenic concerns motivated the work of both Galton and Pearson, particularly regarding the regression to the mean through generational reproduction.

29. Boas, "Human Faculty," 224.

30. Boas, "Human Faculty," 225.

31. Boas, "Human Faculty," 226.

32. As Benton-Cohen has noted in *Inventing the Immigration Problem*, Boas maintained communication with many scholars deeply involved in eugenics.

33. Boas, *Half-Blood Indian*, 761.

34. Williams, *Rethinking Race*.

35. Boas, "Human Faculty," 242.

36. See Zumwalt and Willis, *Franz Boas*, for Boas's visit to Atlanta University in 1906. During the time, W. E. B. Du Bois was teaching in the university as a faculty member in sociology. In his lecture, Boas reiterated the argument of his 1894 address with a focus on Africa. Black students and faculty members responded enthusiastically, as the argument was in line with the ideas espoused by contemporary Black leaders, such as Booker T. Washington. Boas and Du Bois would continue their intermittent correspondence for decades.

37. Minutes of Immigration Commission Meetings, April 1, 1908, Husband Papers, Chicago History Museum; Franz Boas to Jeremiah W. Jenks, March 23, 1908, Franz Boas, American Philosophical Society.

38. See Zeidel, *Immigrants, Progressives, and Exclusion Politics*, 86–96, and Hyatt, *Franz Boas*, 105–12, for the details leading up to Boas's involvement in the Dillingham Commission.

39. Boas, *Changes in Bodily Form*, 5.

40. Boas, *Changes in Bodily Form*, 5.

41. Boas, *Changes in Bodily Form*, 5.

42. Anthropologists have debated the validity of Boas's statistical analysis (Spark and Jantz, "Reassessment"; Spark and Jantz, "Changing Times"; Gravlee, Bernard, and Leonard, "Heredity"; Gravlee, Bernard, and Leonard, "*Changes in Bodily Form*"; Holloway, "Head to Head"), and the debate garnered much popular attention ("A New Look at Old Data May Discredit a Theory on Race," *New York Times*, October 8, 2003). Although critics have argued that Boas's argument on the plasticity of head forms was much exaggerated, if not entirely groundless, Gravlee and his coauthors found that Boas's most important findings were still valid when tested by modern statistical techniques.

43. Hacking, "Bio-Power."

44. Lewis, "Passion of Franz Boas"; Stocking, *Race, Culture, and Evolution*.

45. Boas, "Problem of the American Negro," quoted in Degler, *In Search of Human Nature*, 80.

46. Note that this is very much in contrast with Agassiz's "revulsion" in chapter 1.

47. Boas, "Race Problems in America."

48. Darnell, *And Along Came Boas*.

49. Degler, *In Search of Human Nature*; Yu, *Thinking Orientals*; Stocking, *Race, Culture, and Evolution*; Gordon, *Assimilation in American Life*; Alba and Nee, *Remaking the American Mainstream*.

50. Letter to William I. Thomas from Boas, October 1, 1910, Franz Boas Papers, American Philosophical Society.

51. Degler, *In Search of Human Nature*, 89–90.

52. Stocking, *Race, Culture, and Evolution*, 264.

53. Park, "Racial Assimilation," 66. See J. Kim, *Contested Embrace*, for an account of ideological conformity in the nation-building process in Korea.

54. Carson, *The Measure of Merit*; Gould, *The Mismeasure of Man*.

55. As evidenced by periodic recycling of Richard Herrnstein and Charles Murray's *The Bell Curve*, the popular appeal of racial difference in intelligence did not diminish over time.

56. Gershenhorn, *Melville J. Herskovits*.

57. In a rare gesture for the time, Herskovits's acknowledgments for the book included the names of numerous African American intellectuals who supported him throughout the data collection, including Alan Locke, the unofficial "dean" of the Harlem Renaissance, and Zora Neale Hurston, who was a graduate student of Boas's during the time. Note the contrast with how the Dillingham Commission listed Yamato Ichihashi and his colleagues as merely "special agents" in its reports (see chapter 6).

58. Frazier, "Negro's 'Cultural Past.'"

59. Omi and Winant, *Racial Formation*.

60. Baker, *Anthropology*.

61. Boas's students endearingly referred to him as "Papa Franz" behind his back, but Hurston was the only one bold enough to publicly call him that at a department party. Boas replied jokingly, "Of course, Zora is my daughter. Certainly! Just one of my missteps, that's all." Hurston was the only Black student in both Barnard College and Boas's circle at Columbia. She was possibly one of the few, if not the only, non-White person at the party. See Boyd, *Wrapped in Rainbows*.

62. Hughes, *Big Sea*, 142.

63. Quoted in A. Walker, "In Search of Zora Neale Hurston."

## CHAPTER FIVE

1. Zeidel, *Immigrants, Progressives, and Exclusion Politics*. Benton-Cohen, in *Inventing the Immigration Problem*, highlights the work of female agents hired by the commission.

2. See chapter 1 of Benton-Cohen, *Inventing the Immigration Problem*, for more details on Jenks.

3. W. Jett Lauck, Immigration Commission-Reports and Plans of W. Jett Lauck, box 80, W. Jett Lauck Papers, Special Collections, University of Virginia.

4. The final reports of the commission do not contain the names of the agents. The Lauck Papers feature a number of field reports with authors' names. One recognizable figure among the agents is LeRoy Hodges (1888–1944), a Washington and Lee University graduate who had a prolific career in the state of Virginia and the federal government. While he was still a college student, he was probably hired by Lauck, who had held a faculty position at the university prior to working full time with the commission (see LeRoy Hodges Papers 1908–1942, Special Collections, Washington and Lee University). The other is Erville B. Woods, who later became a faculty member of the Sociology Department at Dartmouth. He received his doctorate degree from the University of Chicago in 1906 (see *University Records*, vol. 10, *July 1905–April 1906*, University of Chicago). He would have likely worked for the commission after receiving his degree. If these two figures are representative of the agents, I suspect that most of the field agents were students or recent graduates who had received at least some training in social science methodology. Benton-Cohen's account in *Inventing the Immigration Problem* corroborates this assertion.

5. "Community Report for Immigration Commission," box 62, William Jett Lauck Papers, Special Collections, University of Virginia Library. The Russell Sage Foundation conducted a similar inquiry, titled the Pittsburgh Survey (Greenwald and Anderson, *Pittsburgh Surveyed*), also in mining towns of Pennsylvania during a similar period (1907–8). The resulting report provides an elaboration on the racial distinction prevalent in the field:

> By the Eastern European immigration the labor force has been cleft horizontally into two great divisions. The upper stratum includes what is known in mill parlance as the "English-speaking men"; the lower contains the "Hunkies" or "Ginnies." Or, if you prefer, the former are the "white men," the latter the "foreigners." An "English-speaking" man may be either native American, or English, or Irish. He may be one of these, or he may be German, Scandinavian, or Dutch. It is sufficient if the land of his birth be somewhere west of the Russian Empire or north of Austria-Hungary. A "Hunky" is not necessarily a Hungarian. He may belong to any of the Slavic races. "Ginny" seems to include all the "Hunkies" with the Italians thrown in. (*The Pittsburgh Survey: The Steel Workers*, 147–48, quoted in Hourwich, *Immigration and Labor*, 164)

Somewhat ironically, the restrictionist ideology dividing new immigrants from old immigrants had some traction in the field, as seen in this quote; however, its scientific elaboration, races or peoples, did not have much standing.

6. Note that the categories shown in figure 10 were slightly different from the original races or peoples scheme (see the beginning of this chapter). All of the non-White races or peoples were missing from the list, and instead there was an "American, negro" category (upper left). The gap between the high theory of racial classification and the reality of data collection was already visible before the agents were sent into the field.

7. *DCR*, 7:225–26.

8. Guglielmo, *White on Arrival.*

9. "Community Report for Immigration Commission."

10. *DCR*, 1:45–47.

11. Zeidel, *Immigrants, Progressives, and Exclusion Politics*, 113–15.

12. *DCR*, 1:49.

13. Benton-Cohen, *Inventing the Immigration Problem*, 235.

14. E. Ross, *Old World in the New*, 144. See also Benton-Cohen, *Inventing the Immigration Problem*, 72. Perlmann's account of the failed attempt to include the "Hebrew" category in the 1910 census in *Americans Classify the Immigrant* suggests otherwise—there was an element of antisemitism in the commission, at least among some executive committee members, such as Lodge.

15. Jenks and Lauck, *The Immigration Problem*, xx.

16. Jenks and Lauck, *The Immigration Problem*, xxii.

17. Jenks and Lauck, *The Immigration Problem*, 49.

18. Jenks and Lauck, *The Immigration Problem*, 68.

19. Jenks and Lauck, *The Immigration Problem*, 285–86.

20. Jenks and Lauck, *The Immigration Problem*, 210.

21. Jenks and Lauck, *The Immigration Problem*, 217.

22. Jenks and Lauck, *The Immigration Problem*, 251.

23. Jenks and Lauck, *The Immigration Problem*, 259.

24. Jenks and Lauck, *The Immigration Problem*, 260.

25. This position did not differentiate Lauck and Jenks from the anti-Asian movement on the West Coast, except that they were willing to admit the supposed greatness of ancient Asian civilizations.

26. Jenks and Lauck, *The Immigration Problem*, 260.

27. Born to a wealthy family in Boston, Emily G. Balch (1867–1961) studied in Paris and Berlin before becoming a professor at Wellesley College in 1896. She participated in numerous investigative commissions, specializing on issues relating to women's labor and immigration. Her 1910 monograph, *Our Slavic Fellow Citizens*, was based on her experience living in immigrant communities across the country. In the introduction, while recognizing the limited scope of her ethnographic fieldwork, Balch writes that "students of immigration are eagerly awaiting the completion of the Commission on Immigration appointed by President Roosevelt" (vi). A close ally of Jane Addams and the settlement house movement, she was also active in the peace movement and received the Nobel Peace Prize in 1946 for her work.

28. Born in Nebraska, the Abbott sisters studied social sciences at the University of Chicago and actively participated in the pro-immigrant organizations of the city, such as Hull House and the Immigrant Protective League. Grace Abbott later left Hull House to lead the Children's Bureau and was for a time the highest-ranking female member of the federal government. Her work largely focused on the rights of immigrants, children, and mothers, whom she deemed vulnerable and requiring protection. Edith Abbott later served as a professor of social welfare at the University of Chicago and is regarded as the founder of the academic field of social welfare in the United States. In her memoir, Edith recalled her sister Grace discussing the interview for the commission job in Boston in 1913, cautiously stating, "I do not think they will want me for their

secretary after they look me over and hear what I have to say—I'll be glad to have a chance to tell them some of the things I think they should do," even though she thought there were "several good people . . . so much better known than I am." To soothe her sister's nerves, Edith went out shopping with her to buy a new hat for the interview. Grace got the job, and in nine months she wrote the *MCR*, which Emily Balch described in her letter to the *New York Times* as the "ablest State paper ever issued in the Commonwealth," presenting over fifty recommendations. Balch saw the proposal as applicable not only to Massachusetts but also nationwide. "Part III New Horizons," February 26, 1950, box 91, folder 1, Edith and Grace Abbott Papers, Hanna Holborn Gray Special Collections Research Center, University of Chicago.

29. Sorensen and Sealander, *The Grace Abbott Reader*.

30. Sorensen and Sealander, *The Grace Abbott Reader*, xxv.

31. Benton-Cohen, *Inventing the Immigration Problem*, 108.

32. In her memoir, Edith wrote about a night when she and her sister had to intervene in a domestic violence incident in an immigrant household, recalling how Grace "firmly and sternly" told the violent husband to "go to bed" to defuse the situation. Sorensen and Sealander, *The Grace Abbott Reader*, 6.

33. Yu, *Thinking Orientals*.

34. Abbott, "Chicago Employment Agency."

35. *The Report of Commission on Immigration on the Problem of Immigration in Massachusetts* (1921, henceforth *MCR*).

36. The Dillingham Commission did take a limited number of photos but did not use them in its reports. See Benton-Cohen, *Inventing the Immigration Problem*, for surviving photographs.

37. Benton-Cohen, *Inventing the Immigration Problem*.

38. *MCR*, 87.

39. *MCR*, 85–86.

40. On moral panic about "white slavery," see Donovan, *White Slave Crusade*. A congressional inquiry on the subject was an immediate precursor to the Dillingham Commission's inquiry. See Benton-Cohen, *Inventing the Immigration Problem*, for details. See Beisel, *Imperiled Innocents*, for a detailed analysis of the class politics surrounding "vice" during this time.

41. Mamdani, *Define and Rule*.

42. Wilde, *Birth Control Battles*; L. Gordon, *The Moral Property of Women*; Beisel, *The Imperiled Innocents*.

43. *MCR*, 67–68.

44. Omi and Winant, *Racial Formation*; Goldberg, *Racial State*.

45. Goldberg, *Racial State*; Fujitani, *Race for Empire*; quisumbing king, *Enduring Empire*.

46. *MCR*, 160–61.

47. For details regarding Hourwich's relationship with the Dillingham Commission, see Perlmann, *Americans Classify the Immigrant*.

48. In the preface, Hourwich thanks W. W. Husband, the executive secretary of the Dillingham Commission, for providing table proofs of the *DCR* in advance of publication. The Husband Papers feature the correspondence between the two federal bureaucrats, and even though they represent different sides of the immigration debate, the exchange feels cordial.

49. For details regarding Hourwich's life, see Perlmann, *Americans Classify the Immigrant*, 161–64.

50. Jenks and Lauck's book (1913) was published later than Hourwich's (1912). The emphasis on "economic concerns" was mentioned in the *DCR* but not as central as in *The Immigration Problem*. But Hourwich correctly predicted that the economic angle would become the main talking point of restrictionists.

51. Hourwich, *Immigration and Labor*, iii.

52. Hourwich, *Immigration and Labor*, 48.

53. In England, Francis Galton and Karl Pearson had already developed elementary forms of regression analyses and methods for controlled comparisons of group-level data. However, these methods were considered cutting-edge techniques, and most of the experts on the Dillingham Commission were not aware of them. One notable exception was Franz Boas. Donald MacKenzie, in *Statistics in Britain*, has chronicled how these techniques were developed for work in race and eugenics. Yu Xie, in "Franz Boas and Statistics," has pointed out the limitations of MacKenzie's approach.

54. Hourwich, *Immigration and Labor*, 23.

55. Hourwich, *Immigration and Labor*, 43.

56. Hourwich, *Immigration and Labor*, 57–58.

57. Hourwich, *Immigration and Labor*, 35.

58. Hourwich, *Immigration and Labor*, 329.

59. Hourwich, *Immigration and Labor*, 499. The Knights of Labor may be an example Hourwich alludes to in terms of labor organizing (Voss, *Making of American Exceptionalism*). See Prasad, *Land of Too Much*, for a sociological analysis of the free silver movement.

60. Kevles, *In the Name of Eugenics*; Baker, *Anthropology*; Muhammad, *Condemnation of Blackness*; Yu, *Thinking Orientals*.

61. Carpenter, *Forging of Bureaucratic Autonomy*.

62. Hirschman, "Rediscovering the 1%."

63. Alba and Nee, *Remaking the American Mainstream*.

64. D. Ross, *The Origin of American Social Science*, 394.

## CHAPTER SIX

1. Stanford economist Harry Millis was listed as the principal investigator in these reports. The report notes that the commission is "under special obligation to four Japanese students who at different times have served it as interpreters and translators" (*DCR*, 23:4). One of them was Ichihashi. According to Ichihashi's accounts, the four students carried out most of the data collection efforts.

2. Chang, *Morning Glory*, 472. Ichihashi, along with three other unnamed Japanese students, was one of the few non-White persons who participated in the commission.

3. Ichihashi, *Japanese in the United States*; Ichihashi, *Emigration from Japan*, ii–iii.

4. Haney-López, *White by Law*. See also Jung, "Constituting the U.S. Empire State," for a critical discussion of racial hierarchy and citizenship.

5. Benton-Cohen, *Inventing the Immigration Problem*; Benton-Cohen, "Other Immigrants."

6. *DCR*, 1:45–49.

7. Azuma, *Between Two Empires*; Alba, "Bright vs. Blurred Boundaries."

8. Haney-López, *White by Law*.

9. *DCR*, 23:5. "East Indians" likely refers to immigrants from South Asia, sometimes also referred to as "Hindoos." This group likely included Muslim and Sikh immigrants as well. See Benton-Cohen, "Other Immigrants," for how the commission treated Mexicans. On the immigrants on the West Coast, see also Barkan, *From All Points*.

10. *DCR*, 24:280.

11. Lew-Williams, *Chinese Must Go*.

12. *DCR*, 25:88.

13. This example also appears on Benton-Cohen, *Inventing the Immigration Problem*, 64–65.

14. *DCR*, 25:291–92.

15. *DCR*, 1:45–48.

16. *DCR*, 23:67; see also 24:31, 58, 108.

17. *DCR*, 24:58.

18. *DCR*, 24:59.

19. *DCR*, 24:59.

20. *DCR*, 23:159.

21. *DCR*, 23:47.

22. *DCR*, 23:82.

23. Gomez, *Picture Bride, War Bride*.

24. *DCR*, 23, see part 2.

25. *DCR*, 24:242.

26. *DCR*, 24:46.

27. *DCR*, 24:597.

28. *DCR*, 24:429.

29. Haney-López, *White by Law*.

30. *DCR*, 24:355.

31. *DCR*, 23:160. *Mikado* (御門) literally refers to the honorable gate of the imperial palace in Tokyo. Figuratively, the term refers to the resident inside the gate, the Japanese emperor.

32. *DCR*, 23:166.

33. *DCR*, 23:162.

34. *DCR*, 23:247.

35. Gordon, *Assimilation in American Life*; Alba and Nee, *Remaking the American Mainstream.*

36. *DCR*, 23:301.

37. *DCR*, 23:278.

38. C. J. Kim, "Racial Triangulation"; Lee and Xu, "Marginalized Model Minority."

39. I borrow this praise from a conversation I had with Michael Omi.

40. Haney-López, *White by Law.*

41. Haney-López, *White by Law*, 56–60, 63. I am indebted to an anonymous reviewer for this quote from the decision.

42. J. Lee and Zhou, *Asian American Achievement Paradox.*

43. Hsu, *Dreaming of Gold.*

44. Azuma, *Between Two Empires.*

45. The details about Ichihashi's life are based on Gordon Chang's biography, *Morning Glory*, as well as the Yamato Ichihashi Papers, SC0071, Department of Special Collections and University Archives, Stanford University. See also chapter 2 in Benton-Cohen, *Inventing the Immigration Problem.*

46. Ichihashi, *Japanese in the United States.*

47. The cartoon is featured in *The Four Immigrants Manga: A Japanese Experience in San Francisco* by Henry Yoshitaka Kiyama. Kiyama arrived at San Francisco in 1904 and studied painting at the Academy of Arts in San Francisco. Inspired by the popular cartoon strips featured in American newspapers, Kiyama produced fifty-two serials of manga that touch on the Japanese immigrant experience from 1904 to 1924. His original intention was to publish the serials in a local Japanese newspaper, but the material was rejected because it was more true-to-life than humorous. With his own funds, he published the manga as a monograph in 1931. The original copy of the manga can be found in the archives of East Asian Library, University of California, Berkeley.

48. The discussion of Asian immigrant settler colonialism is pertinent here. See Azuma, *In Search of Our Frontier.*

49. Azuma, *Between Two Empires.*

50. Esthus, *Theodore Roosevelt*, 147.

51. Svinth, "Professor Yamashita."

52. Jordan's belief in eugenics and racial theory has been a recent topic of discussion at Stanford. See Eugenics at Stanford History Project, "Request to Rename Jordan Hall," February 16, 2019, https://www.stanfordeugenics.com/_files/ugd/124541_b0231655bdfc46f9bada4df5f21e0a06.pdf. Although Jordan generally held non-White

peoples in low regard, he considered the Japanese an exception. See also Miller, *Why Fish Don't Exist.*

53. David Starr Jordan, *The Days of Man*, 5.

54. Burns, *David Starr Jordan*, 64–65.

55. Chang, *Morning Glory.*

56. See chapter 1 of this book for Ripley's theoretical contribution to the Dillingham Commission. In *Between Two Empires*, Azuma presents an interesting case of how Japanese immigrants appropriated the frontier discourse from the likes of Turner to advocate for their belonging on the American West Coast: Essentially, they replaced the figure of the European immigrant and native White settlers with themselves, arguing that the Japanese were the true frontier people embodying a "progressive" spirit and thus deserving of the unclaimed land and honor to be had for making it fruitful. Idiosyncratic as this may sound, Ichihashi's work also followed this line of argument, repeatedly invoking Turner to highlight the frontier spirit of Japanese immigrants.

57. Ichihashi, *Emigration from Japan*, ii–iii.

58. Recall that Edward Ross was fired for his remarks on Japanese immigrants in 1900 (see chapter 1). Ichihashi was hired as a faculty member fifteen years after this. David Starr Jordan hired both men.

59. Ichihashi, *Japanese in the United States*, 400.

60. Ichihashi, *Japanese in the United States*, vi.

61. Ichihashi, *Japanese in the United States*, 155.

62. Ichihashi, *Japanese in the United States*, 44. See Jung, *Reworking Race*, for more on coolie labor.

63. Lee and Zhou, *Asian American Achievement Paradox.*

64. Ichihashi, *Japanese in the United States*, 82.

65. Ichihashi, *Japanese in the United States*, 115.

66. Ichihashi, *Japanese in the United States*, 175.

67. Ichihashi, *Japanese in the United States*, 210.

68. On Ichihashi at the Tule Lake center, see Notes on the Segregation Program, Robert Billigmeier, Japanese American Evacuation and Resettlement Records, BANC MSS 67/14 c, folder R 20.14, Bancroft Library, University of California, Berkeley. See Muller, *The American Inquisition*, for further context on the loyalty questions.

69. Lummis, "Ruth Benedict's Obituary."

70. Yamashita, "Kiss of Kitty."

71. William Pettersen, "Success Story, Japanese-American Style," *New York Times*, January 9, 1966.

72. Wu, *Color of Success.* The scholars of "new assimilation theory" present third- and fourth-generation Japanese children of immigrants as an epitome of assimilation, especially in terms of intermarriage with Whites (Alba and Nee, *Remaking the*

*American Mainstream*). Dana Nakano, in *Japanese Americans*, disproves this point by demonstrating the continuing significance of race in their lives.

## CHAPTER SEVEN

1. Zolberg, *Nation by Design*; D. King, *Making Americans*; FitzGerald and Cook-Martin, *Culling the Masses*; Tichenor, *Dividing Lines*; Handlin, *Race and Nationality*.

2. Ngai, "Architecture of Race."

3. This is in contrast to the domain of jurisprudence on Whiteness, in which the seemingly absurd logic of "common sense" has prevailed (Haney-López, *White by Law*). I argue that this is another instance of racial essentialism presiding over the workings of racial liberalism. In other words, consistency and practicality mattered when it came to European immigration; in excluding non-European migrants, there was no necessity to justify the decision, however random it may seem. See also the discussion of Lodge at the end of this chapter.

4. See FitzGerald and Cook-Martin, *Culling the Masses*, for an argument focusing on eugenics and racism. See Benton-Cohen, *Inventing the Immigration Problem*, as well as Ly and Weil, "Antiracist Origin," for a counterpoint based on a more detailed reading of the history up to the National Origins Quota Act of 1924.

5. See Keyssar, *The Right to Vote*, 86, 99.

6. Hutchinson, *Legislative History*, 465; see also Zeidel, *Immigrants, Progressives, and Exclusion Politics*.

7. *DCR*, 1:14.

8. Hutchinson, *Legislative History*, 154.

9. Tichenor, *Dividing Lines*, 142.

10. Ngai, *Impossible Subjects*, 25–37.

11. Ly and Weil, "Antiracist Origin."

12. *DCR*, 1:47–48.

13. Biographical information obtained from the official homepage of United States Citizenship and Immigration Service, "William W. Husband," National Encyclopedia of American Biography, last updated April 6, 2020, http://www.uscis.gov/history-and-genealogy/our-history-25, and the webpage of the American Catholic History Classroom, "The U.S. Conference of Catholic Bishops and Immigration," last updated October 2, 2024, https://cuomeka.wrlc.org/exhibits/show/immigration/documents/bio-husband.

14. Skowronek, *Building a New American State*.

15. William W. Husband, "How the Quota Limit System of Regulating Immigration Happened," September 4, 1941, box 2, folder 1, Husband Papers, Chicago History Museum. John Higham also corroborates this account by way of the testimony from Richard, Husband's son (*Strangers in the Land*, 393). Husband dates his epiphany to the fall of 1913, whereas Gulick first published his idea of quotas in his 1914 monograph.

16. Most of the staff at the DC headquarters were female employees charged with processing the statistical data. Women in the early twentieth century were regarded as more apt for processing numbers as opposed to highly abstract subjects, such

as philosophy and history. As seen in the commission's organizational structure, numerical data was regarded as low in status compared to politics and theory. See Anderson, "The History of Women." In a sense what I describe as "challenges" of facts to racial ideology mirrors this social divide within the organization of knowledge production.

17. Zeidel, *Immigrants, Progressives, and Exclusion Politics.*

18. See Ly and Weil, "Antiracist Origin," for a discussion on the antiracist origin of the national quota system.

19. Husband, "How the Quota Limit System of Regulating Immigration Happened." The press releases and other related materials are also included in the same folder.

20. Hutchinson, *Legislative History*, 166.

21. Ly and Weil, "Antiracist Origin." However, contemporaries may not have seen it as antiracist, as they lacked a clearly defined concept of racism, which would emerge later (see the conclusion to this book and the discussion of Ruth Benedict). They may have perceived Gulick's idea as focusing less on race than other measures.

22. Gulick, *American Japanese Problem*, 135.

23. Gulick, *American Japanese Problem*, 288.

24. Ly and Weil, "Antiracist Origin."

25. Ly and Weil, "Antiracist Origin."

26. FitzGerald and Cook-Martin, *Culling the Masses*, 100.

27. King, *Making Americans*. See Ngai, *Impossible Subjects*, 33–36, for a critical analysis of Hill's calculations.

28. Ngai, *Impossible Subjects.*

29. Carpenter, *Forging of Bureaucratic Autonomy*; Skowronek, *Building a New American State.*

30. Carpenter, *Forging of Bureaucratic Autonomy*, 21.

31. William W. Husband, "The Immigration Problem of Today," February 1, 1913, address given at the Republican Club of New York, box 1, Husband Papers, Chicago History Museum.

32. William W. Husband, "Immigration Restriction," February 23, 1915, address given at the Fifth Congress of the National Federation of Religious Liberals, box 1, Husband Papers, Chicago History Museum.

33. Arendt, *Eichmann in Jerusalem.*

34. Bonilla-Silva, *Racism Without Racists.*

35. Brown, "Who Is an Indian Child?"

36. Mamdani, *Define and Rule.*

37. Mitchell, "Limits of the State."

38. Goldberg, *Racial State.*

39. Allerfeldt, "And We Got Here First."

40. FitzGerald and Cook-Martin, *Culling the Masses.*

41. FitzGerald and Cook-Martin, *Culling the Masses.*

42. Haney-López, *White by Law.*

43. Daniels, *Politics of Prejudice,* 101.

44. As a few senators pointed out, "grave consequences" in contemporary diplomatic parlance meant no threat of war. Hanihara was a seasoned diplomat fluent in English, and he consulted with Tokyo before writing the letter. In fact, Theodore Roosevelt used the same phrase in 1907 regarding the Gentlemen's Agreement to persuade unwilling Californians. There was no chance that Lodge was not aware of the implication of his actions.

45. Daniels, *Politics of Prejudice,* 101–2.

46. Cong. Rec., 68th Cong., Senate, April 14, 1924 (6308–9).

47. Roger Daniels, in *Politics of Prejudice,* interprets Lodge's action as stemming from political animosity to Coolidge and Hughes (103). He does not, however, explain why Lodge chose the case of Japanese exclusion to express his animosity toward the administration, especially when the senator himself had much experience with the intricacies of the relationship between immigration policy and diplomacy.

48. For instance, Ly and Weil, "Antiracist Origin"; Higham, *Strangers in the Land.*

49. Ngai, "Architecture of Race."

## CONCLUSION

1. Hailing from a German Jewish immigrant family, Weltfish was a student of Boas's specializing in the study of the Pawnee. A longtime adjunct faculty member at the Department of Anthropology at Columbia, she was an active participant in social movements of the day. Later in life, she recalled that she and Benedict had heard of Nazis burning Boas's books and decided to "carry the banner on the race question" by writing *The Races of Mankind.* During the McCarthy era in the 1950s, Weltfish was accused of being a communist and swiftly fired from Columbia. In the process, McCarthy's Senate subcommittee declared *The Races of Mankind* to be "subversive" (Pathe, "Gene Weltfish").

2. Benedict and Weltfish, *Races of Mankind,* 31.

3. Hacking, "Avalanche of Printed Numbers."

4. Baker, *Anthropology;* Alba and Nee, *Remaking the American Mainstream;* Sollors, *Invention of Ethnicity.*

5. Jung, *Reworking Race.*

6. Hattam, *In the Shadow of Race.*

7. Many acclaimed works on immigration have posed a similar question. See Kasinitz et al., *Inheriting the City;* J. Lee and Bean, *Diversity Paradox.*

8. Mamdani, *Define and Rule;* Goldberg, *Racial State.*

9. I elaborate more on this point in Kim, "Blinded by the Facts," while drawing on the evidence presented in this book.

10. Omi and Winant, *Racial Formation,* 142.

11. Bonilla-Silva, *Racism Without Racists;* Alexander, *New Jim Crow;* Goodman, *Deportation Machine.*

12. J. Scott, *Seeing Like a State.*

13. Lamont and Molnar, "Study of Boundaries"; Alba, "Bright vs. Blurred Boundaries."

14. Ngai, *Impossible Subjects*, 5.

15. Jung, "Racial Unconscious."

16. See Bloemraad, *Becoming a Citizen*, for a detailed exposition of differences between these terms. Zolberg, *Nation by Design*, among others, is an important early exception to this tradition. FitzGerald and Cook-Martin, *Culling the Masses*, and Sharma, *Home Rule*, also address this gap.

17. Mamdani, *Define and Rule*; Hattam, *In the Shadow of Race*; Omi and Winant, *Racial Formation.*

18. Treitler, *Ethnic Project.*

19. Hattam, *In the Shadow of Race*; Greene, *Jewish Origin.*

20. Jerome Karabel, in *The Chosen*, pinpoints this moment as the origin of so-called holistic admission.

21. Perlmann, in *Americans Classify the Immigrant*, provides a comprehensive account of how the category of "Jew" was articulated in the Dillingham Commission's period. Influential Jewish leaders and advocacy groups attempted to disassociate the category from the race concept, sensing the pitfalls of essentialism in the latter.

22. Daniel Greene points out that, while their trajectories overlapped, Kallen did not associate or correspond with contemporary Black intellectuals, such as W. E. B. Du Bois or Alan Locke, the leading figure in the Harlem Renaissance movement (*Jewish Origin*, 8). This oversight is notable because they were all concurrently grappling with the question of difference and belonging in elite spaces dominated by WASP men. Victoria Hattam in *In the Shadow of Race* makes a similar point.

23. In fact, Franz Boas and his family were the prime example of such German Jews. They were wealthy, practiced arts and sciences over religion, and politically leaned left. This group had migrated to the United States earlier than Jews from rural areas in eastern Europe. In fact, Boas's uncle, Jacoby, had established himself a secure footing in New York City by the 1880s and subsequently sponsored his professorship at Columbia through donation.

24. Sollors, *Invention of Ethnicity.*

25. Glazer and Moynihan, *Beyond Melting Pot*; Alba, *Ethnic Identity*; Waters, *Ethnic Options.*

26. J. Lee and Bean, *Diversity Paradox.*

27. Mamdani, *Define and Rule.*

28. Poovey, *History of Modern Fact*; Hirschman, "Rediscovering the 1%."

29. Alba and Nee, *Remaking the American Mainstream*; Baker, *Anthropology.*

30. Franz Boas's study in the Dillingham Commission exemplifies this argument. See chapter 4 of this book as well as Benton-Cohen, *Inventing the Immigration Problem.*

31. Ngai, *Impossible Subjects.*

32. Granted, the concept of assimilation had been available since the middle of the nineteenth century, if not earlier. However, as a review from the end of the nineteenth

century shows, the discussion of assimilation was tied to colonial conquest and violent territorial acquisition, often conflating intermarriage ("mixture of blood"), genocide, and changes in language and customs (S. Simons, "Social Assimilation"). The concept of ethnicity made clear the distinction between biology and culture, opening up space for the modern conception of assimilation that focused on peaceful, gradual erosion of group distinction over time.

33. Treitler, *Ethnic Project*; Sollors, *Invention of Ethnicity*; Alba and Nee, *Remaking the American Mainstream.*

34. Benton-Cohen, *Inventing the Immigration Problem*; Jacobson, *Whiteness*; Guterl, *Color of Race*; Roediger, *Working Toward Whiteness.*

35. Omi and Winant, *Racial Formation*; Treitler, *Ethnic Project.*

36. Frankel, *States of Inquiry*, 10; Mamdani, *Define and Rule*; Goldberg, *Racial State*; Omi and Winant, *Racial Formation.*

37. FitzGerald and Cook-Martin, *Culling the Masses.*

38. Goldberg, *Racial State.*

39. See Starr, "Social Categories," and Menjívar, "Immigration Bureaucracies," for broader discussions of categories and governance.

40. Mitchell, "Limits of the State."

41. Oz Frankel, in *States of Inquiry*, presents a similar argument in the context of the nineteenth century.

42. Mandelberg, *The Race Card.*

43. Bonilla-Silva, *Racism Without Racists*; Alexander, *New Jim Crow.*

44. The Hart-Cellar Act abolished the national origin quota based on US population but did retain the numerical cap by country. With the concurrent abolishing of the Bracero program in 1964, this meant that the vast number of Mexican migrant workers in the Southwest had no choice but to become "illegal aliens" to perform the same jobs they had performed for generations. Mae Ngai sees this outcome as stemming from both the liberal critique of racism in immigration policy and consideration of national economic interest (*Impossible Subjects*, 263–64).

45. Mead and Baldwin, *A Rap on Race*, 145.

46. Goldberg, *Racial State.*

47. Patterson, *Slavery and Social Death.*

48. Mead and Baldwin, *A Rap on Race*, 238. See also Wilderson, *Afropessimism.*

49. Mead and Baldwin, *A Rap on Race*, 251.

50. Jerng (*Racial Worldmaking*) stresses the temporal dimensions of racial worldmaking, in which the idea of race is bound up not only with categories and inequalities but also with time progression and corresponding narrative structure. That is, a proper concept of race tells the story of the past and future as well as the present. In this sense, racial liberalism is a well-configured world that paints a temporary suffering and eventually bright future for the racialized. The term *worldmaking* comes from philosopher Nelson Goodman's work (*Ways of Worldmaking*; *Fact, Fiction, and Forecast*). In a series of writings dealing with the problem of induction, Goodman shows that facts become meaningful ("fabricated") only within a specifically configured

"world." The Dillingham Commission's data exemplifies this account: By coming into the discursive network that the commission created, initially meaningless information became a crucial part of a "world" that racial liberalism envisioned and served as a vehicle to tell the story of progress through effort and support.

51. Morris, *Scholar Denied.*

52. Swidler, "Culture in Action."

53. Alba and Nee, *Remaking the American Mainstream.*

54. J. Scott, *Seeing Like a State*; Loveman, "Modern State."

55. Ngai, *Impossible Subjects*, 5.

56. The pioneering work of Cecilia Menjívar, "Liminal Legality," is useful in this regard. See Bialas, *Forever 17*, as well as Bialas, Lukate, and Vertovec, "Contested Categories."

57. Lee and Bean, *Diversity Paradox*; Kasinitz et al., *Inheriting the City*. See also Sharma, *Home Rule.*

58. Carpio, *Migrant Aesthetics*, 4.

59. D. Scott, *Contempt and Pity.*

# Bibliography


Abbott, Grace. "The Chicago Employment Agency and the Immigrant Worker." *American Journal of Sociology* 14, no. 3 (1908): 289–305.

Agamben, Giorgio. *The Signature of All Things: On Method.* Princeton University Press, 2009.

Alba, Richard. "Bright vs. Blurred Boundaries: Second-Generation Assimilation and Exclusion in France, Germany, and the United States." *Ethnic and Racial Studies* 28, no. 1 (2005): 20–49.

Alba, Richard. *Ethnic Identity: The Transformation of White America.* Yale University Press, 1990.

Alba, Richard. *Italian Americans: Into the Twilight of Ethnicity.* Prentice Hall, 1985.

Alba, Richard. "The Twilight of Ethnicity: What Relevance for Today?" *Ethnic and Racial Studies* 37, no. 5 (2014): 781–85.

Alba, Richard, and Victor Nee. *Remaking the American Mainstream: Assimilation and Contemporary Immigration.* Harvard University Press, 2003.

Alexander, Michelle. *The New Jim Crow: Mass Incarceration in the Age of Colorblindness.* New Press, 2010.

Allen, Jennifer, Baird Howland, Markus Mobius, David Rothschild, and Duncan Watts. "Evaluating the Fake News Problem at the Scale of the Information Ecosystem." *Science Advances* 6, no. 14 (2020).

Allen, Shaonta'. "The Black Feminist Roots of Scholar-Activism: Lessons from Ida B. Wells-Barnett." In *Black Feminist Sociology: Perspectives and Praxis*, edited by Zakiya Luna and Whitney Pirtle. Routledge, 2021.

Allerfeldt, Kristofer. "'And We Got Here First': Albert Johnson, National Origins and Self-Interest in the Immigration Debates of the 1920s." *Journal of Contemporary History* 45, no. 1 (2010.): 7–26.

Anderson, Margo. *The American Census: A Social History.* Yale University Press, 1990.

Anderson, Margo. "The History of Women and the History of Statistics." *Journal of Women's History* 4, no. 1 (1992): 14–36.

Anderson, Mark. *From Boas to Black Power: Racism, Liberalism, and American Anthropology.* Stanford University Press, 2020.

Arendt, Hannah. *Eichmann in Jerusalem: A Report on the Banality of Evil.* Penguin, 2006.

Arendt, Hannah. *The Origins of Totalitarianism*. Schocken Books, 1951.

Azuma, Eiichiro. *Between Two Empires: Race, History, and Transnationalism in Japanese America.* Oxford University Press, 2005.

Azuma, Eiichiro. *In Search of Our Frontier: Japanese America and Settler Colonialism in the Construction of Japan's Borderless Empire*. University of California Press, 2019.

Bailey, Thomas. *Theodore Roosevelt and the Japanese-American Crisis: An Account for the International Complications Arising from the Race Problem on the Pacific Coast*. Stanford University Press, 1934.

Baker, Lee. *Anthropology of Racial Politics of Culture*. Duke University Press, 2010.

Baker, Lee. *From Savage to Negro: Anthropology and the Construction of Race, 1896–1954*. University of California Press, 2010.

Balch, Emily. *Our Slavic Fellow Citizens*. University of Michigan Library, 1910.

Baldwin, James, and Margaret Mead. *A Rap on Race*. Lippincott, 1971.

Barkan, Elliot. *From All Points: America's Immigrant West, 1870s–1952*. Indiana University Press, 2007.

Barth, Fredrik. *Ethnic Groups and Boundaries: The Social Organization of Culture Difference*. Waveland Press, 1969.

Bean, Frank, and Jennifer Lee. *The Diversity Paradox: Immigration and the Color Line in Twenty-First Century America*. Russell Sage Foundation, 2012.

Beisel, Nicola. *Imperiled Innocents: Anthony Comstock and Family Reproduction in Victorian America*. Princeton University Press, 1997.

Beisel, Nicola, and Tamara Kay. "Abortion, Race, and Gender in Nineteenth-Century America." *American Sociological Review* 69, no. 4 (2004): 498–518.

Benedict, Ruth, and Gene Weltfish. *The Races of Mankind*. Public Affairs Committee, 1943.

Benton-Cohen, Katherine. *Inventing the Immigration Problem: The Dillingham Commission and Its Legacy*. Harvard University Press, 2018.

Benton-Cohen, Katherine. "Japanese Immigrants in the Dillingham Commission: Federal Immigration Policy and the American West." In *Immigrants in the Far West: Historical Identities and Experiences*, edited by Jessie L. Embry and Brian Q. Cannon. University of Utah Press, 2015.

Benton-Cohen, Katherine. "Other Immigrants: Mexicans and the Dillingham Commission of 1907–1911." *Journal of American Ethnic History* 30, no. 2 (2011): 33–57.

Bialas, Ulrike. *Forever 17: Coming of Age in the German Asylum System*. University of Chicago Press, 2023.

Bialas, Ulrike, Johanna M. Lukate, and Steven Vertovec. "Contested Categories in the Context of International Migration: Introduction to the Special Issue." In "Contested Categories in the Context of International Migration," special issue, *Ethnic and Racial Studies* 48, no. 4 (2024): 1–23.

Biddiss, Michael. *Father of Racist Ideology: The Social and Political Thought of Count Gobineau*. Weidenfeld and Nicolson, 1970.

Blackhawk, Ned. *The Rediscovery of America: Native Peoples and the Unmaking of US History*. Yale University Press, 2023.

Blauner, Robert. "Internal Colonialism and Ghetto Revolt." *Social Problems* 16, no. 4 (1969): 393–408.

Bloemraad, Irene. *Becoming a Citizen: Incorporating Immigrants and Refugees in the United States and Canada*. University of California Press, 2006.

Blumenbach, Johann Friedrich. *On the Natural Variety of Mankind*. In *The Anthropological Treatises of Johann Friedrich Blumenbach*, translated and edited by

Thomas Bendyshe. Longman, Green, Longman, Roberts & Green, 1865. Originally published 1795. https://archive.org/details/anthropologicalt00blumuoft/.

Boas, Franz. *Changes in Bodily Form of Descendants of Immigrants*. Vol. 38, *United States Immigration Commission Report*. General Printing Office, 1911.

Boas, Franz. "The Half-Blood Indian: An Anthropometric Study." *Pop Science Monthly* 45 (1894): 761–70.

Boas, Franz. "Human Faculty as Determined by Race." *Proceedings of American Association for the Advancement of Science* 43 (1894): 301–27. Reprinted in *A Franz Boas Reader: The Shaping of American Anthropology 1883–1911*, edited by George Stockings Jr. University of Chicago Press, 1974.

Boas, Franz. "The Problem of the American Negro." *Yale Review* 10 (1921): 392–93.

Boas, Franz. "Race Problems in America." *Science* 29, no. 752 (1909): 839–49.

Bonilla-Silva, Eduardo. "The Essential Social Fact of Race." *American Sociological Review* 64, no. 6 (1999): 898–906.

Bonilla-Silva, Eduardo. *Racism Without Racists: Color-Blind Racism and the Persistence of Racial Inequality in America*. Rowman and Littlefield, 2003.

Bophal, Raj. "The Beautiful Skull and Blumenbach's Errors: The Birth of the Scientific Concept of Race." *BMJ* 335, no. 7633 (2007): 1308–9.

Bosniak, Linda. *The Citizen and the Alien: Dilemmas of Contemporary Membership*. Princeton University Press, 2008.

Bourdieu, Pierre. *On the State: Lectures at the Collège de France, 1989–1992*. Polity Press, 2015.

Boyd, Valerie. 2003. *Wrapped in Rainbows: The Life of Zora Neale Hurston*. Scribner, 2003.

Bowker, Geoffrey, and Susan Leigh Star. *Sorting Things Out: Classification and Its Consequences*. MIT Press. 1999.

Brace, C. Loring. *"Race" Is a Four-letter Word: The Genesis of the Concept*. Oxford University Press, 2005.

Brilliant, Mark. "Reimagining Racial Liberalism." In *Making the American Century: Essays on the Political Culture of Twentieth Century America*, edited by Bruce Schulman. Oxford University Press, 2014.

Brinton, Daniel. *Races or Peoples: Lectures on the Science of Ethnography*. N. D. C. Hodges, 1890.

Brodkin, Karen. *How Jews Became White Folks and What That Says About Race in America*. Rutgers University Press, 1998.

Brown, Hana. "Who Is an Indian Child? Institutional Context, Tribal Sovereignty, and Race-Making in Fragmented States." *American Sociological Review* 85, no. 5 (2020): 776–805.

Brown, Hana, and Jennifer A. Jones. "Rethinking Panethnicity and the Race-Immigration Divide: An Ethnoracialization Model of Group Formation." *Sociology of Race and Ethnicity* 1, no. 1 (2015): 181–91.

Brown, John. "Jeremiah Jenks: A Pioneer of Industrial Organization?" *Journal of the History of Economic Thought* 26, no. 1 (2004): 69–89.

Brubaker, Rogers, Mara Loveman, and Peter Stamatov. "Ethnicity as Cognition." *Theory and Society* 33 (2004): 31–64.

Burns, Edward. *David Starr Jordan: Prophet of Freedom*. Stanford University Press, 1952.

Camponanes, Oscar. "Images of Filipino Racialization in the Anthropological Laboratories of the American Empire: The Case of Daniel Folkmar." *PMLA* 123, no. 5 (2008): 1692–99.

Canaday, Margot. *The Straight State: Sexuality and Citizenship in Twentieth-Century America*. Princeton University Press, 2009.

Carpenter, Daniel. *The Forging of Bureaucratic Autonomy: Reputations, Networks, and Policy Innovations in Executive Agencies, 1862–1920*. Princeton University Press, 2001.

Carpio, Glenda. *Migrant Aesthetics: Contemporary Fiction, Global Migration, and the Limits of Empathy*. Columbia University Press, 2023.

Carson, John. *The Measure of Merit: Talents, Intelligence, and Inequality in the French and American Republics, 1750–1940*. Princeton University Press, 2018.

Chang, Gordon. *Morning Glory, Evening Shadow: Yamato Ichihashi and His Internment Writings 1942–1945*. Stanford University Press, 1997.

Chavez, Leo. *The Latino Threat: Constructing Immigrants, Citizens, and the Nation*. Stanford University Press, 2013.

Clemens, Elisabeth. "Towards a Historicized Sociology: Theorizing Events, Processes, and Emergence." *Annual Review of Sociology* 33, no. 1 (2007): 527–49.

Cole, Douglas. *Franz Boas: The Early Years, 1858–1906*. University of Washington Press, 1999.

Collins, Harry M., and Robert Evans "The Third Wave of Science Studies: Studies of Expertise and Experience." *Social Studies of Science* 32, no. 2 (2003): 235–96.

Cooter, Roger. *The Cultural Meaning of Popular Science: Phrenology and the Organization of Consent in Nineteenth-Century Britain*. Cambridge University Press, 1984.

Cornell, Stephen, and Douglas Hartmann. *Ethnicity and Race: Making Identities in a Changing World*. 2nd ed. Pine Forge Press, 2007.

Crenshaw, Kimberlé. "Race Liberalism and the Deradicalization of Racial Reform." *Harvard Law Review* 130, no. 9 (2017).

Daniels, Roger. *The Politics of Prejudice: The Anti-Japanese Movement in California and the Struggle for Japanese Exclusion*. University of California Press, 1962.

Darda, Joseph. *The Strange Career of Racial Liberalism*. Stanford University Press, 2022.

Darnell, Regna. *And Along Came Boas: Continuity and Revolution in Americanist Anthropology*. John Benjamins Publishing, 1998.

Davenport, Charles. *Heredity in Relation to Eugenics*. Henry Hold and Company, 1911.

Dawson, Michael. *Behind the Mule: Race and Class in African-American Politics*. Princeton University Press, 1994.

Degler, Carl. *In Search of Human Nature: The Decline and Revival of Darwinism in American Social Thought*. Oxford University Press, 1991.

Deniker, Joseph. *The Races of Man: An Outline of Anthropology and Ethnography*. Scribner's, 1900.

Donovan, Brian. *White Slave Crusade: Race, Gender, and Anti-Vice Activism, 1889–1917*. University of Illinois Press, 2006.

Du Bois, William Edward Burghardt. *Black Reconstruction in America: Toward a History of the Part Which Black Folk Played in the Attempt to Reconstruct Democracy in America, 1860–1880*. Routledge, 2017.

Du Bois, William Edward Burghardt. *Dusk of Dawn: An Essay Toward an Autobiography of Race Concept*. Routledge, 2017.

Dunbar-Ortiz, Roxanne. *Not "a Nation of Immigrants": Settler Colonialism, White Supremacy, and a History of Erasure and Exclusion*. Beacon Press, 2021.

Duster, Troy. *Backdoor to Eugenics*. Routledge, 1990.

Dyer, Thomas. *Theodore Roosevelt and the Idea of Race*. Louisiana State University Press, 1980.

Emigh, Rebecca Jean. "The Power of Negative Thinking: The Use of Negative Case Methodology in the Development of Sociological Theory." *Theory and Society* 26: 649-684, 1997.

Emigh, Rebecca Jean, Dylan Riley, and Patricia Ahmed. *Changes in Censuses from Imperialist to Welfare States: How Societies and States Count*. Palgrave Macmillan, 2015.

Emirbayer, Mustafa, and Matthew Desmond. *The Racial Order*. University of Chicago Press, 2015.

Esthus, Raymond. *Theodore Roosevelt and Japan*. University of Washington Press, 1966.

Eyal, Gil. *The Disenchantment of the Orient: Expertise in the Arab Affairs and the Israeli State*. Stanford University Press, 2006.

Eyal, Gil. "For a Sociology of Expertise: The Social Origins of Autism Epidemic." *American Journal of Sociology* 118, no. 4 (2013): 863–907.

Eyal, Gil, and Larissa Buchholz. "From the Sociology of Intellectuals to the Sociology of Interventions." *Annual Review of Sociology* 36 (2010): 117–37.

Fabian, Ann. *The Skull Collectors: Race, Science, and America's Unburied Dead*. University of Chicago Press, 2010.

Faust, Drew. *A Scared Circle: The Dilemma of the Intellectual in the Old South 1840–1860*. Johns Hopkins University Press, 1986.

Feagin, Joe. *Systemic Racism: A Theory of Oppression*. Routledge, 2000.

Fields, Barbara. "Whiteness, Racism, and Identity." *International Labor and Working-Class History* 60 (2001): 48–56.

Fitch, John. *The Pittsburgh Survey: The Steel Workers*. Charities Publication Committee, 1911.

FitzGerald, David, and David Cook-Martin. *Culling the Masses: The Democratic Origins of Racist Immigration Policy*. Harvard University Press, 2014.

Fleck, Ludwik. *Genesis and Development of a Scientific Fact*. Edited by Thaddeus J. Trenn and Robert Merton. Translated by Fred Bradley and Thaddeus J. Trenn. University of Chicago Press, 1981. Originally published 1935.

Foner, Eric. *Reconstruction: America's Unfinished Revolution, 1863–1877*. Updated edition. Harper Perennial Modern Classics, 2014.

Folkmar, Daniel. *Album of Philippine Types (Found in Bilibid Prison in 1903): Christians and Moros (Including a Few Non-Christians)*. Bureau of Public Printing, 1904.

Foucault, Michel. *Discipline and Punish: The Birth of the Prison*. Penguin, 1977.

Foucault, Michel. *Security, Territory, Population: Lectures at the Collège de France*. Picador, 2007.

Fox, Cybelle. *Three Worlds of Relief: Race, Immigration, and the American Welfare State from the Progressive Era to the New Deal*. Princeton University Press, 2012.

Fox, Cybelle, and Thomas A. Guglielmo. "Defining America's Racial Boundaries: Blacks, Mexicans, and European Immigrants, 1890–1945." *American Journal of Sociology* 118, no. 2 (2012): 327–79.

Frankel, Oz. *States of Inquiry: Social Investigations and Print Culture in Nineteenth-Century Britain and the United States*. Johns Hopkins University Press, 2006.

Frazier, Franklin. "The Negro's 'Cultural Past.' Review of' The Myth of the Negro Past,' by Melville J. Herskovits." *Nation* 154 (February 14, 1942): 195–96.

Fujimura, Joan, Deborah Bolnick, Ramya Rajagopalan, Jay Kaufman, Richard Lewontin, Troy Duster, Pilar Ossorio, and Jonathan Marks. "Clines Without Classes: How to Make Sense of Human Variation." *Sociological Theory* 32, no. 3 (2014): 208–27.

Fujitani, Takashi. *Race for Empire: Koreans as Japanese and Japanese as Americans During World War II*. University of California Press, 2011.

Frymer, Paul. *Building an American Empire: The Era of Territorial and Political Expansion*. Princeton University Press, 2017.

Gaines, Kevin. *Uplifting the Race: Black Leadership, Politics, and Culture in the Twentieth Century*. University of North Carolina Press, 2012.

Gans, Herbert. "Symbolic Ethnicity: The Future of Ethnic Groups and Cultures in America." *Ethnic and Racial Studies* 2, no. 1 (1979): 1–20.

Garland, David. "What Is a 'History of the Present'? On Foucault's Genealogies and Their Critical Preconditions." *Punishment & Society* 16, no. 4 (2014): 365–84.

Garraty, John. *Henry Cabot Lodge*. Knopf, 1953.

Gerstle, Gary. *American Crucible: Race and Nation in the 20th Century*. Princeton University Press, 2002.

Gershenhorn, Jerry. *Melville J. Herskovits and the Racial Politics of Knowledge*. University of Nebraska Press, 2004.

Gilroy, Paul. *The Black Atlantic: Modernity and Double-Consciousness*. Harvard University Press, 1995.

Ginzburg, Carlo. *Clues, Myths, and the Historical Method*. Johns Hopkins University Press, 2013.

Glazer, Nathan, and Daniel Moynihan. *Beyond Melting Pot: The Negroes, Puerto Ricans, Jews, Italians and Irish of New York City*. MIT Press, 1970.

Go, Julian. "'Racism' and Colonialism: Meanings of Difference and Ruling Practices in America's Pacific Empire." *Qualitative Sociology* 27 (2004): 35–58.

Go, Julian. "Thinking Against Empire: Anticolonial Thought as Social Theory." *British Journal of Sociology* 74, no. 3 (2023): 279–93.

Go, Julian, and Anne Foster, ed. *The American Colonial State in the Philippines: Global Perspective*. Duke University Press, 2003.

Go, Julian, and Jake Watson. "Anticolonial Nationalism from Imagined Communities to Colonial Conflict." *European Journal of Sociology/Archives Européennes de Sociologie* 60, no. 1 (2019): 31–68.

Gobineau, Comte de (Joseph Arthur). *Essay on the Inequality of Human Races*. London, 1915. First French edition, Paris, 1853–1855. 4 vols. Available at Internet Archive, contributed by University of North Carolina, Chapel Hill. https://archive.org/details/inequalityofhuma00gobi.

Golash-Boza, Tanya Maria. *Deported: Immigrant Policing, Disposable Labor and Global Capitalism*. New York University Press, 2015.

Gomez, Sonia. *Picture Bride, War Bride: The Role of Marriage in Shaping Japanese America*. New York University Press, 2024.

Goodman, Adam. *The Deportation Machine: America's Long History of Expelling Immigrants*. Princeton University Press, 2020.

Goodman, Nelson. *Fact, Fiction, and Forecast*. 4th ed. Harvard University Press, 1983.

Goodman, Nelson. *Ways of Worldmaking*. Hackett Publishing Company, 1978.

Goldberg, David Theo. *The Racial State*. Blackwell Publishing, 2002.

Gordon, Linda. *The Moral Property of Women: A History of Birth Control Politics in America*. University of Illinois Press, 2007.

Gordon, Milton. *Assimilation in American Life: The Role of Race, Religion, and National Origins*. Oxford University Press, 1964.

Gossett, Thomas. *Race: The History of an Idea in America*. Oxford University Press, 1963.

Gould, Stephen Jay. *The Mismeasure of Man*. Rev. ed. AppLife, 1981.

Gravlee, Clarence C., H. Russell Bernard, and William R. Leonard. "Boas's *Changes in Bodily Form*: The Immigrant Study, Cranial Plasticity, and Boas's Physical Anthropology." *American Anthropologist* 105, no. 2 (2003): 326–32.

Gravlee, Clarence C., H. Russell Bernard, and William R. Leonard. "Heredity, Environment, and Cranial Form: A Reanalysis of Boas's Immigrant Data." *American Anthropologist* 105, no. 1 (2003): 125–38.

Green, Lawrence, Jonathan Fielding, and Ross Brownson. "More on Fake News, Disinformation, and Countering These with Science." *Annual Review of Public Health* 42 (2021): v–vi.

Greene, Daniel. *The Jewish Origin of Cultural Pluralism: The Menorah Association and American Diversity*. Indiana University Press, 2011.

Greenwald, Maurine, and Margo Anderson. *Pittsburgh Surveyed: Social Science and Social Reform in the Early Twentieth Century*. University of Pittsburgh Press, 1996.

Griswold, Whitney. "The Agrarian Democracy of Thomas Jefferson." *American Political Science Review* 40, no. 4 (1946): 657–81.

Guess, Andrew M., Brendan Nyhan, and Jason Reifler. "Exposure to Untrustworthy Websites in the 2016 US Election." *Nature Human Behaviour* 4, no. 5 (2020): 472–80.

Guglielmo, Thomas. *White on Arrival: Italians, Race, Color, and Power in Chicago, 1890–1945*. Oxford University Press, 2000.

Guinier, Lani. "From Racial Liberalism to Racial Literacy: *Brown v. Board of Education* and the Interest-Divergence Dilemma." *Journal of American History* 91, no. 1 (2004): 92–118.

Gulick, Sydney. *The American Japanese Problem: A Study of the Racial Relations of the East and the West*. Charles Scribner's Sons, 1914.

Guterl, Matthew. *The Color of Race in America, 1900–1940*. Harvard University Press, 2001.

Guyatt, Nicholas. *Bind Us Apart: How Enlightened Americans Invented Racial Segregation*. Basic Books, 2016.

Hacking, Ian. "The Bio-Power and Avalanche of Printed Numbers." *Humanities in Society* 5 (1982): 279–95.

Hacking, Ian. "Making up People." In *Historical Ontology*. Harvard University Press, 2002.

Hacking, Ian. *Social Construction of What?* Harvard University Press, 1999.

Hammer, Ricarda, and José Itzigsohn. "Rethinking Historical Sociology: Learning from WEB Du Bois and the Black Radical Tradition." *Du Bois Review: Social Science Research on Race*, October 11, 2024, 1–19.

Hammer, Ricarda, and Alexandre White. "Toward a Sociology of Colonial Subjectivity: Political Agency in Haiti and Liberia." *Sociology of Race and Ethnicity* 5, no. 2 (2019): 215–28.

Handlin, Oscar. *Race and Nationality in American Life*. Anchor Books, 1957.

Haney-López, Ian. *White by Law: The Legal Construction of Race*. New York University Press, 1996.

Hattam, Victoria. *In the Shadow of Race: Jews, Latinos, and Immigrant Politics in the United States*. University of Chicago Press, 2007.

Hawley, Joshua. *Theodore Roosevelt: Preacher of Righteousness*. Yale University Press, 2008.

Herrnstein, Richard J., and Charles Murray. *The Bell Curve: Intelligence and Class Structure in American Life*. Simon and Schuster, 2010.

Higham, John. *Strangers in the Land: Patterns of American Nativism 1860–1925*. Rutgers University Press, 1963.

Hirschman, Daniel. "Rediscovering the 1%: Knowledge Infrastructures and the Stylized Facts of Inequality." *American Journal of Sociology* 127, no. 3 (2021): 739–876.

Hirschman, Daniel, and Isaac Reed. "Formation Stories and Causality in Sociology." *Sociological Theory* 32, no. 4 (2014): 259–82.

Hochschild, Arlie. *Strangers in Their Own Land: Anger and Mourning on the American Right*. New Press, 2016.

Hochschild, Jennifer, and Brenna Powell. "Racial Reorganization and the United States Census 1850–1930: Mulattoes, Half-Breeds, Mixed Parentage, Hindoos, and the Mexican Race." *Studies in American Political Development* 22 (2008): 59–96.

Holloway, Ralph L. "Head to Head with Boas: Did He Err on the Plasticity of Head Form?" *Proceedings of National Academy of Science* 99, no. 23 (2002): 14622–23.

Horsman, Reginald. *Josiah Nott of Mobile: Southerner, Physician, and Racial Theorist*. Louisiana State University Press, 1987.

Hourwich, Isaac. *Immigration and Labor: The Economic Aspects of European Immigration to the United States*. G.P. Putnam's Sons, 1912.

Hsu, Madeline. *Dreaming of Gold, Dreaming of Home: Transnationalism and Migration Between the United States and South China, 1882–1943*. Stanford University Press, 2000.

Hughes, Langston. *The Big Sea*. Hill and Wang, 1940.

Hutchinson, Edward. *Legislative History of American Immigration Policy: 1798–1965*. University of Pennsylvania Press, 1981.

Hyatt, Marshall. *Franz Boas, Social Activist: The Dynamics of Ethnicity*. Greenwood Press, 1990.

Ichihashi, Yamato. "Emigration from Japan and Their Immigration into the State of California." PhD diss., Harvard University, 1913.

Ichihashi, Yamato. *Japanese in the United States*. Stanford University Press, 1932.

Ignatiev, Noel. *How the Irish Became White*. Routledge, 1995.

Immerman, Richard. *Empire for Liberty: A History of American Imperialism from Benjamin Franklin to Paul Wolfowitz*. Princeton University Press, 2010.

Immerwahr, Daniel. *How to Hide an Empire: A History of the Greater United States*. Farrar, Straus, and Giroux, 2019.

Irmscher, Christopher. *Louis Agassiz: Creator of American Science*. Houghton Mifflin Harcourt, 2013.

Itzigsohn, Jose, and Karida Brown. *The Sociology of W. E. B. Du Bois: Racialized Modernity and the Global Color Line*. New York University Press, 2020.

Jacobson, Matthew. *Whiteness of a Different Color: European Immigrants and the Alchemy of Race*. Harvard University Press, 1998.

Jasanoff, Sheila, ed. *States of Knowledge: The Co-Production of Science and the Social Order*. Routledge, 2006.

Jenks, Jeremiah, and W. Jett Lauck. *The Immigration Problem: A Study of American Immigration Conditions and Needs*. Funk and Wagnalls Company, 1913.

Jerit, Jennifer, and Yangi Zhao. "Political Misinformation." *Annual Review of Political Science* 23 (2020): 77–94.

Jerng, Mark. *Racial Worldmaking: The Power of Popular Fiction*. Fordham University Press, 2017.

Jiménez, Tomás. *The Other Side of Assimilation: How Immigrants Are Changing American Life*. University of California Press, 2017.

Jiménez, Tomás, and Adam Horowitz. "When White Is Just Alright: How Immigrants Redefine Achievement and Reconfigure the Ethnoracial Hierarchy." *American Sociological Review* 78, no. 5 (2013): 849–71.

Jones, Donna. *The Racial Discourse of Life Philosophy: Négritude, Vitalism, and Modernity*. Columbia University Press, 2011.

Jones, Jennifer A. "'They Are There with Us': Theorizing Racial Status and Intergroup Relations." *American Journal of Sociology* 128, no. 2 (2022): 411–61.

Jordan, David Starr. *The Days of a Man: Being Memories of a Naturalist, Teacher and Minor Prophet of Democracy*. Vol. 2, *1900–1921*. World Book Company, 1922.

Jung, Moon-Kie. "Introduction: Constituting the U.S. Empire-State and White Supremacy; The Early Years." In *State of White Supremacy: Racism, Governance, and the United States*, edited by Moon-Kie Jung, Joao Costa Vargas, and Eduardo Bonilla-Silva. Stanford University Press, 2011.

Jung, Moon-Kie. "The Racial Unconscious of Assimilation Theory." *Du Bois Review* 6 (2009): 375–95.

Jung, Moon-Kie. *Reworking Race: The Making of Hawaii's Interracial Labor Movement*. Columbia University Press, 2006.

Jung, Moon-Kie, and Yaejoon Kwon. "Theorizing the US Racial State: Sociology since Racial Formation." *Sociology Compass* 7, no. 11 (2013): 927–40.

Kale, Steven. "Gobineau, Racism, and Legitimism: A Royalist Heretic in Nineteenth-Century France." *Modern Intellectual History* 7, no. 1 (2010): 33–61.

Karabel, Jerome. *The Chosen: The Hidden History of Admission and Exclusion at Harvard, Yale, and Princeton*. Mariner Books, 2005.

Kasinitz, Philip, John Mollenkopf, Mary Waters, and Jennifer Holdaway. *Inheriting the City: The Children of Immigrants Come of Age*. Russell Sage Foundation, 2008.

Katznelson, Ira. *When Affirmative Action Was White: An Untold History of Racial Inequality in Twentieth-Century America*. W. W. Norton, 2005.

Kevles, Daniel J. *In the Name of Eugenics: Genetics and the Uses of Human Heredity*. Harvard University Press, 1985.

Keyssar, Alexander. *The Right to Vote: The Contested History of Democracy in the United States*. Basic Books, 2000.

Kim, Claire Jean. *Asian Americans in an Anti-Black World*. Cambridge University Press, 2023.

Kim, Claire Jean. "The Racial Triangulation of Asian Americans." *Politics & Society* 27, no. 1 (1999): 105–38.

Kim, Jaeeun. *Contested Embrace: Transborder Membership Politics in Twentieth-Century Korea*. Stanford University Press, 2016.

Kim, Sunmin. "Blinded by the Facts: Unintended Consequences of Racial Knowledge Production in the Dillingham Commission (1907–1911)." *Theory and Society* 53, no. 3 (2024): 425-464.

Kim, Minaje, Oliver Hahl, Ethan Poskanzer, and Ezra Sivan. "When Truth Trumps Facts: Studies on Partisan Moral Flexibility in American Politics." *American Journal of Sociology* 130, no. 1 (2024).

King, Charles. *Gods of the Upper Air: How a Circle of Renegade Anthropologists Reinvented Race, Sex, and Gender in the Twentieth Century*. Anchor, 2020.

King, Desmond. *Making Americans: Immigration, Race, and the Origins of Diverse Democracy*. Harvard University Press, 2002.

King, Desmond, and Rogers Smith. "Racial Orders in American Political Development." *American Political Science Review* 99, no. 1 (2005): 75–92.

Kiyma, Henry. *Four Immigrants Manga: A Japanese Experience in San Francisco, 1904–1924*. Stone Bridge Press, 1999.

Kolchin, Peter. "Whiteness Studies: The New History of Race in America." *Journal of American History* 89, no. 1 (2002): 154–73.

Koselleck, Reinhart. *The Practice of Conceptual History: Timing History, Spacing Concepts*. Stanford University Press, 2002.

Kramer, Paul. *Blood of Government: Race, Empire, the United States, and the Philippines*. University of North Carolina Press, 2006.

Krause, Monika. *Model Cases: On Canonical Research Objects and Sites*. University of Chicago Press, 2021.

Lala-Milán, Armando, Brian Sargent, and Sunmin Kim. "Theorizing with Archives: Contingency, Mistakes, and Plausible Alternatives." *Qualitative Sociology* 43 (2020): 345–65.

Lamont, Michèle, and Virág Molnár. "The Study of Boundaries in the Social Sciences." *Annual Review of Sociology* 28, no. 1 (2002): 167–95.

Latour, Bruno. *Science in Action: How to Follow Scientists and Engineers Through Society*. Harvard University Press, 1987.

Latour, Bruno. *We Have Never Been Modern*. Harvard University Press, 1991.

Lee, Erika. *At America's Gates: Chinese Immigration During the Exclusion Era, 1883–1943*. University of North Carolina Press, 2003.

Lee, Jennifer, and Frank Bean. *The Diversity Paradox: Immigration and the Color Line in Twenty-First Century America*. Russell Sage Foundation, 2010.

Lee, Jennifer, and Jun Xu. "The Marginalized Model Minority: An Empirical Examinations of the Racial Triangulation of Asian Americans." *Social Forces* 91, no. 4 (2003): 1363–97.

Lee, Jennifer, and Min Zhou. *The Asian American Achievement Paradox*. Russell Sage Foundation, 2015.

Lewis, Herbert. "The Passion of Franz Boas." *American Anthropologist* 103, no. 2 (2001): 447–67.

Lew-Williams, Beth. *The Chinese Must Go: Violence, Exclusion, and Making of the Alien in America*. Harvard University Press, 2018.

Lie, John. *Modern Peoplehood*. Harvard University Press, 2004.

Lieberman, Robert. *Shifting the Color Line: Race and the American Welfare State*. Harvard University Press, 2001.

Link, Arthur S. "What Happened to the Progressive Movement in the 1920's?" *American Historical Review* 64, no. 4 (1959): 833–51.

Lipsky, Michael. *Street-Level Bureaucracy: Dilemmas of the Individual in Public Service*. Russell Sage Foundation, 1980.

Livingstone, David. *Nathaniel Southgate Shaler and the Culture of American Science*. University of Alabama Press, 1987.

Lodge, Henry Cabot. *Early Memories*. C. Scribner's Sons, 1913.

Lodge, Henry Cabot. "The Restriction of Immigration, March 16, 1896." In *Speeches and Addresses 1884–1909*. 2nd ed. Houghton Mifflin, 1909. Available at Internet Archive, contributed by New York Public Library. https://archive.org/details/speechesaddresse00lodg.

Love, Eric. *Race over Empire: Racism and U.S. Imperialism, 1865–1900*. University of North Carolina Press, 2004.

Loveman, Mara. "Is "Race" Essential?" *American Sociological Review* 64, no. 6 (1999): 891–98.

Loveman, Mara. "The Modern State and Primitive Accumulation of Symbolic Power." *American Journal of Sociology* 110, no. 6 (2005): 1651–83.

Loveman, Mara. *National Colors: Racial Classification and the State in Latin America*. Oxford University Press, 2015.

Lummis, C. Douglas. "Ruth Benedict's Obituary for Japanese Culture." *Asia-Pacific Journal* 5, no. 7 (2007).

Lund, John. "Vermont Nativism: William Paul Dillingham and U.S. Immigration Legislation." *Vermont History* 63 (2008): 15–29.

Ly, Son Thierry, and Patrick Weil. "The Antiracist Origin of the Quota System." *Social Research: An International Quarterly* 77, no. 1 (2010): 45–78.

Machado, Maria Helena. "Nineteenth-Century Scientific Travel and Racial Photography: The Formation of Louis Agassiz's Brazilian Collection." Mirror of Race Project, May 8, 2012. http://mirrorofrace.org/machado/.

MacKenzie, Donald. *Statistics in Britain, 1865–1930: The Social Construction of Scientific Knowledge*. Edinburgh University Press, 1981.

Mamdani, Mahmood. *Define and Rule: Native as Political Identity*. Harvard University Press, 2012.

Mandelberg, Tali. *The Race Card: Campaign Strategy, Implicit Messages, and the Norm of Equality*. Princeton University Press, 2001.

Marx, K. F. H. "Life of Blumenbach." In *The Anthropological Treaties of Johann Friedrich Blumenbach*, translated and edited by Thomas Bendyshe. Longman, Green, Roberts & Green, 1865. https://archive.org/details/anthropologicalt00blumuoft/.

McKeown, Adam. *Melancholy Order: Asian Migration and the Globalization of Borders*. Columbia University Press, 2008.

McKinely, William. *Executive Order*, December 21, 1898. https://www.presidency.ucsb.edu/documents/executive-order-132.

Mead, Margaret, and James Baldwin. *A Rap on Race*. J. B. Lippincott, 1971.

Menand, Louis. *The Metaphysical Club: A Story of Ideas in America*. Harvard University Press, 2001.

Mendelberg, Tali. *The Race Card: Campaign Strategy, Implicit Messages, and the Norm of Equality*. Princeton University Press, 2001.

Menjívar, Cecilia. "Immigration Bureaucracies and State-created Categories Across the Globe." In "Contested Categories in the Context of International Migration," special issue, *Ethnic and Racial Studies* 48, no. 4 (2024): 927–47.

Menjívar, Cecilia. "Liminal Legality: Salvadoran and Guatemalan Immigrants' Lives in the United States." *American Journal of Sociology* 111, no. 4 (2006): 999–1037.

Merton, Robert K. "Three Fragments from a Sociologist's Notebooks: Establishing the Phenomenon, Specified Ignorance, and Strategic Research Materials." *Annual Review of Sociology* 13, no. 1 (1987): 1–29.

Merton, Robert K. "The Unanticipated Consequences of Purposive Social Action." *American Sociological Review* 1, no. 6 (1936): 894–904.

Miller, Lulu. *Why Fish Don't Exist: A Story of Loss, Love, and the Hidden Order of Life.* Simon and Schuster, 2020.

Mills, Charles. *The Racial Contract.* Cornell University Press, 2009.

Mitchell, Timothy. "The Limits of the State: Beyond Statist Approach and Their Critics." *American Political Science Review* 85, no. 1 (1991): 77–96.

Moore, Jacqueline. *Booker T. Washington, W. E. B Du Bois, and the Struggle for Racial Uplift.* Rowman and Littlefield, 2003.

Mora, G. Cristina. *Making Hispanics: How Activists, Bureaucrats, and Media Constructed a New American.* University of Chicago Press, 2014.

Morning, Ann. "Does Genomics Challenge Social Construction of Race?" *Sociological Theory* 32, no. 3 (2014): 189–207.

Morning, Ann. *The Nature of Race: How Scientists Think and Teach About Human Differences.* University of California Press, 2011.

Morning, Ann, and Marcello Maneri. *An Ugly Word: Rethinking Race in Italy and the United States.* Russell Sage Foundation, 2022.

Morris, Aldon. *The Scholar Denied: W. E. B. DuBois and the Birth of Modern Sociology.* University of California Press, 2015.

Morton, Samuel. *Crania Americana; or, A Comparative View of the Skulls of Various Aboriginal Nations of North and South America.* J. Dobson, 1839. Available at Internet Archive, contributed by Smithsonian Libraries. https://archive.org/details/Craniaamericana00Mort.

Muhammad, Khalil. *The Condemnation of Blackness: Race, Crime, and the Making of Modern Urban America.* Harvard University Press, 2011.

Mullaney, Thomas. *Coming to Terms with the Nation: Ethnic Classification in Modern China.* University of California Press, 2010.

Muller, Christopher. "Northward Migration and the Rise of Racial Disparity in American Incarceration, 1880–1950." *American Journal of Sociology* 118, no. 2 (2012): 281–326.

Muller, Eric. *The American Inquisition: The Hunt for Japanese American Disloyalty in World War II.* University of North Carolina Press, 2017.

Müller-Wille, Ludger, and William Barr. *Franz Boas among the Inuit of Baffin Island, 1883–1884: Journals and Letters.* University of Toronto Press, 1998.

Murakawa, Naomi. *The First Civil Right: How Liberals Built Prison America.* Princeton University Press, 2014.

Nagel, Joane. "American Indian Ethnic Renewal: Politics and the Resurgence of Identity and Culture." *American Sociological Review* 60, no. 6 (1997): 947–65.

Nakano, Dana. *Japanese Americans and the Racial Uniform: Citizenship, Belonging, and the Limits of Assimilation.* New York University Press, 2023.

Ngai, Mae. "The Architecture of Race in American Immigration Law: A Reexamination of the Immigration Law of 1924." *Journal of American History* 86, no. 1 (1999): 67–92.

Ngai, Mae. *Impossible Subjects: Illegal Aliens and the Making of Modern America.* Princeton University Press, 2005.

Nobles, Melissa. *Shades of Citizenship: Race and the Census in Modern Politics.* Stanford University Press, 2000.

Nott, Josiah. *Types of Mankind, or Ethnological Researches: Based Upon the Ancient Monuments, Paintings, and Sculptures, and Crania of Races, and Upon Their Natural, Geographical, Philological, and Biblical History.* 9th ed. J. B. Lippincott, 1868. Available at Internet Archive, contributed by University of California Libraries. https://archive.org/details/typesofmankindor00nott.

Obasogie, Osagie. *Blinded by Sight: Seeing Race Through the Eyes of the Blind.* Stanford University Press, 2020.

Omi, Michael and Howard Winant. *Racial Formation in the United States: From the 1960s to the 1990s.* 3rd ed. Routledge, 2014.

Pacewicz, Josh. "What Can You Do with a Single Case: How to Think About Ethnographic Case Selection Like a Historical Sociologist." *Sociological Methods and Research* 51, no. 3 (2020).

Painter, Nell Irvin. *The History of White People.* W. W. Norton, 2010.

Park, Robert. "Racial Assimilation in Secondary Groups: With Particular Reference to the Negro." *American Journal of Sociology* 8 (1913): 66–83.

Pascoe, Peggy. *What Comes Naturally: Miscegenation Law and the Making of Race in America.* Oxford University Press, 2009.

Pathe, R. A. "Gene Weltfish (1902–1980)." In *Women Anthropologists: A Biographical Dictionary,* edited by Ute Gacs, Aisha Khan, Jerrie McIntyre, and Ruth Weinberg. Greenwood, 1988.

Patterson, Orlando. *Slavery and Social Death: A Comparative Study.* Harvard University Press, 1982.

Perlmann, Joel. *America Classifies the Immigrant: From Ellis Island to the 2020 Census.* Harvard University Press, 2018.

Perlmann, Joel. *Italians Then, Mexicans Now: Immigrant Origins and Second-Generation Progress, 1890 to 2000.* The Russell Sage Foundation, 2007.

Poovey, Mary. *A History of Modern Fact: Problems of Knowledge in Sciences of Wealth and Society.* University of Chicago Press, 1998.

Porter, Theodore. *Trust in Numbers: The Pursuit of Objectivity in Science and Public Life.* Princeton University Press, 1995.

Portes, Alejandro, and Ruben G. Rumbaut. *Immigrant America: A Portrait.* University of California Press, 2006.

Portes, Alejandro, and Ruben G. Rumbaut. *Legacies: The Story of the Immigrant Second Generation.* University of California Press, 2001.

Portes, Alejandro, and Min Zhou. "The New Second Generation: Segmented Assimilation and Its Variants." *Annals of the American Academy of Political and Social Science* 530 (1993): 74–96.

Poskett, James. *Materials of the Mind: Phrenology, Race, and the Global History of Science, 1815–1920.* University of Chicago Press, 2019.

Prasad, Monica. *The Land of Too Much: American Abundance and the Paradox of Poverty.* Harvard University Press, 2012.

Prewitt, Kenneth. *What Is Your Race? The Census and Our Flawed Efforts to Classify Americans.* Princeton University Press, 2013.

Quadagno, Jill. *The Color of Welfare: How Racism Undermined the War on Poverty.* Oxford University Press, 1996.

quisumbing king, katrina. *Enduring Empire: U.S. Statecraft and Race-making in the Philippines.* Stanford University Press, 2025.

Ramírez, Catherine. *Assimilation: An Alternative History.* University of California Press, 2020.

Rao, Hayagreeva, and Henrich Greve. "The Plot Thickens: A Sociology of Conspiracy Theories." *Annual Review of Sociology* 50 (2024).

Ripley, William. *The Races of Europe: A Sociological Study.* D. Appleton, 1899.

Rodríguez-Muñiz, Michael. "Cultivating Consent: Nonstate Leaders and the Orchestration of State Legibility." *American Journal of Sociology* 123, no. 2 (2017): 385–425.

Rodríguez-Muñiz, Michael. *Figures of the Future: Latino Civil Rights and the Politics of Demographic Change.* Princeton University Press, 2021.

Roediger, David. *The Wages of Whiteness: Race and the Making of American Working Class.* Verso, 1991.

Roediger, David. *Working Toward Whiteness: How America's Immigrants Became White.* Basic Books, 2005.

Romero, Mary. "Crossing the Immigration and Race Border: A Critical Race Theory Approach to Immigration Studies." *Contemporary Justice Review* 11, no. 1 (2008): 23–37.

Ross, Dorothy. *The Origin of American Social Science.* Cambridge University Press, 1992.

Ross, Edward. *The Old World in the New: The Significance of Past and Present Immigration to the American People.* Century Co., 1914.

Roth, Wendy. *Race Migrations: Latinos and the Cultural Transformation of Race.* Stanford University Press, 2020.

Roth, Wendy, and Biorn Ivemark. "Genetic Options: The Impact of Genetic Ancestry Testing on Ethnic and Racial Identities." *American Journal of Sociology* 124, no. 1 (2018): 150–84.

Roth, Wendy, Eleva G. van Stee, and Alenadra Regla-Vargas. "Conceptualizations of Race: Essentialism and Constructivism." *Annual Review of Sociology* 49 (2023): 39–58.

Roth, Wendy D., and Şule Yaylacı. "Genetic Options and Constraints: How Genetic Ancestry Tests Change Ethnic and Racial Identities." *American Journal of Sociology* 129, no. 4 (2024.): 1172–1215.

Roy, Keidrick. *American Dark Age: Racial Feudalism and the Rise of Black Liberalism.* Princeton University Press, 2024.

Rydell, Robert. *All the World's a Fair: Visions of Empire at American International Expositions, 1876–1916.* University of Chicago Press, 1984.

Sáenz, Rogelio, and Karen Douglas. "A Call for Racialization of Immigration Studies: On the Transition of Ethnic Immigrants to Racialized Immigrants." *Sociology of Race and Ethnicity* 1, no. 1 (2015): 166–80.

Saperstein, Aliya, Andrew Penner, and Ryan Light. "Racial Formation in Perspective: Connecting Individuals, Institutions, and Power Relations." *Annual Review of Sociology* 39 (2013): 359–78.

Schaffer, Simon, and Steven Shapin, *Leviathan and the Air-Pump: Hobbes, Boyle, and the Experimental Life.* Princeton University Press, 1985.

Schickler, Eric. "New Deal Liberalism and Racial Liberalism in the Mass Public, 1937–1968." *Perspectives on Politics* 11, no. 1 (2013): 75–98.

Schor, Paul. *Counting Americans: How the US Census Classified the Nation*. Oxford University Press, 2017.

Schor, Paul. "Mobilising for Pure Prestige? Challenging Federal Census Ethnic Categories in the USA (1850–1940)." *International Social Science Journal* 57, no. 183 (2005): 89–101.

Scott, Daryl. *Contempt and Pity: Social Policy and the Image of the Damaged Black Psyche, 1880–1996*. University of North Carolina Press, 1997.

Scott, James. *Seeing Like a State: How Certain Scheme to Improve the Human Condition Have Failed*. Yale University Press, 1998.

Shaler, Nathaniel. *The Autobiography of Nathaniel Southgate Shaler*. Houghton Mifflin, 1909.

Shapin, Steven. "Phrenological Knowledge and the Social Structure of Early Nineteenth-Century Edinburgh." *Annals of Science* 32, no. 3 (1975): 219–43.

Sharma, Nandita. *Home Rule: National Sovereignty and the Separation of Natives and Migrants*. Duke University Press, 2020.

Shiao, Jiannbin Lee, Thomas Bode, Amber Beyer, and Daniel Selvig "The Genomic Challenges to the Social Construction of Race." *Sociological Theory* 30, no. 2 (2012): 67–88.

Simons, Sarah. "Social Assimilation." *American Journal of Sociology* 6 (1901): 790–822.

Skarpelis, Anna Katharina Mosha. "Horror Vacui: Racial Misalignment, Symbolic Repair, and Imperial Legitimation in German National Socialist Political Photography." *American Journal of Sociology* 29, no. 2 (2023): 313–83.

Skowronek, Stephen. *Building a New American State: The Expansion of National Administrative Capacities, 1877–1920*. Cambridge University Press, 1982.

Smith, Rogers. *Civic Ideals: Conflicting Visions of Citizenship in U.S. History*. Yale University Press, 1997.

Sollors, Werner. *The Invention of Ethnicity*. Oxford University Press, 1989.

Solomon, Barbara Miller. *Ancestors and Immigrants: A Changing New England Tradition*. University of Chicago Press, 1956.

Sorensen, John, and Judith Sealander, eds. *The Grace Abbott Reader*. University of Nebraska Press, 2008.

Sparks, Corey, and Richard Jantz. "Changing Times, Changing Faces: Franz Boas's Immigrant Study in Modern Perspective." *American Anthropologist* 105, no. 2 (2003): 333–37.

Sparks, Corey, and Richard Jantz. "A Reassessment of Human Cranial Plasticity: Boas Revisited." *Proceedings of the National Academy of Sciences of the United States of America PNAS* 99, no. 23 (2002): 14636–39.

Spiro, Jonathan. *Defending the Master Race: Conservation, Eugenics, and the Legacy of Madison Grant*. University of Vermont Press, 2008.

Stanton, William. *The Leopard's Spots: Scientific Attitudes Toward Race in America 1815–59*. University of Chicago Press, 1960.

Starr, Paul. "Social Categories and Claims in the Liberal State." *Social Research* 59 (1992): 263–95.

Steinberg, Stephen. *The Ethnic Myth: Race, Ethnicity, and Class in America*. 3rd ed. Beacon Press, 2001.

Stocking, George W., Jr. *Race, Culture, and Evolution: Essays in the History of Anthropology*. The Free Press, 1968.

Stoler, Ann Laura. *Along the Archival Grain: Epistemic Anxieties and Colonial Common Sense*. Princeton University Press, 2008.

Svinth, Joseph. "Professor Yamashita Goes to Washington." *Journal of Combative Sport*, October 2000.

Swidler, Ann. "Culture in Action: Symbols and Strategies." *American Sociological Review* 51, no. 2 (1986): 273–86.

Telles, Edward and Vilma Ortiz. *Generations of Exclusion: Mexican Americans, Assimilation, and Race*. Russell Sage Foundation, 2009.

Thomas, William Isaac, Robert Ezra Park, and Herbert Adolphus Miller. *Old World Traits Transplanted*. Harper and Brothers, 1921.

Tichenor, Daniel. *Dividing Lines: The Politics of Immigration Control in America*. Princeton University Press, 2002.

Tilley, Helen. *Africa as a Living Laboratory: Empire, Development, and the Problem of Scientific Knowledge, 1870–1950*. University of Chicago Press, 2011.

Thompson, Debra. *The Schematic State: Race, Transnationalism, and the Politics of the Census*. Cambridge University Press, 2016.

Torpey, John. *The Invention of the Passport: Surveillance, Citizenship, and the State*. Cambridge University Press, 1999.

Treitler, Vilna Bashi. *The Ethnic Project: Transforming Racial Fictions into Ethnic Factions*. Stanford University Press, 2013.

Treitler, Vilna Bashi. "Social Agency and White Supremacy in Immigration Studies." *Sociology of Race and Ethnicity* 1, no. 1 (2015): 153–65.

Turner, Frederic Jackson. "The Significance of the Frontier in American History." *Proceedings of the State Historical Society of Wisconsin*, 1893.

Valentine, A. B. *Report of the Commissioner of Agricultural and Manufacturing Interest in the State of Vermont*. Tuttle, 1890.

Vaughan, Dianne. *The Challenger Launch Decision: Risky Technology, Culture, and Deviance at NASA*. University of Chicago Press, 2016.

Voss, Kim. *The Making of American Exceptionalism: The Knights of Labor and Class Formation in the Nineteenth Century*. Cornell University Press, 1993.

Wacquant, Loic. *Racial domination*. John Wiley and Sons. 2024.

Wacquant, Loic, and Pierre Bourdieu. *An Invitation to Reflexive Sociology*. Polity, 1992.

Walker, Alice. "In Search of Zora Neale Hurston." *Ms.*, March 1975.

Walker, Francis. "Restriction of Immigration." *Atlantic*, June 1896. https://www.theatlantic.com/magazine/archive/1896/06/restriction-of-immigration/306011/.

Warner, W. Lloyd, and Paul Lunt. *The Social Life of a Modern Community*. Yakee City Series Vol. 1. Yale University Press, 1941.

Waters, Mary. *The Ethnic Options: Choosing Identities in America*. University of California Press, 1990.

Waters, Mary, and Tomás Jiménez. "Assessing Immigrant Assimilation: New Empirical and Theoretical Challenges." *Annual Review of Sociology* 31 (2005): 105–205.

Wiebe, Robert. *The Search for Order 1877–1920*. Hill and Wang, 1967.

Wilde, Melissa. *Birth Control Battles: How Race and Class Divide American Religion*. University of California Press, 2019.

Wilderson, Frank. *Afropessimism*. Liveright, 2000.

Williams, Vernon, Jr. *Rethinking Race: Franz Boas and His Contemporaries*. University Press of Kentucky, 1996.
Wimmer, Andreas. *Ethnic Boundary Making: Institutions, Power, Networks*. Oxford University Press, 2013.
Wimmer, Andreas. "Herder's Heritage and Boundary-Making Approach: Studying Ethnicity in Immigrant Societies." *Sociological Theory* 27, no. 3 (2009): 244–70.
Wimmer, Andreas. "Race-Centrism: A Critique of and a Research Agenda." *Ethnic and Racial Studies* 38, no. 13 (2015): 2186–205.
Winant, Howard. "Race, Ethnicity, and Social Science." *Ethnic and Racial Studies* 38, no. 13 (2015): 2176–85.
Wu, Ellen. *The Color of Success: Asian Americans and the Origins of the Model Minority*. Princeton University Press, 2013.
Xie, Yu. "Franz Boas and Statistics." *Annals of Scholarship* 5 (1988): 269–96.
Yamashita, Karen. "Kiss of Kitty." *The Spectacle*, 2015. https://thespectacle.wustl.edu/?p=256.
Yokota, Karen. *Unbecoming British: How Revolutionary America Became a Postcolonial Nation*. Oxford University Press, 2014.
Yu, Henry. *Thinking Orientals: Migration, Contact, and Exoticism in Modern America*. Oxford: Oxford University Press, 2001.
Zeidel, Robert. *Immigrants, Progressives, and Exclusion Politics: The Dillingham Commission, 1900–1927*. Northern Illinois University Press, 2004.
Ziegler-McPherson, Christina. *Americanization in the States: Immigrant Social Welfare Policy, Citizenship, and National Identity in the United States (1908–1929)*. University Press of Florida, 2009.
Zolberg, Aristide. *A Nation by Design: Immigration Policy in the Fashioning of America*. Harvard University Press, 2006.
Zuberi, Tukufu. *Thicker Than Blood: How Racial Statistics Lie*. University of Minnesota Press, 2001.
Zumwalt, Rosemary Lévy, and William Shedrick Willis. *Franz Boas and W. E. B Du Bois at Atlanta University, 1906*. American Philosophical Society, 2008.

## ARCHIVAL SOURCES

Daniel Folkmar Photographs of Philippine People, circa 1903–1907, NAA Photo Lot 105, National Anthropological Archives.
Daniel Folkmar Papers. The National Anthropological Archives in the records of the Department of Anthropology (Manuscript and Pamphlet File), Smithsonian Institution.
Edith and Grace Abbott Papers. Hanna Holborn Gray Special Collections Research Center. University of Chicago.
Franz Boas Papers, American Philosophical Society.
Immigration Restriction League Records, 1893–1921, MS AM 2245, Houghton Library, Harvard University.
Japanese American Evacuation and Resettlement Records, BANC MSS 67/14 c, Bancroft Library, University of California, Berkeley.
LeRoy Hodges Papers 1908–1942. Special Collections, Washington and Lee University.
Records of the Immigration and Naturalization Service (RG85), National Archives and Records Administration.

*Report of the Commission on Immigration on the Problem of Immigration in Massachusetts*. Wright and Pottery Printing, 1914. Available at Internet Archive, contributed by Cornell University Library. https://archive.org/details/cu31924021185362.

*The Reports of the United States Immigration Commission*. Vols. 1–41. Bancroft Library. University of California, Berkeley.

William Jett Lauck Papers. Special Collections, University of Virginia Library.

William Stiles Bennet Papers, Special Collections, State University of New York, Albany.

William Walter Husband Papers, Chicago History Museum.

Yamato Ichihashi Papers, SC0071, Department of Special Collections and University Archives, Stanford University.

# Index